TO THE MEMORY OF

MY FRIEND AND TEACHER,

JAMES BOWLING MOZLEY,

WHO HAS BEEN CONSTANTLY IN MY THOUGHTS

IN WRITING THESE LECTURES,

I DEDICATE THIS BOOK.

O GOD, who hast made of one blood all nations of men for to dwell on all the face of the earth, and didst send Thy blessed Son to preach peace to them that are far off and to them that are nigh; grant that *all Thy people everywhere* may seek after Thee and find Thee; and hasten, O Lord, the fulfilment of Thy promise to pour out Thy Spirit upon all flesh: through Jesus Christ our Lord. Amen. *

* A prayer of Bishop Cotton's, slightly altered by substituting the words in italics for *all the people of India.*

EXTRACT

FROM THE LAST WILL AND TESTAMENT

OF THE LATE

REV. JOHN BAMPTON,

CANON OF SALISBURY.

—— " I GIVE and bequeath my Lands and Estates to the
" Chancellor, Masters, and Scholars of the University of
" Oxford for ever, to have and to hold all and singular the
" said Lands or Estates upon trust, and to the intents and
" purposes hereinafter mentioned; that is to say, I will and
" appoint that the Vice-Chancellor of the University of
" Oxford for the time being shall take and receive all the
" rents, issues, and profits thereof, and (after all taxes,
" reparations, and necessary deductions made) that he pay
" all the remainder to the endowment of eight Divinity
" Lecture Sermons, to be established for ever in the said
" University, and to be performed in the manner following:

" I direct and appoint, that, upon the first Tuesday in
" Easter Term, a Lecturer be yearly chosen by the Heads
" of Colleges only, and by no others, in the room adjoining
" to the Printing-House, between the hours of ten in the
" morning and two in the afternoon, to preach eight Di-
" vinity Lecture Sermons, the year following, at S. Mary's
" in Oxford, between the commencement of the last month
" in Lent Term, and the end of the third week in Act
" Term.

" Also I direct and appoint, that the eight Divinity
" Lecture Sermons shall be preached on either of the follow-
" ing Subjects—to confirm and establish the Christian Faith,
" and to confute all heretics and schismatics—upon the

"divine authority of the holy Scriptures—upon the autho-
"rity of the writings of the primitive Fathers, as to the
"faith and practice of the primitive Church—upon the
"Divinity of our Lord and Saviour Jesus Christ—upon
"the Divinity of the Holy Ghost—upon the Articles of the
"Christian Faith, as comprehended in the Apostles' and
"Nicene Creeds.

"Also I direct, that thirty copies of the eight Divinity
"Lecture Sermons shall be always printed, within two
"months after they are preached; and one copy shall be
"given to the Chancellor of the University, and one copy
"to the Head of every College, and one copy to the Mayor
"of the city of Oxford, and one copy to be put into the
"Bodleian Library; and the expense of printing them
"shall be paid out of the revenue of the Land or Estates
"given for establishing the Divinity Lecture Sermons;
"and the Preacher shall not be paid, nor be entitled to
"the revenue, before they are printed.

"Also I direct and appoint, that no person shall be quali-
"fied to preach the Divinity Lecture Sermons, unless he
"hath taken the degree of Master of Arts at least, in
"one of the two Universities of Oxford or Cambridge;
"and that the same person shall never preach the Divinity
"Lecture Sermons twice."

PREFACE.

THE following Lectures are a contribution to the comparative study of religion from a Christian point of view. It is a subject that has been ably treated by Mr. F. D. Maurice[a], Archdeacon Hardwick, and others. But it has long been evident that some fresh discussion of it was needed, owing to the new light which has fallen upon it from so many quarters; and Christians have of late been constantly reminded of the misconceptions to which a partial study of the history of religion is liable.

I had for some time, like others, been conscious of the want, but it was not till a few years ago that I felt myself called upon to do the little that I could to supply it. When I was appointed by Dr. Mozley to lecture for him to candidates for ordination in the year 1877, I was anxious to give a systematic and somewhat extended course of theology. The necessary prolegomena to such a scheme seemed to be twofold: first, a series of Lectures on the Evidences for the

[a] In his Boyle Lectures on the *Religions of the World, and their Relations to Christianity*, first published in 1846.

Being and Nature of God and the Future Life of Man (delivered in Michaelmas Term, 1877); and, secondly, a course which covered much the same ground as the present volume. Dr. Mozley's lamented death in January, 1878, cut short my plan at this point; but those who attended the course delivered in the Latin Chapel at Christ Church, in Lent Term, 1878, if any of them should see this book, will recognize a good deal of the same material, as well as a general similarity in the argument. That course has, in fact, been the basis of the present Lectures; but they have, I need hardly say, been wholly re-written, so that both in style and substance they are practically new.

My readers will, I hope, excuse this explanation, which it seemed a duty to make. I have written this book especially for candidates for ordination, and for those recently ordained, some of whom it may help to realize not only that their message is superior to that of other religious teachers, but how and why it is unique and universal. I offer it also more particularly to those who have an interest or a share in foreign missions, from association with whom I have derived constant help and encouragement, for which I should wish in some degree to make a return. It is not too much to say, that without the Oxford Missionary Association of Graduates, of which Dr. Mozley was the first President [b], and without the free use of its library and the stimulus of the frequent intercourse with foreign missionaries, of which it has been the centre, this book would never have been written. I should wish, at any rate, to take this opportunity of thanking most warmly those who have spoken to us there with great frankness and wisdom of their difficulties as well as their encouragements, and who have filled us with a sense of the unity of all Christian work throughout the world.

The book may, I trust, be useful to some who have not access to libraries, though it is far from resting on so broad a basis of study as I could wish. My obligations to many previous writers will, I hope, be pretty evident from the notes and index. If any of them, or of other workers in the same field, at home or abroad, will favour me with corrections or fresh illustrations, I shall be most grateful. Dr. Oscar Frankfurter, who is already favourably known in England as an independent Pāli scholar, has been good enough to supplement my imperfect

[b] Among the first promoters of the association, which was founded in the year 1874, were the late Mr. E. C. Woollcombe, of Balliol College,—whose Christian example was a blessing to all who knew him,—and the present Bishops of Bombay and Colombo. The latter was, I believe, the first who actually suggested such an association.

knowledge of Buddhism with a sketch of its tenets as they appear in the Pi*t*akas, which seems to me as fair and accurate an account of this great system, in its original conception, as it was possible to write in so small a compass[c]. The short paper *On the Notion of Conscience among the Zulus*, with which Bishop Callaway has favoured me, will also be read with great interest[d]. My obligations to private friends are numerous, and not least to those whose help has been given almost unconsciously in the unreserve of conversation, and to those whose intimate relation to myself seems to make a formal and public acknowledgment less appropriate. I am, however, particularly obliged to two friends, Dr. Liddon and Mr. Wace, who have helped me in the correction of the proof-sheets, the former in part, and the latter throughout. This would at any time have been of the greatest value in attaining clearness of thought and precision of style, but it has been an especial benefit to me owing to the circumstances which impeded the delivery of the Lectures, and delayed their passage through the press. A severe accident which happened to me in the Easter vacation, followed by a protracted illness, interrupted the course after three

[c] See below, Appendix I., pp. 337 foll.
[d] Appendix II., p. 354.

only had been given. The series was continued for me, as far as it was complete, during the Summer Term, by the great kindness of the Warden of Keble College, who delivered Lectures IV., V., VI., in my place in the University Pulpit, besides giving me advice on many small points. The last two were unavoidably postponed, but by the goodness of the Vice-Chancellor and Mr. Wace (who yielded me a turn which fell to him as Select Preacher), were delivered informally in the present Michaelmas Term.

It is, therefore, with deep thankfulness to God, the giver of life and strength and love, that I send this book into the world, though not without a natural regret. This year, 1881, will long be remembered in Oxford as a year of changes and losses, and there are eyes which would have looked upon these pages with affectionate interest which are now closed on earth. We that remain, by God's mercy, must strive more earnestly to do the daily tasks to which He calls us.

1 KEBLE TERRACE, OXFORD,
Nov. 7, 1881.

NOTE ON THE TRANSLITERATION OF ORIENTAL WORDS.

IN transliterating oriental words, I have generally adopted the missionary alphabet introduced by Prof. F. Max Müller into his collection of *Sacred Books of the East*, chiefly because I had occasion to quote from it frequently. It has the two advantages of being printed with ordinary type, with few dots or diacritical marks, and of being based on a principle of phonetics. English readers have to remember that italic *k* stands for ch, and *g* for j, and that *s* is to be pronounced like s in sure. Most of us will be sorry to part with ch (or c) and j, but if custom at length decrees that we shall do so, the sounds of *k* and *g* will be easily learnt. I need hardly say that the accented vowels are to be pronounced long, with the Italian or German, not the English, sounds, and that whether we write â, ā or á is absolutely indifferent. It is also to be remarked that short a is very short in Sanskrit, more like English ŭ. I am afraid that I have been careless from time to time, especially in transliterating common words (as Asoka for A*s*oka, Vishnu for Vish*n*u, Pitaka for Pi*t*aka, &c.), and have used different accents rather loosely. I hope the reader will forgive this fault, and not be much the worse.

I append a copy of the missionary alphabet, as

applied to Sanskrit, in the dictionary order of the letters. Cp. *Sacred Books*, vol. i. p. lv. Other languages, such as Zend, Hebrew, Arabic, and Chinese, require of course some additional symbols. Strictly speaking, according to the rules of this alphabet, the vowels e, ai, o, au, ought to have accents, ê, âi, ô, âu, but they are omitted in practice.

Vowels—a, â ⎫
   i, î ⎬ e, ai.
   u, û ⎭ o, au.
   ri, rî.
   li, lî.

Gutturals . . .	k, kh, g, gh, ṅ.
Palatals . . .	*k, kh, g, gh,* ñ.
Cerebrals . . .	t, th, d, dh, n.
Dentals . . .	t, th, d, dh, n.
Labials . . .	p, ph, b, bh, m.
Semivowels . .	y, r, l, v.
Sibilants . . .	s, sh, s.
Aspirate . . .	h.
Anusvâra . .	*m.* Visarga . . *h.*
(*Slight nasal.*)	(*Slight sibilant.*)

I add here a few Corrigenda.

On p. 27, the line of Terence should be printed according to Fleckeisen's text, *Heauton Timorumenos,* 25,—
  "Homo sum : humani nil a me alienum puto."

On p. 57, note 21, for *The Religions of China* read *Religion in China,* the title of Dr. Edkins' book.

On p. 96, last line, Rägnarök should rather be rendered "doom of the gods," or "world-judgment." The last part of the word has nothing to do with "twilight," as used to be supposed, but means judgment. See Dr. Vigfússon's *Lexicon,* pp. 488 and 507.

On p. 165 read, "Chiron willingly giving up his immortality to free Prometheus from the Scythian rock of torture."

On p. 173, note 72, for *Scotland* read *Shetland.*

CONTENTS.

LECTURE I.

INTRODUCTION. PRESENT PERPLEXITIES. THE UNITY OF RELIGION.

The present unsettlement in Religion, p. 1.—Its relation to the movement of civilization, 3.—Sense of injustice often felt in a time of transition.—Book of Job, 5.—Christ, however, connects unbelief and sin, 6.—Moral causes of unbelief, 8, (1) Prejudice, 9, (2) Severe claims of religion, 12, (3) Intellectual faults, esp. Indolence, coldness, recklessness, pride and avarice, 14.—General position of the believer.—Faith belongs to a state of probation, 24.

The present Lectures a contribution to internal evidence, 25.—The call upon us to consider the unity of our race and of religion, 27.—Wonderful advance in knowledge of human nature, 28.—Method of these Lectures.—Superiority of the Biblical idea of God (Lect. II.).—God a God of Truth (Lect. III., IV.), Holiness (V., VI.), and Peace (VII., VIII.), and as such sought by the nations (III., V., VII.), but only found in Christ (IV., VI., VIII.), 31.

LECTURE II.

BIBLICAL THEISM CONTRASTED WITH OTHER CONCEPTIONS OF THE NATURE OF GOD.

The Unity of God witnessed by instinct and reason, but only explicitly and publicly taught by those who acknowledge the Bible, p. 33.—God revealed to Moses as both Infinite and Personal, 38.—Why this unity of attributes is credible, 40.—Departures from this belief on either side, 42.

Pantheism a one-sided exaggeration of His Infinity, 43.—Its danger, 47.—Dualism a step nearer the truth, 49.—Sabellian and Eutychian types of heresy, 51.

Anthropomorphic Deism the antithesis to Pantheism, 55.—Exaggeration of God's personality and of Man's independence.—State religion of China, 57.—Deistic tendencies in Græco-Roman philosophy, and in Judaism, 60.—In later times, outside and inside the Church.—Islam, 63.—Pelagian and Nestorian heresies, and similar movements, 63.—Tübingen School, 65.—Conclusion, 66.

TABLE shewing the chief contrasted types of heresy and false doctrine, 68.

LECTURE III.

THE NATURAL EXPECTATION OF DIVINE TRUTH, AND THE CONFESSION OF HUMAN INCAPACITY OF ATTAINING TO IT.

Innate Passion for Truth, p. 69.—Non-Christian religious systems to be approached with sympathy and reverence, 73. (1.) God speaking in the voices of nature, 74.—Thunder, 74.—Wind.—The Sea, &c., 75.—Light, 76.—Profound character of Vedic Gods, 77.—Apollo and Delphi, 78.—Socrates, 81. (2.) God revealed in human forms, 83.—Heroes.—Kingly Incarnations.—Greece.—Mexico, 83.—Scandinavia.—Egypt, 84.—China.—Rome, 85.—Avatars, 86.—Krishna.—Buddha, 87. (3.) Sacred books, 92: Avesta.—Vedas, 94.—High idea of Inspiration, 95.

Shortcomings of these revelations confessed by the heathen themselves, 96: Plato, 97.—Cicero, 100.—Seneca.—Porphyry, 101.—The poets, 103.—God, who gave much, withheld His best gift of rest, 105.

LECTURE IV.

THE CHRISTIAN REVELATION CONSIDERED AS TRUTH BOTH IDEAL AND PRACTICAL.

"The world by (its) wisdom knew not God," p. 107.—Revelation the just harmony of the spiritual and external, 109.

Ideal Truth (1) *Comprehensive*, 110: the One and the Many, 112.—The Trinity.—Union of the Finite and Infinite in the Incarnation and Atonement, 112.—Christian doctrine of Human Nature: its fearlessness, 113.—(2) *Mysterious*: Mysteries in nature and thought, lead us to accept those of Christian doctrine, 115.—(3) *Inexhaustible*: The Bible compared with other religious books, 118.

Practical Truth (1) *Authoritative*, 122: Our Saviour's claims compared with those of Buddha and Mahomet, 123.—The Prophets.—Miracles, 126.—Instinct for authority in human nature: how it avenges itself if suppressed, 127.—Justin Martyr: freedom in submission to the Truth, 130.—(2) *Definite and intelligible*: Doctrine of the Trinity compared with other religious formulas,

132.—(3) *Permanent and concrete:* combination of flexibility with firmness, 133.—Contrast with other religions, 134.—Union of Fact and Symbol the type of truth, 136.—Biblical history, 137.—St. Paul and St. Ignatius, 139.—Modern Gnosticism, 140.
ADDITIONAL NOTE to p. 121, 141 ; to p. 125, 142.

LECTURE V.

THE NATURAL SENSE OF SEPARATION FROM GOD, AND OF THE NEED OF ATONEMENT.

The altar to the unknown God a true type of heathen worship, p. 143.
1. *The separation from God considered as connected with Sin and Death:* Myths of a golden age, and contrast with later times, 146.—Departure of the gods, 148.—Popular sense of the misery of man, 148.—Sense of sin, especially in classical writers, 149. —Sin a breaking away from God, and leading to death, 153.— Sense of the impurity of death, and of murder, 154.
2. *Attempts at atonement,* especially confession of sin and sacrifice, 156.—*Confession* implied in approach to a priest, 157.— In Assyria, Persia, Mexico, 157. — Extraordinary mixture of ideas in the latter, 159.—*Sacrifice* for sin : ideas implied in it, (1) the most precious thing, (2) a substitution for ourselves, 162.—Bloody sacrifice, why chosen, 162.—Willingness to die, &c., 164.—Climax in human sacrifice : union of best and worst in it, 165.—Reaction against it almost universal, 169.—Mystical theories of sacrifice, miraculous power especially of austerities, and attribution of it to God, 170.—In India and Odin's Rune-Song, 171.—Mexican sacrifices, 174.—Osiris, Adonis, &c., 174. —Not merely pantheistic, but allied to a first principle of Christian theology, 175.
3. *Failure of these attempts :* acknowledged by the best minds of antiquity, 177.—Difficulty of the forgiveness of sin insoluble to the natural conscience, 178.

LECTURE VI.

THE INCARNATION AND ATONEMENT A REVELATION OF HOLINESS, WORTHY OF GOD, AND MEET FOR THE NEEDS OF MAN.

Isaiah's prophecy : God leading man along the way of Holiness, p. 181.
Conflict between Hope and Reason, 183.—(1) *Grandeur and breadth*

of the Doctrine, worthy of God who reveals it, 186.—Majestic power of the Creed, 187.—Objections on the side of Love and of Justice.—Other ways of reconciliation suggested, 189.—(2) *The Atonement and God's Love*, 191.—Inadequate idea of Love in objectors to the Atonement.—Its fiery quality, 192.—Work of sin in the world, 193.—Not to be lightly dealt with, 194.—(3) *The Atonement and God's Justice*, 197.—The innocent suffering for the guilty, 197.—Principle of Mediation, 199.—Willing Sacrifice, 199.—Mystical appropriation of it, 199.

Practical value of the doctrine (1) *Revelation of the guilt and danger of Sin*, 200.—Necessity of this thought, 201.—Horror of separation from God, 202.—(2) *Christ the representative of the race*, 203.—Idea of Representation, 205.—Messianic prophecy, 207.—Fragments of the Idea in heathenism, 208.—Their inadequacy, 210.—Holiness and Humility overlooked, 211.—Testimonies of non-Christian teachers to Christ, 212.—Union of Christians with His work, 215.—(3) *Direct moral example* of the Redeemer; its value to individuals, 215.

LECTURE VII.

The Natural Desire for Peace, and the Inadequacy of Human Efforts to attain it.

I. Social tendency of mankind, p. 218.—The family the basis of society, 219.—Obligations to (1) the ideal of paternal government, 220.—High conception of kingship, 221.—Chinese book of history, 222.—The "Great Plan," 224.—(2) The assertion of individual liberty, 226.—Socrates, &c., 227.—(3) The sense of social duty, 227.—Plato's *Republic.*—Education of children, 228.—Higher position of women, 228.

Nevertheless, the State cannot make men really happy, 230.—Impossibility even of preventing war, 231.—Limit to the power of rewarding virtue, 232.—The wants of the soul untouched, 233.

II. Natural alliance between Religion and Politics, 234.—Three theories of their relation, (1) Popular Religion treated as a preservative of Order apart from Truth, 237.—Ancient philosophers, 238.—Polybius on Roman Religion, 238.—Euhemerism.—Varro, 240.—Italian tendency to subordinate Truth to Expediency, 241.—(2) Religious Reformation imposed upon all citizens, 241.—Plato's *Laws*, book x.: his Religious Discipline, 242.—Mahomet, 244.—Formal character of Islam, 245.—Defective theology and morality.—Want of Love, 246.—Character of Mahomet, 247.—His lapse, 249.—Why not a "true prophet," 250.—How far sincere, 252.—Islam, 1. has stereotyped a low form of social life, 254; 2. has opposed religious and intellectual liberty, 256; 3. is a barrier to the Gospel, 257.—(3) Religion a voluntary society, not necessarily co-extensive with the State, 259.—Polynesian Areoi, 260.—Pythagorean clubs.—The Mysteries, 261.—Private guilds, 263.—Buddhism, 265.—Reasons for its success, 266.—Assertion of free-will and the moral Law, 267.—Not really a religion, 267.—Selfishness and apathy, 273.—Failure, 275.

LECTURE VIII.

THE PEACE OF THE CHURCH AS WORTHY OF GOD WHO GIVES IT AND AS SATISFYING THE NEEDS OF MAN.

Recapitulation, p. 278.—I. Notes of the Church as representing the Divine Nature; (1) *Unity*, (2) *Holiness*, (3) *Catholicity*, 279.

(1.) *Unity*, its double sense, singleness and concord, 280.—Other systems based on human concord.—The Church rests on the Unity of the Blessed Trinity, 281.—Difficulty of present disunion.—Reference to the invisible Church not a sufficient reply, 282.—Answer, 1. the early Church was visibly one, 283.—Tübingen theory not borne out by facts, 284.—2. Unity, on points of faith still very profound.—The schismatic temper, a sort of check on heresy, 285.—3. Prospects of future unity, much advanced by the loss of secular power, 287.—A new period of history began in 1870, 288.—Position of the Church of Rome. —Of our own Church.—The Royal Supremacy, 289.—Future conflict on fundamental truths, 290.—Possible mediation by Church of England, 291.

(2.) *Holiness*, not self-culture or outward law, but the assimilation of divine life, 292.—Coincidence of obedience and freedom in Christ, 293.—Approach to it in Christians, especially near death, 294.—Gradual sanctification of nations.—Christianity and national character, 296.—Christian legislation.—Constantine, 297.—Self-corrective power.—Repentance for negro slavery, 298.—Other social reforms, 299.

(3.) *Catholicity*, an image of God's omnipotence and omnipresence, 300.—Definition of St. Cyril of Jerusalem, 301.—Slowness of the work.—1. Influence of the Church on *action* in social and civil life, 302.—2. Influence on *thought* in doctrine of the Logos, 305.—Necessary overthrow of Scholasticism, 306.—Successive tendencies to Deism, Pantheism, ar d Positivism, 306.—Present demand for a Christian philosophy, 309.—3. Education of *feeling*.—Art and literature, 310.—Call to repentance : work of religious orders, 312.—Place of the charismata, 314.

II. The Church as satisfying Human wants, 314.—Contrast of the Jewish Ark and heathen mysteries, 315.—Dionysiac enthusiasm, 316.

(1.) *Doctrine*.—Faith and scepticism, 318.—Theology recognizes all classes of fact, 320.—Peace given to the Intellect, 321.

(2.) *Sacraments*.—Analogies in heathenism, 322.—Christian Sacraments "an extension of the Incarnation," 324.—Practical value, 325.—St. Cyprian on Baptism, 326.—The Eucharist, 327.—Other sacramental rites, 328.

(3.) *Discipline*.—Apostolicity.—The Gospels "the Institution of a Christian Ministry," 329.—Realization of Christ's presence, 331.—Practical influence, 333.—Conclusion, 335.

ADDITIONAL NOTE to p. 320, 336.

APPENDIX I.—On Buddhism, by Dr. OSCAR FRANKFURTER   337

APPENDIX II.—On the Notion of Conscience among the Zulus, by Bp. CALLAWAY, of St. John's, Kaffraria . . 354

APPENDIX III —The Purusha-Sūktā, from Dr. J. MUIR's Sanskrit Texts 356

INDEX 359

LECTURE I.

PSALM lxxxvi. 9.

All nations whom Thou hast made shall come and worship before Thee, O Lord; and shall glorify Thy Name.

INTRODUCTION. PRESENT PERPLEXITIES. THE UNITY OF RELIGION.

The present unsettlement in Religion.—Its relation to the movement of civilization.—Sense of injustice often felt in a time of transition.—Book of Job.—Christ, however, connects unbelief and sin.—Moral causes of unbelief, (1) Prejudice, (2) Severe claims of religion, (3) Intellectual faults, esp. Indolence, coldness, recklessness, pride and avarice.—General position of the believer.—Faith belongs to a state of probation.—The present Lectures a contribution to internal evidence.—The call upon us to consider the unity of our race and of religion.—Wonderful advance in knowledge of human nature.—Method of these Lectures.—Superiority of the Biblical idea of God (Lect. II.).—God a God of Truth (Lect. III., IV.), Holiness (V., VI.), and Peace (VII., VIII.), and as such sought by the nations (III., V., VII.), but only found in Christ (IV., VI., VIII.)

IF ever we attempt to forecast in detail the future of our race, or of any important section or society within it, we find ourselves very soon in a state of uncertainty and confusion. Darkness and light seem to our imaginations to struggle without any definite issue; broad and brilliant hopes clash with gloomy prognostications; and the only certainty which we attain is that of our own inability to form a picture of what will really happen.

Such a feeling as this may well be specially strong at present in the sphere of politics. Who, for instance, that has witnessed the wonderful changes of the last thirty years, and has noticed what a number of new or long-dormant and untried forces are stirring within the world of nations, can doubt that by the side of more joyous surprises even bitterer disappointments are in store for the generation that is to come after us?

But this feeling is in no degree confined to one region only of the future. The changes which have passed, and are passing, upon us in religious temper and religious belief are no less striking, and are no less unsettling to the minds of those who strive to pierce the mystery of that which is to come. A painful feeling of uncertainty and unrest prevails on many sides, and when it is found too irksome, is often merely exchanged for a strange and criminal indifference. Men are, no doubt, very prone to exaggerate the evils under which they live; and the historical enquirer who looks beneath the surface will frequently find, under the seeming solidity of the so-called "ages of faith," a coarse infidelity or a subtle scepticism, not unlike that of which he is apt to complain as the peculiar disease of his own time. But many witnesses concur to mark out the present age as specially unsettled in religion, and disinclined to look forward with confidence to the fulfilment of such prophecies as that which I have cited from the prayer of David.

There is much in this to create anxiety; and we naturally ask ourselves the cause, in order that we may provide a remedy that will attack the sickness at its root. In such an enquiry we shall perhaps meet with more matter to reassure and console us, than we at first expect. The present age, like many that have gone before it, is a time of transition. We are in many respects passing through a period like that which separates boyhood from manhood. We are exchanging an intuitive instinct and an unquestioning obedience to authority, for a conviction which is the result of reason, and a submission which is based upon experience.

This is part of the great civilizing movement in which, under all perversions and distortions, we clearly recognize the hand of God. It were at once profane and foolish to separate this movement from Him, and to ascribe it to man's unassisted energy. No: it is essentially His work, and is designed to raise the general tone and temper of nations, as that of single men is raised by education and experience of life. Without civilization, there can be no assured level of morality. An isolated act of heroism in a barbarous age may be as lofty as any that we now admire, but the general level is incomparably lower. A Roman "imperator" may sometimes rise to the ideal dignity of the "happy warrior," but at other moments he falls to the standard of an ordinary brigand. The civilizing process is intended, doubtless, to render such a lapse impossible. We must not, then, quarrel with civilization if there follow with it certain mental and moral changes, which at first cause us trouble. For it seems a necessary result of such advances, that some special individual powers should fall into the background, and be exchanged for others. Just as the savage, when raised a few steps above wildness, loses his hunter's instincts and his power of finding his way through tangled forests and over unknown seas, so in more progressive societies the feeling of mental security and prophetic certainty is apt to vanish. But just as a road and a chart and compass are better guides than the instincts of a savage, so reason and experience are more solid supports than mere intuitive certainty and mechanical obedience to law; for when thoroughly established, their action is at once more general and more unfailing.

The period of transition is, however, dangerous and critical, as we see too plainly all around us. Sin lies ever at the door to catch men off their guard. Many lives designed by God to do His work, and endowed with the fairest treasures for its performance, seem to be thrown away, and come almost to nothing. Men, solemnly dedicated to God, relinquish the task to which they have put their hands, or commit moral suicide by submission to ultramontane tyranny, and call it an act of faith to give up faith. Now, as ever, mankind are prone to rebel against the Providence of God under which they live. In their self-will, they prescribe the terms upon which they will believe, and the conditions which must be fulfilled to secure their obedience. They affirm, almost in so many words, "We will be forced into belief, or we will not believe at all." They call upon God to be a despot; they clamour against Him because He is not a tyrant.

I.] *Sense of injustice to be treated with sympathy.* 5

There is, indeed, a sort of childish petulance and passion in many of these complaints, but the issues involved in them are so solemn, that it is sinful to treat them lightly. At the bottom of our hearts we may think, with Bp. Berkeley, that it is as unreasonable for such men to complain of the defect of evidence for revelation, as it would be for a man to deny the brightness of the sun because it only shone upon the surface of things, and sometimes seemed to shine dimly or not at all [1]. But we know that there is much sincere perplexity even under a certain impatience and vehemence of manner, and that from the time of Job a sense of revolt against the dispensations of God has been felt in certain moments by many a true heart that loved righteousness. And here it may be remarked, in passing, that the fact that this feeling has been admitted, as it were, into the centre and core of Holy Scripture, and has there received full justice, is no slight evidence that the Bible is inspired to be the manual of religious truth for all the world. Men are thereby taught that a sense of injustice is a trial which they will have to meet and conquer; that to feel it is no proof that God has deserted them, or that they are unfit to serve Him. Nay, to use the old illustration, by which the Abp. of Paris comforted the sceptical master of theology in the days of St. Louis of France [2], the king is more pleased with him that keeps a frontier castle, assaulted and beleaguered by the enemy, than with him who merely rules a fortress in the midst of the settled land of

---

[1] Berkeley's *Alciphron*, Dial. vi. § 8.   [2] Joinville, *Saint Louis*, near the beginning.

peace. And, consequently, those who do not suffer from a sense of injustice and uncertainty, are warned to be tender and compassionate to those who do so, not judging harshly the irritability or weakness which vexes them and stirs their indignation, but hoping against hope that God will soften even the wayward and the stubborn, and call them gently to work again, even when they seem to have declined His service.

Nevertheless, our most merciful Saviour has so definitely linked together the ideas of sin and unbelief, that we must in very justice to those around us explain to them how and why they are so connected. In those hours when, with the shadow of death upon Him, He opened His heart with such loving unreserve to His disciples, Christ prophesied that the first office of the coming Spirit of Truth would be to establish this connection between sin and unbelief: "When He is come, He will reprove (*or* convict) the world of sin ... because they believe not on Me" (John xvi. 8, 9). Now, before any of you shrink back from the supposed harshness of these words of Christ, consider the value, the admitted value, of the principle on which they rest; and consider also that its establishment is due to Christianity. You will all agree that neglect of truth that it is in your power to obtain is sinful, and sinful in proportion to the value of the subject-matter. This extension of the field of duty so as to include the field of knowledge, is one of the triumphs of Christian moral philosophy, to which modern scientific advance owes more than it is likely to confess. Aristotle said, "All men naturally desire to know;" our Lord said, in fact, "It is the duty of all men to know," and especially to know the highest of all truths, that of religion. If it is culpable for a young man to be ignorant of some book which he offers for examination; if it is more sinful for us who teach here to be ignorant of the subjects which we profess; if it is wrong to be ignorant of the laws of health; and, worse still, to be ignorant of the moral laws which bind man to man: how much more sinful than all is it to be ignorant of our relations to God! Supposing that truth respecting religion is within our reach, and as long as the least hope of obtaining it glimmers before us, we are committing a very grievous sin indeed in resting contented in ignorance. For by so doing we neglect the highest perfection of which we are capable; we distinctly determine to be worse than we have the power of being, less vigorous in our motives, less definite in our hopes of the future, less noble in our aspirations for ourselves and our fellow-men. For we determine to know less and think less of God, from whom all goodness flows, and in whom all hope of joy centres.

It is needless, I suppose, to urge this point further. But here we are met by a difficulty, which presses, as I am well aware, upon many people, especially in societies where the respect for intellect is strong. How is it, we are asked, that such-and-such intelligent and high-minded persons, who profess to give themselves entirely to the search after Truth, whose lives are one continual pursuit of Truth,—how is it that they do not believe in Christ? Can we be right and honest in thinking them sinners? Such men seem to say, "We would willingly believe if we could; we suffer pain from our unbelief, we feel that it separates us from our friends, and renders our lives less free and powerful, and in many ways diminishes our usefulness and success; but it is the very love of Truth which stops our believing."

This is a very serious difficulty, and when it is raised in reference to individuals, I do not think we can give a definite answer to it without pretending to an impossible insight into the secrets of other hearts. Nevertheless, a quiet observation of what goes on about us, and especially a study of the undercurrents which influence our own conduct when we are not thinking of public opinion, but acting as inclination moves us, may suggest at least some reasonable explanation of the moral causes of unbelief.

I say the moral causes of unbelief, because I believe these to be the true causes of permanent alienation. I am speaking not of those who really fight with doubt, but of those who acquiesce in unbelief. It is not so much an observation of the uniformity of nature, or a belief in evolution, that makes them first deny miracles, and then deny God. It is the spirit with which they observe this uniformity and this evolution. Christianity has done as much as science, if not more, to enforce the truths that God is a God of order, and that He makes step follow step in delicate progression. But carrying with it a spirit of love and humility, it recognizes in this order and progress a will to which they are subject, and finds nothing strange, nothing disorderly, in the clearer revelation of this will from time to time in events which we call miraculous. To the eye of faith, both nature and miracle are equally natural and equally miraculous, being the expression of the same divine love and power. But this is not the case with those whose moral sense has been injured or darkened by shocks in the conflicts of the world, or by selfishness and fear of the claims of religion, or by narrow limitation of its field of view.

Let us, then, enumerate a few of the ordinary causes which lead men first to doubt, and then to deny, the truth of revelation.

1. In the first place, it is evident that belief is much weakened by prejudice against the excesses and errors, the vices and crimes, committed from time to time in the name of religion. How often do we hear Lucretius quoted, and not always without justice, to emphasise the greatness of the evil to which superstitious zeal has carried even heroic souls! In some cases, e.g., it is notorious that infidelity is a reaction from an over-rigid or erroneous presentation of the truth. A severe Calvinism, or even a hard Anglicanism, has been thrown aside, and with it Christianity itself has seemed to perish[3]. Sometimes the confusion between sins and legal offences, especially sins of unbelief, which was common to the legislation of many countries, has grown so intolerable to minds in love with freedom, that

[3] The evidence of Mr. J. E. Symes, of Newcastle-on-Tyne, and Mr. Stewart D. Headlam, in their speeches on 'Secularism' before the Leicester Church Congress, Sept., 1880, is well worth considering. They emphasise especially the hard views of some Christians on Inspiration, the Atonement, and Future Punishment, as leading the working-classes to reject belief. (*Report*, pp. 353, 650.)

religion has been identified with a persecuting spirit, and so cast aside as almost absolutely evil. It is difficult to over-estimate the influence, let us say, of the Spanish Inquisition and the Massacre of St. Bartholomew, in turning men with loathing from a profession of religion [4]. When Voltaire calculated that some ten millions of men had been slaughtered under the pretext of the Christian religion, and said, "Religion chrétienne, voilà tes effets!" he was using a very plausible, though a very irrational argument [5]. So again some of our own old penal laws, though laws of State not specially loved or sanctioned by the Church, have had in their own sphere a most disastrous influence. Sometimes (though happily for England the danger is now rare among ourselves) religion has been shunned as tainted with coarse imposture and brutal superstition; sometimes it has been degraded by the character of its ministers. An Alexander VI. and a Cardinal Dubois have done more injury to the Church than Attila or Napoleon; and even in more recent times worldly and selfish ecclesiastics, grasping for place and power, have thrown suspicion upon the morality of their whole order. One detected hypocrite may make a hundred infidels.

[4] Robert Browning has given a concentrated expression of this feeling in his vivid 'dramatic lyric,' *The Confessional* [*Spain*], (Poetical Works, vol. iii. p. 98, Lond. 1870,) beginning,—
"It is a lie—their priests, their pope,
   Their saints, their . . . all they fear or hope
   Are lies," &c.

[5] Quoted by Luthardt, *Fundamental Truths of Christianity*, Lect. ix. note 21, E. T. p. 419, 3rd ed., Edinb. 1873. Cp. on the reply to such cavils, H. Wace, *Bampton Lectures*, pp. 25, 26.

The supposed dulness and ignorance of the clergy is another excuse sometimes urged for infidelity. They are reproached for an unscientific habit of mind, and for bringing everything round to prove a foregone conclusion. There may at times be justice in these aspersions, but a calm review of past centuries will hardly bear out the conclusion that the defenders of Christian truth have been inferior in ability to those who attack it. If, however, the clergy are somewhat slow to embrace new theories, and cling with tenacity to the traditions they have received, is not this far better in them than a rash love of change? If there is one thing you can say with certainty of the books and theories of those whom it is the custom to call "advanced" thinkers, it is that they will soon be superseded. As long as there is anything to be learnt from the past; as long as truth is laboriously built up by the slow and settled results of experience; as long as history is the mistress of life, and custom and positive law the guardians of morality, so long will the best teachers of religion be those who understand, sympathize with, and reverence the past. No doubt a mere dead conservatism turns away the eager and the fervent from religion; but such will not be the temper of the English clergy as long as they retain their connexion with the Universities. To uphold this connexion is simple common sense; and they are no true friends of religion who one moment declaim against the stupidity of the clergy, and the next moment vote the abolition of those endowments which secure them their present measure of enlightenment. Drive them into seminaries, and limit them to a mere professional learning, and you increase tenfold the dangers of infidelity.

2. I have spoken of some common prejudices which foster unbelief. A second sort of difficulty is not to be passed over, though it is not easy to speak of it without offence. I mean a revolt from the severe claims of religion, and a secret inclination to sin which dwells in many hearts. Such an explanation of unbelief is one from which charity and courtesy alike would shrink, and it often seems obviously inapplicable; but a serious testing of what religion is, and of the very heavy strain which it puts upon the believer, must convince us that this difficulty is no imaginary one.

For experience shews us that no amount of intellect, or high culture, or noble ambition, can save a man from grave moral faults; and that even apparently sincere conviction sometimes breaks down, in cases of men who seem entirely raised above temptation. No one, I believe, can really know his own heart, without knowing also that he is by nature capable of almost any sin, and that there is within him a constant pressure, sometimes gentle, sometimes vehement, tending to make light of the responsibility for sin, and to weaken belief in the justice and love of God. This pressure, if once we yield to it, tends directly to unbelief in revelation; for the morbid conscience longs above all things to slumber, and in the full brightness of revelation it cannot rest. If we are once convinced that God has spoken, all hope of peaceful repose in sin is lost; and therefore he whose heart inclines to sin, instinctively veils himself from the knowledge of revelation, just as the sick man tosses uneasily until the stream of sunlight is curtained from his pillow.

This is the interior state; outside, for a time, there is perhaps no apparent change. The force of sinful inclination appears to have spent itself in producing unbelief. The force of habit still remains to balance it. An equilibrium seems to be produced in the man, and no striking and glaring evil marks the moment of lapse into infidelity. It seems almost as if the state of unbelief were not such a bad one after all, and death may intervene before the strife of powers has been decided within the soul. But often, even to our eyes, there comes a sudden collapse, and the apparent peace which preceded it is found to have been merely a quiet rottenness [6].

3. I have spoken of such moral failures as all must

---

[6] Some rather striking evidence on the moral results of infidelity may be found in *The Life of Joseph Barker, written by himself* (London: Hodder and Stoughton, 1880), who was a Methodist, Quaker, Unitarian, and all but an atheist in turn, and finally returned to Christianity. Of America he says (p. 336):—"Often when I came to be acquainted with the men who invited me to lecture [in America], I was ashamed to be seen standing with them in the streets; and I shrank from the touch of their hand as from pollution. . . . . In England, where I expected on my return home to find unbelievers better, I found them worse. I supposed that the Secularists thought as I did with regard to virtue. . . . . And when at length I was convinced past doubt of my mistake, the effect was terribly painful. But it was salutary." He was himself an instance of an infidel who preserved his love of right conduct and domestic purity, and this in the end restored him to Christ, but several incidents in his account of himself shew clearly enough that in many of the more delicate virtues his character degenerated as he became sceptical.

acknowledge when they occur; and, if one case only of infidelity from such a cause is known to us, surely we have a warning from God, which it were in the highest degree foolish and criminal to disregard. But, besides these so-called "moral" failures, there are sins attaching to the intellect, which are as essentially and really acts and states of "immorality" as the grossest outbreaks of vice. Will you pardon me if I point out one which seems the special canker of societies like our own? Many are the faults which disguise themselves as a love of truth, but perhaps none is more frequent than a selfish intellectual indolence. We live amongst men devoted to study, whether for their own sake or as teachers of others, many of whom pass their lives in a somewhat narrow round of philosophy or history, or law or language, or natural science or mathematics, or a mixture of some of these. This is the essence of a University, that it should contain experts and students specially devoted to these subjects, who can be referred to as authorities in their particular spheres: and no one who has imagination or experience enough to give him any sense of the value of such stores of knowledge, lying close together as in a vast treasure-house, can do anything but thank God for the blessings we enjoy in this place, and pray that He may increase them tenfold to our posterity. But this grand artificial society has its peculiar temptations, as all artificial societies have; and one of the strongest, I venture to repeat, is a refined and selfish indolence, disguising itself as a love of truth, or at least of knowledge. For, without doubt, one of the first conditions to success in study is the power of abstraction and attention, the concentration of the intellect on a given area, and the pursuit of the action of certain isolated principles belonging to the science or art which is being studied. By this we see that a direct premium is offered to one-sidedness, if a man will content himself with a temporary success. Clearness, method, systematic power, the ability to strike the imagination and impress the memory of one's pupils, all these things are gained by the adoption of a few simple principles, and the excision of all reference to debateable or inconsistent facts. To men consciously or unconsciously under the influence of these motives, revelation is felt as an awkward disturbing force, rather than as the most helpful energy of their lives.

It appears to them as coming in from outside to dissipate and distract their intellectual vigour, which might otherwise be spent on perfecting themselves and others in some definite line of enquiry. It is seen to involve those who accept it in so many troubles and disputes; it places life so much more at the mercy of alien intruders, it encumbers it with so many engagements. Even the time spent in public or private prayer is grudged. "Why," it is urged, "should I go to college chapel, when I do not really believe more than half that I hear and say there? I had better make up some prayers of my own, such as exactly suit my religious position." But where are these prayers, after half-a-year's absence from college chapel? Gone with the other half of the belief, I fear, in too many cases; or perhaps suspended till

God in His mercy send sickness or sorrow to touch the heart and lift the veil of customary indifference. In the meantime, the stall in chapel and the lowly posture of devotion is exchanged for the seclusion of the study, or self-directed meditation at the fireside. The intellectual exercise of thinking about God takes the place of the humble attitude of listening to His word, and pouring out the soul in prayer, and worshipping before the altar. The sweet charities and sympathies, the mysterious inspirations which flow from the gatherings of the faithful in the presence of God, the tenderness and confidence of sons, are exchanged for selfish isolation. The burning love of souls, the zeal which once glowed for spreading the cause of Christ and of goodness throughout the world, gradually sink to a cold and ashy cynicism. Instead of a duty to God and men, church-going is reduced, by the men of whom we speak, to a rare compliment paid to a preacher whom they wish to study, in the faint hope that he will kindle some sense of languid admiration. Who can wonder that such perverse conduct bears its fruit in a withered, discontented heart, and a stunted and one-sided intellect? As time goes on, the exercise of thinking about God becomes on their part an act of grace and patronage, and then a dry and spiritless formality. At last, too often, His very existence as a personal Being comes to be regarded as a speculation, the decision of which has but little interest for the scientific or literary mind, occupied steadily in such matters as are fairly within its grasp and measure.

Very nearly akin to this intellectual indolence

is the cool, dispassionate candour on which some sceptics plume themselves, as if it were the best method of attaining religious truth. They seem to forget that revelation comes to them, if it comes at all, from above, not from below, and from a Power in whose presence fear is a duty. If it exist at all, which is the question before them, it is a gift for which they ought to be thankful, not a suppliant upon their charity[7]. They tell us that it is their first duty to preserve their minds from prejudice in favour of revelation; that they are responsible for the legal purity and judicial impartiality of their reason, which is to them the sole arbiter of truth. And so they exclude all hope of finding revelation, lest it should delude them into credulity, and all fear of losing it, lest they should be frightened into superstition. The fact is, that in so jealously guarding the supremacy of reason, they are really wronging what they profess to honour, they unduly limit the field of which it ought to take cognizance, and the position it ought to occupy. True, as all wise apologists of all ages remind us, "Reason is a divine reality: and God who purposed, disposed and ordered nothing without Reason, wills that all things should be treated and considered with Reason[8]."

[7] Cp. some excellent remarks on this topic in Newman's *Grammar of Assent* (pp. 420, 421, London, 1870), criticizing Paley's method. See also Pascal, *Pensées*, part 2, article 6, § 5 (p. 188, Didot, 1863), on the low idea of conversion which is entertained by many sceptics.

[8] Tertullian, *de pœnitentia*, § 1, which thus begins:—"Pœnitentiam hoc genus hominum, quod et ipsi retro fuimus, cæci sine domini lumine, natura tenus norunt passionem animi quandam

"Reason is the only faculty we have wherewith to judge concerning anything, even Revelation itself[9]." This is true, however, just because, and so far as, our reason is a guide of our life ever present with us, not a judge deciding in a court outside us. If it is to decide aright, it must take into account all the elements of our complex life, it must measure and balance all the forces that tend to preserve and extend our powers of will and feeling, as well as those which form our purely intellectual conclusions. Right reason cannot be guardian only of the interests of one faculty or portion of the human soul, but is the director of the whole, and it must take cognizance likewise of the whole evidence offered by human nature. Thus the warm personal love felt by the soul to its Saviour is evidence offered not by the intelligence, but by the heart. The impression of a divine voice speaking in a way which commands obedience in the pages of Holy Scripture, is evidence again offered, not so much by the intelligence as by the will and the conscience. But reason cannot, dare not, reject a consideration of either. Right reason on

esse quæ veniat de offensa sententiæ peioris. Ceterum a ratione eius tantum absunt, quantum ab ipso rationis auctore. Quippe res Dei ratio; quia Deus omnium conditor, nihil non ratione providit, disposuit, ordinavit, nihil non ratione tractari intellegique voluit."

[9] Butler, *Analogy*, part ii. chap. 3. Cp. Isaac Barrow, *Sermon* 2, *Of Faith* (vol. ii. pp. 21—23, ed. 1683), and *Sermon* 13, *Of the Christian Religion* (p. 189), and my father's *Letters to M. Gondon*, ed. 2, pp. 49 following. Origen has sometimes been misrepresented as if he admitted Celsus' taunt that Christians believe on mere faith, without examination. He really treats it as a *calumny* (*c. Celsum*, i. 9, 13; iii. 50).

the contrary says, If there is a revelation it will touch the heart, it will speak to the conscience in just such a way as the Gospel does; and, so far, I have the evidence I am bound to expect. Unless revelation did produce these effects, it would be irrational to accept it.

If reason, however, restricts itself to merely intellectual evidence, the case of a man like the late John Stuart Mill, according to his own witness, shews how inevitable is the collapse [10]. Other faculties will have their rights somehow or other, or the man will perish. And even in the interests of pure intelligence, who can say that hope and fear, love and joy, are foes to be excluded? Did not hope enable Columbus to find America? Do not affection and inclination, as well as the expectation of success, play a real part in all scientific discovery? Do not feeling and taste give insight into character and argument? Does not experience shew us daily that only he who loves can understand the language of love [11]? Am I then to

[10] See his *Autobiography*, chap. v., "A crisis in my mental history." He quotes two lines of Coleridge (p. 140) as a true description of what he felt in his intense dejection:—
"Work without hope draws nectar in a sieve,
And hope without an object cannot live."
Unfortunately, the religion to which he turned as an object was not the highest—a mere human affection, however tender. See p. 251, written shortly after the death of his wife:—"Her memory is to me a religion, and her approbation the standard by which, summing up as it does all worthiness, I endeavour to regulate my life."

[11] St. Bernard. Cp. Pascal, *Pensées, part* 1, *art.* 3 (pp. 30, 31, Didot, 1863), "qu'il faut aimer (les choses divines) pour les connaître," and *art.* 6, § 13 (p. 64) on the will as an organ of belief. See also the last pages of Mozley's *Bampton Lectures.*

drive away all my best thoughts, all the quickening impulses of spiritual life, all my fears of losing man's highest good, and even turn against them and hate them as misleading falsities, because they do not happen to be arguments of a peculiar type, reducible to a certain form of syllogism? Am I to call this a reasonable state of mind? No, rather I should be utterly unreasonable if I did so. Surely it is much wiser to hold with the most profound of living poets [12],—

> " I say, the acknowledgment of God in Christ
> Accepted by thy reason, solves for thee
> All questions in the earth and out of it,
> And has so far advanced thee to be wise.
> Wouldst thou unprove this to re-prove the proved?
> In life's mere minute, with power to use that proof,
> Leave knowledge and revert to how it sprung?
> Thou hast it; use it, and forthwith, or die.
> For this I say is death, and the sole death,
> When a man's loss comes to him from his gain,
> Darkness from light, from knowledge ignorance,
> And lack of love from love made manifest."

This intellectual coldness seems, in fact, to be as sinful as intellectual indolence. Yet some people tacitly make the assumption that the intellect is outside morality; that you have but to follow your own bias and instinct in its sphere, and to disregard the consequences. This is, indeed, a very narrow system of ethics. Let us suppose a man to receive a letter

---

[12] R. Browning, *A Death in the Desert;* a wonderful ideal description of the last hours of St. John, in which he is supposed to review his life, and to meet possible future objections to his Gospel: Poetical Works, vol. vi. p. 127 (Lond., 1870), or Selections, Second Series, pp. 316, 317, (Lond., 1880).

purporting to come from his father, and containing a promise of something which he much desired, which would be a great comfort to him to have, and which the father was specially able to bestow. What should we say of such a man, if he submitted this letter to a purely intellectual test, and decided that the very suitability of the promise to his wants and wishes was a reason for doubting, if not rejecting it? We should call him unfilial and brutal, as well as stupid [13]. And yet this is what these coldly-intellectual persons say with regard to what we tell them of their heavenly Father's message. In them "lack of love" comes " from love made manifest."

There are other sins besides these, to which the intellect is liable, such as recklessness, pride, and avarice, all of which may be disguised as love of truth. Thus there is a mere taste for adventure in the pursuit of knowledge, which is akin to the common passion for hunting and mountaineering, where the object is not the result obtained, but the lively agitation of spirits which is created by the act itself.

[13] Pascal says on this point, with righteous indignation (*Pensées*, part 2, art. 2, (p. 152) :—" Cette négligence en une affaire où il s'agit d'eux-mêmes, de leur éternité, de leur tout, m'irrite plus qu'elle ne m'attendrit; elle m'étonne et m'épouvante; c'est un monstre pour moi." And further on (p. 158) :—" Rien ne marque davantage une extrême bassesse de cœur que de ne pas souhaiter la vérité des promesses éternelles; rien n'est plus lâche que de fair le brave contre Dieu," &c. It is probable that in all ages of the world a certain connection between infidelity and this "bassesse de cœur," of which Pascal speaks, has been observable. On the duty of hope and of noble wishes, cp. the fine passages of Mozley's University Sermons on *Eternal Life* (pp. 75 foll.) and *The Strength of Wishes* (pp. 250 foll., first ed., 1876).

The end is in the means, and nothing beyond. This love of adventure lends a certain air of grace and nobility to a man; it makes him brave weariness, physical pain and danger, with a light heart, because he sets them against the power of excitement which fills and masters him, and carries him outside himself. So it is in those who value the search after truth, more than truth itself. They point, perhaps, to the pains they undergo as a justification of their integrity, and ask us, it may be, to sympathize with them in their failures. But we are tempted to reply, "You have obtained all that you desired. You do not really care for truth. You do not believe in the power of attaining it. All that you have aimed at was a refined form of intellectual excitement and amusement. In so doing you are doubly guilty, both in cheating yourself of success, which might have been yours if you had sought the truth, not its shadow; and in deluding your neighbours, who have judged you really in earnest, when you were only aiming at a vain and selfish pleasure."

Again, that the intellect is liable to pride is, of course, notorious; and was, I suppose, a fact as much recognized by the better heathens as by ourselves. In the search after truth, that is to say, the pride of intelligence invests what it obtains with a kind of halo of interest as its own property; just as men, proud in this world, get to respect what lies about them, because of its nearness to the glories that flow from their own persons. The proud man seems to himself a sort of centre of light and dignity, from which an effluence pours forth upon all which he touches, or at least gathers to himself; and this sentiment is hardly less common in the intellectual than in the secular sphere of life. This fault, in another type of character, becomes rather a species of avarice. Truth is looked upon as a kind of property, of which so much may be obtained by diligent and acquisitive habits [14], and as a property which lends glory to its possessor, just as acquired capital does honour to the successful merchant. But in either case truth is regarded as valuable, chiefly because of its relation to the man, not because of its objective worth and dignity. And this is the great difference between the selfish and the Christian pursuit of truth. *We* do not look for a mere discovery, an ornament, a treasure, but an objective personality outside us and above us, to which we bow in reverent adoration; a light which is both liberty and law; a power which finds and chooses us, and is not found and chosen by us; a moulding and informing presence, which is none other than the might of Christ our Lord.

In some such way, then, as this we may point out

[14] These topics are treated with great force by Dr. Mozley, in his interesting review of *Blanco White's Autobiography;* Essays, vol. ii. cp. especially p. 146 :—" Here is the point. The fact is, that the love of truth, especially in fallen man, is a corrupted affection, just as natural love is. It betrays the selfish element. His mind annexes truth to itself, and not itself to truth. It considers truth as a kind of property; it wants the pride of making it its own; it treats it as an article of mental success; it does not reverence truth as an object, but appropriates it as a thing; it loves it as its own creation, and as the reflection of itself and its labours. The merchant sees himself in his capital, the parent in his child; every one has the image of himself in the shape of some issue from himself; and there is a philosophy which sees such an issue in truth, and makes it, in its sphere, the very embodiment of that of which truth divine is the extinction—the principle of self."

whereabouts may probably be found the answer to the question, "How can the unbelief of really intelligent men be sinful?"

This may be of some help to the wavering. But they require also a positive support, and it has usually been held to be the function of Lectures such as these to give that help in the form demanded by the necessities of the day. To a specific portion of that task I desire, with God's blessing, to address myself; but first I would remind you, in few words, of that general and familiar truth which is the foundation of all such undertakings.

We cannot look on human life as anything else than a state of probation, that is to say, a state in which we are tried and strengthened by use and exercise of the less, before we are put in possession of the more [15]. Faith, not compulsion, is the true means of development suitable to a moral being. In this way, and in no other that we can conceive possible, are the powers of our nature brought to their fullest maturity. In this way, both the more passive qualities of trustfulness and trustworthiness, and the more active energies of the will, are educated in the service of God. In our relations with God, as well as in our relations to one another, we are men, not machines; and as long as faith and hope, and a reliance upon the unseen and unknown, have their place in social intercourse, so long must they have a place, and a foremost place, in religion [16].

---

[15] Cp. Butler's *Analogy*, part i. chaps. iv. and v., on "A State of Probation," and "Moral Discipline."

[16] For a fuller statement of this topic, nothing can be better than Mr. Wace's very forcible paper in reply to Prof. Clifford's *Ethics*

You will pardon me for stating a truth, I had almost said a truism, which has so often been urged from this place, and which so many able apologists have handled elsewhere, age after age. But simple as it is, it is daily in danger of being forgotten. It is one of those first principles which the indolence and negligence of mankind are ever ready to let drop out of sight. It is so much easier to be querulous because you have not received off-hand a complete and absolute demonstration, than to pursue a long course of arguments, in which a number of different lines converge upon a given point, and in which the careful judgment of a variety of moral questions is involved.

To recall this primary fact to mind is the first duty of the Christian apologist. Let him force it clearly into the understanding of the opponent or doubter with whom he is arguing, and then he will have some chance of making an impression by means of the particular arguments which ought to follow. These, as we are all aware, are of two kinds, external and internal; the first appealing to the authority of witnesses to facts outside us, the second shewing the intrinsic or inward reasonableness of the Christian revelation. Both of these methods of argument are necessary, and Oxford perhaps needs the first quite as much as the second. But on the present occasion

of Belief, read before the Victoria Institute, and reprinted as note 6 to his *Bampton Lectures*, pp. 242—258. The germ of this argument is in Origen *contra Celsum*, i. 11. Cp. also S. Irenæus *adv. hæreses*, ii. 28, § 3, who extends the offices of faith and hope (as well as love) to another world, that God may be always our teacher, and we may be always waiting upon His bounty.

I shall beg your attention to a portion rather of the internal evidence, which I propose to treat from a special point of view. I need scarcely say to those about me at this moment what motives induce this choice of subject. There are times of life to some men (with which most of us here are very familiar) when the intellect is in a state of passionate activity, when it throws itself upon the world with instinctive self-assertion, and desires to create, out of the mass of fragments which seem to lie about it, an ideal truth which shall be all its own. In times like these, the voice of authority has a distant, unmeaning sound; its light for the time is eclipsed, its assertions merely irritate. The most conclusive external proofs are powerless; and the whole fabric of past experience seems on the point of crumbling into dust.

What are we Christian teachers to do in these critical moments? Are we simply to stand apart, till weariness or disappointment suggest a return to the old paths? May we not do more, by placing ourselves side by side with these eager strivings? We shall at least gain the influence which is the prerogative of sympathy, and the respect which is given to those who are thorough believers in the validity of their message. Our attempt to construct a Christian philosophy of religion may not be, in any sense, a final one; yet, by God's grace, it may be a bridge, for some at least, over that dangerous gulf in which so many barks have gone down, which set forth in the morning with sunlit sails, a passage over those dark waters in which so many strong swimmers have lost their lives.

Unity of human nature and of religion.

I desire, then, to be permitted to hold up to such seekers after God the beautiful form of Christianity as the one normal or standard religion of the human race. I assume, with them, that religion is not only possible, but is the great end for which mankind were created; that it is reasonable to believe with David, that all nations whom God has made will be brought to worship Him together and to glorify His name. I cannot suppose that any of us, at least in our better moments, will be behind the Platonist and the Stoic in their aspirations after one law and one doctrine [17]. I address myself, therefore, to those who feel the need of religion, and who believe in the essential unity of religion, but who desire to be Christians by conviction, and with a reasonable grasp of the intrinsic pre-eminence of the Church's faith. Further, and more particularly, I address those who feel with myself that they are now called upon to consider their faith in the new light which is thrown upon it by the simultaneous researches into all the faiths, new and old, that claim the allegiance of mankind. I speak to those who feel that the old adage,—

"Homo sum: nihil humani a me alienum puto,"

[17] On the heathen sentiment as to the unity of belief, see Maximus Tyrius, *dissert.* 17, ch. 4 and 5, where he imagines a sort of congress of nations voting unanimously on religion; Plutarch, *de fortuna Alexandri*, 6, on the Stoic polity (Wytt., vol. 2, p. 349), *de Iside et Osiride*, 67 (vol. 2, p. 546); Numenius ap. Euseb., *præp. Evang.*, ix. 7; Celsus ap. Origen., *c. Celsum*, i. 14, vi. 80. All these writers, however, lived after the Gospel had spread belief in the unity of the human race and of religion. Cp. Th. Keim, *Celsus Wahres Wort*, p. 213 (Zürich, 1873).

acquires daily fresh force from the multitudinous facts which pour in on every side to witness that man is everywhere the brother and like of man.

Consider for a moment what a marvellous knowledge we now possess in this department. In the first place, there is now no race upon the globe of anything like even third-rate importance which is unvisited and undescribed; there is none whatever, we may feel perfectly sure, which, when visited, will be very dissimilar to those already within our view. Everywhere, within certain limits, the same religious and moral nature appears, even when it is overlaid and degraded, and all but obliterated. Even in minute details of mythology and custom, we find an extraordinary unanimity of ideas between the remotest tribes. The dwellers in distant corners, hunted and trodden down by stronger races, the very bywords of humanity—the Bushmen, the Andamans, the Veddahs, the Australians, the Fuegians, the Botocudes, the Eskimo [18], and if there be any lower than these—when approached with sympathy and insight,

---

[18] E.g. the Bushmen and the Eskimo are said to be the races which have the greatest natural capacity of forming mental images of things they have seen, and therefore of making drawings, maps, &c. The Christianisation of the Fuegians is one of the greatest triumphs of modern missions in an apparently hopeless field. Mr. Darwin, it is said, thought it impossible, but afterwards became a contributor to the funds of the mission. The Queen recently sent a token of her approval to those natives who were formerly wreckers, but on a late occasion humanely succoured some English sailors cast upon their inhospitable shore, and took care of their property after their death. (Speech of Rev. R. J. Simpson before Oxford Missionary Association of Graduates, Jan. 30, 1880).

I.] *Manifold advance of the study of Human Nature.* 29

shew themselves truly human types, with some qualities defective or imperfect, but with others more than usually vigorous, and all, at any rate, with a personality and a creative power which proves them all equally formed in the image of God [19].

[19] On this topic it is sufficient to cite three well-known witnesses, Dr. Theodor Waitz, Dr. James Cowles Prichard, and Professor A. de Quatrefages of Paris. The former thus sums up the discussion which is the principal subject of the first volume of his very valuable *Anthropologie der Naturvölker* (Eng. tr., p. 327, Lond., 1863):—"On casting a retrospective glance at the numerous facts and the various points of view from which we have endeavoured to elucidate the main question, we are irresistibly led to the conclusion that there are no specific differences among mankind with regard to their psychical life. The great difference in civilization amongst peoples of the same stock, testifies that the degree of civilization does not chiefly depend on organization or mental endowment."

Dr. Prichard thus concludes his *Natural History of Man* (vol. ii. pp. 713, 714, ed. Norris, Lond., 1855):—" We contemplate among all the diversified tribes who are endowed with reason and speech, the same internal feelings, appetences, aversions; the same inward convictions, the same sentiments of subjection to invisible powers, and, more or less fully developed, of accountableness or responsibility to unseen avengers of wrong and agents of retributive justice, from whose tribunal men cannot even by death escape. We find everywhere the same susceptibility, though not always in the same degree of forwardness or ripeness of improvement, of admitting the cultivation of these universal endowments, of opening the eyes of the mind to the more clear and luminous views which Christianity unfolds, of becoming moulded to the institutions of religion and of civilized life: in a word, the same inward and mental nature is to be recognized in all races of men. When we compare this fact with the observations which have been heretofore fully established as to the specific instincts and separate psychical endowments of all the distinct tribes of sentient beings in the universe, we are enabled to draw confidently the conclusion that all human races are of one species and one family."

M. de Quatrefages says (at the end of book i. of his treatise on

And while we have this flood of light thrown upon the present state of the human family, we have yet more marvellous discoveries in the ancient histories of Egypt, Assyria, Babylonia, and other great nations, carrying us back two or even three thousand years before the birth of Christ [20]. And just at the same moment we have unbiassed and authentic accounts of the great religions of the East, long imfectly known to us, of Persia, India, and China; enabling us to reach deep into the heart of the patient millions of Eastern Asia, and to know their springs of motive and action better even, it may be, than they know themselves [21].

The Human Species, pp. 87, 88, London, 1879):—" In every case crossings between human groups exhibit the phenomena characteristic of mongrels, and never those of hybrids.

"Therefore these human groups, however different they may be, or appear to be, are only *races of one and the same species*, and not *distinct species*.

"Therefore, there is but one human species, taking this term species in the acceptation employed when speaking of animals and plants."

He also says, speaking generally, that " what science may affirm is that *from all appearances* each species has had, as point of departure, a single primitive pair," (p. 84). He naturally concludes, therefore, for one centre of appearance in the case of man, which he inclines to place in Northern Asia (p. 178).

[20] According to Mr. Renouf's estimate (*Hibbert Lectures*, 1879, pp. 49, 50, Lond., 1880), our knowledge of Egypt goes back to beyond 3000 B.C. Dr. Legge places the invention of the Chinese primitive characters at about the same date; *Religions of China*, pp. 8, and 59, 60. (London, 1880.)

[21] It is scarcely necessary to mention the series of *Sacred Books of the East*, edited by Prof. Max Müller, and the unpretentious but very useful manuals published by the Society for Promoting Christian Knowledge, on *Non-Christian Religious Systems*, besides the

Lastly, a re-reading of the old classical mythologies seems to bring the whole mass into focus, and to present us with a lively picture of the unity of the religious instincts and aims of the great family of mankind. This generation, whatever its losses in respect to traditional reverence, has at least this enormous gain, that, for the first time in the history of the world, it can survey the whole field of natural theology, with a fair certainty that it is not being deceived.

Such, then, is the matter before us. The method I shall pursue in dealing with it is a simple one, and will, I hope, commend itself to your judgment.

In my next Lecture I shall lay the foundation for the whole argument, by comparing and contrasting the Christian and Biblical idea of God with the chief non-Christian and heretical conceptions which claim to take its place. In those that follow, I shall consider in turn the three great positions which seem to be assumed as fundamental in all religions.

The *first* of these is, that God wills to make Himself known to man; that He is a God of Truth, and a giver of revelations (Lectures III. IV.).

The *second*, that sin separates man from God, and that atonement for it must be made by sacrifice (V. VI.).

The *third*, that men may find peace and favour with God in this life, and a better life with Him after death (VII. VIII.).

These three propositions, if summed up in one sentence for the sake of clearness, amount to this, viz.

mass of separate publications, many of which will be referred to in the notes to the following Lectures.

that God is the God of Truth, of Holiness, and of Peace, and as such wills to unite man to Himself in truth, holiness, and peace. As the God of Truth, He deigns to satisfy the cravings of the soaring intellect, which He has created to look upwards to Himself, and to find rest in no lower sphere. As the God of Holiness, He wills that the heart and affections, which have been turned away from Him by sin, should be brought back and reconciled to His Fatherly love. As the God of Peace, He desires that the will of man should be ordered and disciplined for ever in His ways; that death should be no bar to our advancement, but that we should be carried onward into the freedom and blessedness of eternal life; that the Church on earth should lead upward to the Church in heaven.

Taking these propositions as the groundwork of my Lectures, I shall endeavour to prove under each of these three heads in turn:—

Firstly, that non-Christian religious systems assume or bear specific witness to these general convictions; while they fail, often by their own admission, to satisfy the yearnings to which they give utterance (Lectures III. V. and VII.).

Secondly, that the Christian revelation, in each of these respects, does represent the nature of God in a manner befitting His glory, and does give the true and blessed answer to the needs and hopes of man (Lectures IV. VI. and VIII.).

LECTURE II.

EXODUS iii. 13, 14.

And Moses said unto God, Behold, when I come unto the children of Israel, and shall say unto them, " The God of your fathers hath sent me unto you ;" and they shall say to me, "What is His Name?" what shall I say unto them?

And God said unto Moses, "I AM THAT I AM:" and He said, Thus shalt thou say unto the children of Israel, " I AM hath sent me unto you."

BIBLICAL THEISM CONTRASTED WITH OTHER CONCEPTIONS OF THE NATURE OF GOD.

The Unity of God witnessed by instinct and reason, but only explicitly and publicly taught by those who acknowledge the Bible.—God revealed to Moses as both Infinite and Personal.—Why this unity of attributes is credible.—Departures from this belief on either side.

Pantheism a one-sided exaggeration of His Infinity.—Its danger.—Dualism a step nearer the truth.—Sabellian and Eutychian types of heresy.

Anthropomorphic Deism the antithesis to Pantheism.—Exaggeration of God's personality and of Man's independence.—State religion of China.—Deistic tendencies in Græco-Roman philosophy, and in Judaism.—In later times, outside and inside the Church.—Islam.—Pelagian and Nestorian heresies, and similar movements.—Tübingen School.—Conclusion.

INSTINCT, reason, and revelation all combine to speak to us of one God. The soul of man, at least in this regard, (as Tertullian[1] well teaches us,) is "naturally Christian." Monotheism, though it is the public creed only of those races who pos-

---

[1] *Apologeticum*, chap. 17, a passage enlarged in his interesting treatise, *De Testimonio animæ*.

sess (or, like the Mahometans, at least acknowledge) the Scriptures[2], is, nevertheless, clearly the normal religion of mankind. It is assumed, or implied, in the ordinary religious language of every nation; it is everywhere a sort of quiet background of belief, waiting to be called into actuality at the approach of light; it is that to which the best thought of the best minds in every age is everywhere distinctly tending. To this truth bear witness the general names for God existing in so many languages, and the appeals to His universal power and justice, His omniscience and His mercy, His will and goodness, which burst from the heart of man whenever he is deeply stirred, and caught (as it were) off his guard[3].

[2] Islam is, of course, no exception, even if the Moslem idea of God was less faulty than it is. For Mahomet acknowledged both the Jewish and the Christian Scriptures, and considers that the Koran is confirmatory of them. See *Sura*, v. 50—52 (Rodwell, ed. 2, p. 545), a passage ending, "To thee we have sent down the Book *of the Koran*, with truth confirmatory of previous Scripture and its safeguard." Cp. *Sura*, ii. 130 (p. 383); iii. 79 (p. 432): "Say: We believe in God, and in what hath been sent down to us, and what hath been sent down to Abraham, and Ismael, and Isaac, and Jacob, and the tribes: and in what was given to Moses, and to Jesus, and to the Prophets, from their Lord. We make no difference between them. And to Him are we resigned (Muslims)." Cp. Max Müller on Semitic Monotheism, which he traces to the faith of Abraham, and ascribes to a 'special revelation:' *Selected Essays*, vol. ii. pp. 433 foll. (reprinted in 1881). The modern Pārsīs may seem to be an exception, but they have come too much in contact with Christian and Mahometan theists to be cited. See below, p. 50.

[3] Cp. Minucius Felix *Octavius*, c. 18, "Audio vulgus, cum ad cælum manus tendunt, nihil aliud quam deum dicunt, et 'deus magnus est' et 'deus verus est,' et 'si deus dederit.' Vulgi iste naturalis sermo est, an Christiani confitentis oratio?" Similarly, Tertullian, *de testimonio animæ*, c. 2, and *Apol.*, c. 17.

Hear on this point a Kaffir,—one of that race which has often been calumniated as atheistic,—who thus adds his contribution to the great testimony of the "consensus gentium[4]:"—

"We had this word [the name of God] long before the missionaries came: we had God (Utikxo) long ago: for a man, when dying, would utter his last words, saying, 'I am going home, I am going up on high.' For there is a word in a song which says:—

> 'Guide me, O Hawk!
> That I may go heavenward,
> To seek the one-hearted man,
> Away from the double-hearted men
> Who deal in blessing and cursing.'

* * * *

"So we say there is no God who has just come to us. Let no man say, 'The God which is, is the God of the English.' There are not many Gods: there is but one God. We err when we say, 'He is the God of the English.' He is not the God of certain nations; just as man is not English and Kosa; he is not Fingo and Hottentot; he is one man, who came forth from one God."

It would be difficult to put this great truth more powerfully and succinctly than it is stated by this Kaffir theologian, the first-fruits of a race just brought to Christ. We cannot fail to recognize in these simple words the real instinctive voice of natural piety which has already thrilled us in so many other languages. And the persistent tes-

---

[4] Translated by Bp. Callaway, in the *South African Folk-Lore Journal*, vol. ii. p. 56, foll. (Capetown and London, Nutt, 1880.) Cp. also his lecture *On the Religious Sentiment among the Tribes of South Africa*, recently published in the *Cape Magazine*, of which he has kindly sent me a copy.

timony of instinct is reinforced by that of reason. The well-known arguments from nature and human nature can never be effete. On the one hand, a view of nature teaches us, first, that all things have a Cause, which is itself uncaused, Eternal, and Infinite, and is the efficient and adequate cause of all that is, whether intelligent or unintelligent; and secondly, that all things have an End, or (as it is often called) a final Cause, and that end a fulfilment of the will of God. On the other hand, a survey of human nature, quite apart from our own instincts or conclusions, and regarding it as a field of scientific enquiry, teaches us other lessons of the same kind. We see that man, considered as a reasoning animal, and, therefore, certainly not made in vain and to no purpose, exhibits two great tendencies. The first is Dependence upon the unseen, leading him to prayer and humble reverence to the author of his life; the second is the pursuit of an Ideal of moral goodness, leading him to sacrifice and its correlative rites, and to an enunciation of the dictates of his conscience as a Divine law. These four methods of argument, viz. from Causation and Design in Nature, and from the sense of Dependence and of the Moral Law in Man, when combined together, carry us nearly to that belief in God, which we learn from Holy Scripture. They teach us that there is one Supreme Being, at once Infinite and Personal, who is perfect in power and perfect in moral nature.

Yet it needs little or no imagination to understand that this great truth gains a much more powerful and decisive hold upon the minds of men when explicitly declared as a truth of revelation.

"Though the works of nature (says Locke [5]) in every part of them sufficiently evidence a Deity, yet the world made so little use of their reason, that they saw Him not, where, even by the impression of Himself, He was easy to be found." "Native and original truth is not so easily wrought out of the mine as we, who have it delivered ready into our hands, are apt to imagine [6]."

Accordingly, as we have already said, as a matter of historic fact, only those peoples who acknowledge the Scriptures have made public profession of Monotheism. Even in the case of this most simple and fundamental principle of religion, a revelation was necessary to formulate and establish what all nature and all experience was tending to teach. This must strike us, even at first sight, as a great point in favour of the Scriptures considered as a body of doctrine. We cannot imagine this superiority to be an accident, or to be confined to one division only of the massive and coherent structure of Scriptural theology. There is, as we very soon recognize, a vital connection between belief in one God, as taught in the Bible, and all the other articles of our faith. He who accepts the first is naturally led on to accept those that follow. Nor shall we err in thinking, that if we grasp aright the doctrine of one God as taught in the Bible, we shall be able also to understand the

---

[5] *Reasonableness of Christianity*, § 167. [6] Ibid., § 170, speaking of moral truths.

unique superiority of our creed, and to distinguish it from all false and defective systems.

To make clear this distinction is the task which we have before us this morning. Let us first ask what is the essence, or inner principle, of the Biblical conception of God. To discover this, we naturally look to the great revelation of the Divine name made to Moses on Mount Sinai. "What shall I say unto the people when they ask the name of their fathers' God?" is the prophet's question. The answer is, "I AM THAT I AM." .... "I AM hath sent me unto you."

It can hardly escape any one here that this Divine name, when analysed, presents us with a twofold mysterious idea, that of Infinity and Personality in combination. In this name, "I am that I am," or, as we should say in modern English, "I am that which I am," we are first taught that God is absolute, independent, self-existent, eternal. His nature can be expressed adequately in no other terms than those of a comparison with Himself. All other things have a limit outside them; they are finite, that is to say, bounded and conditioned, produced by, or tending to, or supported by something else. But it is not so with God, who alone is Infinite, who depends on nothing, while all other things depend upon Him; who alone is that which He is, and not what others are.

Other things are defined in terms of something higher and more generic. But God can only be defined as being that which He is,—the First, the Midst, and the Last, *of* whom, and *through* whom, and *to* whom are all things (Isa. xliv. 6; xlviii. 12; Rev. i. 8; Rom. xi. 36).

This is one thought suggested by reflection on the revelation made to Moses. The other, and the complementary thought to it, is that of the Personality of God. There is, as we have said, nothing, however awful and mysterious, with which God can be compared except Himself; and further, that self is, as far as language can assert or imply anything, asserted or implied to be a Personal one. The "I" which appears both in the subject and the predicate of the sentence, i.e. both in the first and second clauses, can bear no other meaning. It assures us that the God of Israel desires to be known as one who is conscious of His own Being, and who distinguishes His will from that of His creatures.

This is the meaning of the first utterance. The second carries it on, and enlarges it. "Thus shalt thou say unto the children of Israel, I AM hath sent me unto you." Here we have the assertion of God's will in action, of His regard for His creatures, and desire to make Himself known for their good. And this emphatic assertion of personal interest and loving care pervades the whole Bible; and is fundamental to the whole Hebrew and Christian conception of the Divinity.

Let us, then, this morning start with the doctrine of Biblical Theism, and consider its central position and value as the foundation-truth of religion. But first we must dispose of an obvious objection which is constantly made to it. God, as revealing Himself to Moses, speaks as both Infinite and Personal. Is there, or is there not, an inconsistency between these attributes?

Infinity (as we have seen) asserts the absence of limit: nothing exists outside it; and, in the words of St. Paul, the infinite God is He in whom we all live, and move, and have our being (Acts xvii. 28). Personality, on the other hand, is unknown to us by experience, except in connection with limit. One person, or "I," is limited by another; and consciousness, as far as we understand it, suggests definitely an acknowledgment of such limitation, an apprehension of the difference between self and something outside self, or, as philosophers say, between the I and the not I. Thus, while the truth of the Infinity of God teaches us, for example, that all things do His will, the truth of His Personality teaches us to distinguish His will from the wills of His creatures.

There is absolutely no way, as yet known to us, out of this difficulty. If we seek to explain this apparent inconsistency, we are brought face to face with a problem, insoluble to our present reasoning powers. That is to say, we are not capable, being men, of understanding the "how" and the "why" of what is so much above us. Yet, none the less, we are capable of believing in the fact of this union of apparent opposites in the Divine nature. And thus much we can say in explanation—and this goes a long way in pointing to the direction where the solution of the problem lies. Divine Personality differs ineffably from that of those created beings whose experience we use in forming our idea of what is personal. The limits of the Divine Being, in His relation to other dependent beings, are only such as He chooses to impose upon Himself, while all other beings rest within the limits He fashions for them and outside them. It is His infinite will that certain finite wills should subsist in time, distinguishable from His own.

And surely even our own experience supplies some faint analogy, some degree of likeness, to this transcendent marvel of the unity of the Infinite and the Personal. The higher and nobler the nature of a human being, the broader and deeper is its sympathy. We have an expansive power by which we can enter into the thoughts and feelings of others, and as we approach to God, we experience at once a deeper feeling of our own personality, and a greater facility in passing outside it. The character of finite being is intensified, while its limits are extended, indefinitely if not infinitely, by Love.

This mystery, then, is a perfectly credible one, though completely inexplicable; and it is credible, not only because it has the stamp of the highest authority, and is established by a concordance and intimate coherence of those rational arguments to which I have alluded, but also *because* it is to us inexplicable. The old sayings, *Credo quia absurdum, Credo quia impossibile*, which have been often ridiculed, and often (it must be confessed) misused, have, like almost all sayings current in the Church, a great deal of the soberest common sense at the bottom of them. The object of thought in this case is the nature of God, and the persons engaged in contemplating it are men, that is to say, beings of short life and very limited intelligence, and puny faculties of all kinds; creatures who can hardly think for a few hours in succession without a head-ache, utterly powerless to make the merest insect, and a mystery to themselves and to one another.

These men, it is confessed, come from God, live in dependence upon Him, and can look forward to no higher immortality than that of daily growing nearer to Him, and knowing and loving Him more profoundly. Such men cannot believe in a merely obvious and trivial account of God. Where would be the disparity of powers, if the creature at once understood the nature of the Creator? Where would be the mysterious fulness of the idea of God, of which the fulness of His world seems to be so natural an image? Where would be the inexhaustible depth and riches of His nature, answering to the illimitable periods of eternal life that lie before our view?

We believe, then, in the union of Infinity and Personality in God, for this, among other good reasons, that it absolutely removes God from any comparison with ourselves. It puts Him upon a level of being utterly above and beyond us, it exalts Him to a throne which is worthy of the Lord of heaven and earth.

But it is not strange that other religious systems have failed to grasp the fulness of this mysterious truth. Mankind is prone to be one-sided; and in this especially, as in other things, error has come from exaggeration of a part, while truth is only to be found in the comprehension of the whole.

Of this error, the two extreme and most clearly antithetical forms are Pantheism and anthropomorphic Deism [7]; each of them in its way a logical and natural system, but each perfectly irrational as a religion. Representing, as they do, the two opposite tendencies of the human mind, they may be said to stand on the extreme left and right of the central truth. They are opposed, that is to say, in religion, as synthesis is to analysis, as the combinative is to the separative process in philosophy. Pantheism generalises, or is synthetic; while Deism particularises and discriminates, or, in other words, is analytic. Pantheism seizes on the idea of Universality and Infinity, and exaggerates it out of all sense and measure; while Deism grasps that of separate Personality, and developes it with equal onesidedness and unreason. Pantheism, that is to say, represents God as Infinite, without being Personal, as the one substance of which all things that exist are modifications; while Deism sets Him before us as Personal, but limited and separated from His creatures, — in other words, denies His Infinity, and treats Him as one who is to be

---

[7] For a clear statement of this antithesis, compare H. L. Mansel, *Second Letter to Prof. Goldwin Smith*, p. 2, (Oxford, 1862); a letter directed against the tendency which he calls "Anthropomorphism," and defending himself against the criticism upon his Bampton Lectures. See also Th. Christlieb, *Modern Doubt and Christian Belief*, Lecture III., on *Modern non-Biblical Conceptions of God*, especially the latter half (pp. 161—209, E. T., Edinburgh, 1874), which traverses much the same ground as the present Lecture.

judged as one of ourselves. Between the two come various phases of belief, approaching the truth more or less on either side, but all tinged with one or other of these two colours.

I need not occupy your time with long descriptions of all these types of erroneous doctrine. A scheme or table may be presented [8], from which it is easy to see at a glance the general connection of the principles of the different schools of thought both within and without the Church. It will now suffice to give a rapid sketch of the most prominent opinions. Those to whom the subject is new, will find it helpful to remember, that the pantheistic tendency inside the Church is due mainly to the adoption of pagan modes of thought, and to the reception of many half-converts from heathenism within her fold. Deistic leanings, on the other hand, were closely connected with the Jewish elements in Christendom, especially in those early believers (the Ebionites), who accepted Jesus as the Messiah, but did not recognize in Him the eternal Son of God.

To begin with the extreme left, or Pantheism. This may be said to be the natural result of unchecked meditation on the unity and continuity of nature, and upon the interaction of natural forces, without adequate regard to the culture of the will and the heart. Pantheism, in its baldest form, asserts that the universe and God are convertible terms; that God is everything, and everything is God. More philosophically stated, it teaches that

---

[8] See the table at the end of this Lecture.

II.] *Various forms of Pantheism.* 45

there is only one eternal and infinite substance [9], of which all things that exist are modifications, with no permanent individual existence. It matters little in what form this belief is held, or how the relation of the One to its subordinate and constitutive many is conceived [10]. It may be under the comparatively childish hypothesis of emanations, which is that of some of the Hindu Upanishads, which suppose the visible universe to grow out of the unseen Divine substance, as the web is drawn out of the spider, as plants spring out of the ground, or as hairs grow upon a living being [11]. It may be the fashionable sentiment of the age of Nero:—

"Jupiter est quodcumque vides quodcumque moveris [12]."

[9] Spinoza, *Ethics*, i. prop. xiv.: "Præter Deum nulla dari neque concipi potest substantia."

[10] ἓν καὶ πᾶν is the motto of Greek pantheism, attributed to Xenophanes of Elea. See Zeller, *Pre-Socratic Philosophy* (tr. by Alleyne, vol. i. pp. 562, 563, Lond., 1881), who thinks this was said in a pantheistic sense, notwithstanding some striking theistic expressions of Xenophanes, e.g. those quoted by Clemens Alex., *Strom.*, v. p. 601 C.

[11] *Mundaka Upanishad*, i. 1. 7, quoted by Dr. Kay in his excellent papers in the *Missionary*, p. 35, (Calcutta, 1853.) Cp. Monier Williams, *Indian Wisdom*, p. 39; and Max Müller's *Upanishads*, p. 205 (*Sacred Books*, vol. i. 1879). "The seed of Pragâpati are the Devas (gods). The seed of the Devas is rain. The seed of rain are herbs. The seed of herbs is food. The seed of food is seed. The seed of seed are creatures. The seed of creatures is the heart. The seed of the heart is the mind. The seed of the mind is speech (Veda). The seed of speech is action (sacrifice). The action done (in a former state) is this man, the abode of Brahman." (*Aitareya-Arânyaka*, ii. 1. 3.)

[12] Lucan, *Pharsalia*, ix. 579: from Cato's speech to Labienus against consulting the oracle of Hammon, a speech which the poet considers equal to any revelation.

It may be the literary commonplace of the eighteenth century :—

> "All are but parts of one stupendous whole,
> Whose body nature is, and God the soul [13]."

It may be the vague idealism, dear to the hearts of some modern poets, which supposes spirit to be everything and matter nothing, and explains our perception of things to be merely an illusion of the senses and the understanding, and that the world is a place

> "Where nothing is, and all things seem,
> And we the shadows of the dream [14]."

It may be the Tao or immaterial potentiality of the Chinese Laotse, which, coming from non-existence into existence, returns again to nothing [15].

It may be the theory of the Vedantist that God willingly and intentionally, for amusement, loses Himself in nature, imposing ignorance upon Himself, and, as we may say, ignoring Himself in His manifestations [16]; or, it may be the converse theory of the Hegelian, that God is the pure idea realizing

---

[13] Pope, *Essay on Man*, Epistle 1, near the end.

[14] Shelley, *The Sensitive Plant; Poems*, p. 497, (Lond. 1853). The likeness of this thought to the Hindu *Māyā*, or illusion, is very noticeable.

[15] See *Confucianism and Taouism*, by R. K. Douglas, p. 214.

[16] The two great maxims of this sect are, "One only Essence (or Being) without a second,"—the famous "Ekam evādvitīyam," —and "Brahma is true, the world is false, the soul is only Brahma and no other," (M. Williams, *Indian Wisdom*, p. 113). On the principle of Avidyā, which represents God as *ignoring* Himself in developing the phenomenal world, see *ibid.*, p. 118.

II.]   *Pantheism : its disastrous Results.*   47

itself in the progress of human consciousness, and so finding His true self in mankind [17].

But in every case the God of Pantheism is a principle, not a person, however reverent language may, from time to time, be used concerning Him.

It is not difficult to see the disastrous results of this exaggeration. This eternal substance, or Spirit, has no true choice of will, no desire for good, no providence, no moral attributes of any kind.

This philosophy thus cuts away the whole basis of morality, the distinction between right and wrong, and between good and evil. For if these differences do not exist for the whole, which is the highest, why should they exist in the parts? In the same way, it destroys the whole idea of Free-will, and of Responsibility. For if we are but parts of a vast machine, or rather of a general process of being or becoming, we cannot have a freedom greater than is possessed by the whole; and so, again, we cannot be responsible for our actions to a being which has no personal existence.

Thus, for the Pantheist, if he be really consistent and logical, the whole of Life and Nature is but a meaningless vision, from which all will and purpose are removed. He has nothing final

---

[17] Hegel himself (*Religions philosophie*, section headed *der speculative Begriff der Religion,* Works, vol. xi. p. 200, Berlin, 1840), speculatively defines religion as "the self-consciousness of the absolute Spirit," and as "the self-knowledge of the divine Spirit through the medium of the finite Spirit." Hegel frequently defends himself from the charge of Spinozism, and he certainly feels after a more living God than Spinoza; but the general tendency of his teaching seems to be pantheistic. Cp. J. A. Dorner, *System of Chr. Doct.,* E. T., vol. i. p. 400 (Edinb., 1880).

before him, either to hope or to fear. If he be a man of higher type of mind, the best that he can do is to sit down in ecstatic contemplation and adoration of something—he knows not what. If he belongs to a lower order, he plunges into every form of enjoyment or worldly pursuit, into mere materialism and secularity. He is like a sailor without a definite port to steer to, sometimes eagerly pursuing this or that, sometimes idly drifting with the current; sometimes wildly sensual, sometimes fantastically refined; sometimes eager for knowledge, sometimes curious in asceticism; but in every case, without principle and without determination.

The two great historical examples of the working out of this tendency are to be found in India and ancient Egypt, which are the two chief types of really intelligent and powerful heathenism, running their full course in the world. In both, a comparatively simple worship of the forces of nature has been developed among the people into a great system and world of gods, and an elaborate and pedantic ritual. But side by side with this has grown up an esoteric doctrine or philosophy of religion, with a general pantheistic colouring, but having all varieties of shades down to pure sensuality and hopeless atheism [18]. And what has taken place in these countries

---

[18] On the Hindu philosophy, see J. C. Thompson, introduction to translation of the *Bhagavad-Gítá* (Hertford, 1855); K. M. Banerjea, *Dialogues on the Hindu Philosophy* (Williams and Norgate, 1861), and M. Williams' *Indian Wisdom* and *Hinduism*. On the tendency to Atheism in India, cp. Max Müller, *Hibbert Lectures*, 1878, pp. 298 foll. On similar tendencies in Egypt, see Renouf's last lecture in the same series. It has sometimes been said that the esoteric doctrine of Egypt was pure monotheism, and the

is found more or less constantly in all heathen nations at all advanced in civilization. There is an inner doctrine for the wise, which does not rise above a conception of the Infinity of God, and often falls below it.

But everywhere, when men have recoiled from the vulgar worship of many gods, or from the pride and self-assertion of their fellows, or from a crude state-religion, Pantheism has been the fancied harbour of refuge, which has proved a fatal gulf to many thoughtful minds. It is found amongst Jews, Mahometans, and Christians, under various names, but everywhere with the same deadening and disastrous results. It sheds an evanescent rainbow light over certain schools of poetry and art; it creeps into the ritual of the Church, and into the discipline of the convent; it takes shelter alike in the epicurean rose-garden, and in the cell of the mystic; but it withers (thank God!) when the heart is stirred by the call of duty, and when active, self-sacrificing love to man is recognized as the true expression of love to God.

Nearer to the Truth than Pantheism, but obviously on the same side, comes Dualism; that is to say, a separation of the Divine Being into two elements, or principles, variously contrasted as good and evil, as procreation and destruction, as light and darkness,

phrase, "nuk pu nuk," often put into the mouth of the gods, has been translated, "I am that I am." It is accepted, for instance, by Bp. Ellicott, *The Being of God,* p. 39 (S.P.C.K., 1880). Mr. Renouf, however, tells us it simply means, "I even I" (*Hibbert Lectures,* 1879, p. 244, compared with his letter in the *Academy* for June 26, 1880, p. 475).

or as spirit and matter. Here we see the moral sense rejecting the miserable helplessness and confusion of Pantheism; but, through its inability to rise to the idea of a Creator of perfect power (though it ascribes to Him the perfection of goodness), it has assumed that good and evil are co-eternal, and that there is a perpetual warfare between them. The result of this belief has been, while setting the human will in some measure free, to leave it still in doubt as to its power or its responsibility. For sin is treated by the thorough-going Dualist as an involuntary pollution or uncleanness from contact with the realm of darkness, as something, therefore, external and physical, rather than as a voluntary act of the soul: and, further, a sharp line is drawn between those creatures who belong naturally to the one kingdom and to the other, a line which limits the sympathies and the hopes of men to the inner circle of the servants of light. The chief historical manifestation of Dualism has been in the old Persian or Zoroastrian religion [19], which under Darius (if not so certainly under Cyrus) appeared to be verging towards monotheism, and which still exists, with much of its early dogmatism purged away under persecution

---

[19] On Ormazd and Ahriman see James Darmesteter, translation of the *Zend-Avesta* (*Sacred Books of the East*, vol. iv.), Introduction, pp. lxx. foll., and a separate essay on the same subject, *Ormazd et Ahriman* (Paris, 1877). Cp. Monier Williams, *The Religion of Zoroaster*, in the *Nineteenth Century* for Jan., 1881, vol. 9, pp. 155—176, whose conclusions are somewhat different.

On Cyrus and Darius, with reference to the inscriptions, see Mr. T. K. Cheyne's Essay in his *Prophecies of Isaiah*, vol. ii. pp. 264—270 (Lond., 1881).

II.] *Sabellian and Eutychian types of Heresy.* 51

and exile, so that it has become chiefly a superstitious theism [20]. But the real influence of Dualism has been rather in the form of an under-current of heresy, just on the verge or within the pale of the Christian Church, sometimes in the glaringly repulsive speculations of Gnostics and Manichæans [21], sometimes in the more insidious forms of antinomian assertions of sinlessness in the elect and reprobation of the lost, or in a belief in the efficacy of sacraments and charms, apart from holiness of life.

Nearer yet to Christianity, but still on the same Pantheistic side, come the philosophical heresies, which we may call by the quasi-generic names of Sabellian when they relate to the Trinity, and Eutychian when they concern the person of Christ. They are remnants, that is to say, of the Pantheistic love of oneness, of identification, of confusion disguised under Christian formulas. It is worth while to see this clearly, for a great many persons covertly hold these doctrines, without understanding why they are in the wrong.

[20] See Max Müller's *Chips*, vol. i., article on *The Modern Parsis*. On p. 173 he quotes a catechism, distinctly teaching belief in one God the creator of all things, and repudiating belief in any other. Cp. Haug's *Essays*, ed. 2, p. 53; Darmesteter, *Zend-Avesta*, pp. lxxxiii. foll.; M. Williams, *The Pārsīs*, in *Nineteenth Cent.*, March, 1881, p. 506 foll.

[21] The Alexandrian Gnostics were more theoretically Pantheistic, and thought that evil arose from the last link of a series of emanations,—growing enfeebled by distance from the primal source,—and dropping into the chaos of matter. The Syrian Gnostics, and specially the Manichæans, were more decidedly Dualist. See the interesting passage in Neander's *Church History*, vol. ii. pp. 11—17, E. T., ed. Bohn, 1851; and Dr. Mansel's *Lectures*.

According to the Sabellian theory, the Holy Trinity is thus reduced to three phases or manifestations of one substance. In the Eutychian class of heresies, the continued existence of the human nature of Christ is denied, or considered as swallowed up and absorbed by the divine, "like a drop of honey cast into the sea [22]." It needs some little stretch of thought to see the real bearing of these heresies, which at first sight have an appearance of being tolerable speculations on obscure subjects. But a short reflection will shew that they have really a definite connection with false principles of a far-reaching and practically evil tendency.

Consider first how Pantheism is encouraged by the Sabellian theory, which makes God only one absolutely in Himself, and threefold merely in His temporal manifestations. It takes away that power of conceiving the existence of God apart from the world, and from His revelations in the world, which the true Trinitarian doctrine affords, and which is essential to a real belief in His personality. For, by the help of the doctrine of the Trinity, as explained by the Church, we are able to conceive of God as perfect and complete in Himself from eternity, and as wanting nothing for His display or de-

---

[22] This comparison is attributed to the Eutychian speaker in Theodoret's *Eranistes*, dial. 2 (ed. Schulze, iv. p. 114). Cp. Dorner, *Person of Christ*, E. T., div. ii. vol. i. p. 84, who says that, although Eutyches himself may not have used this simile, "yet no comparison of the view as set forth by him, can be more relevant than that to such a chemical permeation of the human nature by the divine, as allowed the former still continuing in some sense to exist."

II.] *Sabellian and Eutychian types of Heresy.* 53

velopment. God is not presented to us as existing in cold and barren isolation, but as having a fulness and blessedness of loving relations *within* His own nature. The Father is ever truly Father, because He sees Himself ever reflected in His express image and likeness in the Divine Son, and there never was a time when the Father and the Son were not bound together by the co-operation of the Holy Spirit, "searching the deep things of God" (1 Cor. ii. 10). God, then, lay under no necessity to create the world: creation added nothing to His glory or His blessedness. But to the Sabellian all this is otherwise. To him, God without the world is an undeveloped monad, to whom creation is a necessary act of self-unfolding, and to whom the universe supplies a theatre for His complete expansion and manifestation[23]. The world is to the Sabellian, not indeed precisely an emanation from God in the Pantheistic sense, but at least a necessary condition of His development; and God is, therefore, brought under the dominion of an impersonal principle, or fate, superior to Himself. The transition from this to Pantheism is very easy, as we see in Schleiermacher[24] and some who follow him.

[23] On the pantheistic tendencies of Sabellius, cp. Dorner, *Doctrine of the Person of Christ*, E. T. vol. ii. p. 157 foll., and pp. 288, 473. St. Athanasius, *contra Arianos*, iv. 11—14, tries to fix on him the doctrine that creation is a self-evolution of the Monas, which he compares to the Stoic 'expansion.'

[24] On the Sabellian leanings of Schleiermacher, see Ueberweg, *Hist. of Philosophy*, vol. i. p. 311, E. T. On his anticipation of Strauss, and admiration of Spinoza, *Ib.*, ii. pp. 248, 249, e.g.: "Offer reverentially with me a lock to the manes of the holy, rejected Spinoza! He was filled with the lofty world-spirit, the

To the Sabellian, therefore, God is not so much a creator as a generator, or producer; and the world is His son rather than His creature, brought into being because, otherwise, the Divine nature would be sterile and incomplete. To the Christian, on the other hand, creation is an act of pure love, and the first of those external acts of love which make God's other acts of revelation to His creatures so credible and so reasonable.

The Eutychian or Monophysite class of heresies are in Christology what Sabellianism is in theology proper, they confound the human and divine natures of the Saviour, just as that confounds the persons of the blessed Trinity. It is easy to perceive the result of this insidious mistake. With the loss of the human nature, the life of Christ readily becomes an idea instead of a fact, a myth or poem, the details of which may be as unreal as those of the romantic life of Buddha. The connection of this heresy with the Pantheistic school is self-evident, and the example of Strauss may shew that men, who begin by professing reverence for religion, and who claim to be merely seeking to discover its central Idea freed from illusions and strained from foreign matters, may end in blank atheism.

Such is in outline the character of the pantheistic

infinite was his beginning and his end; the universe his only and eternal love," &c. Cp. Pfleiderer, *Religions philosophie*, pp. 115, foll. (Berlin, 1878); Dorner, *System of Chr. Doct.*, i. p. 401. It may be remarked that the Scotist theory of the Incarnation may possibly be connected with Sabellian tendencies. But the drift of Scotus' philosophy seems rather to be Deistic, as far as it is exposed to criticism. See below, p. 63.

side of heresy. We must now turn to its opposite, anthropomorphic Deism, and to the allied and neighbouring forms of error. While Pantheism practically ignores the will, either in God or man, and confuses all things together, Deism gives man an exaggerated independence, and discriminates with excessive sharpness in the interests of human Pride. To the narrow, selfish mind of the Deist, God appears chiefly as an enlarged man, and as a being to be kept jealously at a distance. He is regarded not only as distinct from the world, but as outside it. He is not only supramundane, but extra-mundane. He is the Creator of the universe, which He leaves to itself without further interference on His part, to act according to the Laws of Nature, which He has imposed. Hence, to the Deist, miracles, though not theoretically impossible, are not to be expected; and whatever redemption is necessary, is left to man to work out for himself. The idea of the Christian revelation is abhorrent to him; all that man requires, in his opinion, is to use his natural reason, and to follow the teaching of the inward light.

Historically speaking, Deism has not had such a definite, systematic existence as Pantheism. It has been rather a hard rust or canker, hindering the action of other religions, than a religion in itself. Wherever men are found of strong powers and nervous energies, especially when joined to a cold temperament, Deism has come in to intensify and deepen the gulf between God and man, and to represent His relation to us as that of an external Lawgiver, rather than one of ever-present and ubiquitous contact. In cases like this, the feeling of God's *grace* has disappeared, and a scheme of moral duty has been erected in its place, which man is declared capable of fulfilling in his own strength. In the higher schools of Deism this law of conduct is regarded as divine, though communicated to man only through his conscience, or by the agency of great human teachers, of whom our Saviour is indeed considered the best and greatest. Hence we get the various attempts which have been made to establish religions of morality without a creed, and Churches ruled by a merely human order and discipline. In the lower schools of Deism, both religion and religious discipline are given up, and morality is based simply on expediency, with considerable deference to the will of the stronger and of the majority, and little or none to the will of God. The descent from this to the democratic secularism, which is the ideal of so many of our working-men, is easy enough; and this is perhaps the most imminent danger of our own age and country.

Let us now, in pursuance of our method, refer to some of the manifestations of this tendency in earlier times, and to the forms of it which gradually approach Christian truth. As a general rule, pre-Christian religions tended to polytheism, pantheism, or dualism. There is one, however, which is an exception, and which presents us almost with pure Deism, namely, the State religion of China, which we sometimes rather inexactly call Confucianism.

II.]   *State Religion of China.*   57

This creed recognizes God (Tî or Shang Tî)[25] or Heaven (Tien) as one and supreme, but removes Him far from ordinary life. He is worshipped publicly by the Emperor alone on behalf of the State, and only at the great sacrifices at the solstices and the beginning of spring[26]. The language of some of the prayers, composed for this service about the time of our own Reformation, has recently been quoted by a well-known authority, and is too remarkable to be passed over. Though comparatively recent, there is no reason to suppose them other than a fair representation of this worship at a much earlier date. I venture to repeat a few of the most striking sentences[27] :—

"Thou hast vouchsafed, O Tî, to hear us, for thou regardest us as our Father . . . ."

" When Tî, the Lord, had so decreed, He called into existence the three powers (heaven, earth, and men). Between heaven and earth He separately disposed men and

[25] The name of God in Chinese has been a fertile subject of dispute among missionaries. But the practical question what word should be used in modern translations of the Scripture is one thing, and that of the meaning to be attached to Tî or Shang-Tî in the Chinese Classics is another. Supposing Shang-Tî to be now the name of an idol, that does not prove that it was not originally the name of God. I think it therefore quite safe to follow Professors Legge and Max Müller in regard to the old religion, without entering upon the practical question. See the introduction to the *Sacred Books of China*, (Oxford, 1879).

[26] A detailed description of these services is given by Dr. Edkins, *The Religions of China*, chap. ii. entitled ' Imperial Worship' (ed. 2, Lond., 1878). There are at present separate altars for the Spirits of Heaven and Earth, but this was not the original intention : ibid., p. 29.

[27] Dr. J. Legge, *Religions of China*, pp. 47 foll. (London, 1880).

things, all overspread by the heavens. I, His small servant, beg His (favouring) decree to enlighten me His vassal; so may I for ever appear before Him in the empyrean."

And again :—

"The service of song is completed, but our poor sincerity cannot be fully expressed. Thy sovereign goodness is infinite. As a potter hast Thou made all living things. Great and small are curtained round (by Thee from heaven). As engraven on the heart of Thy poor servant is the sense of Thy goodness, but my feeling cannot be fully displayed. With great kindness Thou dost bear with us, and notwithstanding our demerits, dost grant us life and prosperity [28]."

There is a grave and manly tone about these prayers, which seems the expression of sincere feeling, though even in its highest utterances we may detect a want of enthusiasm. But the great defect is the rarity of the service of the God who is so highly honoured, and the absence of anything like a continuous impulse to communion with Him. The people know nothing of Him, except in the vague references to heaven in their life and conversation [29]. Confucius himself avoided using the personal name of God [30], and the ordinary worship of this religion is that of a multitude of celestial and terrestrial spirits and departed ancestors, including Confucius himself. These beings are arranged in de-

---

[28] J. Legge, *Religions of China*, pp. 49, 50.   [29] Ibid., pp. 251, 252.

[30] Ibid., p. 139. In his *Life and Teaching of Confucius*, p. 100, ed. 3, 1872, Dr. Legge says:—"I would say that he was unreligious rather than irreligious: yet by the coldness of his temperament and intellect in this matter, his influence is unfavourable to the development of true religious feeling among the Chinese people

partments and offices like Ministers of State, and stand between the people and the sovereign God, very much as local officials do between the provincials and the unseen Emperor. Further, the Chinese sacred books are not supposed to be inspired, or to contain the record of a revelation, in the way that those of other nations are said to be and to do [31]. Nor is there anything like the usual feeling of the guilt of sin or of the need of sacrifice and atonement, expressed in them, though these ideas are not absolutely wanting. And hence follows that self-satisfaction and want of sensibility to supernatural life, to break down which is found so hard a task by Christian missionaries. Yet the character of the Chinese is by no means so wanting in mobility as we are sometimes prone to believe. The rational State-religion shares its claims upon their allegiance in common with Taoist and Buddhist superstition, both of which in great measure owe their success to the revolt of human nature against the coldness of the older creed. We cannot doubt, then, that China will one day become Christian. May God grant that some of ourselves may be instrumental to her conversion!

This great people, as we have said, forms the exception to the general character of heathenism. But if China is the only pre-Christian nation with a really

generally, and he prepared the way for the speculations of the literati of medieval and modern times, which have exposed them to the charge of atheism."

[31] J. Legge, *The Sacred Books of China*, part i. p. xv. (Oxford, 1879).

deistic religion, all stronger and more progressive nations have shewn a large infusion of deistic feelings. This is the case, for instance, in the philosophy of Aristotle, and the Stoics in Greece and in the Roman empire. With all their differences of detail, they agree in assuming the law of duty, and the ability of man to fulfil it in his own strength. No one can read the description of Aristotle's characters, or those of the ideal Stoic and Cynic in Seneca and Epictetus, without feeling that we are in a very different atmosphere from that of Hindu pantheism. The conceptions of a law of nature and of nations, of a hero, of the typical good man, of the typical wise man, of virtue as a habit of moral choice, the doctrine of the mean, of the limitation of knowledge to what is in our power to know, in fact, all the furniture of the Aristotelian and the Stoic moral philosophy, is deistic, though it is grafted on a religious theory which is technically of another kind.

This tendency of the philosophy of the great European nations aided, it would seem, in bringing about a partial fusion of deistic principles with Jewish and Christian monotheism, especially in certain schools. The connection of Judaism with Stoicism [32] is obscure, and its exact bearings can perhaps never be fully known. There is not sufficient material to define precisely which was the borrower and which the lender.

[32] Josephus, *Life*, § 2, compares the Pharisees to the Stoics. [Bp.] Lightfoot in his essay on *St. Paul and Seneca* (*Philippians*, p. 297), calls attention to the Eastern and Semitic origin of Stoicism, and believes that some of the coincidences of language between Seneca and the New Testament "can hardly be considered accidental."

It is, however, I believe, indubitable that the later Stoics were influenced by Jewish and even Christian ideas, if not by direct contact, at any rate by that subtle infiltration of thought which makes contemporaries sympathetic without conscious communication. More obvious, however, is the Deistic influence of certain Jewish schools in the Christian Church. Amongst the Pharisees the Mosaic law, which was intended to break the neck of Pride, was perverted into an instrument of Pride. The command, "This do, and thou shalt live," was twisted into an assumption that man was able in his own strength to work out his own salvation. The Pharisees looked upon God as a Being whose only relation to themselves was a formal one, who could be treated as fully known and accounted for, who could be cheated with subterfuges like that of Korban, and so be practically left out of consideration. They could reckon up their duty to Him as to a man, and so eliminate all mystery from religion. Hence they shrank from any further revelation, and preferred to treat our Saviour as an impostor and deceiver of the people; or, if they were to some extent attracted by His presence, they wished to lay down the terms of miraculous evidence on which they would consent to believe. The Pharisees asked for a sign, somewhat in the spirit which now requires that a miracle should be performed in London or Paris, such as would satisfy the tests of a commission of scientific men[33]. Their opponents, the Sadducees,

---

[33] Cp. Renan, *Les Apôtres*, p. xliv. ed. 1, 1866; "Un miracle à Paris, devant des savants compétents, mettrait fin à tant de

to whose sect the chief-priests belonged, went even farther in their contempt [34]; and having made up their minds that a miracle was out of the question, openly mocked the Crucified, and called upon Him to come down from the Cross. In them, Deism led to mere brutality.

Such was the wretched condition of those who professed themselves heirs of the faith of Abraham and Moses. Such, too, is the influence of Deism in other places. If we trace the working of this spirit through the centuries behind us, we shall find it everywhere shewing an abhorrence of mystery, deifying common sense, and rationalizing away everything that can wound human self-satisfaction. Outside the Church, it has had immense power in forming the eclectic religion of Mahomet, which is above all things a religion of Pride and of formal works, though its doctrine of divine decrees, when interpreted in a fatalistic and necessarian sense, gives it a Pantheistic impulse which has been developed in Sufiism [35].

doutes! Mais, hélas! voilà ce qui n'arrive jamais." In censuring such a sentiment, we must not forget the provocation given by the pious frauds and credulities of some ·modern popular shrines in France.

[34] It is a mistake to confuse the attitude of the Pharisees and the Sadducees to our Lord and to miracles, though this is often unconsciously done. The contrast between them appears, e.g., in the case of Nicodemus, and in the different conduct of the two parties in the Sanhedrim. (Cp. Westcott on John xi. 46—49, xii. 19.)

[35] On the Divine decrees (Taqdi'r), see T. P. Hughes, *Notes on Muhammadanism*, p. 98, ed. 2, Lond. 1877. On Sufiism, or Mysticism, which teaches that God "is in all things, and all things in Him, and all created beings visible and invisible are an emanation from God, and not really distinct from Him," see *ibid.* pp. 227 foll. The doctrine of Divine decrees has, however, a deistic side (when

II.] *The Jewish Sects. Islam.* 63

But in the Koran, the character of God is chiefly an extension of that of man, and, as has been well observed [36], it has "raised a notion of the Supreme Being which is rather an extension of the large-minded and sagacious man of the world, than an extension of man's virtue and holiness..... Such a man is indulgent as a simple consequence of his knowledge, because nothing surprises him. So the God of Mahomet forgives by reason of his vast knowledge."

Inside the Church, this deistic spirit is found dominating many heresies. We find it in the Arian and Macedonian conceptions of the Blessed Trinity, in the ruder Ebionite Christology and the more plausible speculations of Nestorius, and in their revival in Spanish Adoptionism. We find it germinant in the Antiochene school of biblical interpretation, and bursting out again and again in Pelagian self-sufficiency in morals. It meets us in Abelard, and, to some extent, in Duns Scotus [37] amongst the schoolmen, and in Socinus, Zwinglius, and perhaps Arminius amongst the reformers. It startles us in the strangely exaggerated cultus of the Blessed Virgin [38] in the Church

---

they are interpreted as arbitrary motions of God's will), as we see in the theology of Duns Scotus. Cp. Dorner, *System of Chr. Doct.*, i. pp. 428—431.

[36] Mozley, *Bampton Lectures on Miracles*, Lect. VII., p. 142, ed. 3, 1872.

[37] Ueberweg, *Hist. of Philosophy*, i. p. 456 bottom, E. T., (Lond., 1872). Cp. Dorner, *Person of Christ*, div. 2. vol. i. pp. 342—346, for the Adoptionist leanings of Scotus, and their connection with Mariolatry; and *ibid.*, vol. ii. p. 260 foll., for his position as a precursor of Socinianism.

[38] Dr. Newman, in his *Essay on the Development of Christian*

of Rome, in the erection of the pope into an idol, and in the whole formal system of morals which has weakened that Church so much in the eyes of thoughtful men. It lays a heavy grasp upon English thought, first in Lord Herbert of Cherbury and in Thomas Hobbes, and then in the band of eighteenth-century writers, who are generally, but somewhat loosely, called the Deists. It hardens the theology of the orthodox, and drives popular religion into a fanatic and pietistic reaction. It becomes popular and practically powerful in Voltaire, and in the revolutionists that followed him, and professorial in the German school of rationalists. It confronts us in our own day in that destructive criticism of the New Testament, which is specially the creation of Baur and his associates in the school of Tübingen—criticism which is sometimes acute and vigorous, but more often captious and unhistorical; and it insinuates itself, with yet more intolerable self-confidence, in the highly-varnished romances of the French academician, who, with the false courage of the study, dares to patronize our Lord and His Apostles [39].

Doctrine (p. 405, ed. 1), made a strong point of the cultus of the Blessed Virgin taking the place of Arianism. The fact is probable; but it is surely to be interpreted in a sense very widely different from that in which he took it. Indeed, to an ordinary mind, this part of the Essay seems to tell astonishingly against the general argument of the author, and to shew the great danger of a corrupt development, when theology follows a mere popular instinct. Cp. Dr. Mozley's criticism in his article on *The Theory of Development* (pp. 53—73, reprinted in 1878 from the *Christian Remembrancer* of Jan., 1847, vol. xiii. p. 154 foll.).

[39] M. Renan might, perhaps, seem to some to belong rather to the pantheistic side. He talks of the "Père céleste" in the same

Time would fail us to speak in any detail of these various movements of thought; but I would venture to impress upon you the great value of a connected study of such things. When, for example, we treat Nestorianism and Pelagianism side by side, then we understand why the condemnation of Nestorius was necessary, at once as a dogmatist who did not rightly apprehend the Creed, and as a moralist, who gave countenance and support to those who exaggerated human independence, and depreciated the marvels of Divine grace [40]. Or again, when we find deistical writers, like Hobbes, making a strong point of proving the late date and unauthentic character of the books of the Bible, we learn the animus and tendency of much modern criticism in the same direction, and have some reason to suspect it of preju-

breath as he says, "la terre est une bonne mère" (*Les Apôtres*, p. lxi. ed. 1, 1866). In him the influence of Strauss and the Hegelian "left" coalesces with that of Baur; but his attempt to reduce our Lord to a position purely within the lines of human history, leads me to rank him in this place with the Deists. We find the same combination of different heretical positions, as early as the time of Cerinthus; and there is, I believe, nowadays an increasing tendency to unite an Ebionitic, or purely humanitarian conception of "the life of Jesus," with a Docetic or ideal Christology. Cp. Dorner, *System of Chr. Doctrine*, i. p. 415, note.

[40] The relation of these heresies is put very powerfully in an article on *Theodore of Mopsuestia and Modern Thought*, in the first volume of the Church Quarterly Review. This valuable paper [by my friend, Dr. L. G. Mylne, Bp. of Bombay, then a Tutor of Keble College] was one of the fruits of Dr. Mozley's work as Professor with a class of Graduates, who used to meet on Monday afternoons at his lodgings in Christ Church. Those who formed this class read papers of their own in the Summer Term. In the other Terms, he gave us lectures of his own on Old Testament History (since published), and on St. Augustine.

F

dice, even though the prejudice may be unconscious. Members of that school, at least, which makes so much use of the argument of dogmatic prepossession in order to throw doubt upon the character and truthfulness of what we hold to be the inspired Scriptures, cannot wonder if we apply the same test to themselves, and learn to doubt the absolute scientific impartiality of their methods, when we find them deeply imbued with the deistic dislike of revelation.

These are merely instances of the manner in which a connected historical review of doctrines may help to confirm faith. For any one who has once thoroughly perceived the intellectual obliquity, the one-sidedness, and the deterioration of character, to which both Deism and Pantheism lead, will not hesitate to turn away from anything which can be seen to tend, even remotely, to either of them. If a man will but make up his mind not to drift in questions of religion, but to make his belief a matter of deliberate moral choice, founded on a comparison both of principles and results, he will certainly choose that religion which gives the fullest satisfaction and exercise to all his powers. He will determine not to be one-sided, not to yield to the pressure of inclination or mental habit, but with the help of God's grace to form of himself a full-grown, complete, and, in the Biblical phrase, a perfect man. And, without doubt, the foundation of this completeness is to be found in the truth revealed to Moses. For that truth makes known to us a God who is omnipresent and universal in His activity, whose grace touches and sustains us at every point, who is at once by His power in the grain of dust at our feet and in the immeasurable grandeur and distance of the stars, in the stillness of the everlasting hills and in our own beating hearts. It teaches us also of One who is the Author of law and order, who imposes a limit even upon Himself in His revelations, who does nothing arbitrarily, accidentally, or unreasonably, and who wills that His creatures should feel themselves free even in His awful presence.

	PANTHEISTIC TENDENCY.			THE ONE RELIGION.	DEISTIC TENDENCY.		
	Pantheism.	Dualism.	Gnostic, or Heathen Type of Heresy.	Christian Truth.	Pelagian, or Jewish Type of Heresy.	Islam.	Deism.
	1	2	3		(3)	(2)	(1)
	Infinity without Personality.	God, perfect goodness, but not perfect power.	The Trinity a triple manifestation of one person. Noetians, Sabellians, Patripassians, &c.	God Infinite and Personal. The ONE in THREE.	The Trinity a union of diverse and subordinated natures. Arians, Macedonians (The Word and the Holy Spirit not perfectly one with God).	God, perfect power, but not perfect goodness.	Personality without Infinity.
	The ONE without the MANY.	Spirit and matter, good and evil, co-eternal.	Christ not perfect man. Docetæ (His body a phantom). Apollinarians (no human reason united by Love.	God above all things, yet all things have their being in Him. The kingdom of God in the world, but not of the world. Faith and works united by Love.	Ebionites. Photinians (Christ a mere man).	An arbitrary line drawn between good and evil.	The MANY without the ONE. God and Nature sharply divided.
	God and nature consubstantial.	Strong sense of uncleanness without sense of sin as voluntary.				Sense of sin very slight. God forgives 'as a sagacious man of the world.'	History a conflict of free-will and self-acting law.
	History a course of necessity and evolution. Development without morality.		Eutychians (human nature absorbed). Monothelites (human will absorbed). Antinomians, the elect above Law.	CHRIST, the Truth, the Word and Wisdom of God, the one Mediator, uniting the two Natures in One Person.	Nestorians (two persons). Adoptionists (Christ, in His humanity, the adopted Son of God). Pelagians (man self-redeemed).	CHRIST a prophet, but no mediation is required between God and man.	Morality without religion. CHRIST a good man. The Gospels of late date, and unauthentic.
	CHRIST a myth. The Gospels legendary impostures.	CHRIST a Redeemer, but only of those born in the spiritual class.					
	The Church an idea, not a fact.	The Church the society only of the spiritual.		The Church both an idea and a fact.	Hope in excess leading to pretended assurance.	The Church the society of those who do certain acts and profess certain doctrines.	The Church a human society.

Note.—The columns marked 1 (1), 2 (2), 3 (3), should be more particularly compared as antithetical to one another.

LECTURE III.

ACTS xvii. 24, 26, 27.

God that made the world and all things therein, ... hath made of one blood all nations of men for to dwell on all the face of the earth, and hath determined the times before appointed, and the bounds of their habitation; that they should seek the Lord, if haply they might feel after Him, and find Him, though He be not far from every one of us.

THE NATURAL EXPECTATION OF DIVINE TRUTH, AND THE CONFESSION OF HUMAN INCAPACITY OF ATTAINING TO IT.

Innate Passion for Truth.—Non-Christian religious systems to be approached with sympathy and reverence. (1.) God speaking in the voices of nature.—Thunder.—Wind.—The Sea, &c.—Light.—Profound character of Vedic Gods.—Apollo and Delphi.—Socrates. (2.) God revealed in human forms.—Heroes.—Kingly Incarnations.—Greece.—Mexico.—Scandinavia.—Egypt.—China.—Rome.—Avatars.—Krishna.—Buddha. (3.) Sacred books: Avesta.—Vedas.—High idea of Inspiration.

Shortcomings of these revelations confessed by the heathen themselves: Plato.—Cicero.—Seneca.—Porphyry.—The poets.—God, who gave much, withheld His best gift of rest.

THE one blood of all nations, the unity of the human race, of which St. Paul spoke so stirringly before the Athenian people, is no abstraction of philosophy or theology. It is a fact, which meets us wherever we turn; and not least in that universal eagerness for knowledge to which the great heathen teacher testifies: " All men " (it is confessed) "by nature desire knowledge[1]." This desire may aim high or low; it may be a generous ardour, or a mere curiosity; but all men have it in some form. To possess the truth gives us something to build upon; we reach down to the solid substance of things; (to speak reverently) we touch and find the eternal God.

This thought explains why there is so much of passion aroused by disputes respecting truth and falsehood. We are like people battling for standing-ground on a rock in the midst of the waters; and if our neighbours deceive us, they push us back, as it were, into the ocean of uncertainty. And so, from childhood onwards, we ask with eager anxiety, "Is it true?"; we vehemently denounce a supposed liar as one who defrauds us of our rights; and we are feverishly desirous of knowing anything that is purposely concealed from us, even when it is probably of small importance.

Much more are we roused if the mystery is one which specially affects our profession, or our prospects in life. Such enquiries produce a stir in the blood, and a sleepless excitement, quite unique in the scale of human feelings; and disappointment in the pursuit is allowed to be, of all others, perhaps the most bitter. But nowhere is this feeling of desire for truth so universally active as in what we more definitely call religion. For nothing obviously so much concerns us (when once we are roused to perceive it) as religious truth; and our

---

[1] Aristotle, *Metaphysics*, opening sentence.

desire to know it is always stimulated by a sense of mystery and concealment. For religion does not, like philosophy, display to us an abstract relation of the finite to the infinite, but a personal relation of man to God, of finite man to the Infinite and Personal God. No relation, it is clear, can be so important, or so wonderful as this. Even in human relationships there is a strange indefinable mystery, a natural drawing and passing of soul towards soul, wondrous as the way of a bird through the air, or of a serpent on the rock; how much more when we are pressing forward to know our Maker and our Judge, and our own eternal condition in regard to Him!

The object, then, of the present Lecture is, in the first place, to put before our eyes a faithful picture of the way in which the nations of the world—whose times God has allotted, and whose bounds He has set—have experienced this mysterious drawing towards Him, and have felt, as it were, with their hands, after Him, and not all in vain have sought to find Him. Yet if we listen attentively, we shall hear a sad epilogue to all these strivings, a confession wrung with tears from many noble souls, that what they found did not satisfy the tests which truth should satisfy, that the living rock was not reached, that God was not clearly known. Such will be the argument before us this morning. In the next Lecture, we shall endeavour, with God's grace, to shew that the truth which the heathen looked for with such ill-success has been found in the creed of Christendom; at any rate, that it bears upon it the marks which, to a reasonable mind, religious truth would and should bear.

Our first thesis, that man naturally considers God as his teacher and guide, is capable of almost endless illustration. We see it most simply, perhaps, in the revelations which men have drawn from external nature, from signs and omens and sacrifices, from oracles and divinations; we find it taking another shape in the belief in incarnations of the deity, and the help afforded by Gods and sons of Gods come down in the likeness of men; and lastly, we perceive it in its most powerful and permanent form, in the inspiration attributed to particular books and writings. On all these topics you may naturally expect some details.

But, before entering upon them, I would call your attention to one necessary caution. Let us, when considering these phenomena, remember that the study of their so-called origin is one thing, and a right estimate of their religious value another. It is at present far too common a habit of mind to be satisfied with tracing out the conditions and circumstances under which a belief or a religious custom arises in the world. Some men exhaust themselves in classifying the phenomena of religion under this or that heading of myth or symbol. They are careful, for instance, to assign their due influence to fetishism on the one hand, and to animism on the other; they distinguish the various phases of belief in God, and the growing perceptions with which it is accompanied; they have carefully framed theories of prayer and sacrifice;

they trace the steps by which the self-regarding morality of the family or tribe rises to a feeling of universal duty. But, when they have done all this useful work — and very useful and necessary it is —they are in danger, and leave their readers in danger, of tacitly assuming that the subject is closed, and that religion is a natural development, out of which the positive action of God, as a real existing Being, is excluded. Their mouths are full of the various ways in which other men have thought of God, but He Himself is far from their own thoughts. His Name is constantly on their lips, but some of them would know more of Him in reality, if they were "pagans suckled in a creed outworn."

Let us, at any rate, as Christians (which should be, amongst other things, equal to saying 'as reasonable men'), let us, I say, avoid this folly. We cannot be content with a mere museum of religious beliefs, however scientifically arranged, and grateful as we must be to those who have toiled so patiently to fill it. To us Christians the religion of heathenism is rather a mysterious, half-ruined temple; and one in which it is more meet to fall down and worship, than to wander unawed and unabashed, noting each column and capital, each change of style and variation of artistic finish, without thinking of Him for whose glory it was reared.

1. Such a caution as this may enable us rightly and reverently to pass on to a study of those historical facts, which otherwise might seem a mass of even ridiculous superstitions. First of all then, let us say a few words on the consciousness of God's pre-

sence, which has been roused in men by the voices of nature. Who does not feel instinctively with David, when he cries out: "It is the Lord that commandeth the waters: it is the glorious God that maketh the thunder. It is the Lord that ruleth the sea; the voice of the Lord is mighty in operation, the voice of the Lord is a glorious voice"? (Ps. xxix. 3, 4, P.-B. V.)

So, also, our ancient Aryan forefathers seemed to hear the heavy rolling of the chariot-wheels of Indra[2], of Zeus, or of Thor[3], and were solemnized at his presence, as he drew near to visit or to judge them. And the Hindus especially connected this feeling of awe with faith. The old Vedic poet exclaims, "Men have faith in the fiery Indra, when he hurls again and again his destroying thunderbolt;" and once more, as he pours his solemn libation, the worshipper cries, "Poured out with holy words, with truth, with faith, with austere fervour, O Soma, flow for Indra[4]."

It was but a step further to read in these thunderings and lightnings a voice intended to guide and reprove, and to construct something of that theory of auspices with which we are familiar in classical writers. The oldest oracle of Greece, that of Dodona, was perhaps originally a thunder-oracle, though intimations of the Divine will were sought in historical times in the whispering oak-leaves, and in other

---

[2] Muir's *Sanskrit Texts*, v. p. 84 foll.

[3] Grimm, *Teutonic Mythology*, tr. by Stallybrass (Lond., 1880), i. p. 166, foll.

[4] Muir, v., pp. 103, 104; *Rig-Veda*, i. 55, 5; ix. 113, 2.

III.] *God speaking in the Voices of Nature.* 75

ways[5]. But above all was regard paid to such things in Italy, and the most practical people of antiquity dissolved their public assemblies when Jove thundered and lightened.

All the elemental forces, in fact, seemed to mankind to be instruments of Divine speech. To the Chaldeans, on their broad and featureless alluvial plain, the orbs of heaven—with their intricate motions and varied brilliancy, ruling hours, days and months in their course—seemed palpably and above all other powers to proclaim the will of Heaven. To our Aryan forefathers, the ruder and less formal elements of nature seemed more vocal to the wise than the single points of light.

Thus the wind is addressed in the Vedas as the "Breath of the Gods and germ of the universe, the God who moves as he lists, whose voices we hear, though his form is not seen[6]." The roaring mysterious sea was the home of many oracular deities, Nereus, Proteus, Glaucus, and the like. In India the River Goddess is also the Goddess of Speech; and in the great Epic (Mahābhārata) she is called "the mother of the Vedas," and is invoked as a muse[7]. In Greece, too, the waternymphs are supposed to seize men and inspire them with a sort of frenzied gift of prophecy. Fire, again,

[5] F. W. Myers, on *Greek Oracles*, in *Hellenica*, p. 440, (Rivingtons, 1880). They are more fully described by C. Carapanos, *Dodone et ses Ruines*, pp. 164 foll. (Paris, 1878).

[6] From the Vedic hymn to Vāta the Blest, *Rig-Veda*, x. 168. Cp. Max Müller, *Hibbert Lectures*, p. 210; Muir, vol. v. p. 146.

[7] Muir, l. c. p. 342. Sarasvatī was identified with Vāch in the later mythology.

was conceived as the messenger of the Gods, and its motions, especially in sacrifice, were held to be of the highest value in the ancient arts of divination [8]. The Hindu personification of fire — Agni — is specially striking, and is in many respects like the Greek Prometheus [9], only at an earlier stage of mythology. He is the sage, the divinest among sages, who rectifies all mistakes and teaches men the rules of worship. He conveys to the Gods the hymns and sacrifices, and summons them to meet their worshippers; and yet he lives as a kinsman and friend in the midst of every family [10]. But most of all, to our Aryan ancestors, the more ample personifications of the sky and of light were conceived to be the givers of truth to men.

Even to the present day the Brahman, as he recites his morning devotions, utters as his most sacred text the following prayer to the Sun-God: —"Let us meditate on that excellent glory of the Divine vivifier (Savit*ri*). May he enlighten (*or* stimulate) our understandings [11]."

But it is characteristic of India, that the Gods

---

[8] Soph. *Antigone*, 1005 foll., &c.

[9] Cf. Æsch. *Prom.*, 484 foll. The name Prometheus appears in Sanskrit as pramanthas, 'a fire-stick,' derived from a root signifying 'to churn,' 'to agitate,' 'to rub violently.' We may compare the personification of Soma, the Indo-Iranian libation, who becomes a powerful God. [10] Muir, vol. v. pp. 202 foll.

[11] This is called the Gāyatrī, and is taken from the Rig-Veda, III. 62. 10. Cp. Monier Williams, *Indian Wisdom*, p. 20; and Muir, *Sanskrit Texts*, iii. p. 263, who gives rather a different translation. The Sun-Gods, Sūrya, Savit*ri*, and Pūshan, are in the Vedas, however, comparatively subordinate Gods: see the passages collected by Muir, vol. v., under these heads.

most invoked, even in the earliest times, have a philosophical cast. Thus, in the Vedas, the highest and truest conception of God is apparently that of Varuna, — etymologically the same as the Greek οὐρανός,—the God of the over-arching all-embracing sky, and therefore not so much the God of garish day, as of the deep mysterious night, when the myriad stars lead our thoughts back and back into the abysses of space. He is the God of deep thought and wisdom, who reveals himself to the pondering sage, while Mitra, the God of day, calls men to activity and joy [12]. Varuna is everywhere, and knows everything. Where two men are devising something in secret, there he is as the third. "His messengers descending from heaven traverse this world; thousand-eyed they look across the whole earth [13]." But to the man who looks up to him with faith, he reveals himself in the most intimate and loving communion [14].

It is certainly very astonishing to observe the growth which solemn and mysterious ideas have attained in the better parts of these Vedic hymns. We can hardly find elsewhere anything so striking

[12] Muir, vol. v., esp. the quotation from Professor Roth on p. 70.
[13] Ibid., p. 64.
[14] See especially the hymns of the rishi or sage Vasishtha, quoted by Muir, vol. v. pp. 66, 67. His words make us think, partly by way of contrast, of Abraham, the 'friend' of God. Cp. esp. *Rig-Veda*, vii. 88 :— " Where are those friendships of us two ? Let us seek the harmony which (we enjoyed) of old. I have gone, O self-sustaining Varuna, to thy vast and spacious house with a thousand gates. He who was thy friend, intimate, thine own and beloved, has committed offences against thee," &c.

as the prominence given to Aditi, the mother of the Gods, the "womb of the morning," who becomes the personification of Infinity; and *Rita*[15], at first the sun's allotted path through the sky, and then a general name for order and rightness, almost an anticipation of that ideal Duty, of whom it is said,—

> "Thou dost preserve the stars from wrong,
>   And the most ancient Heavens through thee are fresh
>   and strong."

We trace, even here, the dangerous tendency to abstractions which has in the end, by a one-sided development, entangled a most religious people in the net of pantheism; and yet they are abstractions of wonderful beauty, telling us of the richness and ripeness of the Hindu intellect, and filling us with brilliant hopes for the future of that race, when it has received the proper balance of Christian doctrine.

If we turn from India to Greece, we perceive at once the difference in the prominence of the Sun-God Apollo, as the mediator and revealer, conceived as a figure of youthful human beauty, born amongst men, working for them and with them, and dwelling in their midst in his oracular shrines[16]. Delphi becomes the religious centre of Greece, and, we may

---

[15] Max Müller, *Hibbert Lectures*, No. 5; Muir, vol. v. sect. 3.

[16] The Ion of Euripides gives a bright picture of the life of Delphi, and of the kind of affectionate sentiment with which the "common tripod of Hellas" was regarded. In the hands of this poet the religious feeling is, however, much alloyed with those "modern" elements,—the romantic, the sceptical, and the picturesque, which are so natural to him. It is much to be regretted that we do not possess a play of Æschylus or Sophocles on a like subject.

III.]   *The Delphic Oracle.*   79

almost say, of the Mediterranean nations[17]. It is appealed to on the highest State questions, of war and peace, of building cities, sending out colonies, and the like; and also in private difficulties of every kind. The method of consulting this oracle may be described, as it is the best example of the ideas of oracular inspiration generally prevalent in heathenism, shewing its weakness even in its stronghold. The ceremony began by sacrificing a victim, which was required not only to bow its head, as in other sacrifices, but to tremble all over as the libation was poured upon it. This was considered a sign that the God was about to give a response[18]. The Pythia, or prophetess, prepared herself for executing her office, by chewing laurel-leaves (the tree specially sacred to the God), and drinking from the Castalian spring. Being thus, as it were, in communion with him, she took her seat upon the tripod, which was set over a chasm, from which a certain intoxicating vapour or gas was known to issue[19]. The reception of this was supposed actually to fill her with the divine afflatus; she fell into an ecstasy, and uttered strange words with foaming mouth, an excitement which sometimes even resulted in death[20]. These words

[17] The best summary of facts on the subject of Greek Oracles, with which I am acquainted, is Mr. F. W. H. Myers' Essay in *Hellenica*, (Rivingtons, 1880); Cp. Dr. Mozley's Prize Essay, *The Influence of Ancient Oracles in Public and Private Life* (Oxford, printed by Baxter, 1835).
[18] Plutarch, *de defectu oraculorum*, § 46, p. 435 C; § 49, p. 437 A.
[19] Origen, *c. Celsum*, vii. 3; Diodorus Siculus, pp. 523, 524. Cp. Virgil's "plena deo."
[20] Longinus, c. 13. Plutarch, *de defectu orac.*, § 51, p. 438 A. Cp. Döllinger, *Heidenthum*, p. 188.

were taken down, and turned into metre by a prophet or poet, who stood by to listen to her utterances.

The whole scene is repulsive, and it is easy to imagine the few downward steps which lead from the sanctuary of Apollo to the caves of witches and necromancers, that peep and mutter in the corners of the earth. Nor were priestess and prophet free from all suspicion of bribery and undue influence in their answers. Here, as elsewhere, the enemy of mankind stepped in, to mar man's approach to the kingdom of God.

Nevertheless, Delphi, on the whole, plays a noble part in Greek history. It concentrates the rival states, as it were, round one hearth and home; it is a spiritual, vivifying influence; it witnesses to the deep ineradicable belief that God wills to teach and guide men in their difficulties. Even the sceptical Heraclitus confessed its power when he said:—

"The King, whose oracle is in Delphi, neither speaks nor conceals, but signifies."

And again:—

"The Sibyl, with raving mouth, while she utters unlovely, unadorned, and inelegant words, yet, by the power of the God, reaches with her voice to the distance of a thousand years[21]."

But the highest testimony is that given by Socrates, who, above all his countrymen, combined faith and common sense in due proportion. The famous text written up in the shrine at Delphi, "know thyself," was often referred to by him as the foundation of his

[21] *Heracliti Ephesii reliquiæ*, ed. Bywater, pp. 11, 12.

philosophy [22]; and the answer given to his friend, "that no one was wiser than Socrates," was wisely interpreted by himself in no boastful spirit, and determined the direction of his whole career [23]. Hence we are not surprised at finding him refer to oracles and portents, in dealing with a sceptic, as some of the best proofs of the existence of a Divine Providence [24].

"What will convince you (says Socrates) that the Gods really have a care for you?"

"When they send, as you say they send, counsellors to teach us what to do and what to avoid."

"But (rejoins Socrates) when the Athenians ask them some question, and they reply by means of the art of divination, do you not think that they really speak to you also? Or when they send portents to warn the Greeks, or it may be all mankind, of something which is coming, do they except you alone, and neglect you? Or do you think that the Gods would have given mankind an innate opinion that they were able to do them good and evil, if they had not the power, and that men would have been deceived continually, and never have found out their mistake, if it were not so [25]?"

The whole passage from which this is an extract is well worth reading; and our confidence in Socrates is heightened, when we find that he made a wise distinction between questions which should and should not be referred to the God, refusing to ask for revelation, where the exercise of good sense and

---

[22] Xenophon, *Mem.* iv. 2. 24; Plato, *Phædrus*, p. 229 E, &c.

[23] Plato, *Apol.*, p. 20 E.   [24] Xen., *Mem.* i. 4. 15.

[25] The Stoics argued the converse proposition. The Gods love men, therefore they give man a knowledge of the future, which is so advantageous to him. Cicero *de Divinatione*, i. 38.

judgment would suffice [26]. But, over and above this good sense and judgment, he believed himself to possess a certain Divine monitor, which is best described as a supernatural voice, generally taking the form of a restraint from some dangerous course of action [27]; and answering nearly to the Christian's trust in the directing grace of the Holy Spirit.

This faith on the part of Socrates had, no doubt, great weight with his chief disciple, the most brilliant representative of Greek religious thought. Plato had the natural contempt of a thinker for what seems irrational and ecstatic, and puts the inspired seer low down in the scale of those who have had any vision of Truth [28]. But he, nevertheless, acknowledged the art of divination to be a channel of truth, and declared it to be the office of the intellect and reason to collect and criticise the revelations made in these states of troubled fancy [29]. And further, in his mature treatise on the Laws, he prescribed resort to Delphi for the whole body of the sacred ordinances of a state [30].

Facts like these, chosen from a multitude, may serve to illustrate the trust in oracles entertained by some of the highest minds of antiquity.

2. Something of this kind forms, perhaps, the first

---

[26] Xen. *Mem.* i. 1. 6—9.   [27] Plato, *Phædrus*, p. 242 B; *Rep.* iv. p. 496 C; *Euthyd.*, p. 272 E; *Apol.*, p. 40. Plato limits the δαιμόνιον to restraint, while Xenophon, *Mem.* i. 4, iv. 3. 12, extends its action to command also.
[28] *Phædrus*, p. 248 D; *Timæus*, p. 71 D, E. Cp. John Smith's *Select Discourses*, p. 187, 2nd ed. (Camb., 1673); Westcott, *Study of the Gospels*, p. 6.   [29] Cp. *Charmides*, p. 173 C.   [30] *Laws*, v. p. 428; vi. pp. 759, 914.

step in the aspiration after religious certainty in almost every race. For it is an old observation, that most men rely upon themselves when things go smoothly, and all turn to God in difficulties. Less absolutely universal, but not less striking, is that anthropomorphic instinct which grasps at a vision of God in concrete and even tangible forms; an instinct to which we owe alike what is most beautiful, and what is basest in heathenism. On the one side, you have the radiant vision of Gods of light and song; on the other, hideous and grotesque idols, and the worship of beasts and bestial nature, and the deification of cruelty and lust. The whole Græco-Roman mythology, with its world of Gods and heroes, travelling about to teach men arts and letters, like Demeter and Hermes and Apollo, to build their walls and roads, and to help, like Herakles, in the destruction of monsters, and to join with them in the contests of love and war, shews us this feeling working itself out with a peculiar simplicity, sometimes delightful, but often frivolously and childishly immoral.

Very curious, too, are the parallels to all this in far-off Mexico, where the travels of the Gods, and their residence amongst men, sometimes as teachers, sometimes as cruel and destructive magicians, form, perhaps, the staple of the Aztec mythology. Nay, so simple and quaint was this belief, that stone seats were fixed at the corners of the streets for the highest of their Gods[31] to rest upon; seats canopied

[31] Tezcatlipoca: see the authorities in H. Bancroft, *Native Races of the Pacific States*, vol. iii. p. 239 (New York, 1875). The same

over with green boughs, constantly renewed, and rigorously kept from human occupation.

The same easy commerce between earth and heaven, with a somewhat grayer and ruder colouring, appears in the old Norse legends of Thor, Odin, and Loki [32] walking the earth, or Heimdall begetting the three races of men [33]. This latter idea, that all men are in general, and some men specially, the children and representatives of the Gods, is another and a very widespread issue of this instinct. The deified monarchs of Egypt, China, and Rome; the "Jove-born kings" of Homer; the standing title, "Father of Gods and men;" and the myth of the origin of the four Hindu castes from different parts of the body of Brahmā [34], are cases which occur to every one.

The divinity ascribed to Egyptian kings is, indeed, marvellous in its audacity, and dates from the earliest times of which we have monumental evidence, some 3,000 years, it is said, before the Christian Era [35]. The sovereign of Egypt is usually styled the son of Rā, and "great God." He is seated upon the throne of Horus, and claims authority over all nations of the world. He is the "emanation" of

chapter contains the myths of other gods, esp. the gentle Quetzalcoatl, who forbade human sacrifice. See below, Lecture V. Cp. C. Hardwick's *Christ and other Masters*, pp. 372 foll. ed. 3, 1874.

[32] Cp. Grimm, *Teutonic Mythology*, vol. i. p. 337, E. T.

[33] See the *Rígsmál* in Sæmund's Edda (Thorpe's translation, pp. 85—90, Trübner, 1866).

[34] See the passages collected in Muir's *Sanskrit Texts*, vol. i. chap. i. ed. 2, 1872.

[35] See Renouf, *Hibbert Lectures*, p. 161 foll. 1880.

III.] *Deified Kings in Egypt, Rome, and China.* 85

the Sun-God, and his living image upon earth. "All lands, all nations, the entire compass of the great circuit [of the sun], come to me as my subjects;" such is the language of an Egyptian king [36]. And this language, strange and awful as it may seem, does not appear to be merely official grandiloquence, or courtier-like adulation, it reads like a genuine expression of belief that the king is a true impersonation of the deity, whose goodness penetrates everywhere, whose eyes see everything, and whose ears hear every secret [37].

The other country to which we should turn, expecting to find similar expressions, is China, where, at the present day, "Son of Heaven," and "august or mighty God" (Hwang Tî), are common titles of the Emperor.

The phenomenon here and at Rome is, indeed, different from that in Egypt. It arose rather in policy of state than in simple impulse, when a comparatively late dynasty wished to establish its position by claiming equal prerogatives with an old and deified race of heroes [38]. Yet, even in this degraded and artificial form, it could not have taken root without some foundation in natural feeling. In both countries, this divinity ascribed to the

[36] Amenophis II.; Renouf, l. c. p. 163.

[37] Cp. Mr. Goodwin's remarks, quoted by Renouf, l. c. p. 165; and the ode to Pharaoh, in *Records of the Past*, vol. vi. p. 101.

[38] Cp. Legge, *Religions of China*, p. 10, 1880; and especially Introduction to the *Shû-King*, pp. xxv. foll., in *Sacred Books of the East*, vol. iii. 1879. The title Hwang Tî, was taken, B.C. 221, "by the founder of the short-lived dynasty of *Kh*im, avowedly that he might appear equal to Fû-hsî, and other ancient sovereigns."

Emperor, bears witness to the deep sense of the people that sovereign power is a reflection of the Divine nature, that God is a God of order, and speaks to man by and through man, and that He cares for and watches over the regular political life of His creatures. When, indeed, we consider the marvellous fact, absolutely unparalleled, I suppose, in history, that China has been a settled state, in which dynasties have followed dynasties for the whole known period of perhaps 5,000 years, during which we have details and records of human society; that it began to be thus settled as early as Egypt, and has outlasted the Romano-German empire; we cannot wonder that men should form even this terribly exaggerated estimate of the divinity of government. Much less can we doubt that from that country will issue, in God's good time, some new and glorious type of the Christian polity, when Christ shall be recognised as the mighty God and Son of Heaven, whose dominion is an everlasting dominion, and His kingdom that which shall not be destroyed.

But even more remarkable than this sort of king-worship is the doctrine of Incarnation which has prevailed in the later periods of Hinduism. Every one has heard of the avatârs, or descents of Vishnu, by which he has appeared from time to time at great crises, to shew his love for men, and his condescension to their wants, sometimes in human form, sometimes in that of animals [39]. In the majority of

---

[39] The ten avatârs are enumerated by Hardwick, *Christ and other Masters*, p. 196, ed. 1874; and Monier Williams, *Indian Wisdom*, p. 329 foll. 1875, &c.

these, he is thought to have exhibited only a portion of his essence; but in that of Krishna, the supreme God actually becomes man. There is something attractive and Apollo-like in this figure of the "dark God," which has made him the most popular deity of great part of the peninsula; but in his manifestations he does not rise above the ordinary heathen level. His legend is full of strange exaggerations, and freaks of licentious passion. He dies by a chance shot from a hunter's hand, and leaves the world to the desolation of the last, or Kali age [40].

The other great quasi-Incarnation of the eastern world, that of Sakyamuni, or Gotama Buddha, belongs to a different, and certainly to a higher order of things. Gotama was, we can hardly doubt, a real man—the son, as is supposed, of a king in northern India, contemporary with Pythagoras in Greece, and Confucius in China. He died after a long life of some eighty years [41], the greater part of which had been spent in philosophic teaching, about the year

[40] The legend of Krishna is comparatively modern. See H. H. Wilson, *Essays on the Religion of the Hindus*, vol. ii. pp. 66 foll., ed. 2, 1862. He believes the Puranas to be none of them older than the eighth or ninth century A.D. Cp. Banerjea, *On the Hindu Philosophy*, pp. 517 foll.

[41] *Mahâ-Parinibbâna-Sutta* (Book of the Great Decease), ed. T. W. Rhys Davids, chap. v. § 62; *Sacred Books*, vol. xi. p. 106:—

"But twenty-nine was I when I renounced
The world, Subhadda, seeking after good.
For fifty years and one year more, Subhadda,
Since I went out, a pilgrim have I been
Through the wide realms of virtue and of truth,
And outside these no really 'saint' can be."

480 B.C.[42], almost at the same time as Confucius. He was, in many respects, like the philosophers of his age and country, and under the dominion of the same prepossessions, especially that of a belief in transmigration. But his sympathy with human life was much deeper and wider, and his moral sense much keener. He longed to deliver his countrymen from a double slavery—at once religious and social. Imagining himself to be possessed of perfect knowledge, acquired by meditation and self-conquest, he proclaimed that he could free men from the necessity of repeated births, with their attendant misery, and at the same time break down the bondage of caste, by preaching a universal brotherhood. His words are thus recorded:—

"It is through not understanding and grasping four Noble Truths, O brethren, that we have had to run so long, to wander so long in this weary path of transmigration, both you and I.

"And what are these four?

"The noble truth about sorrow; the noble truth about the cause of sorrow; the noble truth about the cessation

---

[42] On this date, see the evidence in Max Müller's *Dhammapada, Sacred Books*, vol. x. p. xxxvi. foll. (Oxf., 1881), a volume to which (with part of vol. xi.) he has most kindly given me access before its publication. He dates the death in 477 B.C., which nearly agrees with Dr. O. Frankfurter's date, B.C. 483. Mr. Rhys Davids puts it, however, about 412. Cp. the *Appendix on Buddhism* at the end of this volume. The date of Pythagoras' death is put at 497 B.C. in Eusebius' Chronicle, but it may have been earlier or later: see the discussion in Zeller, *Pre-Socratic Philosophy*, i. pp. 324 foll., E. T., 1881. Confucius was born B.C. 551, and died B.C. 478: see J. Legge, *Life and Teachings of Confucius*, pp. 57 and 87. Hardwick, in his *Christ and other Masters*, called attention generally to this synchronism of great teachers and great religious movements in different countries.

of sorrow; and the noble truth about the path that leads to that cessation. But when these noble truths are grasped and known, the craving for existence is rooted out, that which leads to renewed existence is destroyed, and then there is no more birth [43]."

Hence he taught that if any man put implicit faith in him as supremely Blessed, Holy and Enlightened, and believed that he has proclaimed a universal Truth, 'of advantage in this world, passing not away, welcoming all, leading to salvation,' and has set up a Church which is the 'supreme sowing-ground of merit for the world,' such a man need not fear the misery of re-birth.

Any one, of whatever race or position, who believes in Buddha, his Law and his Church, can triumphantly say,—

"Hell is destroyed for me; and re-birth as an animal or a ghost or in any place of woe. I am converted; I am no longer liable to be re-born in a state of suffering, and am assured of final salvation [44]."

What strikes us, first of all, in looking at this pretended revelation, is the awful audacity and self-reliance of this great teacher, the absence of anything like gratitude to God, or dependence upon Him —which is a redeeming feature in Mahomet, and is not absolutely wanting in Confucius. Gotama either denied or ignored the two great motive and ennobling truths of the existence of God and of the hu-

[43] *Mahá-Parinibbána-Sutta* (Book of the Great Decease), ed. T. W. Rhys Davids, chap. ii. § 1; *Sacred Books*, vol. xi. p. 23. Cp. the same editor's *Buddhism* (S.P.C.K., p. 48).
[44] *Mahá-Parinibbána-Sutta*, ut supra, ch. ii. § 8, p. 27.

man soul[45],—truths which were doubtless terribly obscured by the Brahmanism of his day, but were certainly not unknown to many of his Hindu countrymen. He offered a refuge from misery by turning away from the positive to the negative side of life. He was a thorough-going pessimist, believing, as his Hindu education inclined him to conclude, that the supreme force in the world was that of action (karma)[46], not of love; and having had burnt into him the misery and sorrow which follows action, he taught that a state of apathy, of death in life, the extinction of passion and delusion (or, as he called it, Nirvāna) was the highest goal of existence, and the true escape from repeated births. Believing also that he, as man, had reached, by his own strength, a summit which placed him above all other beings, whether Gods or men, he turned the attention of his disciples entirely on the attainment of merit and wisdom, 'each one for himself.' Buddhism, in one main aspect, is Pelagianism run mad, tempered with this proviso, that directly a man reflects on his own merit, he entirely loses the benefit which it was earning for him. On the other hand, Buddha himself was possessed by so elevating and self-sacrificing an

---

[45] Metaphysical Buddhism denies the existence of the soul: see the quotations in Rhys Davids' *Buddhism*, pp. 93 foll. But there are verses in the *Dhammapada* (160, 165, and 323) which speak of 'self' in a way rather inconsistent with this. Cp. Max Müller, *Selected Essays*, ii. p. 303.

[46] *Sutta-Nipâta*, ed. Fausböll, verse 653 (*Sacred Books*, x. 2, p. 116): "By work the world exists, by work mankind exists, beings are bound by work as the linch-pin of the rolling cart (keeps the wheel on)."

III.]   *Religious Doctrines of Buddha.*   91

impulse, and by so mystical and even spiritual a character, that his precepts are superior to those of most heathen teachers, and have attracted many who have no turn for his philosophical doctrines.

The fact that he felt himself bound to resort to these terrible and cruel extremes, enables us, to some extent, to measure the corruption of the doctrines from which he fled. He seems to have felt that destruction was the only possible process of dealing with the current notions of Brahmanism.

His followers have, to some extent, filled the gap thus created within them, either by deifying their master, as some of the Northern Buddhists do[47], or at least by exalting him above all things in heaven and earth, by worshipping his supposed relics, and inventing a vast amount of romantic legends about him, from which the earlier records of his life are comparatively free[48]. But the ma-

---

[47] The Aiśvarikas of Nepal, who worship an Ādi-Buddha: see B. H. Hodgson, *Illustrations of the Literature and Religion of the Buddhists* (Serampore, 1841), and later works. Cp. Max Müller, *Selected Essays*, ii. p. 222, and the quotations from Clement of Alexandria (*Strom.* i. 15, § 71, p. 131 Sylb.), and Megasthenes (ed. Schwanbeck, p. 139), who, after mentioning the Brahmans and the Samanas, say that "there are also some of the Indians who are followers of the commands of Butta, whom through excessive veneration they have honoured as a god." See also Rhys Davids' *Buddhism* (S.P.C.K.), chap. 8, and Hardwick, *Christ and other Masters*, p. 162 foll., ed. 3.

[48] The *Dhammapada*, a collection of ethical sayings, contains none. The *Sutta-Nipâta* has, I believe, only an instance of levitation, a common Hindu belief at the present day. The *Mahâ-Parinibbâna-Sutta* has more, but they are trifling compared with those of the later *Lalita-Vistara*, which is the ordinary source of

jority of them seem to have kept but too faithfully to his negative doctrines, and where Buddhism is really prevalent, there life, if less actively vicious than elsewhere, is generally weak and childish. We shall have occasion to return to this subject again; but so much must now be said to introduce to your notice the founder of the system which claims the largest number of adherents of any one religion on this earth, that strange figure of selfish unselfishness, and austere gentleness which is, alas! to perhaps five hundred [49] millions of mankind the pattern ideal man, the light of the world, the way, the truth, and the life, the supreme wisdom, the teacher and deliverer of the human race.

3. What has already been said under the two previous heads, with regard to elemental voices and Incarnations, will enable you to grasp more readily the third point, viz. the doctrine of Inspiration which has prevailed in non-Christian lands. The sacred books of the world are the third and final expression

the romance. Those of the *M. P. S.* are described in *Buddhism* (S.P.C.K.), p. 188, perhaps with too great a tendency to assimilate them to the supposed Gospel parallels. The *Mahâ-Parinibâna-Sutta* or *Great Decease*, the earliest biographical treatise of Buddhism, is allowed to be certainly not older in its present form than the age of Sandracottus, *circa* B.C. 300, on account of the title, *K*akravarti, or "King of Kings," there frequently mentioned: see the note, ch. v. § 25; *Sacred Books*, vol. xi. p. 92. But no Buddhist books at all can be traced beyond the Council of Asoka, about B.C. 250. See *Buddhism*, p. 86, and the Babra inscription, which refers to certain Buddhist treatises at present difficult to identify, *ibid.*, p. 224 foll.

[49] See the calculation in Max Müller's *Selected Essays*, vol. ii. pp. 224 foll., 1881.

of the feeling that God has spoken to man. Whether in the form of mythical History or of sacred Law, of Hymns or collections of Prophecy and Oracles, they all bear witness to the same sentiment. They represent to us not the direct and special interference of the Divine voice at scattered moments, nor the temporary appearance of the Divinity in human form at certain crises of the world's history, but the interpenetration of the human spirit by the Divine, so as to produce a general and systematic form of religious temper and religious thought and policy. Fragments of this kind of literature meet us (it may be said) in all countries; and it is often little more than an accident that we possess the Scriptures of one nation and not those of another.

Men from the beginning have seen something Divine in the use of language, especially of impassioned or disciplinary language. They see certain of their fellows rising above the seen and the actual, carried by faith to the near presence of God, grasping human life in its great issues, gathering up its past in myths, reading with keen eye the lessons of its present history, summing up the relations of class to class and of person to person, in laws which will satisfy the mass of individual instincts of right and wrong, foreseeing the glories and catastrophes of the future in the germs of existing tendencies. Observations of this sort have led everywhere to a belief in inspiration. Thus almost all early poetry and early law is ascribed to the assistance of a Divine, indwelling Spirit, a breath of God swaying and directing human breath.

This is true, even in those nations whose thoughts of God were somewhat wanting in awe. When Homer and Hesiod invoke the muse, when Numa consults Egeria for his laws, or when the old Norse tale-teller [50] relates his journey to Asgard, the home of the Gods, there is more in it than literary commonplace or fanciful ornament. Under somewhat different circumstances, any of these books might have formed part of a regular collection of sacred texts. But the feeling that meets us in Persia and India, in the Avesta, and especially in the Vedas, (not to speak of the Koran,) is certainly much deeper, and is connected with a more permanent hold of the forms of religion upon the mind. The dialogues of the old Persian lawgiver, Zoroaster, with the supreme Being, have, in the midst of much that is trivial and exaggerated, something of the simple grandeur of Moses and the Prophets. But of all pre-Christian religions, that of India has had the completest and most unchecked history, and particularly in regard to its sacred books.

The word Veda means "knowledge," and is etymologically connected, as you know, with the common Greek and Latin words for knowing and seeing, and with our own 'wit' and 'wisdom'; and in the Vedas, the Hindus suppose themselves to possess a perfect system of truth. These books are so sacred, that for many centuries they were handed down by word of mouth without manuscripts, yet in a form which even western criticism supposes to be very little changed

---

[50] Snorri, the collector of the Prose Edda. Cp. Thorpe, *Northern Mythology*, vol. i. p. 133.

III.] *Idea of an Eternal Word in the Vedas.* 95

by tradition. Thus they embody the idea of reverence for the Word of God rather than for Scripture, for speech rather than writing. So far is this thought carried, that Hindus generally believe them to be an actual articulate sound, emanating from the Divinity [51]. Some suppose this sound to be itself eternal, others that it is a spirit, or breath, issuing from a personal God; others that it was produced from the elements; while others derive it from the mystical victim (Purusha), begotten in the beginning [52], to whom we shall have occasion to refer hereafter.

But with all these varieties of opinion, the recognition of the Divine authority and infallibility of the Vedas was, till quite lately, characteristic of all Hindu sects, and was thought to be so self-evident as to require no more proof than that the sun shines [53], i.e. it was one of those things that proved itself. Even now the Vedas, little as they are known to the mass of the people, form probably the chief spiritual link which binds the various forms of Hinduism together. Hence follows clearly the immense importance of a knowledge of their contents to any

[51] For the different theories of inspiration, reference should be made to Muir's *Sanskrit Texts*, vol. iii., which is entirely occupied with this subject. Cp. Monier Williams, *Indian Wisdom*, pp. 7, 8.

[52] *Rig-Veda*, x. 90; the *Purusha Sukta*: see Appendix to this volume. Cp. Muir, vol. iii. p. 3, and Banerjea, *Arian Witness*, p. 204.

[53] See the quotation from Sankāra Achāryya (8th or 9th cent. A.D.) and from Sāyana's Introduction to his Commentary, (14th cent. A.D. acc. to Muir), *Sanskrit Texts*, vol. iii. p. 62, &c. Cp. S. John viii. 12, 14: "I am the Light of the world . . . Even if I bear witness of Myself, My witness is true,"—perhaps as the Light which proves itself by its mere shining.

who would preach Christ, the true Word, in India. We have the people with us (thank God!) in their deep conception of an eternal Word; we have them with us in the thought that all things in heaven and earth are filled by its sound and speak of it, that its shining presence is more than any logical proof; and surely, on the basis of this real agreement, we can bring them to acknowledge that, while their own sages have heard from time to time echoes of the Divine voice mixed with more earthly tones, we have the true and full harmony in the Bible and in the Church of Christ.

Up to this point we have been tracing the belief of mankind outside the Church in its main outlines. We have indicated the chief forms in which men have supposed that God has made Himself known, and with Himself has brought them truth. At the same time, we have pointed out the kind of errors which have interfered with their grasp of truth, the evil forms of superstition and delusion, of diabolic lust and cruelty, of passion and policy, which rise up like so many spectres to mock the enquirer. Nor must we imagine that the insufficiency of their supposed revelations was unperceived by the wiser among the heathens themselves[54]. They, too, have

---

[54] This feeling shews itself in a common belief in the death and passing away of the older gods: see an interesting passage in Max Müller's Essay on *Buddhist Pilgrims, Selected Essays*, ii. p. 241 foll. The scepticism of the Peruvian Inca, who 'threw doubts upon the divine nature of such an unquiet thing' as the sun appeared to him to be, is paralleled by the familiar facts of Greek mythology, the succession of Kronos, Zeus, &c., and by the Rägnarök, or so-called "twilight of the Gods," in the Teutonic my-

III.] *Heathen Criticism of their own Revelations.* 97

criticised and censured their own shortcomings; they have passed through all forms of disappointment, sorrow, doubt, and scepticism, often ending in philosophic atheism and blank materialism. I will conclude by some examples of this despondency from the great writers of Greece and Rome, not because the feeling did not exist elsewhere, but because their ability and high character stamp their sayings with a value for the whole human race.

Look first, then, at the testimony of Plato, whom we may fairly name the most religious mind of classical antiquity. If you read his writings, you will perceive how saturated he is with the old poets, how much weight he attaches to their writings, how much wisdom he finds in the myths they relate, quoting them almost as we quote from the Bible[55].

Yet Plato, when he is devising a perfect scheme of education, is constrained to forbid the admission of the poets. And why is this? Because of the laxity of their moral teaching with regard to the Gods, and the low idea of Truth which they

---

thology, by the tendency to atheism in India and Egypt (see above, Lect. II., note 17), and by the spontaneous destruction of their idols on the part of the Sandwich Islanders. On *Indian Theistic Reformers*, and their criticism of the traditional doctrines of their country, see Monier Williams in *Journal of Royal Asiatic Society* for Jan., 1881, which contains some account of Rāmmohun Roy and the development of the Brāhma Samāj. This unitarian sect has worked out the principles of the Vaishṇava reformers of the twelfth, thirteenth, fifteenth, and sixteenth centuries (Rāmānuja, Madhva, Vallabha and Chaitanya), by the help of intercourse with Christians.

[55] On this point cp. C. Ackermann, *The Christian Element in Plato*, Eng. Tr., p. 53. (Clark, Edinburgh, 1861.)

embody. He professes himself shocked at the myths which represent the Gods as doing acts of fraud and violence and cruelty. For God cannot be the author of evil, but of good only. He cannot be like a magician, appearing insidiously, now in one form and now in another. He cannot be willing to lie or to deceive. For he says—

"God is perfectly simple and true, both in deed and word; he changes not; he deceives not, either by dream or waking vision, by sign or word [56]."

We know the charges which infidels sometimes bring against the Bible, but imagine a sincere Christian solemnly forbidding the use of the Bible in education, and you have a parallel to what Plato actually does, and not without very good and practical reason [57]. And lest we should think that he was more certain about his own possession of truth, of which he has so magnificent an ideal, turn to that most pathetic story of the trial of the greatest and best man he knew, the trial of Socrates. How does he represent his master? As willing certainly to die, as happy in suffering death in the cause of duty, as reasoning calmly about a future state, but really uncertain whether it would be better than the present life. Socrates goes through all the reasons which make him die peacefully, but his alternative is between annihilation and Elysium.

[56] Plato, *Republic*, ii. at the end, pp. 377—383. Cp. *Laws*, book xii. at the beginning; Zeller's *Plato*, Eng. Tr., by Alleyne and Goodwin, p. 497.

[57] For other instances of this feeling of the danger of the myths, see Döllinger, *Heidenthum*, p. 255.

III.]   *Plato's Dissatisfaction and Uncertainty.*

He comforts himself with the thought that his inward monitor had not restrained him from the course which led to his condemnation, and that a good man can never suffer evil in life or death, or be neglected by God; yet, after all, his last words are :—

"It is now time for us to depart, for me to go to death, for you to remain in life, but whether of us goes to a better fortune, none can tell but God [58]."

Plato, then, was one of those who, with all his respect for the early poets and for the oracles, could not rest his faith upon them. He felt that it was his own duty (to use the words which he puts into the mouth of Simmias in the *Phædo*) "to take the best and most irrefragable of human words," namely, philosophy, "and to make the hazardous voyage of life upon it." But still, before his eyes there floated the vision of a safer vessel, a Divine word as yet unrevealed to the sons of men [59].

In other philosophers this dissatisfaction meets us still more strongly. We find them agreeing in little else except in confessions of their impotence to give any religious knowledge worthy of the name. We find them sometimes making a dogma of scepticism with the Pyrrhonists, sometimes taking refuge in probabilities with the Academics, sometimes denying or doubting immortality and particular providence with the Stoics, sometimes denying a future life and a providence alto-

---

[58] Plato, *Apology*, pp. 40—42.
[59] See the famous passage in the *Phædo* (Simmias' Speech), p. 85.

gether with the Epicureans. In this conflict of opinions, no wonder that probability should seem the best form of truth attainable. It is surely not by accident that Cicero, living in the maturity of Roman thought, leaves the summing-up of his dialogue on the nature of the Gods, which is a discussion between an Epicurean, a Stoic, and an Academic, to Cotta, the representative of the latter school. It is worth while to listen to the words in which he takes for granted that wisdom or certain truth does not exist in philosophy, for this may be held to be the practical judgment of unprejudiced men just before the Christian era.

"If folly (says Cotta) is allowed by all philosophers to be a greater evil than all other evils of fortune or body together, while yet as a fact no one attains to wisdom, it follows that all we, whom you (Stoics) say are so well looked after by the Gods, are after all in the most evil case. For just as it makes no real difference whether as a fact no one is in health, or whether it is abstractedly impossible to be in health, so I can see no difference whether we assert that no one actually is wise, or that no one can be wise [60]."

This uncertainty about providence was naturally accompanied, as we have seen, with an uncertainty about personal immortality. The Stoics, who asserted the noble truth, "that no great man ever existed who was not to some extent inspired [61]," and who were more dogmatic in their definitions of religious truth than many of the ancients, wavered weakly on this subject. Yet what is inspiration worth, if it can tell

---

[60] Cicero *De Nat. Deorum*, iii. 32. 79.

[61] "Nemo vir magnus sine aliquo afflatu divino umquam fuit." Cic. *De Nat. Deor.*, ii. 66. 167.

nothing on a topic so important to every man? Seneca, you will remember, paints his own state of mind on this subject in memorable language:—

"I was delighting in the discussion about the eternity of souls, or rather in the belief of it. For I gave ready credence to the opinion of great men, who promise, rather than demonstrate, a thing which it is very agreeable to believe. I gave myself up to this magnificent hope. I already began to despise my present self, and to look down upon the poor remains of my weak life, as I thought of the passage to immeasurable time, and the possession of eternity; when suddenly I was roused by the receipt of your letter, and lost so fine a dream."

He goes on, indeed, to attempt to restore his dream, and dwells specially on the thought of death being a birth into another existence in almost apostolic language ("dies iste quem tamquam extremum reformidas æterni natalis est"), but his proofs are rather aspirations than arguments; it is a dream, and a 'perhaps'; and elsewhere in his writings doubts are thicker than beliefs [62].

We have given instances of dissatisfaction and even despondency, from two great periods in which the strength of the human mind was at its height. I will add a third, which discloses the state of the heathen heart just before the triumph of Christianity throughout the Roman empire — the case of Porphyry. This man lived at the end of the third century of our era, and was the pupil and

[62] Seneca, *Ep.* 102; cp. Cicero, *Tusc.* i. 11. 24, a criticism on Plato's *Phædo*. For further references see Döllinger, *Heidenthum*, p. 589 foll.

literary heir of Plotinus, who, coming as the successor of a long series of religious thinkers, had made prodigious and even gigantic efforts to establish heathenism on a rational basis. But Porphyry longed for something more than Plotinus could give him. He saw, like Justin Martyr, that the revelation of prophecy was the real satisfaction needed by mankind. But, unfortunately, the principles of his school, which was founded on the doctrine of the transcendence of the Deity [63], forbade him to accept the Incarnation and the Gospel message; nay, they converted him into a bitter enemy of the faith. So he turned for a substitute to the heathen oracles. His confident expectations, in so doing, may be seen in the preface to the collection which he made.

"The man is secure and firm," says Porphyry, "who starts from this ground, as one who draws his hopes of being saved from the only secure source..... And how useful such a collection may be, those will know best who, with painful longings after truth, have prayed that some special vision of the Gods might be vouchsafed them, in order that by the sure instruction of such teachers they might obtain rest from their doubts [64]."

[63] Cp. Ueberweg, *Hist. of Philosophy*, i. p. 245, lower part, on the doctrine of Plotinus.

Porphyry's books against the Christians were written 267—270 A.D., in Sicily.

[64] Euseb., *Præp. Evang.*, iv. 7. The fragments of his book, περὶ τῆς ἐκ λογίων φιλοσοφίας, *de philosophia ex oraculis haurienda*, have been edited by Gustav Wolff (Berlin, 1856). Cp. an interesting passage of Celsus on the blessings which have resulted from oracles, ap. Origen, *c. Cels.*, viii. 45; see also Plutarch, *de defectu oraculorum*, § 46, p. 435 D. The last writer, however, clearly recognizes the diabolical element in popular religion, *ib.*, § 14, p. 417 C.

Yet, after all these attempts to assure himself and to touch the rock of truth, Porphyry was constrained to confess that the way of salvation, the liberation of the soul, on which he prided himself so much, was not to be discovered in the doctrines of any one sect or religion; that no single philosophy or mode of life, neither the asceticism of India nor the learning of Chaldea, nor any other way of thinking, was universal in its scope, and that he knew of none, either in fact or theory, which was adequate to human needs [65].

This sad confession of the most religious among philosophers is re-echoed by the voices of the poets, from the beginning to the end of classical literature:—

"There is no prophet of mortal men," cries Hesiod, "who can know the mind of ægis-bearing Zeus [66]."

Solon, again, simply asserts,—

"The mind of immortals is altogether concealed from men [67]."

And Pindar, after his fashion, moralises upon the same theme:—

"Why do you imagine that to be wisdom in which one man a little excels another? For the counsels of the Gods cannot be scrutinized by the understanding of a man, the offspring of a mortal mother [68]."

It would be easy to add to these assertions of igno-

---

[65] Quoted by St. Augustine, *de Civitate Dei*, x. 32.
[66] Hesiod ap. Clem. Alex., *Strom.*, v. 14, § 130, p. 727, Potter.
[67] Solon ap. Clem. l. c.   [68] Pind. fr. 39 [33] ap. Stob., *Ecl. Phys. et Eth.*, ii. 1, § 8, a chapter containing much similar matter.

rance on the part of the poets [69]. The ways of God were dark to them; they owned it with sadness; a tinge of melancholy clouds their songs, and often

> "medio de fonte leporum
> Surgit amari aliquid quod in ipsis floribus angat."

"The world by its wisdom knew not God,"—this is confessed by the wise men themselves. The world knew not whether there was one God or many, whether He cared for men at all, or whether He cared for great things and neglected little ones. They knew not whether they should die at once in soul as well as in body, or whether they should live for a time disembodied, and be burnt up in a great world-conflagration, or after numberless transmigrations be absorbed into the great Being from which they sprang. They had no certainty in these things. And what the heathen world knew not, our modern non-Christian philosophers are equally ignorant of [70].

---

[69] A good collection of these sayings may be found in Tholuck's useful little book, *Guido and Julius*, translated by J. E. Ryland, and published by Wm. Ball (London, 1836).

[70] See their statements about the future life, as quoted by the late [Dean] Mansel, *Letter to Goldwin Smith*, 1861, p. 30:—"When even in this nineteenth century, I see one disciple of an advanced school of progress arguing that the human soul, as having a beginning and a development, must necessarily also have an end [Blasche, *Philosophische Unsterblichkeitslehre*, § 16]; when I find another assuring me that the belief in the remedy of wrongs in a future life is a great hindrance to repentance and amendment in this life [F. Richter, *Lehre von den letzten Dingen*, i. p. 107]; when a third asserts that the belief in a true death, which completely ends the life of the individual, can alone render men capable of true religion and self-denial [Feuerbach, *Ueber Tod und Unsterblichkeit*, p. 11]; when a fourth proclaims that the last enemy that shall be destroyed by Criticism is the belief in a future existence [Strauss, *Glaubenslehre*, ii. p. 739]; when a fifth teaches that individual ex-

It is only since the Incarnation, and for those who believe in it, that light and immortality have been brought to light through the Gospel. It is this only which enables men of all nations to tread firmly among things unseen, and to rest in the knowledge of God, as seen in the face of Jesus Christ. And so God poured out His riches of strength and beauty, of wisdom, honour and pleasure, upon the nations of the world, but did not give them the last best gift of rest: and men tried one after another of the avenues to divine truth, and turned back from them disappointed and discouraged. Thus God in His wisdom had decreed, as our poet words it so well,—

> "For if I should (said He)
> Bestow this jewel also on My creature,
> He would adore My gifts instead of Me,
> And rest in nature, not the God of nature:
>   So both should losers be.
>   Yet let him keep the rest,
> But keep them with repining restlessness:
> Let him be rich and weary that at least,
> If goodness lead him not, yet weariness
>   May toss him to My breast [71]."

istence is the error from which it should be the aim of life to extricate ourselves [Schopenhauer, *Die Welt als Wille*, ii. p. 494]; and a sixth boasts of the moral superiority of a subjective immortality in the minds of others, over the old objective immortality which is radically selfish [Comte, *Catéchisme Positiviste*, Préface, p. xxxvi.];—I am thankful that God has not left men, even in this enlightened age, to grope after their future destiny by the feeble rays of their unassisted reason, whether speculative or moral."

[71] **George Herbert,** *The Pulley.*

LECTURE IV.

PSALM cxix. 129, 130.

Thy testimonies are wonderful: therefore doth my soul keep them.

The entrance of thy word giveth light: it giveth understanding unto the simple.

THE CHRISTIAN REVELATION CONSIDERED AS TRUTH BOTH IDEAL AND PRACTICAL.

"The world by (its) wisdom knew not God." Revelation the just harmony of the spiritual and external.

Ideal Truth (1) *Comprehensive:* the One and the Many.—The Trinity.—Union of the Finite and Infinite in the Incarnation and Atonement. — Christian doctrine of Human Nature: its fearlessness.—(2) *Mysterious:* Mysteries in nature and thought, lead us to accept those of Christian doctrine.—(3) *Inexhaustible:* The Bible compared with other religious books.

Practical Truth (1) *Authoritative:* Our Saviour's claims compared with those of Buddha and Mahomet.—The Prophets.—Miracles. —Instinct for authority in human nature: how it avenges itself if suppressed.—Justin Martyr: freedom in submission to the Truth.—(2) *Definite and intelligible:* Doctrine of the Trinity compared with other religious formulas.—(3) *Permanent and concrete:* combination of flexibility with firmness. — Contrast with other religions.—Union of Fact and Symbol the type of truth.—Biblical history.—St. Paul and St. Ignatius.—Modern Gnosticism.

THE substance of our former Lecture may be summed up in two well-known sentences of St. Paul. In the first, as you will remember, he speaks of the nations of the world as moved by the Lord to seek Him, if haply they might feel after Him and find Him (Acts xvii. 24 foll.). In the second He declares that "in the wisdom of God, the world by (its) wisdom knew not God" (1 Cor. i. 21). It was God's will that the heathen should seek Him, and seek Him hopefully, in oracles and portents, in the forms of kings and heroes and helpful deities, and in the supposed inspirations of lawgivers and prophets. It was His will also that they should not find Him by efforts which they might call and fancy to be their own. Hence all the long periods of heathenism, both past and present, may be considered by the Christian student as periods of probation, in which the Divine Logos, or Reason, is drawing out and establishing the character of each race and nation; teaching sometimes by hope and sometimes by disappointment, till the time of His revelation should be full, and the race be ready to accept the Incarnation of the Son of God in Jesus Christ. Then comes the harvest of souls, and the known or unknown labourers, who have worked for a "Saviour of the world" whose name they never heard, have their work at last crowned and blessed (John iv. 38, 42). Then God-fearing men leap forward to the Light and embrace the Truth, because they find in it such marks of heavenly beauty as they longed to find, and found not, in the phantoms they were pursuing.

Some of these marks I propose, if God gives me strength, to set before you to-day. No one can profess to enumerate them all, and therefore I must beg your indulgence if I pass over many a subtle and delicate element, many a delightful and lovely feature of Divine Truth, which your hearts individually prize and cherish. But I trust that those chosen will at any rate be distinctive and significant. Nor do I suppose that there will be any dispute as to the fundamental principle, which indeed involves all the rest, that the one true revelation must be at once Ideal and Practical, both the highest philosophy and the most salutary discipline. This is the point, as all doubtless have perceived, on which the poet of Holy Scripture, the writer of the 119th Psalm, has rested for the moment in the verses of my text. He is filled in the inner man with the mystery, depth and richness of the revelation, which is the mirror of the incomprehensible and inexhaustible fulness of God the giver of Truth. "Thy testimonies are wonderful: therefore doth my soul keep them." Then he turns round and looks outside him, and observes that character of direct utility, of power in the regulation of life, which adapts God's Law to the every-day needs of human kind. "The entrance of Thy word giveth light: it giveth understanding unto the simple." Revelation, as he saw it, and as we see it, is fitted both for gentle and simple, for the wise and the unwise, the philosopher and the peasant. It is the right and well-proportioned mixture of the internal and external, lifting the people to that which is inward and spiritual, and bringing down the proud to the practical and positive, and is only complete because it unites both [1].

[1] Cp. Pascal, *Pensées*, part 2, art. 4, § 3, p. 167:—"Les autres religions, comme les païennes, sont plus populaires; car elles consistent toutes en extérieur : mais elles ne sont pas pour les gens habiles. Une religion purement intellectuelle serait plus propor-

I.

Under these two great heads, then, of Ideal and Practical Truth, I shall offer to your notice some of the most striking characteristics of Christian doctrine. And first, out of the marks which Ideal Truth should bear, I have chosen three, which a very slight reflection will prove to be necessary to any system which should claim our allegiance. Ideal truth, I say, must be *comprehensive*, must be *mysterious*, must be *inexhaustible*, and Christian doctrine has all these qualities far above any other religious system of which the world has ever even dreamed.

1. *It must be comprehensive.*

No one, I presume, will throw doubt on this in an age when to be "one-sided" is generally recognized as an obvious defect: and in speaking of Pantheism and Deism, we have already pointed out the dangers of "one-sidedness" in religion. Some men see only one substance in the universe, and reduce everything to a vague indifference, a featureless oneness, from which will and morality are absent. Others, in their cold and proud deism, see in the world many parallel wills and powers, of which God's is the first and greatest, but the most distant and the least practically important. Now it is clear that Pantheism and Deism, the assertion of the one with-

---

tionée aux habiles ; mais elle ne servirait pas au peuple. La seule religion chrétienne est proportionée à tous, étant mêlée d'extérieur et d'intérieur. Elle élève le peuple à l'intérieur, et abaisse les superbes à l'extérieur ; et n'est pas parfaite sans les deux : car il faut que le peuple entende l'esprit de la lettre, et que les habiles soumettent leur esprit à la lettre, en pratiquant ce qu'il y a d'extérieur."

out the many, and the assertion of the many without the one, being mutually exclusive opposites, cannot both be true. Yet, if mere simplicity were to be considered a mark of truth, either of these rival theories might be thought superior to Christian doctrine. But so far from being true, each of these systems, as we have seen, contradicts or overlooks fundamental facts of reason and experience, and leads directly to moral consequences of the most obviously evil kind. We have seen also that Pantheism and Deism are the underlying principles of the various religious systems or heretical doctrines which lie to the right and left of Christian doctrine. It is clear, then, that mere simplicity, that is to say, the adoption of a single principle to explain all that exists, is no sure test of ideal truth.

Yet I am far from supposing that the natural tendencies of human belief, whether philosophical or theological, which Christians are called upon to controvert, are necessarily devoid of truth. On the contrary, it seems a certain axiom, that whatever large bodies of men are prone to believe, has in it an element of truth. Even of individuals we feel bound to say that none is so depraved as not to be, to some extent, a mirror of Divine truth. Only Ideal Truth will combine all these varied and partial rays and reflections into a white and steadfast light, such as seems truly to be an effluence from the throne of God.

For consider this, that God has fashioned all the minds of men created in His image, so that all their thoughts are in some true sense His thoughts. He it is alone who has given them the power with which they grasp this or that side of His glory and His beauty. We could think nothing without His will. Must not, then, ideal truth unite all these different points of view, and combine all that can be shewn to be natural for man to think or believe about Him?

It is not difficult to shew that such ideal comprehensiveness is a distinctive mark of the Christian creed, which being equally opposed to Pantheism and Deism, combines the two opposite apprehensions of the One and the Many.

Take, for instance, the cardinal Christian doctrine of the Trinity in Unity. Does not this involve the assertion, that in the most profound object of faith there is found co-existing Unity and Multiplicity, the One and the Many? Or take the other great doctrines of the Incarnation and Atonement. The most astonishing thing about them is their conciliation of what seems most opposite. In the Incarnation we have offered to our belief the absolute Union of the Infinite with the Finite, of the Divine Nature with the Human, in one Christ. In the Atonement, we have the single perfect mystical sacrifice "slain from the foundation of the world" (Rev. xiii. 8), and offered eternally in heaven, yet complete in the short moments of the historical and exemplary death of Jesus on Calvary. So, again, we have the one Christ dying once[2] for all in perfect obedience, yet summing up and representing the successive death to

---

[2] *Romans* vi. 10 (ἐφάπαξ); *Hebrews* ix. 28 (ἅπαξ), x. 10 (ἐφάπαξ); 1 *Peter* iii. 18 (ἅπαξ).

IV.] *Comprehensiveness of Christian Doctrine.* 113

sin of each individual of the human race[3], and extending the power of His reconciling blood even to angels, principalities, and powers, and the whole created universe, seen and unseen[4].

Look, again, at the Christian doctrine of human nature, how fearless it is, how unlike the temporizing, tentative expedients of human systems. What other religion has anything like the same breadth of view on this mysterious subject? None can speak in stronger terms of the constraining power of Divine grace, of the absolute necessity of the Father's "drawing" before a soul can come to Christ (John vi. 44), of the inability of man to do any good action without God's help (Eph. ii. 8, &c.); yet none is so jealous in asserting human free-will, and so intolerant of a depressing philosophy of fatalism. But lest it should be said that the doctrine of grace is held by one sect of believers and the doctrine of free-will by another, look at Jeremiah, who has no sooner told us of the potter's vessels, made and marred at pleasure, than he asserts the universal power of repentance (Jeremiah xviii. 1—10). Or recollect St. Paul's striking aphorism to the Philippians, in which he co-ordinates grace and free-will: "Work out your own salvation with fear and trembling: for it is God which worketh in you both to will and to do of His

---

[3] 2 *Cor.* v. 14: "For the love of Christ constraineth us: because we thus judge, that if one died for all, therefore all died" (Rev. v.) *Rom.* vi. 6: "Our old man is crucified with Him," &c.

[4] In *Col.* i. 20 St. Paul speaks of the blood of the cross reconciling all things to God, "whether they be things in earth or things in heaven." Cp. *Rom.* viii. 19, "the earnest expectation of the creature," i.e. of creation, with *Mark* xvi. 15.

I

good pleasure" (Phil. ii. 12, 13). Had but Buddha been able to say this, how different might have been the condition of the Eastern world[5]!

Nay, even in those Christians who have a stronger tendency to one side of this conception than to the other, the balance of the Biblical idea has not been without its effects in steadying them. It must never be forgotten that St. Augustine, who was the champion of grace against the Pelagians, was equally the champion of free-will against the Manichæans.

It would be easy to multiply illustrations of this topic, but enough has been said by way of example [6]. The outsider may come to these doctrines with a prejudice against them. He may naturally incline to one or other form of heresy respecting them. His sympathies may be Sabellian or Arian in regard to

---

[5] His principles were:—" Well-makers lead the water (whereever they like); fletchers bend the arrow; carpenters bend a log of wood; good people fashion themselves."—*Dhammapada*, verses 80 and 145. " By oneself the evil is done, by oneself one suffers; by oneself evil is left undone, by oneself one is purified. Purity and impurity belong to one self; no one can purify another."— *Ibid.*, 165. Cp. *Mahá-Parinibbána-Sutta*, ii. 9, p. 27, where he defines faith as " believing the truth to have been proclaimed by the Blessed One, of advantage in this world, passing not away, welcoming all, leading to salvation, and to be attained to by the wise, each one for himself." It is also one of the principles of Buddhism that any one can become a Buddha, as good as Gotama.

[6] The reader may be referred particularly to [Abp.] Trench's *Hulsean Lectures* for 1845, especially Lectures 2 and 3 on the " Unity of Scripture" and " the Manifoldness of Scripture," for many beautiful thoughts bearing on this topic; and to Dr. Liddon's *University Sermons*, 2nd series, pp. 83 foll. (1879), on the Bible as it is, with its exhaustless variety and living, spiritual unity, contrasted with the Bible such as man would probably have made it on an *a priori* system.

the Trinity; Eutychian or Nestorian in respect to the Incarnation; Calvinistic or Pelagian on the question of human freedom. But even if he cannot readily accept the fulness of the Catholic doctrines, he cannot deny the immensity of their grasp, the wonderful sweep of vision with which they combine all elements of thought which can be brought before the mind. He cannot hesitate to admit that some such breadth of doctrine is at least more like Divine truth than any that can be put in comparison with it.

2. *Ideal Truth must be mysterious.*

Truth of any kind, that is really comprehensive, cannot fail to contain an element of mystery. This second attribute follows naturally and inevitably from the first, and is no speciality of theology as distinct from other sciences. Even the simplest and most abstract study, that of pure number, which seems to make no assumptions, has its marvels and its surprises: and as we advance in the scale of sciences, taking into account time and space and organisation, and life and thought, the mysteries thicken about us. Thus most schoolboys are familiar with the lines in conic sections which are always approaching and never meeting[7], two properties which naturally seem quite inconsistent. Or, to use another illustration which recent speculation has well-nigh established, you take up a crystal, and perhaps view it poetically as a type of coldness and hardness, of stillness and repose. But we are now told[8] that the molecules

[7] The hyperbola and its asymptote.
[8] See *The Atomic Theory*, by Prof. Ad. Wurtz, in the International Scientific Series, pp. 310—314.

or aggregates of atoms which compose it are in perpetual vibration and rotation, and that the very constancy and regularity of their agitation is the cause of the apparent solidity of the substance.

And when from inanimate things we pass to life and thought, we find mysteries increase. The simplest instance of the union of the one and the many is inexplicable. Philosophers have never settled the much-vexed question of what is the import, what the idea, underlying the common names given to a class or genus. Men are in turns Realists, Conceptualists, Nominalists, or what you will, but the battle between them is still undecided; and in point of fact it makes very little difference to the mystery what theory you hold. Take a number of persons, and ask yourself what is meant by the common name "Man," what, in fact, is human nature? The Nominalist will tell you that it is a mere abstraction; but it is just as astonishing a thing, whether you call it an abstraction, or prefer to describe it, with Plato, as an eternal idea. The fact that given a man, of whatever race, you can talk to and have sympathy with him, because he is a man, not a beast or a stone, is a mystery attaching to human nature, however we may describe it. Yet individuality is more characteristic of human beings than of any others of which we have immediate experience. No two men are alike, and the better we know them, the greater differences we perceive between them. The student, then, of human nature is daily becoming more conscious of this mystery that the human race is one with an extraordinary oneness, while the individuals who compose it are many and diverse from one another with a marvellous diversity.

It is therefore mere common sense to believe that in the highest of all regions of Truth, that which concerns the nature of God Himself, there should be such mysteries as the Christian creed proclaims. The fact that revelation speaks to us of what is so infinitely above our scope and measure, makes it absolutely certain that mystery is to be expected in the message. Hence the trained and balanced mind finds no shock in the doctrines of the Union of Three Persons in One God, or in the co-ordination of perfect Justice and perfect Love in the Deity, or in the entrance of man into covenant with God, or in the Union of the Divine and Human natures in the one Christ, or in His mysterious presence in the Eucharist as taught by the Church of England, or in the dispensation of the Holy Ghost by the agency of His Church.

The mystery (I say) is no shock to a reasonable man. Nay, it is rather one of the signs or marks which he naturally expects; and the contraries of all the positions which I have just enumerated, would be discredited by the very fact of their supposed greater transparency to the human understanding. Who would not at once doubt, for instance, if we taught that God was Love without Justice, or Justice without Love? Who does not see that, as our reformers say, "Transubstantiation destroys the nature of a Sacrament," that is, removes it from mystery to one-sided marvel, or at least tends to do so? While the coldly transparent idea of a mere commemoration is unfitting, on the other hand, to the highest act of communion with God. So it is also with regard to the other doctrines which I have mentioned.

Of course, all these articles of faith are supported by other evidence, internal and external, and could not be received without it [9]. All that I am here arguing is, that their mysteriousness is *pro tanto* in their favour, and not, as some superficial thinkers hold, adverse to their credibility.

3. *Ideal Truth must be inexhaustible.*

Here we take another step onward, as by a natural ascent, from what has just been admitted; and this attribute is as clear a reflection of the nature of the Deity as either of the foregoing. As God comprehends everything, and is in a region high above our understandings, so also He is the ever-fresh and living fountain of life and grace. We expect, therefore, that ideal Truth should have the same freshness, that it should never be effete, that it should adapt itself to all ages and characters and nations and climes, with new and unexpected vigour.

This is true, undoubtedly, with respect to the Gospel message.

We see it, perhaps, most clearly and astonishingly in the Holy Scriptures, which, though they have been

---

[9] The defect of evidence, or rather the strong contrary evidence, at once separates the true mysteries of the Christian creed from false ones, like the Immaculate Conception of the Blessed Virgin and Papal Infallibility. But apart from other evidence, they have a one-sided artificial character which ought to strike the trained theologian, just as in the case of the doctrine of Transubstantiation.

IV.] *Inexhaustibility of Holy Scripture.* 119

read and commented on with such close, eager, and intelligent criticism by the men of almost every race, and with such immense and wonderful patience, as no other books in the world have ever had expended on them, yet after two and three thousand years of experience, are continually yielding fresh treasures to those who study them patiently, and enter into them with humility and love. This is a matter of simple observation, which is daily being tested. The inexhaustible riches of the Law struck the imagination of the writer of the 119th Psalm, who has recorded his impression in terms which are themselves an example of the eternal force and power of Biblical language. But how much clearer is this richness to us who have the key to the Law in the Gospel, and who have the substance of the Gospel itself. Ask those who really try and test it, ask any devout sick person, any reverent and learned student, any painstaking preacher, and they will tell you that they daily find a new beauty and a new use, a new music and a new instruction, in their reading.

It is true that other religious bodies speak even more highly of their sacred books, and treat them with a superstitious and exaggerated reverence. The Vedas, as we have seen, are thought to be the eternal voice of the Divine Being. The Koran is similarly regarded as the uncreated word of God[10]; while the Granth of the Sikhs, which no Western can read with patience[11], is actually worshipped.

[10] Tiele, *Outlines of Hist. of Religion*, § 63, p. 100, E. T. 1877; cp. T. P. Hughes, *Notes on Muhammadanism*, ed. 2, pp. 14 foll.

[11] See Dr. E. Trumpp's Preface to his translation of the *Adi Granth*, p. vii. (Lond., 1877):—"It is for us occidentals a most painful task to read only a single Rāg; and I doubt if any ordi-

But how formal, how unreal, is the use of these books to the worshippers themselves, compared, for instance, with our own use of the Psalter [12]! Most of them are actually in a dead language to those who hear or recite them, and no more suit even the formalities of the present day than so much jargon. But were they never more living? No doubt they were, but only with a very meagre and impotent life. For us at least it is impossible to read a few pages merely of these writings without feeling wearied and critical. This is confessed by all who have taken the greatest pains to make them known, and to popularize them among us. This is the verdict of the editor of the Sacred Books of the East, whose fairness and peculiar competency as a witness on such a point no one is likely to call in question [13]:—

"No doubt (he says) there is much in these old books that is startling by its very simplicity and truth, much that is elevated and elevating, much that is beautiful and sublime; but people who have vague ideas of primeval wisdom, and the splendour of Eastern poetry, will soon find themselves grievously disappointed. It cannot be too strongly stated, that the chief, in many cases the only, interest of the Sacred Books of the East is historical; that much in them is extremely childish, tedious, if not repulsive; and that no one but the historian will be able to understand the important lessons which they teach."

That this criticism could be applied to the Bible even by its worst enemies seems impossible. But

nary reader will have the patience to proceed to the second Rāg, after he shall have perused the first."

[12] See Dean Church's two Lectures on *The Sacred Poetry of Early Religions* (Lond., 1874), esp. pp. 37 foll. and 77.

[13] Prof. F. Max Müller, in his *Preface to Sacred Books of the East: Programme of translation*, vol. i. p. xliii. Oxf. 1879.

here you have the best friend amongst Europeans of the sacred books of the East, including the Vedas and the Koran, warning their readers not to expect much from them, except a few scattered beauties, and a certain amount of hardly-won historical information. Infidels may scoff at portions of the Bible: they may attack detached pieces of its morality, or laugh at details of its history, or bring out with triumph the supposed incongruity of some of its doctrines—all this and more they have done and will continue to do, but if they have any remains of fairness, they will at the same time admit the marvellous literary supremacy of the Bible, even in translations, its unique power to soothe and to alarm the conscience, its extraordinary unity of tone from Genesis to Revelation, its adaptation to the genius of every nation into whose language it has been rendered, its authority at every stage of civilisation [14]. To win this concession is to win perhaps as much as we have any right to expect. For in argument, we can never absolutely and beyond self-willed contradiction prove the occurrence of any long-past events, or the morality of past actions, nor can we give men, who may have vitiated their perception of truth by scoffing and self-assertion, the clearness of vision which is

---

[14] The only conceivable parallel to the literary supremacy of the Bible is to be found in the Homeric ;poems. But these fall at once into the background when considered as religious books, and as such were condemned by the higher moral sense of the Greek nation itself, or allegorized into fancies far removed from the poet's own intention. The Bible has sometimes suffered from excessive allegorizing, but the primary sense is always fruitful in moral lessons. See additional note, p. 141 foll.

necessary for the acceptance of Christian mysteries. What we can do is to observe, and make others observe, the power of facts present before our eyes; and these do exhibit to us a virtue and potency in the Bible which is Divine, if there be such a thing as divinity anywhere in operation in the world.

II.

Such, then, is the character of wondrous fulness and inexhaustible profundity which we naturally ascribe to ideal Truth, and which we find really in the Christian revelation. There is also a light-giving simplicity, expected by the reason as the complement to these qualities, the presence of which is equally marked. Let us consider this under the three heads of 1. *authority;* 2. *definiteness;* 3. *permanence:* which are, as you will perceive, the proper practical counterparts to the three qualities we have just been considering in the first part of this Lecture. They are such as fit the message, which we have shewn to be worthy of the Infinite God, to the needs and capacities of finite man.

1. That the Christian revelation is *authoritative* in a distinct and superior manner no one, I presume, will be likely to dispute. Other religious systems may indeed claim and receive as great or greater external reverence. The flesh may be kept in perpetual bondage to false gods, or false and imperfect creeds. But the soul does not receive that support and motive-power from them which it is the true function of authority to give. Authority is not tyranny, but transmitted power, which we accept and incorporate

with our own powers. And this power is certainly possessed by our Master in a degree to which none other can approach.

The reason of this is clear. Christ alone, of all teachers who have made any serious claim to be the instructors of the souls of men, has proclaimed Himself the Son of God, one with the Father[15]. Setting aside the purely legendary creations of mythology, and the hollow pretences of kings and emperors, and the vulgar fanaticism of false prophets like Simon Magus, what do we find to be the case with those teachers who have made an abiding impression as founders of religions? There are but two, namely Buddha and Mahomet, who have any right even to be discussed, and they most distinctly limit their claims to the narrow circle of human powers. Buddha is reverenced just because his death was a more complete annihilation of his personality than that of any man before or since. In his triumph-song he glories in destroying the principle of individual life so entirely, that he can never rise again in any form.

> "Many a house of life
> Hath held me—seeking ever him who wrought
> These prisons of the senses, sorrow-fraught;
> Sore was my ceaseless strife!
> But now,
> Thou builder of this Tabernacle—Thou!
> I know Thee! never shalt thou build again
> These walls of pain,
> Nor raise the roof-tree of deceits, nor lay
> Fresh rafters on the clay;

---

[15] Cp. the interesting short passages of Origen *c. Celsum*, vi. 11; and Lactantius, *Divin. Instit.* v. 13; and the full statement of Dr. Liddon's *Bampton Lectures*, Lect. iv. pp. 163—190, 2nd ed. 1868.

> Broken thy house is, and the ridge-pole split;
> Delusion fashioned it!
> Safe pass I hence— deliverance to obtain [16]."

And though Buddha (if we may trust the Pitakas) makes absurd pretensions to knowledge and virtue, and on the day of his death outbrags a rival teacher as to his successful attainment of a useless and selfish apathy [17], and calls on all men who wish to attain the like state to put faith in him—yet he did not imagine himself to be by any means an unique person. It is one of the doctrines of the Buddhists that any one can become a Buddha [18], as powerful as Gotama, by the suppression of desires, just as the humanitarian Ebionites held that any Christian could become a Christ by keeping the Law [19].

Mahomet, for his part, though apparently a vainer

---

[16] From Edwin Arnold's poem, *The Light of Asia*, fourth ed., 1880, p. 178. The words, of which this passage is a pretty close poetical version, occur in the *Dhammapada*, verses 153, 154, and are supposed to have been uttered by Gotama on attaining Buddhahood under the Bo-tree forty-five years before his death. Cp. Spence Hardy, *Manual of Buddhism*, p. 180; *Buddhist Birth Stories*, i. p. 103, ed. Rhys Davids (1880). According to the *Lalita-Vistara*, however, the words then uttered were:—"The vices are dried up; they will not flow again;" Max Müller, *Dhammapada*, p. 13, note. The "house-builder" is probably the spirit of desire (tamhâ), perhaps here identified with Mâra, the Tempter. Craving, Discontent and Lust (Tamhâ, Aratî and Ragâ) are sometimes called daughters of Mâra (*Buddhist Birth Stories*, p. 107).

[17] *Mahâ-Parinibbâna-Sutta*, ch. iv. §§ 35 foll. pp. 76—79. The comparison is between Âlâra-Kâlâma, who was not aware when 500 carts passed by, and himself, who was unconscious of a great storm of rain, lightning and thunder, which killed two peasants and four oxen close to him.

[18] See *Dhammapada*, ch. xiv., called *The Buddha*.

[19] S. Hippolytus, *Refutatio omnium hæresium*, vii. § 34, p. 406.

IV.] *Inferior claims of Buddha and Mahomet.* 125

man and actuated by more selfish motives, never professed to work a miracle, while he admitted the miracles of Christ and of the Old Testament [20]. He does not attempt to rise above the position of a prophet. Such, too, he remains in the traditions of his followers outside the Koran, even though marvels have been added to ornament and illustrate his story. Yet it is striking that this same tradition, which tacitly but clearly allows sinlessness to Christ, who is called the Servant, the Apostle, the Spirit and the Word of God, should speak of Mahomet himself merely as "a servant whose sins God has forgiven [21]."

There is little need to remind you how different from these are the claims of our Blessed Saviour. He declares Himself the only source of light and life and love and joy and peace to men; He is their Lawgiver, Redeemer, King, and future Judge. He

[20] He frequently finds fault with those who pressed him for signs, declaring the Koran itself to be quite a sufficient attestation of his mission: see *Sura*, vii. 156, xxvi. 1—5, and cp. J. W. H. Stobart, *Islam and its Founder*, S.P.C.K., pp. 111 foll. For his acceptance of the miracles of Christ, including some of those of the Apocryphal Gospels, see *Sura*, iii. 41, v. 110—114. Cp. Hughes' *Notes on Muhammadanism*, pp. 256 foll. References to the Old Testament miracles are frequent. See additional note on p. 142.

[21] This remarkable Hadís, or tradition, is given by T. P. Hughes, *l. c.* p. 258 foll. At the resurrection Musalmans will not be able to move, and will go from one prophet to another to intercede for them. Adam, Noah, Abraham, Moses, in turn will remember their sins, and send them on to another. Moses, remembering the slaughter of the Egyptian, "will say 'Go to Jesus, He is the servant of God, the Apostle of God, the Spirit of God, and the Word of God.' Then they will go to Jesus, and He will say, 'Go to Muhammad; who is a servant, whose sins God has forgiven both first and last.' Then the Musalmans will come to me, and I will ask permission to go into God's presence and intercede for them." Thus Mahomet ascribes sin to all the prophets and to himself, but not to Jesus.

commands unquestioning obedience to Himself as having all power given to Him in heaven and earth, and as knowing and being known by the Father with a fulness of reciprocal knowledge which none can attain, except as He wills to reveal it (Matt. xi. 27 foll.; Luke x. 22; Matt. xxviii. 18). The souls that are given to Him are taken as His royal possession, and none can pluck them out of His hand. His they are now, and His they will be at the judgment-day.

And these tremendous claims and promises come not alone, but as the climax of a long series of miraculous manifestations of power, and of prophetic utterances in the Church of Israel. Here had been, for many generations, the home and seat of religious authority, expressing itself in divers modes, sounding differently in the Patriarchs and in Moses, in Samuel, in David, in Elijah, in Isaiah, in the other prophets, but intensely authoritative in all. Each of these witnesses confirms those that have gone before him, yet each points onward to a mightier that is to follow, till all are summed up in Christ. And He, speaking as never man spake, and confirming His word with signs that exactly harmonised with the truths He taught, and which are in themselves parables, prophecies, and instructions, as well as miracles, has never ceased by the voices of His ministers to claim the same absolute authority over the souls of men, and to promise them the same certainty of rest upon His word as perfect Truth.

So much is commonly acknowledged, whatever gloss or interpretation sceptics may put upon it; and few, if any, will doubt that claims like these, supported by the guarantees of prophecy and miracles, are exactly fitted to carry home truth to expectant human hearts. Experience shews that men have an indomitable instinct, which assures them that if God speaks to them at all, He will speak so as to make Himself felt, and will not leave them in uncertainty [22].

But those who suppress this instinct in one direction, find themselves suffering its vengeance in another. The man who shuts up all revelation within the limits of scientific or metaphysical discovery, is in dire danger of becoming practically

[22] This position is assumed or asserted by the generality of writers on evidences. See, for a full statement, Dr. Mozley's first Lecture, *Miracles necessary for a Revelation*, and the passages quoted in the notes, esp. note 1. I will add two from writers earlier than those he refers to, John Locke and Samuel Clarke. The passages of Locke are in his *Reasonableness of Christianity*, §§ 165 and 169, and *Discourse on Miracles*, pp. 59, 60. (London: W. Smith, 1839.) In the last he speaks of miracles as "the basis on which Divine mission is always established, and consequently that foundation on which the believers of any Divine revelation must ultimately bottom their faith." Locke, though apparently inclined to Arianism, and a strong opponent of "priestcraft," was a serious believer in a miraculous revelation.

Much the same argument is used by Dr. Samuel Clarke in his *Evidences of Natural and Revealed Religion*, prop. ix. p. 320, 7th ed., 1728. "[A revelation] must, moreover, be positively and directly proved to come from God by such certain signs and matters of fact, as may be undeniable evidences of its author's having actually a Divine commission. For otherwise, as no evidence can prove a doctrine to come from God, if it be either impossible or wicked in itself; so, on the other hand, neither can any degree of goodness or excellency in the doctrine itself, make it certain, but only highly probable, to have come from God; unless it has, moreover, some positive and direct evidence of its being actually revealed."

an atheist, of imagining that everything has a history, and that belief in God and morality, like other things, is a simple matter of spontaneous development. He is apt, at least, to lose all the freshness of his interest in the masses of his fellow-men [23]. Or his instinct for external authority, missing its rightful satisfaction in the historic Christ of the Gospels, forces him into the deification of the human race, or of some conspicuous part of it. He worships the Idea of Law and Order, as the heathen world, in the first centuries after Christ, worshipped the Roman Emperor and the genius of the city of Rome, which spread material peace and prosperity. Or like the modern Positivists, with their "ghost" of a religion, he worships the so-called great being of humanity [24].

Or, it may be, finding no rest in merely human characters and institutions, however careful he may be to select the best and noblest for his calendar of saints, he entirely loses his judgment, and sinks into gross credulity and superstition. He collects trumpery oracles with Porphyry; he descends into caves, and receives monstrous rites of initiation with Julian; he asks for a sign from heaven, to sanction the publi-

---

[23] Cp. Origen *contra Celsum*, vi. 1.

[24] Positivism is a remarkable product of the heathen sentiment, which has lingered long after the supposed Christianisation of Europe. In its religious aspect it is essentially an extreme form of idolatry or creature-worship. The curious sympathy which A. Comte felt for the Roman Catholic system, is perhaps due to some extent to the common element in both, derived from the extinct Roman empire. The expression "ghost" I borrow from T. Carlyle's *Reminiscences*, vol. i. p. 338 (1881).

cation of a deistic book with Lord Herbert[25]; or he is the dupe of mediums and necromancers, with some of the would-be enlightened men and women of our own day.

Or if he is a man of a different and higher temper, he takes refuge in an ideal Christology; and with one hand on Kant and Schleiermacher, and the other on St. Paul, accepts what he believes to be the Christian life and spirit, and some part of Christian worship, without the Christian creed,—destined to the sad disappointment of being unable to transmit to others that subjective faith which he prizes so highly as his own. History has not a few examples of philosophic theologians of this class who have started aside from the historic Christianity in which they were

[25] In his *Autobiography* (p. 242, London, J. Warwick, 1824) he tells us that he was in doubt whether to publish his book, *de Veritate*, criticizing the ordinary theories of revelation, and stating his own modicum of supposed Truth; and that he prayed to God, kneeling down with the book in his hand, his "casement being opened towards the south, and the sun shining clear, and no wind stirring." In his prayer he declared that he was not satisfied whether to publish his book or not, ending:—"If it be for Thy glory, I beseech Thee to give me some sign from heaven; if not, I shall suppress it.

"I had no sooner spoken these words, but a loud, though yet gentle, noise came from the heavens (for it was like nothing on earth), which did so comfort and cheer me, that I took my petition as granted, and that I had the sign I demanded, whereupon also I resolved to print my book: this (how strange soever it may seem) I protest before the eternal God is true, neither am I in any way superstitiously deceived herein, since I did not only clearly hear the noise, but in the serenest sky I ever saw, being without a cloud, did to my thinking see the place from whence it came." Lord Herbert was brother of George Herbert, but was a man of conceited, self-willed temper.

nurtured, and to which they owed their strength; who have, for a time, roused and warmed the society in which they lived with a generous passion for ideals, but have been unable to build up a working moral system, not to speak of a religion, without the foundations of belief in objective fact which they disdained.

Or, lastly, (and God has cheered us, no doubt, with some instances of this kind even in our own experience), many a man having tried these systems and discovered their inevitable failure, after having suffered and struggled, at last escapes all snares, and submits to the simplicity of the Gospel. Instances of this are familiar to readers of early Church history, to some extent in the author of the Clementines, and more strikingly still in Justin Martyr. We all know how the latter went through every form of belief that heathen philosophy could offer, unable to find rest and certainty in any. His longing was never stilled, till one day he met an old man upon the sea-shore, who told him of the prophets, the truth of their predictions, the wonders they wrought, and their testimony to God and Christ. "Immediately," he writes [26], "a fire was kindled in my soul, and a love possessed me for the prophets and those men who are the friends of Christ: and revolving with myself what he had told me, I concluded that this alone was a safe and serviceable philosophy." Happy are they who are enabled thus to accept as reasonable that sweet and gentle authority of the Son of God and Son of Man, which is

[26] *Dialogue with Trypho*, ch. 8, p. 225 B.

IV.] *Freedom in the Truth.* 131

harmonious in all its parts, which has nothing lurid or artificial in its light, nothing strained or one-sided in its burden, but is the peace and rest for every believing soul.

"Ye shall know the truth, and the truth shall make you free" (John viii. 32). The authority of Christ (imperious as it is in its demands) is, as I have said, no tyranny, but it is a gift of power to our souls, enabling them to work with freedom. It is a burden which, unlike other burdens, gives rest, a supernatural source of strength, which when once thoroughly accepted, can only be lost by our own wilfulness. Surely this power is a characteristic of ideal truth, which none other than the religion of Christ can shew [27].

2. The characteristic of authority which we have just been discussing is the natural complement of the quality of comprehensiveness. The quality of mystery, of which we spoke in the former part of this Lecture, has as its practical correlative *definiteness* and *intelligibility*, of which we must now proceed to speak.

This attribute of truth is clearly connected with the foregoing, and flows from it. For if God deigns to speak to men with authority, so as to relieve their souls from uncertainty in the discovery of truth, it is reasonable to suppose that He will also speak in a manner that they can understand. While we assert that the truths of revelation, whether spiritual or moral, are mysteries which men were incapable of finding out for themselves, we assert also that,

[27] Cp. Mozley, *Miracles*, Lect. VII. pp. 143 foll.

when made known, they have innumerable points of contact with human life and reason, and are consonant with all the facts of our experience[28].

Compare, for instance, and it is the supreme instance, the Christian creed as comprised in the formula, "I baptize thee in the Name of the Father, and of the Son, and of the Holy Ghost," with the creeds of Pantheism and of Islam. "There is one only being without a second," or, "No substance can be supposed or conceived besides God[29]," says the Pantheist. He wraps you in a cloud of mystery. What natural knowledge can we have of an universal substance? For all practical purposes, the Pantheist might as well bid you step from a balloon upon the vapours which surround you, as be baptized into this faith. The disciple of Islam, again, bids you accept the utterance, "There is but one God, and Mahomet is His prophet;" and for any response that the latter part of this utterance rouses in your soul, he might as well pierce you with the sword with which he enforces his argument.

The words which he uses are indeed intelligible enough, but they do not come home to the natural reason. What do we know of Mahomet except from books? But the Christian creed finds natural ac-

---

[28] Cp. Dr. S. Clarke, l. c. prop. ix. p. 319. He enumerates, among the necessary marks or proofs of a religion coming from God, "that the Doctrines it teaches be all such; as though not indeed discoverable by the bare Light of Nature, yet when discovered by Revelation, may be consistent with and agreeable to sound and unprejudiced Reason. For otherwise no Evidence whatsoever can prove that any Doctrine is true."

[29] Spinoza, *Ethics*, part i. prop. 14, vol. i. p. 197 (Lipsiæ, 1843).

ceptance in the intelligence of the meanest. The merest child knows what it is to have or to want a father, and to feel as a son, and to know itself as a being or spirit distinct from other spirits. Human nature supplies the elements of the notion of the Trinity. Without requiring any knowledge of history, without any metaphysical conceptions of the nature of being or substance, without travelling beyond the simplest relations of life, we can teach an infant that God is at once our Father, our Brother, our Better-self, our Creator, Redeemer, and Sanctifier.

As soon as any thoughts at all can enter the mind, and concurrently and sympathetically with those that first enter, this supreme doctrine of the Trinity, which has sometimes been censured as a metaphysical absurdity, can be imparted to the youngest and the feeblest, and yet it is a mystery which archangels cannot fathom. The simplicity of other creeds, such as it is, is due to their intangibility or their shallowness. It is the prerogative of the Christian creed to inculcate such ideas as can be taught wherever there are the rudiments of human instincts, wherever the elements of reverence, love, and desire for holiness are found; while yet they afford food for lifelong and progressive meditation to the saint and the scholar. Its truth is apprehended by the Melanesian or Swahili boy, as really as by Origen or Aquinas. It is plain to both; it can never cease to be an eternal mystery to either.

3. Lastly in this series of attributes comes that of *permanence*. God is eternal, but the human race is like a flowing stream, no one drop of which is ever

exactly the same as another. A revelation of truth for man must somehow counteract this flux of human life, which tends to render all his ideas unstable and unbalanced. Truth, while it accompanies him in his changes and his progress, and offers an inexhaustible supply of Divine riches, must also establish itself permanently in history. There must be something monumental, something outwardly impressive in its form, if it is to arrest the attention of all men, and to be sustained in their midst. We cannot, indeed, determine *a priori* how this sustenance of truth must be secured: but we can readily see that other religions than the Christian have flexibility without permanence, or stability without adaptation to changing needs; while it alone has both.

If we take the case of religion in India (which is of so much interest to many here), we shall find an unbounded flexibility, joined to an almost entire absence of historic fact. Childish myths, gross symbols, vulgar charms, tedious and effete rituals, absurd claims of a sacerdotal caste, dispute the ground with an exalted and vague philosophy and a highly-strained idealism. There is something to suit every sort of character. Yet things highest and lowest, virtue and vice, self-discipline and self-indulgence, are all confused together under the common name of religion. The grasp of truth and of fact, as distinct from falsehood and fiction, is thus very seriously weakened, since everything may have its place in the world of ideas. There is no criterion by which to distinguish a true religious instinct from the corrupt motions of the human heart. Even secular history,

IV.] *Opposite Defects of Hinduism and Islam.*

including biography, has no existence in India before the Mahometan invasions, except to some extent in connection with Buddhism, or as it may be gleaned from the accounts of foreign visitors. India itself has no native annals. Yet it is clear that there are few countries in which thought has been more active, or the minds of men more alive to religious impressions. But speculation has unfortunately been dominated by the false idea that nature is everything, and the individual man nothing; that the present life is only a vague episode in an endless series of changes; that God and Providence are only names for the impersonal processes of being.

Hence India has sects and monasteries of ascetics, but no Church; it has sacraments and symbols, but no historical festivals. It has a priestly caste, but no High Priestly Redeemer, no apostolic succession, or popular confirmation of its ministers. It has atonements, but no Mediator; it has prophets, but no Holy Spirit; it has, in fact, a religion of nature, but no worship of the living God and Father of men.

It would be easy to shew, on the other hand, how the Chinese State religion, with its intensely historical character, is almost entirely wanting in the ideal elements which should fit it to go along with the growing needs of the people. We have seen already how this want has thrown the populace into the arms of Taoists and Buddhists. Similarly, in Islam, you have a striking contrast to the flexibility of Hindu Pantheism. Here you have history from the Hegira to the present day, the annals of conquest, the self-assertion of conquerors, a Prophet claiming a direct commission from God, whose life is as well-known as that of Augustus or Julian, a Law everywhere received and read, an established Church, a list of saints and confessors, memorial festivals, and many other elements of permanence. But the result is a fatal stiffness and inflexibility. There is no proper progress, no growth in spiritual knowledge, no belief in grace, hardly any sacramental or sacrificial system. Hence comes the absence of a true development of religious life within the bounds of Islam itself, and a spirit of unyielding pride, which makes conversion to a higher religion little short of a miracle, wherever Mahometans are, or have long been, the dominant race.

It is, on the contrary, the union of historical reality, and those conditions of permanence, to which reference has been made, with the fullest spiritual progressiveness, that is the special privilege of the Church of Christ. And by the "Church" I mean (of course) not only that which has existed since the Incarnation, but that which in idea and in fact has been the place of the covenant, or meeting-ground of God with men, since the promise that the seed of the woman should bruise the serpent's head. Its distinctive character throughout has been the combination of profoundest symbolism with plainest fact. As far as the history of this Church is contained in the Bible, from the first chapter of Genesis to the last chapter of the Apocalypse, there is everywhere a correspondence of outward things, visible and tangible, with the mystery by them signified.

A continuous thread of historic fact runs through

IV.] *Union of Symbol and Fact in Bible History.* 137

the whole. It may, indeed, possibly be the case that the beginnings of things are, by some law of God's ordinance, almost as obscure to us as their endings, and that the representations of the Fall and of the early history of man, up to the time of Abraham, with whom detailed history begins, are more like to the descriptions of the Apocalypse and other prophecies of the judgment, than they are to exact photographs or annals of what we call historic times. But making whatever allowance may fairly be made for differences of method in the Biblical narrative, it is clear that what is related in the first part of Genesis is not, like the early history of other religious books, a confused medley of myths about the sun and the dawn and the constellations and the other forces and phenomena of nature, mixed up with grotesque observations of human life. No doubt Genesis contains a record of some of the facts which, in the memory of other nations, have been allied to natural phenomena; thus the first murder is connected by many mythologies with the constellation of the Twins[30]. But this is not so in Genesis, except in the opinion of some who may almost be called mythological fanatics[31]. Here we have no-

---

[30] M. Fr. Lenormant has made a very valuable collection of this kind of material in his recent book, *Les Origines de l'Histoire d'après la Bible.* (Paris, 1880.) It is by no means a complete book, but is interesting and valuable as the attempt of a believer to shew that perfect scientific freedom is compatible with Christian faith.

[31] Lenormant, *on the whole,* takes the view in the text, making some exceptions in detail, e.g. he agrees with the mythologists in seeing the day and night in the names of Lamech's wives, Adah

thing but the mere facts of human life observed as working under the simplest conditions, and so exhibiting a picture which is also a prophecy of the whole course of man's after existence. The elements of all sin are in the Fall: the first murder gives the secret of Christ's rejection for envy; the elements of all history are in the parallel between the city of God and the city of this world in the times of Seth and Cain; the final judgment of all men is foreshadowed by the Flood; the final triumph of the Church is prefigured by the ark riding upon the waves, and settling on Ararat. It is difficult, if not impossible, to determine how far the facts here recorded happened literally as they are described; for my own part, I venture to hold that the literal acceptance of them is nearer the truth than any other interpretation as yet propounded. But what is of the greatest importance, is to understand that facts of human life, not ideas of natural phenomena, are represented by these narratives, whatever varieties of method may at length be discovered in them by a profounder and more learned exegesis.

But if this is the case in the first chapters of Genesis, much more clearly is it so in the narratives that follow. The patriarchs are as real men to us as those who lived yesterday; Abraham, Moses, David, are indeed in some ways much more living men to

(beauty) and Zillah (shadow). (*Origines de l'Histoire*, p. 183.) Is it not much more probable that the first polygamist is described as attracted by contrasted types of female loveliness? Lenormant agrees that "sauf ces appellations elles n'ont plus absolument rien d'un semblable caractère (i.e. caractère mythique) dans le livre sacré."

most of us than Pericles or Cicero. The facts of their lives fit into the facts of ours as closely as two portions of a broken stick, notwithstanding all the social differences of the times that lie between us. In the same way, the whole of the Jewish and Christian religious system of festivals, rites, and ceremonies, is (as I shall shew more in detail hereafter) a linking together of definite concrete material facts with the most profound thoughts. Lastly and chiefly, the reality of the facts of the life of Christ is the true safeguard of the doctrines which rest upon them, as all Christian teachers, from the days of St. Paul and St. Ignatius, have asserted. Thus St. Paul insists on the historical fact of Christ's resurrection against an incipient Gnosticism. "If Christ be not raised; your faith is vain, ye are yet in your sins [32]." And St. Ignatius, in a later stage of the same conflict, writes to the Smyrneans [33], in words which cannot be too often repeated, asserting the literal truth of the passion and resurrection:—

"All these things He suffered for our sakes, that we might be saved. And He suffered truly, as He also truly raised Himself, not as some faithless men say, that He suffered only in seeming, themselves being but a seeming. ... For I know and believe His existence in flesh even after His resurrection. And when He came to Peter, and those with him, He said 'Take, handle Me, and see that I am not a spirit without a body;' and immediately they touched Him and believed, being united both to His flesh and to His Spirit. Wherefore also they despised death, and were found superior to death. And after His resurrection He ate with them and drank with them as fleshly, though being spiritually made one with the Father."

[32] 1 Cor. xv. 17.　　[33] *Ad Smyrnaeos*, ch. 2—4.

"And these things I warn you brethren, knowing indeed that you too hold as I do. But I forearm you against those wild beasts in human form, whom you must not only not receive, but if possible not even meet, but only pray for them, if it may be that they will repent, which is hard. But over this Jesus Christ has power, who is our true Life. But if these things were done by our Lord in seeming, then these bonds of mine are also seeming. And why have I given myself up to death, to fire, to sword, to wild beasts? But near the sword, near to God; with the wild beasts about me, God about me. Only in the name of Jesus Christ I will bear everything that I may suffer with Him, while He gives me strength who was made perfect Man."

Such Gnosticism as this, which the earliest age had to combat, is not extinct, alas! among us, nor can we afford to lay aside St. Ignatius' warning as out of date. We still hear the assertion paraded as the secret of the universe, that thoughts are the only realities, and things are unreal. Yet we may ask the simple question of such would-be philosophers, "How can those who talk like this believe in the immortality of the soul?" for the soul, though it be not material, is a thing quite as much as it is a thought. And so we know where we should be led by the supposed philosophy of religion, which talks of God's teaching only by means of a series of "illusions[34],"

---

[34] Dr. Abbott, in his book, *Through Nature to Christ*. The germ of this book appears (if I mistake not) in a sermon of the late F. W. Robertson's, *Third Series*, No. 6, entitled *The Illusiveness of Life* (London, 1878, pp. 77—89). But Mr. Robertson's view of the subject seems to me much sounder than Dr. Abbott's, e.g. in his remarks on what the Israelites found in Canaan, bottom of p. 86, compared with Dr. Abbott, p. 77. The latter seems to overlook the real satisfaction which God gave to the desires of His people, partial as it no doubt was, and very far from final.

and of a "spiritual," as distinct from a "material," incarnation [35] of Christ.

Such a philosophy as this may have its vogue for a season, but it will soon pass to the same gulf as the speculations of Valentinus and Basilides. The faith which the Apostles preached, for which the martyrs suffered, and in which we bury our dead, is a faith resting on historical facts; and it alone will continue, it alone will move the world. The Psalmist's words can never be obsolete, and Christians of every age will sing, as their fathers have sung before them:—

> "Thy testimonies are wonderful: therefore doth my soul keep them.
> The entrance of Thy word giveth light: it giveth understanding unto the simple."

The Bible reconciles the two, when it tells us that the Lord gave the people rest under Joshua (Joshua i. 13, 14; xxi. 44; xxii. 4; xxiii. 1), and that Joshua did not give them rest (Heb. iv. 8). Dr. Abbott overlooks also the reason why God did not fulfil many of His promises, viz., the rebellion and unfaithfulness of His people.

[35] *Through Nature to Christ*, pp. 459, 460.

Additional note to page 121, *note* 14.

In *Christian Evidence Lectures*, Series 2, pp. 291—340 (London, 1879), there is an interesting Lecture by Sir Bartle Frere on *Christianity suited to all Forms of Civilization*, which may be referred to in illustration of the text.

Instances of the power of the Bible to effect conversion could very readily be multiplied. The case of the profligate John Wilmot, Earl of Rochester (ob. 1680), has often been quoted. He said to Burnet that as he heard the 53rd chapter of Isaiah read "he felt an inward force upon him, which did so enlighten his mind and convince him, that he could resist it no longer: For the words had an authority which did shoot like Rays or Beams in his Mind; so that he was not only convinced by the Reasonings he had about it, which satisfied his understanding, but by a power which did so effectually constrain him, that he did ever after as firmly believe in his Saviour, as if he had seen Him in the Clouds." (*Some Passages of the Life and Death of John, Earl of Rochester*, by Gilbert Burnet, pp. 141, 142, 5th edition, London, 1700).

The following is from Miss Bird's *Unbeaten Tracks in Japan*, vol. ii. p. 301, (London, 1880). Some books of the New Testament, and other Christian books, found their way, almost accidentally, into the hands of a prisoner at Otsu, a scholar, incarcerated for manslaughter. "A few months ago, a fire broke out, and 100 incarcerated persons, instead of trying to escape, helped to put out the flames, and to a man remained to undergo the rest of their sentences." It turned out that the possessor of the books had used them to teach his fellow-captives, "and Christian principles, combined with his personal influence, restrained them from defrauding justice. The scholar was afterwards pardoned, but remained in Otsu to teach more of the 'new way' to the prisoners."

Additional note to page 125, *note* 20.

The comparison between Christianity and Islam in respect to miracles, to the disadvantage of the latter, seems to me very forcible. It has been argued, however (by Professor Tyndall), that Mahometanism has spread without miracles, and therefore Christianity may have done the same. But the cases are not parallel. If Christianity had appealed to the sword, and had enforced a mere outward obedience to a law, and had made the concessions to human selfishness that Islam has done, in respect e.g. to polygamy, the argument might be, to some extent, admissible. But Christian morality triumphing over the flesh, and yet nurturing a sense of perfect freedom, could not have succeeded (humanly speaking) without miraculous assistance. Cp. Mr. Benjamin Shaw's argument, *Christian Evidence Lectures*, Series 2, pp. 427 foll.

Further, at least three stupendous miracles, the Incarnation, Resurrection, and Ascension, are essential parts of Christianity, regarded merely as a moral system. Those who do not believe in those lesser $\sigma\eta\mu\epsilon\hat{\iota}\alpha$ of Christ, which are commonly called "miracles," generally end by disbelief in the truth of these essentials.

LECTURE V.

ACTS xvii. 22, 23.

Then Paul stood in the midst of Mars' hill, and said, " Ye men of Athens, I perceive that in all things ye are too superstitious. For as I passed by, and beheld your devotions, I found an altar with this inscription, TO THE UNKNOWN GOD."

THE NATURAL SENSE OF SEPARATION FROM GOD, AND OF THE NEED OF ATONEMENT.

The altar to the unknown God a true type of heathen worship.
1. *The separation from God considered as connected with Sin and Death:* Myths of a golden age, and contrast with later times.—Departure of the gods.—Popular sense of the misery of man.—Sense of sin, especially in classical writers.—Sin a breaking away from God, and leading to death.—Sense of the impurity of death, and of murder.
2. *Attempts at atonement,* especially confession of sin and sacrifice.—*Confession* implied in approach to a priest.—In Assyria, Persia, Mexico.—Extraordinary mixture of ideas in the latter.—*Sacrifice* for sin: ideas implied in it, (1) the most precious thing, (2) a substitution for ourselves.—Bloody sacrifice, why chosen.—Willingness to die, &c.—Climax in human sacrifice: union of best and worst in it.—Reaction against it almost universal.—Mystical theories of sacrifice, miraculous power especially of austerities, and attribution of it to God.—In India and Odin's Rune-Song.—Mexican sacrifices.—Osiris, Adonis, &c.— Not merely pantheistic, but allied to a first principle of Christian theology.
3. *Failure of these attempts:* acknowledged by the best minds of antiquity.—Difficulty of the forgiveness of sin insoluble to the natural conscience.

THE sermon which St. Paul preached on this text had, we know, at first very little success. Yet few utterances have been more powerful or more blessed in the eventual issue. Let this thought comfort us defenders of the faith in this age, as it and others like it has comforted our fathers in the past.

The secret of St. Paul's final success lies in this, that under the common phenomena of heathen life he read the true inner feeling. He shewed to men the real character of their worship. "I perceive (he said to the Athenians) that in all things ye are too superstitious (δεισιδαιμονεστέρους)." Many critics are indeed inclined to see a mistranslation of our Authorized Version here [1], as if he rather praised than blamed them for their religious temper. It may possibly be so: but I venture on the whole to think that our translators were right, and that he *is* blaming the Athenians for superstition and ignorance, when they might really, if they had followed their better guides and truer lights, have had confidence and knowledge. St. Paul, we know, thought highly of the natural evidences of religion open to men as men [2]. He thought that the being and nature of God was clearly enough revealed to human kind, and that creature-worship was inexcusable. Hence he seems to censure rather than praise the altar on which he had cast his eye as he passed, it may be from the port where he landed, or through the Agora, or up the slope of the Areopagus. This censure, moreover (generous as it essentially was) to a great degree explains his temporary ill success, as its intrinsic truthfulness accounts for his eventual triumph.

[1] The new revision has "somewhat superstitious" with "religious" as an alternative in the margin. Cp. p. 177, note 75.
[2] Rom. i. 18—21.

The altar which he saw was probably no very important monument in itself. None exactly like it has come down to us, though altars to "the unknown gods[3]," and to a being addressed as "whether god or goddess[4]," are well known from other sources. The feeling which gave rise to the erection of such an altar is common indeed in heathenism, and is involved in its whole conception of practical religion. The heathen world feels itself estranged from God. It knows that God is angry with sin; it feels itself punished, or likely to be punished, by a power which has retired into a mysterious and awful cloud of reserve; it stretches out its arms into the darkness, vainly trying to propitiate the offended majesty. Surely it is with perfect truth to nature that Isaiah, in describing the coming over of the nations to the Messianic kingdom, represents them as exclaiming, "Verily Thou art a God that hidest Thyself, O God of Israel the Saviour[5]."

This deep feeling of the heathen world is the subject of my lecture to-day. It may be conveniently considered under three heads:—

[3] They are mentioned by Pausanias, i. 1, as at the Piræus, and v. 14, at Olympia; by Philostratus, *Vita Apollonii*, vi. 3 (p. 232, ed. Lips., 1709), as at Athens; and by S. Jerome, *on Titus* i. 12, as at Athens.

Diogenes Laertius, in his *Life of Epimenides*, chap. 3, mentions altars erected by his orders on the Areopagus, τῷ προσήκοντι θεῷ, 'to expiate a pestilence.' Pseudo-Lucian, *Philopatris*, 9 and 29 (νὴ τὸν ἄγνωστον ἐν Ἀθηναῖς), probably refers to this passage of the Acts, and may be fairly said to confirm it.

[4] Wilmanns *Inscr. Lat.*, 48, 2884, 2885. Compare my *Early Latin*, p. 410.

[5] Isaiah xlv. 14, 15.

1. The separation from God considered as connected with sin and death.
2. The attempts to obtain reconciliation by sacrifice, and other methods of purification.
3. The manifest failure of these methods.

1. *Heathen sense of Separation from God.*

Myths of a golden age, long since passed away, in which gods and men lived in closer union, and happiness and justice prevailed on earth, form the background of most, if not all, heathen religious systems. Such a background is apparent in the theory of a primeval revelation, which, as a competent authority [6] has told us, is found "both among the lowest and amongst the most highly civilised races. It is a constant saying among African tribes, 'that formerly heaven was nearer to men than it is now, that the highest God, the Creator Himself, gave formerly lessons of wisdom to human beings; but that afterwards He withdrew from them, and dwells now far from them in heaven [7].' The Hindus [8] say the same, and they as well as the Greeks [9] appeal to their ancestors, who had lived in closer community with the gods, as their authority on what they believe about the gods."

---

[6] Max Müller, *Hibbert Lectures*, p. 170, 2d ed. (Lond., 1878).

[7] Waitz, *Anthropologie der Naturvölker*, ii. p. 171.

[8] *Rig-Veda*, i. 179, 2; vii. 76, 4. Muir's *Sanskrit Texts*, iii. p. 245.

[9] Nägelsbach, *Homerische Theologie*, p. 151. [Cp. Plato, *Philebus*, p. 16. Socrates speaks of "a gift of heaven which, as I conceive, the gods tossed among men by the hands of a new Prometheus, and therewith a blaze of light; and the ancients who were our betters, and nearer the gods than we, handed down the tradition to us," &c.]

The description of the golden age amongst the Greeks is only a reflection of a common belief. In the first days, according to these legends, God Himself was the shepherd of men, and ruled over them [10]. Life was a happy time, free from care and pain; old age did not hinder the free exercise of the limbs in games and dances; the seasons were temperate, earth brought forth of itself for man's delight, and what work was needed was a pleasure and not a toil. Death was for men a lying down to sleep, a happy passing away, followed by their glorified existence as beneficent spirits, the watchers over right and justice on earth [11]. Other traits of this picture are the ascription of great intellectual power to the men of early ages, who were able without let or hindrance to turn their minds in every direction, and to see into the inner truth of things, and to acquire in a lifetime knowledge that ten or twenty lives now go to furnish. They lived in perfect peace and harmony with one another, and with the wildest and fiercest animals, and sacrifice and the eating of animal food was unknown [12].

Those who give us these pictures contrast with

---

[10] Plato, *Politicus*, pp. 271, 272.

[11] Hesiod, *Works and Days*, 109 foll. Cp. Preller, *Griechische Mythologie*, i. p. 69. The phrase θνῆσκον δ' ὡς ὕπνῳ δεδμημένοι and the lines that follow it, are a striking illustration of the meaning of the promise to Abraham, "thou shalt go to thy fathers in peace," and other things of the kind in the Old Testament, where we are to see a clear belief in a future life.

[12] Empedocles ap. Mullach, *Frag. Philosophorum Græcorum*, i. p. 13. Cp. Dicæarchus in Porphyrius, *de Abstinentia*, iv. 2, ed. Nauck, (Lips., 1860). The picture of happy life under Quetzalcoatl among the Toltecs is very similar; Bancroft, iii. pp. 250 foll.

them the miserable state in which themselves are living. The well-known lines of Hesiod upon the iron age remind us strongly of the prophecies of the latter days in the New Testament. The sense of separation from God, and consequent alienation between man and man, is strong upon him. The gods have all but left the earth, and last of all the twins Reverence and Justice, covering their faces with their robes, will quit our dark abodes for a better society, and leave us to a misery with which we cannot cope [13].

This belief in a total severance of God and man is remarkable as occurring in Greek mythology, where the sense of sin is on the whole superficial. But with all the lightness of temperament which this great people exhibit [14], there is in their best writers an under-current of melancholy, bearing witness that man is in a state which is very different indeed from his ideal, and has lost his happiness.

Side by side with the assertion that nothing is more wonderful than man, we find the counter statement, that nothing is more miserable. Even joyous, straightforward Homer makes Zeus exclaim—

"Than man more wretched nought, I ween, is found
Of all that breathes the air and walks the ground [15]:"

and the astonishing sentiment that "not to be born is the best fate of all, but next best is to die as soon

---

[13] Hesiod, l. c. 172—199. Cp. Theognis, 1135—1150, who tells us that Hope is the only god remaining: see below, p. 184, note 4; Ovid, *Met.*, i. 150; Juv. vi. 19.

[14] This lightness is well shewn by Mr. Percy Gardner, in an article on *the Greek mind in the presence of death*, Contemp. Rev., Dec., 1877, vol. xxxi. p. 144 foll.

[15] Hom., *Il.*, xvii. 446.

as may be," is almost a commonplace of Greek poetry, and was considered as an oracular utterance [16]. A similar note of sadness runs, it may be noticed, through much of popular music, pitched in its weird minor keys, and through the ballad literature of many countries, with its images of death and terror.

But it is not only poets who speak thus:—

"What is man?" (asks the most reserved of philosophers —Aristotle) "A pattern of impotency, a prey of accident, a plaything of fortune, an image of mutability, a mark for envy and misery to aim at, and for the rest phlegm and gall [17]."

This assertion of the universality of sorrow is matched by hardly less striking language on the universality of sin. It would be but a shallow supposition that Christianity had invented the idea of sin in order to commend the remedy for it offered by our Saviour. It has indeed profoundly deepened and widely enlarged the consciousness of sin, but the recognition of the fact of human wrong-doing is perfectly independent of Christian teaching [18]. To quote

---

[16] We learn that it was considered an oracle from Cicero, *Tusc.*, i. 48, 115, and Plutarch, *Consol. ad Apoll.*, c. 27. It is found substantially in the following poets, Bacchylides ap. Stob., *Flor.*, 98, 27; Theognis, 425; Soph., *Œd. Colon.*, 1226; Eurip., *Cresphontes*, frag. 10. Cp. Plin., *N. H.*, vii. 1, where the old naturalist waxes eloquent on the miseries of human nature, and xxviii. 2, where he treats suicide as the most blessed remedy discovered by mankind.

[17] Ap. Stob., *Florilegium*, 98, 60—a remarkable chapter.

[18] Cp. Liddon, *Elements of Religion*, Lect. iv. p. 129 foll.; Luthardt, *Saving Truths of Christianity*, Lect. 2, *Moral Truths*, Lect. 8, and notes; F. A. O. Tholuck, *Guido and Julius*, ch. 2 (already referred to, p. 104), a valuable little book (first pub. in 1823, in reply to one of De Wette's), the fuller title of which is *The Doctrine of Sin and the Propitiator, or the True Consecration of the Doubter*. It may be read in a translation by J. E. Ryland, (Lond., 1836).

only a few familiar instances. You remember the speech of Diodotus, as reported by Thucydides (iii. 45)—

"All men both as individuals and public bodies are prone to sin, nor is there any law that can restrain this tendency; since men have gone through all forms of punishment, continually augmenting them, with the hope of being less injured by evil-doers. . . . In short, it is an impossibility and a mark of great simplicity to suppose that any one can keep back human nature, when it is vehemently set upon a thing, either by force of law or any other menace."

And Crates puts epigrammatically the presence of corruption everywhere:—

"It is impossible to find a man without blemish; but just as is the case with the pomegranate, every man has in him one rotten grain [19]."

"Let no man think lightly of evil" (says Buddha from the other side of the world), "saying in his heart, It will not come nigh unto me. Even by the falling of water-drops a water-pot is filled: the fool becomes full of evil, even if he gather it little by little [20]."

Nor are there wanting striking descriptions of the struggle between the knowledge of good and the passionate desire for evil, which is, as it were, the central fact of Christian psychology, as traced by the master-hand of St. Paul.

The two horses of the soul of Plato's *Phædrus* [21], the "cords and strings which pull us different and opposite ways and to opposite actions, ... making a man superior or inferior to himself," of which we read in his *Laws* [22], the "two souls" of Xenophon's

---

[19] Ap. Diog. Laert., *vit. philosoph.* vi. § 89.
[20] *Dhammapada*, verse 121; *Sacred Books*, x. p. 34.
[21] *Phædrus*, p. 253 D. [22] *Laws*, i. pp. 644, 645.

Araspes [23], which make a man wish and not wish the same things at the same moment, will occur to many of us. So it is also among the Romans. Even worldly and sensual poets have written with a deep sense of this truth. Ovid's lines have become proverbial,—

"Nitimur in vetitum semper cupimusque negata,"

and the still more often quoted,—

"Video meliora proboque Deteriora sequor [24]."

Cicero, too, tells us mournfully of the poor little sparks of light which nature has given us, and which we hasten to extinguish by immoralities and false notions [25].

And while this is the judgment of the most enlightened ancients, it coincides with the simple reflections of the heathen of South Africa. The Kaffirs have just the same thought of a good heart and a bad heart in every man; the good heart having a small and gentle voice, very easily overpowered; while the bad heart, like Plato's dark-coloured horse, is blustering and passionate [26].

Especially was this feeling of human sinfulness strong in Rome in the latter half of the first century of our era, when history was written more as a bitter record of vices and crimes than as the chronicle of glory and progress. Not only satirical poets like

[23] Xen., *Cyrop.* vi. 1. 41.   [24] Ovid, *Amores*, iii. 4. 15; *Metam.*, vii. 20, 21. Cp. Hor., i. *Od.* 3, 25 foll.

[25] Cic., *Tusc.* iii. 1. 2.

[26] This I learn from Bp. Callaway (March, 1881), who tells me that he was long in discovering how to speak of conscience to his native hearers, but when he spoke of these two hearts the heathen immediately understood him. See *Appendix* II. to this volume.

Persius and Juvenal, but standard prose writers like Paterculus, Seneca, and Tacitus, are full of the wickedness of the age. A Christian apologist with great point says of one of these:—

"If any one wishes to know all that can be said [against heathenism] let him take up the books of Seneca, who was both the truest describer of public morals and vices, and their most stern accuser [27]."

An example of this description may be taken from Seneca's book *on Anger* [28]:—

"All things are full of crimes and vices; more wrongs are committed than can be righted by any penalties. Men vie with one another in a monstrous contest of wickedness; every day the love of sin grows greater, and shame grows less. The respect for what is good and just is repudiated, and desire fastens eagerly on every fancy. Nor are crimes now done in stealth; they brave our sight. And so public is wickedness, such a strong hold of all hearts has it acquired, that innocence is not only rare, but has ceased to exist ('ut innocentia non rara sed nulla sit'). Shall I say that individuals or some few men have broken through the law? on every side, as if at a given signal, they have united to confuse the principles of good and evil."

It would be easy to add to these dark pictures of human life, in many of which it is clear that the uneasy conscience of the writer tries to relieve its own sense of guilt by painting all round it as black and vicious.

Nor was the better mind of heathenism unaware that sin is so bitter because it is a transgression of

---

[27] Lactantius, *Div. Inst.* v. 9: "Qui volent scire omnia, Senecæ libros in manum sumant; qui morum vitiorumque publicorum et descriptor verissimus et accusator acerrimus fuit."

[28] *De ira*, ii. 8.

V.] *Sin a breaking away from God.* 153

the law of God. God (says Plato, in a famous passage) holds in His hand the beginning, middle, and end of all that is:—

"Justice always follows Him, and is the punisher of those who fall short of the divine law. To that law he who would be happy holds fast, and follows it in all humility [30] and order; but he who is lifted up with pride, or money, or honour, or beauty, who has a soul hot with folly, and youth, and insolence, and thinks that he has no need of a guide or ruler, but is able himself to be the guide of others, he, I say, is deserted of God, and being thus deserted, he takes to himself others who are like himself, and dances about, throwing all things into confusion; and many think that he is a great man, but in a short time he pays the penalty which justice cannot but approve, and is utterly destroyed, and his family and city with him [29]."

And he goes on to argue that "he who would be dear to God must be like Him, and such as He is [30]."

In a similar spirit the Stoic Cleanthes, the successor of Zeno and author of the famous hymn to Zeus, declares "that every sin is an impiety, and as such displeasing to the gods [31]."

[29] *Laws*, pp. 715, 716 (Prof. Jowett's translation). The use of ταπεινός in a good sense in the second sentence is remarkable. Plutarch has imitated it, *de profectibus in virtute*, § 10, p. 81 E. Celsus quoted this passage of Plato as the origin of the Christian doctrine of humility, Origen *c. Celsum*, vi. 15. It would be difficult to find a similar thought elsewhere in the classics. Lao-tse, the Chinese Plato, has, however, some striking parallels. See below, Lecture VI., p. 209, and the passages there referred to.

[30] Cp. *Rep.* ix. p. 589, "Is not the noble that which subjects the beast to the man, or rather to the god in man; and the ignoble that which subjects the man to the beast?" Cp. the description of the injustice of the multitude, *Rep.* ii. p. 365; and of desire seizing upon an empty soul, *ib.* viii. p. 560.

[31] Cleanthes in Stobæus, *Eclogæ Physicæ et Ethicæ*, ii. 6, § 6, p. 217, ed. Heeren.

These men, and others with them, were thus on the track of the principle of revelation that sin leads on to death, and that death is the punishment of sin. This principle indeed lies deep in the heart of man, who turns instinctively to God as the author of life, and feels that he was made to hold communion with Him [32]. But men know that they have started away from this communion, they have broken the chain that binds them to heaven, and so they regard death naturally as an avenger, not as a friend.

In the golden age death is a natural passage to a better life—

"They died as men o'erpowered by sleep lie down;"

but in later ages he comes as an executioner [33], as a punisher of irreverence, following on a state of mutual warfare and distrust, and removing his victims to a dark and terrible Hades, over which is cast a veil of impenetrable gloom.

This thought of death as a punishment of sin and the mark of separation from God, explains the constant popular feeling of the impurity of the unburied corpse. All contact with it is to be kept far from the worship of God, and from His priests and ministers. You remember how Euripides has given a fine expression to this thought in the *Alcestis* and *Hippolytus* [34]. In the first, Apollo leaves the house of

---

[32] Cp. Delitzsch, *Christliche Apologetik*, pp. 132 foll. (Leipz. 1869).

[33] Cp. Horace, *Odes*, i. 3. 25 foll.: "Audax omnia perpeti Gens humana ruit per vetitum nefas," &c.

[34] Cp. the picturesque legend of the death of Philemon, the comic poet, and many others.

V.]   *The connection of Sin and Death.*   155

Admetus, where he has sojourned so long, when he sees Death approaching to claim its mistress as his victim:—

> "I, lest uncleanness touch me in this house,
> Must leave the roof of these beloved halls.
> For yonder close I see the approach of Death,
> The dead man's priest, who comes to carry her
> Far down to Hades."—(*Alcestis*, 22 foll.)

And at the close of the *Hippolytus*, Artemis takes leave of her favoured servant, who is dying from the misadventure brought on him by his father's mistaken curse:—

> "Farewell! I must not look upon corruption,
> Nor soil mine eyes with thine expiring breath.
> And thou, I see, art not far off this evil."
> (*Hippolytus*, 1437—1439.)

Even ordinary men and families were defiled by contact with a dead body, and required to be purified, much as we read in the books of Moses[35]. I need not multiply instances of this familiar sentiment, which in some religions, like that of the Pārsīs, is carried to a great height of extravagance[36], though

---

[35] Cp. Döllinger, *Heidenthum*, p. 198, quoting Eur., *Iph. Taur.* 380; and Pollux, *Onomasticon*, 8. 7. Similar instances may be found in Thuc. iii. 104 (purification of Delos); Festus, s. v. *Aqua et igni;* Virg., *Æn.* vi. 149, 150 (Misenus); Liv. ii. 8 (Horatius interrupted while dedicating the Temple of Jupiter Capitolinus).

[36] See esp. *Vendîdâd, Fargard*, iii. 14 foll. p. 26, ed. Darmesteter, and almost the whole of *Fargards* v.—xii. Cp. Darmesteter's Introduction, v. 20, esp. p. xcviii.: "No one should wonder at the unqualified cleanser being put to death who reads Demosthenes' *Neæra;* the Persians who defiled the ground by burying a corpse were not more severely punished than the Greeks were for defiling with corpses the holy ground of Delos [Diodorus, xii. 58], or than

having parallels even in its extravagances in other details of Aryan legislation. Nor will it be necessary to remind you of the special horror attaching to homicide, particularly to malicious and premeditated murder. You know how in many nations the manslayer becomes an outlaw and a fugitive, and is debarred from hearth and altar, and is ordered to be slain by the next of kin as a sacred duty. The man who of his own will causes death is thus confessed to be a chief, if not always the chief, of sinners, because he not only takes a step towards death, as all sinners do, but audaciously introduces it into God's world of life and freedom.

2. *Attempts at Atonement.*

Such being the heathen conscience of sin and of separation from God, we must next proceed to enquire what means were resorted to in the hope of healing the breach. Four of these stand out with great clearness in almost all nations, viz. (1) Confession of sin; (2) lustral washings and purifications; (3) bodily penances, such as fasting; (4) sacrifice. To give an account of all these would be almost to write the history of non-Christian rituals. I can at present merely indicate some of the more prominent instances, and the thoughts that seem to underlie

the conquerors at Arginousæ; nor would the Athenians, who put to death Atarbes [Ælianus, *Hist. Var.* v. 17], have much stared at the awful revenge taken for the murder of the sacred dog. There is hardly any prescription in the Vendîdâd, however odd and absurd it may seem, but has its counterpart or its explanation in other Aryan legislations; if we had a Latin or a Greek Vendîdâd, I doubt whether it would look more rational."

them, especially the first and fourth, which are the most important.

With regard, first, to confession of sin, we must recollect that it is presumed as the foundation of all rites of atonement, even when not expressly mentioned. When a man fled to the priest of Apollo (let us say) to be purified of a murder, he went *in forma pœnitentis*. His very presence was a confession of impurity. When we see him touched by the sacred laurel bough, we are instinctively reminded of the first murderer, Cain, under sentence of banishment, crying to God, "My guilt is greater than I can bear," and receiving from Him a mark or sign, lest any finding him should kill him[37]. The Greeks and Romans have, however, a very slight sense of the importance of confession of sin compared with many other nations.

Amongst the Assyrians, for instance, we find litanies of deprecation, which for depth and force of feeling come perhaps nearest to the Psalms of any heathen utterances. The following passages of the lamentation of a sinner cannot have been written except by one who had a genuine idea of the relation between God and man:—

"I lay on the ground, and no man seized me by the hand.
I wept, and my palms none took.
I cried aloud: there was none that would hear me.
I am in darkness (and) trouble: I lifted not myself up.
To my God my (distress) I referred: my prayer I addressed.

[37] The word ('*avôn*) which we translate "punishment" seems more probably taken to mean "guilt." Cp. Lenormant's parallels in his book above cited, *Les Origines de l'Histoire*, pp. 172 foll.

The feet of my goddess I embraced.
To (my) God who knew, (though) I knew not, (my prayer) I addressed.
To (my) goddess, who knew (though I knew not, my prayer) I addressed."

And after a little,—

" O Lord, Thy servant Thou dost not restore.
In the waters of the raging flood seize his hand.
The sin (that) he has sinned to blessedness bring back.
The transgression he has committed let the wind carry away.
My manifold affliction like a garment destroy.
O my God, seven times seven (are my) transgressions, my transgressions are before (me).
[(To be repeated) 10 times.]
O my goddess, seven times seven (are my) transgressions [38]."

Next to them, and little if at all inferior to them, appear to be the confessions of sin amongst the Old Persians and Mexicans. The former attached great spiritual efficacy to repentance, as appears in the Avesta, where the following words are ordered to be spoken over the corpse of one declared by their law to be a great criminal, and as such just barbarously executed:—

"The man here has repented of all his evil thoughts, words and deeds. If he has committed any other evil deed, it is remitted by his repentance: if he has committed no other evil deed, he is absolved by his repentance for ever and ever [39]."

---

[38] Portions of an *Accadian Penitential Psalm*, tr. by Prof. A. H. Sayce in *Records of the Past*, vol. vii. pp. 154, 155. Cp. vol. iii. p. 136, where a quotation nearly to the same effect is given by Mr. H. Fox Talbot. Fr. Lenormant has some striking short quotations, *Origines de l'Histoire*, pp. 173—175.

[39] *Vendîdâd, Fargard* iii. 21, pp. 27, 28, ed. Darmesteter; cp. *Fargard* v. 26, p. 57, and Introduction, v. 22,

V.] *Assyrian, Persian, and Mexican Confessions.* 159

The more modern Patets, or confessions, are extremely full, and specially concerned with sins of thought as well as word and deed, and are more directly connected with the Creed of Parsism than is the case with other religions; for there the confession of faith leads up, as in our Liturgy, to the confession of sin [40], a fact which stamps the practical theology of the people as of a very high kind.

The Mexican confessions, collected by the Franciscan Bernardino de Sahagun, are, if genuine, some of the most remarkable religious documents in the world [41]. They are, I think, probably none the less real from the extraordinary mixture of refined spirituality with abominable superstition which they exhibit—a combination which is characteristic of the nation in which they appear. One remarkable point about the act of confession was that it could never be repeated: it could only be performed once in a lifetime, and set free from civil and temporal as well as spiritual penalties—not, as among the Pārsīs, from future punishment only in another world. The ceremony consisted in long addresses on the part of the confessor, first interceding with the god for the penitent, and then turning to him to emphasize the blackness and self-will of his crimes.

"Of thine own will and volition thou hast defiled and stained thyself, and rolled in filth, and in the uncleanness of the sins and evil deeds that thou hast committed and

[40] These Patets may be found in Spiegel's *Avesta*, tr. by A. H. Bleeck, vol. iii. pp. 153, 171 (Hertford, 1864).

[41] They may be found in H. H. Bancroft's *Native Races of the Pacific States*, vol. iii. pp. 220 foll., 280 foll. (New York, 1875), a wonderful digest of information.

now confessed.... Verily, thou hast come to the fountain of mercy, which is like very clear water, with which filthinesses of the soul are washed away by our Lord God, the protector and favourer of all that turn to him.... Thou hast snatched thyself from Hades, and hast returned again to come to life in this world as one that comes from another. Now thou hast been born anew, thou hast begun to live anew, and our Lord God gives thee light and a new sun" (p. 223).

He then goes on to caution him against pride, and to bid him beware of the invisible tortures of another world :—

"Therefore I intreat thee to stand up and strengthen thyself, and be no more as thou hast been in the past. Take to thyself a new heart and a new manner of living, and take good care not to turn again to thine old sins."

He is then directed to sweep and cleanse his house, that it may be pleasing to the invisible God, who is ever walking amongst men; and further, he is enjoined to offer a human sacrifice: "Seek out also a slave to immolate him before God; make a feast to the principal men,"—no doubt on the flesh of the victim,—" and let them sing the praises of our Lord." The man himself is further advised to do penance in the temple, wounding himself, and pricking himself with thorns, and passing osier twigs through holes which he has made in his tongue and his ears. He is lastly ordered to give alms to the hungry and to clothe the naked :—"Look to it : for their flesh is like thy flesh, and they are men as thou. Care most of all for the sick, they are the image of God" (p. 225).

In other cases fasting was enjoined as a penance, and certain smaller offerings to the god or goddess supposed to be interested in the special class of sins confessed (pp. 233, 234).

I must not attempt to cite other formulæ of confession, such as those of the Vedic hymns [42] (with which many here are familiar), or the curious negative confession of the Egyptian ritual of the dead, which is so remarkable a mirror of the self-satisfaction of that haughty people, even while testifying to the fact that sin separates from God [43].

I must also pass over the very interesting subject of lustrations and penances, which by their similarity everywhere testify so strikingly to the unity of the human race, and to the common sentiment of a taint of sin clinging to our nature in birth, in its passage through this world, and in its transit by death to another [44]. For, interesting as these things are, the

[42] They are quoted by Prof. Max Müller, *Chips*, vol. i. pp. 39—41 (London, 1868); *Selected Essays*, ii. 148 foll., and elsewhere.
Cp. Dean Church, *The Sacred Poetry of Early Religions*, p. 30 foll.
The following prayer is at present used after the Gāyatrī [see above, p. 76, note 11] by many religious persons among the Hindus (acc. to Prof. Monier Williams, *Indian Wisdom*, p. 146, note 1):—
"I am sinful, I commit sin, my nature is sinful, I am conceived in sin. Save me, O thou lotus-eyed Hari [Vishnu], the remover of sin."

[43] Contained in the *Book of the Dead*, ch. 125 (tr. by Birch in the last vol. of Bunsen's *Egypt*), and in the later *Book of Respirations*, tr. in *Records of the Past*, vol. iv. p. 127. Cp. Renouf, *Hibbert Lectures*, p. 195 foll.; Döllinger, *Heidenthum*, p. 430; Duncker, *Hist. of Antiquity*, tr. by E. Abbott, vol. i. p. 179.

[44] E.g. Mr. H. H. Bancroft (a perfectly unbiassed witness) writes:—"The fact that infants were baptized [among the Mexicans] immediately after birth, proves that these people believed with the Christians and Jews that sin is inherited."—(*Native Races of the Pacific*, vol. iii. p. 439.)

culminating point of these efforts of natural penitence is found with even greater unanimity in sacrifice, and that of a peculiar kind. All sacrifice, indeed, is founded upon the same moral motive of self-denial. This appears in the thank-offering for the harvest, and in the homage-sacrifice, by which man dedicates himself to a particular protecting deity, quite as certainly as in the sin-offering or expiation; and it is a very feeble theory of natural religion which sees only a gross materialism in the lower forms of sacrifice. But it is with sin-offerings that we are mostly concerned to-day, as embodying the deepest feelings of the human conscience [45].

Two ideas specially underlie this class of sacrifices:—

(1.) That the most efficacious sacrifice is the most precious, the best, purest, nearest, dearest, most like ourselves, or what we should wish to be, that in which our heart and will is most bound up.

(2.) That the sin or guilt is laid upon the victim, and carried by it, and so passes away from him who offers to that which he consecrates and presents in his stead; in other words, the idea of vicarious atonement or substitution.

These two ideas explain the general resort to bloodshedding in sin-offerings. The blood is identified with the life. It is at once the seat of the passions which have caused the sin, and of the soul, which, as the most valuable and irrevocable gift we know, is poured out to atone for the wrong committed. The

---

[45] On this subject in general cp. Delitzsch, *Christliche Apologetik*, pp. 167—177 (Leipz., 1869).

V.]   *Ideas underlying Sin-offerings.*   163

heart, again, for a like reason, is especially chosen as the portion to be presented to the god, it is most scrupulously examined for omens, and a victim without a heart is supposed to be a particularly bad sign, as if it could be no proper representative of the feeling of the penitent. The offering of the blood, the pouring of it on the altar, the sprinkling of it upon the penitent, the actual washing in it in some cases [46], are further symbolic of the attempt of the man who has done the wrong to identify himself with the victim that suffers the penalty. Another symbolic action of the same sort is the imposition of hands upon the head of the victim, which Herodotus (ii. 39) tells us was practised by the Egyptians, no doubt to imply transmission of guilt. The Hindus in the same way teach with great clearness the ideal identity of the sinner with the sacrifice he offers. "The sacrificer himself is the victim," we are told in one of the Brāhmaṇas; "it takes the very sacrificer himself to heaven [47]:" and again: "Whoever is initiated in divine service, virtually devotes his soul to all the Gods [48]." And, without this philosophic idealism, the same sentiment appears amongst the Romans in the well-known lines of Ovid :—

---

[46] See the quotations in Müller's *Eumenides,* p. 124, E. T., and Döllinger's *Heidenthum,* pp. 203, 626 foll. The Taurobolia and Criobolia were actual baths of blood, in which the penitent or receiver of a supposed new birth stood in a hole in the ground. They are described by Preller, *Röm. Myth.,* p. 738 foll. Similar things are common elsewhere.

[47] *Taittirīya Brāhmaṇa,* p. 202, quoted by Banerjea, *Arian Witness,* p. 206.

[48] Banerjea, l.c., p. 211.

164 *The natural sense of Separation from God.* [LECT.

"This heart for ours; this flesh for flesh receive:
This, for a better life, to you we give [49]."

So the Rabbinical Jews at the present time, on the day of atonement, sacrifice a cock, and say, "Let this be my substitute, this my expiation [50]."

In consequence of this feeling great pains were taken, wherever religious awe was strong, to secure the most beautiful and unblemished, or the most appropriate victim, varying with the sin to be expiated and the attributes of the deity requiring to be propitiated. The white bull and the ram, emblems of light, beauty, and strength, are perhaps especially prominent; and amongst the old Hindus and Northmen the horse [51] was a favourite sacrifice for the same reason. In most sacrifices, too, a great point is made of willingness to die. It was a bad omen when the victim struggled in going to the altar, and amongst the Greeks it was not slaughtered till, by an inclination of the head (generally obtained by a trick of the attendant), it seemed to give its consent to the stroke of death [52].

This attempt to find atonement in the surrender of

[49] Ovid, *Fasti*, vi. 161, 162:—
"Cor pro corde precor: pro fibris sumite fibras.
Hanc animam vobis pro meliore damus."

[50] Delitzsch, *Christliche Apologetik*, p. 354 (Leipz., 1869). On the Moslem feast of sacrifice, see Hughes' *Notes*, p. 173 foll.

[51] On the asva-medha, see Monier Williams, *Indian Wisdom*, pp. 31, 343, &c. On horse sacrifices amongst the old Germans, &c., J. Grimm's *Teutonic Mythology*, tr. by Stallybrass, i. p. 47 foll. (Lond., 1880). On the curious sacrifice of the "October horse" at Rome, see Preller, *Römische Mythologie*, p. 323.

[52] Döllinger, *Heidenthum*, p. 209, quoting Plutarch, *quæst. symp.*, 8. 8. 3; *Scholia in Apollonii Argonautica*, i. 415. A little water was thrown into the ear.

V.]   *Self-devotion.*   165

life for life reaches its climax in the offering of man as the true and best substitute for man, in which the superstition of most nations has for a time culminated. Human sacrifice is an extraordinary mixture of what is highest and lowest, most glorious and most detestable. As a voluntary act of self-surrender it stirs our deepest feelings. Even legends like that of Chiron willingly taking the place of Prometheus upon the Scythian rock of torture [53], and Alcestis dying for her husband, Admetus, move every one who hears them to sympathy. Much more do we feel this when we read in history of a king like Codrus offering himself to die for his people, or a general like Decius for his army, or the Chinese Emperor Thang [54] devoting

[53] Cp. Æsch., *Prom.*, 1026 foll.; Preller, *Griech. Mythol.*, i. p. 79. Two lines of Sophocles, *Œd. Colon.*, 498 foll., have also been well quoted in this connection (by Luthardt, *Saving Truths*, Lect. v. note 8, p. 322, E. T.), where Œdipus requests one of his daughters to worship the Eumenides in his place, as he is old and blind:—
   "For e'en for myriads, I suppose, one soul
   Might do this service if its will were true."
[54] See for this interesting story Prof. James Legge, *Sacred Books of China*, pp. 90, 91 (Oxford, 1879), and *Religions of China*, pp. 54, 55 (Lond., 1880).
   When he had taken possession of the throne (B.C. 1766), from which he had driven the previous dynasty, he made a remarkable announcement, in which the following sentences occur:—
   "It is given to me the one man to secure the harmony and tranquillity of your states and clans; and now I know not whether I may not offend against (the powers) above and below. I am fearful and trembling, as if I were in danger of falling into a deep abyss. .... When guilt is found anywhere in you who occupy the myriad regions let it rest on me, the one man," &c.
   For seven years after his accession (B.C. 1766—1760), says Dr. Legge, there was a great drought and famine. It was suggested at last by some one that a human victim should be offered in sacrifice to Heaven, and prayer made for rain. T'ang (or Thang)

himself as a victim for his famine-stricken subjects. Such things are true types, in their measure and degree, of the self-surrender of the Son of Man for His brethren. These, or others like them, were those exceptions to human selfishness of whom St. Paul thought when he was extolling the magnificence of the love of God, in that while we were yet sinners Christ died for us (Romans v. 7). But human sacrifice, as a ritual institution, in which unwilling victims are slaughtered, like sheep and oxen, is to the reflective mind the most abominable and even diabolic crime. It is further not unfrequently connected with cannibalism. It has nevertheless (as we have said) prevailed at some time or other in almost all nations [55]. In Mexico alone it was calculated that

said, "If a man must be the victim I will be he." He fasted, cut off his hair and nails, and in a plain carriage drawn by white horses, clad in rushes, in the guise of a sacrificial victim, he proceeded to a forest of mulberry trees, and there prayed, asking to what error or crime of his life the calamity was owing. He had not done speaking when a copious rain fell. The ideas of substitution and consecration are thus to be found in the history of China, but they have not found their way into its religious ceremonies. Delitzsch, *Chr. Apol.*, p. 171, mentions the smearing of temples and temple vessels with blood of a sacrifice, as the relic of a deeper feeling about sin-offerings; and alludes (without quoting his authority) to the brother of an Emperor Wu-wang, as devoting himself to save some sick people: *ibid.*, p. 183.

[55] On human sacrifices generally amongst the "native races," see Georg Gerland's excellent Essay, *Ueber das Aussterben der Naturvölker*, pp. 73—78 (Leipzig, 1868), and many passages of Waitz's *Anthropologie*; cp. Tylor, *Primitive Culture*, vol. ii. pp. 271, 385, 389, 398 (children), 403 (do.). For India, see H. H. Wilson, *Essays*, vol. ii. No. v., *Human Sacrifices in the Ancient Religion of India*. On such sacrifices amongst the Mediterranean nations, see the collections from Porphyry, Clement, Diony-

some 20,000 persons were sacrificed annually, in the years which preceded the Spanish conquest, and seventy or eighty thousand were butchered at the dedication of a single temple [56]. And these were not only men who might presumably be slaves or captives or criminals, but women and infants—the latter in large numbers. The ceremonies at some of these grim festivals cannot be read without an indescribable loathing [57]. Yet it is possible to trace the steps between the two poles of best and worst, and to imagine how the too superstitious penitent, standing before the altar of the unknown God, might even come to think the sacrifice to Moloch a service pleasing to an offended

sius, Diodorus, &c., in Eusebius, *præp. Evang.*, iv. 16; Lasaulx, *Die Sühnopfer der Griechen und Römer*, pp. 8—13 (Würzburg, 1841); Döllinger and Preller, *passim*. Human sacrifice was forbidden at Rome in B.C. 97 (see note 64), but Cassius Dio tells us (xliii. 24) that two mutinous soldiers were sacrificed publicly in the Campus Martius by the Pontifices and Flamen of Mars, after the triumph of Julius Cæsar, B.C. 46. The story that Augustus immolated 300 prisoners at the "Perusinæ aræ" to Divus Julius is less probable. It is mentioned however by Suetonius, *Octav.*, 15; and Dio, xlviii. 14; and taken for granted by Seneca, *de Clementia*, i. 11. See the remarks in Merivale, *Romans*, ch. 27, vol. 3, p. 244, ed. 1865. The sacrifice of a condemned criminal (bestiarius) to Jupiter Latiaris went on still in the time of Porphyry (*de Abstinentia*, ii. 56). See the Christian authorities in Marquardt, *Römische Staatsverwaltung*, iii. p. 285 note; cp. Preller, *Röm. Myth.*, pp. 104, 191. Heliogabalus reintroduced the sacrifice of children into Italy from Syria (Lampridius, *Heliogabalus*, ch. 8), and such things, though illegal, continued long as a matter of private magic. For the practice of the northern nations, see J. Grimm, *Teutonic Mythology*, tr. by Stallybrass, vol. i. pp. 44—46, (Lond., 1880).

[56] Bancroft, l. c., iii. pp. 442 foll., &c.; cp. Mozley's *University Sermon*, on the Atonement, p. 186 foll., ed. 1, 1876.

[57] See the details, Bancroft, l. c., pp. 330—334, 354 foll., 387, &c.

deity[58]. The primitive and uncultured man is apt to regard children and slaves so little as independent beings, so much as appendages and attributes of their father or master, that he has scarcely any feeling of injustice in disposing of their lives[59]. When the king of Moab offered up his eldest son on the city wall in the sight of the invading host[60], and when Manco Ccapac in Peru[61], or Thoro the Dane[62], did a similar act, we have no right to suppose that they were, or appeared, simply cruel and heartless. The innocence of children makes them seem, like the unblemished and snow-white animal, a peculiarly fitting sacrifice for sin. The very point which makes us shudder so much, the guiltless suffering of these poor babes, was the attraction of the rite to superstitious minds. Men saw that a pure and holy thing was a better substitute for sinners than an unclean one. So it is also that superstition assigns great weight to the rank or status of the victim. A guest has sometimes been sacrificed simply because of the peculiar sanctity attaching to hospitality, and a king because his office is so highly honoured. When the Swedes in a grievous famine sacrificed their king, Domaldi[62], they felt perhaps not so very differently

---

[58] Cp. Porphyrius, *de Abstin.*, ii. 56; S. Augustine, *de Civ. Dei*, vii. 19; Diodorus Sic., xx. 14, &c. "The image was of brass, with its hands outstretched towards the ground, in such a manner that the child when placed upon them fell into a pit full of fire." Smith's *Bible Dict.*, s. v. *Moloch*, p. 404.

[59] See on this topic Dr. Mozley's *Old Testament Lectures* (The Sacrifice of Isaac), pp. 37—48, (Lond., 1877).

[60] 2 Kings iii. 27.

[61] Tylor, *Primitive Culture*, ii. 385.

[62] These two instances are given by Grimm, l. c., p. 48.

from the Chinese, when they looked on Thang disappearing in the forest, or the Roman soldiers who suffered Decius to throw himself upon the Samnite spears, and Curtius to leap into the gulf. Nor are there wanting cases in which merely religious fervour has led people to sacrifice themselves, without any special motive of good to be gained by the action for themselves or others [63]. Such, then, is the fatal strength of this practice, and the deep seat which it has obtained in the human conscience. Yet the better feeling of men has happily prevailed in many instances to stop or mitigate such practices. An echo of the angel's voice which bade Abraham withdraw his hand from slaying Isaac, was heard in India, and Greece, and Italy, and Egypt, and even in Mexico and Polynesia, telling men that such sacrifices were contrary to nature [64]. They had been tried and found wanting.

Human sacrifice, then, is the climax of superstition. It is an awful, a miserable thing, and men have re-

[63] E.g. those mentioned by Bancroft, *Pacific Nations*, ii. p. 336, and those who are popularly supposed to throw themselves beneath the car of Jagannāth. (See however Hunter's *Orissa*, vol. i. ch. 3, p. 133 foll., 1872.) For other cases, cp. Delitzsch, l. c., p. 174.

[64] On the cessation of human sacrifice in India, see the *Aitareyabrāhmana*, as quoted by Monier Williams, l. c., p. 31. In Egypt it was stopped by Amosis acc. to Manetho, and in Cyprus by Diiphilus, in the time of Seleucus (Porph., *de Abstin.*, ii. 55). It was forbidden by a decree of the Roman Senate, B.C. 97, Plin., *N. H.*, xxx. 1. The puppets thrown into the Tiber, the 'mænæ' and the 'ver sacrum,' are familiar instances of the same feeling. In Mexico, the gentle god or hero-king, Quetzalcoatl, dissuaded men from such rites and other cruelties; Bancroft, vol. iii. pp. 250, 269, 282, &c. Gerland notices a re-action against it amongst the Fijians, *Aussterben der N. V.*, p. 76.

volted from it with almost the same unanimity of feeling as they have resorted to it. With this revolt we may perhaps connect some remarkable mystical theories of sacrifice, in which, as it would seem, the higher minds of paganism have sought to find that better theology of atonement, the image of which was for ever floating before them.

Of these conceptions we receive hints from many quarters, especially from India, in which so many truths and half-truths are found overgrown with a luxuriant mass of error. In the first place, sacrifice, especially in the form of austere self-denial ('tapas'), is looked upon by the Hindus as an instrument of mysterious and even immeasurable power. It is by sacrifices (they say) that the gods have attained to heaven, and have overpowered the spirits of evil. This idea is indeed, by itself, the parent of many dangerous consequences. What can be used for a good end can be used for a bad one also, and Hindu mythology tells us of the demon Rāvaṇa [65], who by his austerities obtained a selfish control over the world, and even over the gods; and Hindu practice issues too often in the senseless devotion of the Yogis, or ascetics. Nevertheless there is also a truth in the idea, which must be laid hold of by all who wish to raise their fellow-men. "It *is* more blessed to give than to receive." Self-denial, which is the moral part of sacrifice, does strengthen the will and enlarge the powers of being, doing, and suffering in such a marvellous way, as not remotely to suggest the idea of magic. The practice of giving (for instance), as many

[65] M. Williams, *Indian Wisdom*, pp. 344, 345.

V.] *Mythical theory of Sacrifice in India.* 171

persons have experienced, may be extended almost indefinitely, and is by no means inconsistent with economical saving, and becomes a sort of self-acting habit. So it is also with other acts of sacrifice and self-surrender, which may be practised to a degree quite undreamed of by the slothful and the careless.

We cannot wonder, then, that the Hindus, with their tendency to push principles to extremes, should impute miraculous properties to the act of sacrifice, even apart from the motive. But they have gone further still, and with a wonderful theological audacity have ascribed the highest act of self-denial and self-sacrifice to the Supreme Being Himself. This point has been brought out in a remarkable book by Mr. Banerjea, of Calcutta, called the *Arian Witness*[66],—a book which (whatever be the value of its ethnological theories) contains theological material of no slight importance. Thus we read in the Brāhmanas (as cited by him):—

"The Lord of creatures offered himself a sacrifice for the gods."—(*Tāndya Mahā Brāhmana*, vol. i. p. 410.)

And again:—

"To these (i.e. the gods) the Lord of creatures gave himself. He became their sacrifice; sacrifice is food for the gods. He having given himself to them, made a reflection of himself, which is sacrifice. Therefore they say, the Lord of creatures is a sacrifice, for he made it a re-

[66] *The Arian Witness, or The Testimony of Arian Scriptures in corroboration of Biblical History and the rudiments of Christian Doctrine, including dissertations on the original Home and early Adventures of the Indo-Arians*, by the Rev. K. M. Banerjea, (Calcutta and London, Trübner, 1875). See esp. pp. 203—206.

flection of himself; by means of this sacrifice he redeemed himself from them."—(S'*atapatha Brāhmana*, p. 836.)

The Prajā-pati, or Lord of Creatures, according to the same writer, is called *ātmadā*, or "giver of self," even in the Rig-Veda, "whose shadow, whose death is immortality (to us)," (x. 121, 2)[67].

Elsewhere, in a more complicated form, we read of the sacrifice of Purusha, that is "person," the ideal man or soul of the world, "begotten in the beginning[68]."

"When the gods celebrated a sacrifice with Purusha as their oblation, the spring was its butter, summer its fuel, and autumn its (supplementary) oblation. When the gods, celebrating the sacrifice, bound Purusha as the victim, they immolated him, the sacrifice, on the grass—even him, the Purusha, who was begotten in the beginning. With him as their offering, the gods, the Sādhyas[69], and the Rishis[70], also sacrificed."—(*Rig-Veda*, x. 90, 6 and 7; *Taittirīya Āranyaka*, pp. 331—333.)

These striking texts, and others like them, shew a deeper view of this rite and its correlatives than

[67] Banerjea, l. c., p. 213. On Prajāpati, see Muir, *Sanskrit Texts*, vols. iii. p. 4 foll., iv. 15—30, 45 foll., v. 390 foll. Muir, however, translates (iv. p. 16): "He who gives breath, who gives strength, whose command all, [even] the Gods, reverence, whose shadow is immortality, whose shadow is death." *Ātmadā* may mean "giver of life" or "giver of self." The former meaning is the only one recognized in Monier Williams' dictionary, but the cognate word *ātmadāna* is translated "gift of self," "self-sacrifice."

[68] *Rig-Veda*, x. 90, the Purusha-Sūkta: see Muir, i. pp. 8 foll., and Appendix III. to this volume.

[69] Sometimes translated "regents of the sky." For a discussion of the original meaning, see Muir, l. c., vol. v. p. 17, note 26.

[70] The Rishis are the inspired seers or prophets of the Vedas. For the supernatural character attributed to them, see Muir, vol. iii. pp. 245 foll.

even the self-devotion of a Decius or a Regulus. The idea seems to be that sacrifice on earth is the representation of some divine process which goes on, or has gone on in heaven; and that the deity is virtually and sacramentally present in or with the victim. "In some sense (says a modern writer) God was offered up to God"[71]. And in the later mythology, Vishnu, the second member of the Brahmanical triad, "is repeatedly spoken of as being present in, and offered up with the victim; he is also said, through virtue of his sacrifice, to have obtained pre-eminence among the gods."

And this conception, though perhaps most clearly expressed in India, is by no means confined to it. One of the most striking parallels to the self-sacrifice of the Lord of creatures, meets us in the strange Rune-song of Odin in the Edda ("the High One's Lesson"). Many readers will be inclined to suspect a Christian influence in the poem; but reflection will, I think, convince them that this influence, though it may colour, yet does not originate the myth, and that we have here a foretaste of that philosophic view of religion which has been so strongly developed amongst the modern Teutons. It may be translated as follows [72]:—

"1. I mind that I hung on the gallows-tree,
Nine whole nights,
Wounded with the spear, and to Odin offered

[71] Vaughan, *The Trident, the Crescent, and the Cross*, p. 70 and note; cp. Muir, vol. iv. p. 125, for sacrifice of Vishnu.

[72] I have to thank Dr. G. Vigfússon for his kind help in this translation. The poem has lately been discussed by Karl Blind, *Discovery of Odinic Songs in Scotland* (*Nineteenth Century*, No. 28,

Myself to myself—
On that tree of which none knows
From what roots it sprang.
2. They gave me no loaf, they held no horn to me.
I peered down, I caught up the runes (mysteries)
With a cry; then I fell back [i.e. descended].
3. I learnt nine songs of might from the son
Of Balethorn Bestla's father,
And I got the draught of the precious mead
Blent with inspiration (Odreari).
4. Then I became fruitful and wise,
And waxed great and flourished:
Word followed fast on word with me;
And work followed fast on work with me."

Here Odin is represented as hanging on the tree with unknown roots, that is, Yggdrasil, the great ash, which symbolises the world, and offering himself to himself; the result being the production of thoughts and deeds, i.e. revelation of the divinity in nature and concrete fact, especially in the form of the mystic runes. The same conception of a suffering God meets us in another form in the myths of Osiris and of Adonis, in the self-immolation of Herakles, and to some extent in the myth of Prometheus, and in a number of other stories—generally connected with the changing phenomena of the seasons, and similar natural facts. It comes to us again in the strange world of Mexican mythology, where we find a stated festival called "killing the god Huitzilopochtli, so that his body might be eaten [73]"—in which an image made of dough was pierced with

June, 1879, vol. v. p. 1093), but apparently without sufficient knowledge or judgment.

[73] Bancroft, vol. iii. p. 299. Cp. p. 315 for his comments; and vol. ii. pp. 329, 330.

a dart or spear, and afterwards parted as a sacrament amongst the king and people.

It meets us yet more wondrously in a similar festival, in which such an image of the God of fire was raised upon a cross-shaped tree, and then broken in pieces, and thrown upon the ground—a most curious illustration of the myth of Odin [74]. Lastly, it is not out of place to recall the custom of adorning human victims with the emblems and insignia of the God to whom they are dedicated; and thus making them, as far as possible, his living images and representatives.

What is to be said of all this?

No doubt (as we shall be told by comparative mythologists) there is a pantheistic element in these myths. They have many of them a directly naturalistic tendency, and some are vitiated by those unholy associations which cling to most forms of nature-worship. They might at first sight seem little more than parables of the supposed process by which infinite being or substance contracts itself, and by an act which may be described as self-surrender, expresses itself in concrete forms. Yet it is surely

[74] Bancroft, vol. iii. pp. 508, 509: "The feast of the maturity of fruit was dedicated to Xiuhtecutli, God of fire, and therefore of fertility or fecundity. The principal feature of the feast was a tall, straight tree; which was stripped of all its branches except those close to the top, and set up in the court of the temple. Within a few feet of its top a cross-yard, thirty feet long, was fastened; thus a perfect cross was formed. Above all, a dough image of the God of fire, curiously dressed, was fixed. After certain horrible sacrifices had been made to the deity of the day, the people assembled about the pole, and the youth scrambled up for the image, which they broke in pieces, and scattered upon the ground."

unreasonable for us to consider this a full account of the matter. What is the case, then? The philosophical pantheist speaks of God losing Himself or finding Himself in the natural universe, and so outrages the fundamental truth that God is eternally Personal as well as eternally Infinite. But he is, nevertheless, feeling after a truth which is latent also in these myths, and is the foundation of all Christian theology. It is this, namely, that God, being Infinite, has stooped by creation to enter into intimate relations with the Finite. And further, that the condescension of God in creation is akin to the act of sacrifice, or self-surrender, as practised by His creatures, and is a natural prelude to the whole economy of His revealed covenants with man, and specially to the Incarnation and Atonement of the Son of God. This fundamental mystery of the union of the Infinite with the Finite is travestied and misapplied by Pantheism, and appropriated unfairly, as if it were the property of a particular philosophic school. But it is the basis of all Christian theology and philosophy. Without it we are in hopeless confusion; with it we can see something of the reasons of God's patience, and more of the astonishing love which is expressed by His eternal counsel to redeem the world, and of the manner in which it is carried out in time.

We perceive, then, even in these distorted myths, a vague groping after some higher form of atonement, than that which was offered by bloody sacrifices heaped one upon another with all the energy of conscience-stricken superstition.

The true explanation of them is not a mere hopeless, helpless reference to an impersonal process of nature, which does not at all harmonise with the feelings which drive men to sacrifice. Their real meaning is found in the evangelic proclamation of the eternal love of God, the Creator, Redeemer, and Sanctifier. Let those who go forth from hence tell the Hindus (as they will tell them) that God, who has stooped to make the world, has stooped also to die for it; that in His eternal counsel the Lamb of God, the Lord of creatures, the giver of self, was slain before the world was; and that He died in fact and deed on Calvary, that He might raise all created things in heaven and earth a pure sacrifice to God the Father.

3. This thought naturally leads us to the conclusion, which requires very few words to demonstrate, namely, the obvious failure of these efforts, by themselves, to obtain reconciliation with God. The natural conscience cannot, in fact, conceive of the remission of sin.

We have seen something of the terrible course which superstition has run in this world, and of the revolt of a better feeling against its extravagances. The evils of overstrained religion were apparent not only to earnest Epicureans like Lucretius, or self-contained Moralists like Confucius, but to the most religious minds of antiquity, as Plato and Plutarch.

The latter has written a striking treatise on Superstition, which he compares with Atheism [75].

[75] *De Superstitione*, vol. i. p. 651 foll., ed. Wyttenbach (Oxon., 1795). Cp. Theophrastus' character of the Superstitious Man.

The former, as I need scarcely remind you, puts into the mouth of one of his characters an eloquent protest against the popular misuse of religious rites in the interests of injustice. He expresses something like prophetical indignation at those who think that the gods can be bought over by sacrifices and atonements, and who say that injustice is better than justice, for "if we are unjust we shall keep the gains, and by our sinning and praying, and praying and sinning, the gods will be propitiated, and we shall be forgiven [76]." This and like passages will occur to many of you. In his latest scheme of a polity, he sums up the matter in the same strain of dignified common-sense, which practically rejects sacrifice as useless, and leaves us with the impression that pardon for sin is all but impossible:—

"You should first attempt to teach and persuade us that there are gods by reasonable evidences, and also that they are too good to be unrighteous, or to be propitiated, or to be turned from their course by gifts. For when we hear these and like things said of them by those who are esteemed to be the best of poets, and orators, and prophets, and priests, and innumerable others, the thoughts of most of us are not set upon abstaining from unrighteous acts, but upon doing them and making atonement for them [77]."

The tendency, then, of heathen feeling was, if not altogether to give up the practice of sacrifice, yet to restrain it, and especially to drop those bloody sin-offerings [78] which had been entered upon with so

---

[76] *Rep.*, ii. p. 366, a speech put into the mouth of Adeimantus, brother of Glaucon.   [77] *Laws*, x. p. 885.

[78] Cp. Dean Merivale in *Chr. Evidence Lectures*, ser. 2, pp. 364 foll., and Porphyrius, *de Abstin.*, ii. chaps. 11, 12, 33, 43.

V.] Confessions of the uselessness of Sacrifice. 179

much zest and hopefulness. They had been tried, and found wanting. They did not give man, what his conscience told him was the real thing necessary, a sense of righteousness and holiness, which could make him stand cheerfully before an offended God. The superstitious man, with his eternal anxiety to have every little detail of the sacrificial act correct, and his fear lest some point might be omitted, some name or word unuttered, some god not invoked, was a perpetual evidence of their uselessness. St. Paul, when he criticized the altar to the unknown God, was only saying what the stronger, saner-minded heathens were saying all about Him. But these men could not but feel that they were involved in an insoluble difficulty. Man is confessed to be sinful, and all the ritual of atonement is pronounced useless or immoral. What, then, is to become of the

On the uselessness of sacrifice and means of purification as held by the Buddhists, see *Dhammapada*, ch. viii.; *Sacred Books*, x. p. 32;—" Whatever a man sacrifice in this world as an offering or as an oblation for a whole year in order to gain merit, the whole of it is not worth a quarter (a farthing); reverence shewn to the righteous is better." Also v. 127, p. 35: "Not in the sky, not in the midst of the sea, not if we enter into the clefts of the mountains, is there known a spot in the whole world where a man might be freed from an evil deed." Their theory of the origin of sacrifice in Brahmanical covetousness is given in the *Brâhmana-dhammika-sutta* of the *Sutta-Nipâta*, *ib.*, part 2, p. 50. Slaughter of animals was entirely prohibited by the Girnar edicts of Priyadarsî, or Asoka, tablet i.: see *Archæological Survey of Western India*, p. 98 foll., ed. Jas. Burgess (India Office, 1876); or Wheeler's *History of India*, vol. iii. p. 458, 1874. In India, bloody sacrifices are at present abolished, except at the altars of the hideous goddess Kālī or Durgā, and are repugnant to the feelings of the better classes of Hindus: Monier Williams, *Hinduism* (S.P.C.K.), p. 42.

guilty, that is, of all men? How are sinners to obtain remission of sins? It is very well for an accomplished poet to sing,—

> "The sprinkled salt, the votive meal,
> As soon [God's] favour will regain,
> Let but the hand be pure and leal,
> As all the pomp of heifers slain [79];"

but what of those myriad hands which are not pure or leal, amongst which the poet in his graver moments must assuredly have numbered his own?

The human conscience, then, without the Christian revelation, has before it these two great facts, that God is holy and man is sinful; but it is incapable of reconciling them. Man, therefore, alternates between presumption and despair, between incredulity and superstition. His conscience speaks to him of punishment and death, and yet he feels that he was not meant by God to die, but to live. He tries all means of self-torture and asceticism in vain; he confesses sin, and purifies himself in vain; he frequents secret mysteries, and plunges into fanatic orgies, and heaps rites on rites in vain; he forms mystic theories of sacrifice in vain; nothing will give him the holiness he so eagerly and rightly desires, but union by faith with the self-sacrifice of the Son of God.

---

[79] Horace, *Odes*, iii. 23, last stanza, Conington's translation. I have substituted "God's" for "their," referring in the original to the Penates, in order to make the sentiment more generally intelligible.

LECTURE VI.

ISAIAH xxxv. 7, 8.

The parched ground shall become a pool, and the thirsty land springs of water: in the habitation of dragons, where each lay, shall be grass with reeds and rushes.

And an highway shall be there, and a way, and it shall be called The way of holiness; the unclean shall not pass over it; but it shall be for those: the wayfaring men, though fools, shall not err therein.

THE INCARNATION AND ATONEMENT A REVELATION OF HOLINESS, WORTHY OF GOD, AND MEET FOR THE NEEDS OF MAN.

Isaiah's prophecy: God leading man along the way of Holiness. Conflict between Hope and Reason.—(1) *Grandeur and breadth of the Doctrine*, worthy of God who reveals it.—Majestic power of the Creed.—Objections on the side of Love and of Justice.—Other ways of reconciliation suggested.—(2) *The Atonement and God's Love.*—Inadequate idea of Love in objectors to the Atonement.—Its fiery quality.—Work of sin in the world.—Not to be lightly dealt with.—(3) *The Atonement and God's Justice.*—The innocent suffering for the guilty.—Principle of Mediation.—Willing Sacrifice.—Mystical appropriation of it.

Practical value of the doctrine (1) *Revelation of the guilt and danger of Sin.*—Necessity of this thought.—Horror of separation from God.—(2) *Christ the representative of the race.*—Idea of Representation.—Messianic prophecy.—Fragments of the Idea in heathenism.—Their inadequacy.—Holiness and Humility overlooked. — Testimonies of non-Christian teachers to Christ.—Union of Christians with His work.—(3) *Direct moral example* of the Redeemer; its value to individuals.

IN this delightful prophecy, Isaiah describes the condition of the redeemed in the Messianic age.

It is a restoration of Paradise. The creative, renovating power of God shall again be visible in nature and in man. All diseases shall pass away. Nature shall no longer deceive us, or the beasts be at war with us. The mirage shall become a lake, and the desert shall no longer cause us to go astray. A clear road of holiness shall lead up to the Temple. God shall be upon it, walking in the way to guide the infirm and the simple (so the Hebrew seems to be most clearly and truly interpreted)[1]. "And the ransomed of the Lord shall return and come to Zion, with songs and everlasting joy upon their heads. They shall obtain joy and gladness, and sorrow and sighing shall flee away."

This morning I wish specially to call your attention to the fulfilment of this prophecy in the work of our Lord and Saviour Jesus Christ. In Him the mirage has become a lake; in Him we see God walking with weak and erring man, and guiding him along the way of holiness.

In our last Lecture we saw man wandering in the burning sands of the desert, alienated from God, and

[1] v. 8 is literally rendered, "And a raised way shall be there, and it shall be called The holy way; that which is unclean shall not pass over it, *and he for them* (*shall be*) *walking* [sing.] *in the way*, and even fools shall not go astray." Mr. Cheyne sees a probable corruption in the words which I have italicised; but I venture to doubt this judgment. My own opinion is worth little on such a point, but I have the support of Dr. Neubauer in so translating, regardless of the Masoretic punctuation, and in referring the words "for them" to the blind, deaf, lame, and dumb mentioned above, verses 5 and 6. God, that is to say, shall be their guide, walking for them in the way,—a very beautiful and natural sense to give to the words, "v'hû lâmô holek derek."

constantly deceived by the mirage of superstition. The hazy glamour of beautiful pools, in which he hoped to wash and be clean, and slake his thirst for God, drew him on step after step, only to lead to disappointment. But Christ promises us living waters. He bids all the weary come to Him. He is Himself our guide upon the way of holiness. He goes before us to the heavenly city, and there offers Himself a sacrifice for all, and bids all men share in it and unite themselves to it. We have before us to-day the great mystery of His Incarnation and Atonement: may God give us grace to look upon it as He would wish, who has given so wondrous, so ineffable a gift to the sons of men!

At the close of the last Lecture we saw that the natural conscience is left with an insoluble problem before it. God is holy and man is sinful, but all known ways of atonement are incapable of reconciling him to his maker. Nevertheless, man feels that he was made to be at one with God; he deserves death, but he was intended for life. In other words, God is both just and loving; yet how can He exhibit His justice towards sinners without disappointing the expectation He has given them of His love, and how can He proclaim His love without prejudice to His justice? The heart revolts from the idea of humanity left simply to itself, adding sin to sin, and so going further and further, deeper and more deep, upon the horrible road to death. Tradition tells us, instinct tells us, that we were made in God's image, that we are "His offspring," and that our truly natural state is to be in union with

184 *The Christian Revelation of Holiness.* [LECT.

Him. Life is no true life without Him. Nay, with all our misery we have, under His providence, discovered many palliations and even cures for natural evil[2]. As Sophocles well reminds us in his noble choric song on the wondrousness of man :—

> "In all things provident, in none
> Without provision, he doth rise
> To meet the future, and alone
> 'Gainst Death he shall bring in no remedies;
> Yet of diseases dire escapes he doth devise[3]."

God has helped us already, and at the bottom of all our troubles, as in Pandora's box, hope still remains[4] that He will help us further. But then Conscience turns round and reminds us that even if we repent and amend, we can but touch the future. The past still remains as it was. The terrible form of the act done, which cannot be undone, the spectral image of what the Buddhists call *karma*[5] (literally "doing"), with its eternal consequences, starts up against us. "Whatsoever a man soweth that shall he also reap," seems like a law of nature from which there is no escape. Repentance may, indeed, help to check the tendency to future crimes,

[2] Cp. Butler's *Analogy*, part 2, chap. 5, § 3.
[3] Soph. *Antigone*, 360 foll.
[4] Hesiod, *Works and Days*, 94. Preller treats this as a mere false, empty hope; comparing Æschylus, *Prometheus*, 252, &c. But he refers also to the interesting poem of Theognis, 1135—1150, in which Hope is described as the only God left amongst men. Cp. esp. 1143, sq.—

> Ἀλλ' ὄφρα τις ζώει καὶ ὁρᾷ φάος ἠελίοιο,
> εὐσεβέων περὶ θεοὺς, Ἐλπίδα προσμενέτω.

[5] On *Karma*, see T. W. Rhys Davids' *Buddhism* (S.P.C.K.), pp. 101—103; and above, *Lecture* iii. p. 90.

but it cannot have a retrospective action to destroy the past. Humanly speaking, it is a mere cessation from sinning; for to repent and reform is an obvious duty, and not to repent is to add another sin to those we have already committed[6]. An old proverb, indeed, tells us, in words which our hearts echo, though we cannot rigidly justify them:—

"Quem pœnitet peccasse pæne est innocens."

But penitence is at best only an approach to innocence. There always remains the *almost* to discriminate it. And how rare, how nearly unknown, is perfect, genuine repentance!

At this point of suspense comes in the Christian doctrine of the Atonement effected by Jesus Christ, who, being both God and man, of His own free-will offered a perfect and sufficient sacrifice acceptable to the Father, to reconcile the creature with the Creator. It declares that He is able to save all to the uttermost that come unto God by Him, and that him that cometh unto Him He will in no wise cast out.

The heart leaps to embrace this hope. Is it also a doctrine which it is a duty for the reason to accept? This is the question before us this morning.

In treating this high argument, I shall follow the

---

[6] I have here paraphrased some sentences of [Bp.] Edward Steere *On the Attributes of God*, p. 199, a valuable book, which I venture to hope he will some day find time to re-issue, enriched with that deep knowledge of the natural heart of man, and of its growth under divine grace, which his almost unique experiences in Central Africa would furnish. We are both here following St. Anselm, *Cur Deus Homo*, i. 20, and Butler, *Analogy*, pt. 2, ch. 5, § 4.

method of the corresponding Lecture on the gift of Truth, and shew, first, that the doctrine is worthy of the glory and majesty of Him who gives it; and secondly, that it satisfies the needs of man who receives it.

I.

The Atonement considered as a Gift of Holiness, worthy of God who gives it.

1. In the first place, we cannot fail to be struck with the *grandeur and breadth of the doctrine*. We have already to some extent anticipated this topic in speaking of the glorious comprehensiveness of Christian Truth[7]. Whatever objections may be made to the doctrine on other grounds, none surely can lie against the magnificent fulness and richness of result which the New Testament ascribes to the work of Christ, as the prophets had foreshadowed it. It takes into its view the whole human race, from first to last (Romans v. 18, 19; 1 Tim. iv. 10). And not only does it extend to all the sons of Adam, but it has a gracious influence upon the highest angels, nay, upon the inanimate creation also. It is, to use St. Paul's glorious language, the recapitulation, the re-union of all things, both that are in heaven and are on earth (Eph. i. 10; Col. i. 20). It is a revelation of love made to the powers on high, as well as to ourselves. It is one of the things which "angels desire to look into" (1 Pet. i. 12). It is the mystery hidden from the ages which the Church is now commissioned to reveal, and by it is manifested to all powers and authorities of heaven the manifold

[7] See above, Lecture iv. pp. 112, 113.

wisdom of God (Eph. iii. 10). It brings together past, present, and future in such a marvellous completeness, that all the energies of human language are exhausted in describing it "I am Alpha and Omega, the First and the Last;" "I am He that liveth and was dead, and behold, I am alive for evermore" (Rev. i. 11, 18). It is the "love of Christ which passeth knowledge," which fills us "with all the fulness of God" (Eph. iii. 19).

Would to God that it were possible to rouse ordinary Christian people—who too often say the Creed as if it were an old and common-place form, to be hurried over and got rid of—to a sense of the ineffable, the infinite greatness of this mystery! The saying of the Creed is, in some respects, the most important part of the public service, and should form a portion of our private devotions far more often than it usually does. It seems to bring us into the presence of God even more than prayer, because prayer is narrow, and often selfish; prayer, though it ought to be the voice of the Eternal Spirit, is too often an echo of our own worldly temper; but the Creed is God's voice speaking in us. It is something above us and beyond us, holding us up with a supremely powerful grasp. If we are true Christians, we feel that in the Creed "Mercy and Truth are met together, Righteousness and Peace have kissed each other." God has done for us great things of which we can never weary, whose riches we can never fathom. This sustaining, satisfying power of the Creed belongs, indeed, in a measure to all confessions of faith and hope which have been distinctly conceived. We have seen how, in his confession of sin, the old Persian leant upon his Creed: "I confess myself a Mazdayaçnian," he says, "a Zarathustrian, an opponent of the Dævas, devoted to belief in Ahura, for praise, adoration, satisfaction, and laud;" and then he goes on to acknowledge his sins[8]. We may learn even from the atheistic Buddhist, who so constantly throws himself outside himself for protection: "I take refuge in the Buddha; I take refuge in the Law; I take refuge in the Congregation[9]."

No doubt these things are apt to become formal in the repetition, but they were not formal at first; and we who look at them from the outside have the privilege of seeing them in their original freshness. They may help to refresh us, just as the face of a chance-met stranger may revive the recollection of a beloved friend. They may fill us with a sense of our immeasurable blessing in not having to create for ourselves a theory of redemption, but in having so grand, so noble, so infinitely worthy a revelation set before us in the triumphant record of Him "who for us men and for our salvation came down from heaven, and was incarnate, and was made man;" who for us was crucified, rose again, and ascended,

---

[8] *Khordah-Avesta; Patet Aderbat,* Bleeck's *Avesta,* vol. iii. p. 153 (Hertford, 1864).

[9] See Rhys Davids' *Buddhism,* p. 160; and above, Lect. iii. p. 89. The three refuges (Buddha, Dharma, and Saṅgha) are called Trisarana. They are referred to in the *Dhammapada,* verse 190; *Sutta-Nipâta,* pp. 37, 38, &c. As the Triratna, or Trinity, they are worshipped by northern Buddhists: Eitel's *Three Lectures,* pp. 91 foll.

and whom we look to see coming again to claim us as His own in glory.

Such is the majestic breadth of this doctrine of the Incarnation and Atonement. There are, however, two well-known objections to it as a revelation of God's nature, which attack it from very opposite sides. The first puts forward as its pretext the beautiful attribute of Love, and asks, Why was there this need of a great sacrifice for sin? Cannot God reconcile us to Himself by some other means more purely benevolent, such, for example, as a proclamation of His pardon, an illumination of the conscience, and the like?

The other objection takes the converse side, and attacks the Atonement as not satisfying the idea of justice. How can God, it is asked, accept the suffering of Christ in our place? Is it not unjust for the innocent to suffer for the guilty? Would not some other way be preferable? Ought not all men to suffer for their own sins?

Both of these, you see, suggest some other way, as if we were sufficient judges of all that goes on in earth and heaven[10]. But if the Atonement is,

[10] Cp. Butler's *Analogy*, part 2, ch. 5, § 5, note, p. 247, ed. Bohn, where he mentions such questions as this, "which have been, I fear, rashly determined, and perhaps, with equal rashness, contrary ways. For instance, whether God could have saved the world by other means than the death of Christ, consistently with the general laws of His government." And he rejects it as one which cannot "properly be answered without going upon that infinitely absurd supposition that we know the whole of the case. And perhaps the very enquiry, *what would have followed if God had not done as He has*, may have in it some very great impropriety, and ought not to be carried on any further than is necessary to help our partial and inadequate conceptions of things."

what we have seen that it is proclaimed to be, an act influencing the whole creation, it touches a very large region of which we have only the faintest conception. We cannot be judges at all of its propriety, except in so far as it directly influences ourselves; and even here we have no power of judging how other untried means would have succeeded. But, as far as Scripture is concerned, the path seems closed against considering whether other means would, or would not, have been worthy of God.

When we read of the "Lamb slain from the foundation of the world[11]," of the "eternal counsel[12]," of the "it must be[13]," several times repeated by our Saviour in reference to His sufferings, we cannot doubt that such questions of other possible ways are altogether beyond the scope of Christian theology.

But, whilst we deny that any other way of atonement is knowable to ourselves, and must decline to discuss so idle a question, we are bound to reply to any specific objections made to the one which we assert God to have revealed. In the present case there are, as we have seen, two in particular before us, one which finds fault with Biblical Redemption as too hard and unloving; the other, which cavils at it for not being just enough. They are, therefore, in some sense mutually exclusive; and this is one of those many cases where the remark long

---

[11] *Rev.* xiii. 8; cp. xvii. 8, "Whose names were not written in the book of life from the foundation of the world."
[12] πρόθεσις τῶν αἰώνων, *Eph.* iii. 11.
[13] *Matt.* xxvi. 54; *Mark* viii. 31; *Luke* ix. 22, xvii. 25, xxiv. 7, 26, 44, 46, in all of which δεῖ is used.

ago made holds good, that Truth takes a middle course between two different and opposing errors.

2. *The Atonement and God's Love.*

What shall we say, then, to those who think the Atonement a hard and unloving doctrine, and desire rather a proclamation of pure benevolence as characteristic of our heavenly Father?

This difficulty seems to arise from an inadequate idea of the nature of love [14]. It is confused with a mere dispassionate benevolence, with a general wish to make everything comfortable, with a state of mind and feeling not very far removed from the quiet restfulness of the gods of ancient Greece, as conceived by the philosophers. The God of Plato in this differed not so very widely from the God of Aristotle [15]. The latter, κινεῖ ὡς ἐρώμενον, moves others, as the thing loved moves by the force of the desire it excites, but He for His own part has no personal action or movement towards them. The God of Plato is more active, but is too self-contained, to force himself in any way upon the love of men. But the true God is very different from these. He not only wills that we should know Him, but that we should love Him. "We love Him because He first loved us," and willed to make a conquest of us by His love. It is this expansive, penetrating, fiery love of God that is the hope of the Christian,

---

[14] Cp. on this topic Martensen, *Christian Dogmatics*, § 157, p. 303 foll., E. T., and p. 280 foll. of the German ed. (Berlin, 1870).

[15] See his *Metaphysics*, book xi. chap. 7, containing the famous thesis about God as the prime mover.

and supplies the explanation of his attitude towards the mystery of the Incarnation and Atonement.

True love is not benevolence : it is a burning fire, a passionate eagerness to possess the souls of those whom it loves, a grasping after love in return.

It is, therefore, closely allied in God to anger. For He who loves us for our entire good, cannot but be indignant at any hindrances which we create to baulk Him. He is wroth with those who love Him not, with those whose sins interpose a thick cloud, so that His grace cannot shine through. Such love is akin also to grief: it chafes at the barriers set up by self-will; it is distressed by the meanness, the impurity, the deadness of those objects on which we set so much affection, on which we waste so much of that power of loving, which was created to return to Him who gave it. It is this fuller and riper idea of love that enables Prophets and Psalmists to speak in such glowing terms both of God's love and God's anger, without seeing any contradiction between the two. Thus, in the great proclamation made to Moses, we have the attributes, "merciful and gracious, long-suffering and abundant in goodness and truth, keeping mercy for thousands, forgiving iniquity, and transgression, and sin," followed without a break by the other side, "and that will by no means clear (the guilty); visiting the iniquity of the fathers upon the children, and upon the children's children, unto the third and to the fourth generation" (Exod. xxxiv. 6, 7). The same lips which asserted the solemn truth, "our God is a jealous God," and "our God is a consuming fire," found nothing in this belief to prevent them ascribing the tenderest mercy and compassion to the Lord. "Yea, like as a Father pitieth his own children, even so is the Lord merciful unto them that fear Him. For He knoweth whereof we are made; He remembereth that we are but dust" (Psalm ciii. 13, 14).

When once we have risen to the height of this conception of fiery love, we have less difficulty in understanding the condescension and self-sacrifice of the Son of God. Sin had erected a huge barrier between God and man; day after day it was growing in bulk; all the assaults made on it by punishment were unavailing. Man had nothing of his own to offer. His very obedience was tainted with sin, and certainly could not take away the guilt of previous disobedience. And then think of this condition as contrasted with God's glorious design. Man was made to be a reflection of God, to shine back upon Him as an image of all His imitable excellencies. Each human being might have been, as it were, a separate, flawless crystal, distinct, and yet perfect in its kind. The whole race might have been one in its service, one in its historical progress. When viewed from eternity, it might have been a perfect and compact body, a living organism, in which every joint and member, every race, and tribe, and family, contributed to the fulness and warmth of life. How deep a gulf is there between this divine ideal and the reality! How many flaws and rents in each individual! How many retrogressions in the history of progress! How many terrible breaks in the unity and love which ought to bind man to man!

We see also how the Fall of man, which some thinkers have almost divinised as the first giant step of progress [16], so far from contributing to our civilization, deadens and weakens the whole after-life of the race.

Who has not felt the depressing, devilish influence of an atmosphere of sin; the taint contracted from a bad man, or a bad book; the unspeakable, hideous fascination of a wicked thought? Contrast this broken, ruined condition of single persons, and of the race, with the design of God's love for its perfection, and then, if you can, associate it with progress.

Yet of all this perfection which lay, and still in great part lies before him, man has deprived His Creator by his sin and disobedience. As St. Anselm well says: "Abstulit Deo quidquid de humana natura facere proposuerat" (*Cur Deus Homo*, i. 23). Sin thus acquires an ideal character: it ceases to be a collection of single acts of offence; it becomes a malignant spiritual force, fighting everywhere against God. The reconciliation of this sin, then, is no slight and simple problem. It is a great occasion. It is not merely a matter of passing over a slip here, and a fault there; but the whole relation of God to man is involved in it. Is the reconciliation to be one in which His nature shall appear in its

---

[16] E.g. Schiller and Hegel, quoted with approbation by Pfleiderer, *Religions Philosophie*, p. 505, (Berlin, 1878). The mistake seems to arise from the confusion of that external knowledge of evil, as a foe to be combated, which man was obviously intended to have, with the interior, sinful, sympathetic knowledge of it, which was the consequence of the Fall. The former is necessary to progress; the latter hinders it.

fulness and its strength, in the plenitude of its mysterious energy; or is it to be displayed as a weak and barren proclamation of forgiveness? The whole idea we are to form of God is involved in the answer to this question. And we may make bold to reply, that a simple proclamation of release would have been at least as inadequate a satisfaction of our thought of Him as the highest excellence, as would be the release of prisoners at the beginning of a reign, or a general remission of taxes to an empire, if put forward as an act of the highest political wisdom in an earthly sovereign.

For the vague benevolence remitting to man the punishment of sin, because, through his own fault, he was unable to pay his debt of love to God; and the gift to him of happiness, from which he had broken away, without the fulfilment of any of the previous conditions on man's part, would be a kind of mercy unworthy of God. Here, again, listen to St. Anselm [17] : "If God remits what man ought, of his own accord, to pay, merely because man is incapable of payment, what is this, except to say that God remits what He is unable to recover?" that He acts like a man, who yields to the inevitable, and gives up a debt which He finds it impossible to make good. "It is ridiculous," says St. Anselm, "to attribute mercy of such a kind to God." And again: "If God remits the punishment which He was going to

---

[17] "Si dimittit quod sponte reddere debet homo, ideo quia reddere non potest, quid est aliud quam dimittit Deus quod habere non potest? Sed derisio est ut talis misericordia Deo attribuatur." (L.c. i. 24.)

inflict, namely, the deprivation of happiness, and remits it on account of man's inability to pay his debt, this is really to act unjustly, and to make man happy on account of sin, that is, because he has an incapacity, which is his own fault [18]."

Both the remission of sin and the gift of happiness, on these terms, would appear to be the acts of a God who confessed Himself worsted by His creature; who began with a great design, but was not able to accomplish it; who wished for innocence and justice, but was compelled by force of circumstances to be content with guilt and injustice; who wished to bless a creature and a race of beings made after His own image, but was forced, in default of them, to crown with eternal happiness a corrupt and crooked mass of half-dead and deformed creatures [19].

[18] "At si dimittit quod invito erat ablaturus [sc. beatitudinem] propter impotentiam reddendi quod sponte reddere debet, relaxat Deus pœnam et facit beatum hominem propter peccatum, quia habet quod debet non habere" . . . "verum huiusmodi misericordia Dei nimis est contraria justitiæ illius, quæ non nisi pœnam permittit reddi propter peccatum." (L.c. i. 24.)

[19] Cp. Mr. T. T. Carter, *Instructions on the Divine Revelation*, pp. 151, 152. "The conception both of the holiness and the truth of God would suffer, if sin could pass unpunished, and be forgiven, without the exaction of any penalties, and by a simple exertion of remedial power. There could, in such case, be no security for law, no trust in eternal righteousness, no consistency between the character of God and the government of His creatures. But in surrendering His only Son to the death of the Cross, Almighty God shewed, by an irrefragable testimony, that the judgments which guard the laws of His kingdom cannot be withdrawn, notwithstanding His decrees of mercy to free the sinner from the consequences of the Fall."

3. *The Atonement and God's Justice.*

We now pass to the opposite objection, viz. that it is unjust to accept the punishment of the innocent Saviour for the guilty race; that man does not really pay the debt, if it is paid for him. I need not dwell long upon this point in the presence of those who are familiar with what has been so well said upon it by Bp. Butler and Dr. Mozley. The former, as you will remember, calls attention to the fact that in the course of nature the innocent frequently suffer for the guilty; and therefore, if there is any force in the objection, it applies equally to the whole method of Divine Providence [20].

It constantly happens that men bear, and have to bear, labour, and injury, and loss for others with whom they are connected by family or social ties. The loss of one is the gain of another in a thousand ways. Yet we are not shocked by this. It is part of what we are accustomed to see and speak of as natural. Even when it takes the extreme form of a dread calamity falling upon one generation of a people, as the result of a great war, we regret the misery that occurs, but we do not accuse Providence of injustice; unless, perhaps, we happen to be among the immediate sufferers. The surrender of precious lives, tearing the very heart out of a thousand homes, may be the only possible way, in a sinful world like ours, of fusing the sympathies and bracing the energies of the whole nation, and of bringing it to a conscious-

---

[20] *Analogy*, part 2, chap. v. p. 254, ed. Bohn. Cp. Dr. Mozley's Sermon on the Atonement, in his *University Sermons*.

ness of its destiny. Such a sacrifice may be the turning-point in its history, for which age after age has waited; and now that it has come, the whole after-life will have a vigour till then unknown. Yet those who profit by the sacrifice will not have paid it in person; they will only unite with it in sympathy. Thus the self-denying struggles of the Athenians in the great Persian war were the necessary prelude to the age of Pericles. So, again, we at this day benefit wonderfully by the sacrifices made by our fathers in their resistance to Napoleon, and in the abolition of slavery, and the like. But few ever think it unjust in the Creator to have so ordered it.

Yet if we compare such human cases with the Atonement, we shall see that the plea of injustice is really more plausible with regard to the ordinary suffering of man for man. Human suffering is rarely quite voluntary. When a father or mother is made miserable by the extravagance or dissipation of their son, or a physician dies from a disease he has caught in attending the sick, or half an army perishes while the other half enjoys the victory,—we know that the sufferers would in most cases have chosen, if possible, not to suffer. But the sacrifice of Christ was self-chosen and voluntary, contemplated from the beginning of His ministry, though His complete humanity was shewn in the agony and heart-broken bitterness through which He passed in completing the great act of love. Such vicarious offerings as these have always been held not only perfectly legitimate, but most satisfactory to the natural conscience

VI.] *Christ's willing Sacrifice and Mediation.* 199

of right and wrong. Even in the mythical or semi-mythical shape of a Chiron, an Alcestis, or a Codrus, a Quintus Curtius, a Regulus, or a Decius, they have a strong hold upon our feelings. We should revolt and feel injustice done if they were not successful.

We can even understand the anxious superstition of the heathen, which required a semblance of willingness in the animals they sacrificed, and thought a victim without a heart a disastrous portent. We assume it to be a law of God's ordinance that mediation and intercession have a value, that faithful effort and self-denial for others must meet with its reward. Hence, when we think that He who suffered for us upon the cross was the Son of God, "the first-born of every creature," and our future Judge, we feel that the purchase of remission of sins and potential happiness for all mankind is but a just return and reward. That such an act should not gain its end would surely fill us with a sense of injustice, terror, and despair [21].

If the doctrine, indeed, ended here, it would be incomplete. If Christ suffered, and we merely reaped the benefit, as some Christians are too lightly and lazily inclined to think is the case, the enemy might indeed find something to censure. But I need not remind any here, that though a certain degree of present benefit is felt by all men, whether they have heard the name of Christ or not, owing to the greater diffused happiness which Christianity has

---

[21] Cp. some eloquent pages of Mr. R. W. Dale's Lectures on *The Atonement*, at the end of Lect. ix., in reply to Mr. Martineau, *Studies of Christianity*, p. 188.

brought into the world, yet the mystical death to sin with Christ, and the rising again to righteousness, is the only revealed condition of our final salvation. We are saved by faith; we are judged according to our works. The redemption effected by Christ does not dispense with a change of mind in the sinners who are redeemed. It alters the regard with which God looks at men; and now He accepts our repentance, and all the blessed fruits of a holy and peaceful life that follow it.

This is the Gospel message. How God will deal with those who do not hear it or understand it in this world, we know not; but that Christ died for all men, and that those who are saved will be saved by faith in Christ, here or hereafter, of this we are sure.

This thought of the practical correlations to the idea of the Divine mercy, naturally leads us on to the second part of our argument.

II.

We now turn to the blessed effects which this doctrine has, as a revelation meet for human needs.

1. Consider the great value of the doctrine of the Incarnation and Atonement, *as a revelation of the guilt and danger of sin.*

An age like the present, which dislikes the name of sin, which is conscious of many good impulses, and rests leisurely upon an external and conventional morality, is not likely, perhaps, to view this proposition with favour. Yet, even if we take the men of our time at their own valuation, and approach them upon their own principles of historic candour, they cannot fail to see at least something in our statement. "Your excellent impulses are not your own, but are inherited from the past," so we may reason with them; "and the sweet social quietness on which you repose, could not have existed without that idea of a death to sin and a new birth to righteousness, which we can shew historically to have come into the world with belief in the Incarnation, Death, and Resurrection of the Saviour." Even now, when by a natural reaction from puritanism, sad and painful thoughts are being driven by many first from daily life and then from religion, it ought not to be difficult for any, even of the most frivolous, to see the enormous practical gain of the reinforcement of the law of duty by the Life and Passion of Christ. "What the Law could not do," writes St. Paul, "in that it was weak through the flesh, God, sending His own Son in the likeness of sinful flesh, and for sin, condemned sin in the flesh: that the righteousness of the Law might be fulfilled in us, who walk not after the flesh, but after the Spirit" (Romans viii. 3, 4). The clear condemnation of sin in actual visible fact in the flesh of Christ, is a lever of enormous power, possessed by no other religion, and one which has been wielded with vast success by Christian moralists.

But if this will be confessed by those who stand apart from positive belief, how much more is it felt by us Christians, who realize something of what the Saviour meant when He said, "The Son of Man is come to seek and to save that which was lost"

(Luke xix. 10). We know that the first step in deliverance, both for ourselves and for those whom, after our Saviour's example, we love and fain would save, is only found by genuine personal acknowledgment of sin and of the horrors which attend a separation from God. "The incarnation shews to man the greatness of his misery, by the greatness of the remedy which was required to heal it[22]." It is like a light let down into a dismal and narrow pit, revealing its hideousness, and so stirring those who dwell there to desire their escape. It shews also how impossible escape is by our own unaided efforts. When our eyes are opened by Christ, we see that heaven is so far away. We may climb laboriously upwards from rock to rock, and from ledge to ledge, along the sides of our prison-house, but we shall not be appreciably nearer the stars above us, where we know that our true home lies[23]. Only by the coming down of Christ among us, and taking us by the hand, can we be truly lifted up.

The horror of separation from God is certainly not the highest motive, but it is practically inseparable, in almost all cases, from the love of God. The two are brought to our knowledge at once by Christ, and he must be but a lukewarm Christian who does not thank Him for this help to holiness. The place of punishment, the outer darkness and eternal night, were not indeed made for man, but for spiritual beings of a darker and deadlier criminality than ours[24]; but they will be the destiny of impenitent

---

[22] Pascal, *Pensées*, part 2, art. 5, § 8, p. 184. [23] Cp. Tholuck, *Guido and Julius*, E. T., p. 172. [24] St. Matthew xxv. 41.

sinners [25]. Men knew not this, or only knew it in myths and legends, which they were too ready to disbelieve and discredit as children's fables, that they might sin with greater freedom. It was natural, indeed, that God should not reveal the full terrors of His wrath, and the severity of His judgment, till He could reveal them by one who was the Saviour as well as the Judge. But when the fulness of the time came, He sent forth Him who was "acquainted with grief," as none of created beings could be; Him who knew the secrets and depths of sin, and the origin of the place of torment, to call men to repentance. He knew the perfection of love in the bosom of the Father, and He knew the other side too, the tremendous fall of the angels, the ruin of men which followed, the grief of eternal regret, eternal remorse, eternal despair, eternal self-will and rebellion. He knew the feeling of madness, rage, confusion and shame, which make the bitter cup mixed for the ungodly. Hence it is that Jesus Christ our Saviour, who is the Divine Love incarnate and the one offering for sin, is also for our salvation the sternest, because the calmest and most clear-sighted, prophet of the wrath of God.

2. Consider the blessing which we possess in *Christ as the true representative of the race.*

The subject of redemption is the whole race, not single individuals. The one religion must certainly proclaim this. We instinctively reject the ideas of

---

[25] On our Lord as the revealer of future punishment, see Bp. Milman's *Love of the Atonement*, chap. xii., headed "A Man of sorrows and acquainted with grief."

Gnostic or other Dualists, who speak of a special creation of spiritual men, in whom alone God is interested; and the separate selfishness of Buddhist and other ascetics, who are bidden to wander alone in search of salvation, each for themselves [26]. The one religion takes the two great facts of the unity of the race and of the universality of sin, and deals with them in a unique and consistent manner, unknown in any other of the attempts to find redemption.

The problem presented by these two facts is this: How can the whole race make a reparation to God, and be presented to Him? It cannot obviously, as the world is now constituted, be all collected in one place, and be presented at one moment, and by a solemn act of penitence offer to God the homage of a contrite heart. There is, indeed, a marvellous force and power in such common acts, as when so many thousand turbaned heads are bowed to the ground at one instant in the courtyard of the mosque at Delhi, or the Pope blesses the bending multitude from the balcony of St. Peter's Church at Rome. But even if such an act were possible for all the world, the momentary enthusiasm of a crowd is not the highest type of a great religious action. Christianity has, indeed, this enthusiasm amongst its powers, but it has something better and more lasting, above and beyond it. This is found in the principle of Representation, which is a principle specially

---

[26] Cp. *Sutta-Nipâta, Sacred Books*, vol. x. part 2, esp. the *Khaggavisânasutta*, p. 6 foll., the verses of which end, "let him wander alone like a rhinoceros," and the *Munisutta*, p. 33 foll.

bound up and connected with the two greatest of human powers, reason and faith. Christ Jesus is our representative, who being one stands for us all, and in our place offers to God that reparation which we could not otherwise find a means of paying.

But in what manner is He our representative? It is necessary to ask this question, for representation is obviously of two kinds: firstly, natural and of inherent right; and secondly, positive, and resting generally upon some kind of compact.

A representative of the first kind is, for instance, a father acting for his children, a king for his people, a priest for his congregation. The second is the office of a deputy or delegate, elected under certain conditions by the votes of his constituents. This latter sort of delegation is very familiar to us in this country; but even in our political life we readily perceive that it is not a complete form of representation. A mere delegate, who simply acts as a mouthpiece, and re-echoes the sentiments of those who send him, is not considered a political success. Every good representative of the second class must have some of those moral and spiritual qualities which ought to dignify one who belongs to the first class.

This is specially the case when the matter in which we are to be represented lies near our heart, and concerns our deepest interests. Then we feel that only he who is truly worthy can really act for us. But when he does appear to act for us, then we are satisfied. We transfer to him our own impulses, and feel that they add force to his actions. We cannot account for the feeling, or understand the method of the transfer. But we know that the world is God's world. And just as we offer our prayers to Him in faith, without the least understanding how they can prevail, so we give our secret suffrages to that man who defends the cause we approve, and are assured that God will reckon our sympathies amongst the moral forces that He permits to co-operate with His Providence.

It has been well said, that "the disposition to look for such a type or pattern, in which may be properly expressed what each man's consciousness imperfectly witnesses, lies deep in human nature [27]." It expresses itself in our admiration for national heroes, or for leaders in any department of thought or feeling. Such men have fought for us, pleaded for us, reasoned for us, hoped and loved for us, fixed the hues of the sunset, or the tones of unutterable passion,—all without any delegation of ours,—by their inherent natural right as princes and prelates of God's world. In them myriads, who for themselves could never have found a tongue, have made themselves heard and listened to. Yet these representative heroes took the office upon themselves, as God gave them a work to do and a power to do it. They acted most probably under the pressure of unconscious impulse, without thinking of the far-reaching effect of what they were doing; but in them we recognize fathers and brothers, who have vindicated for us a position which for ourselves we could never have attained.

[27] Robert Isaac Wilberforce, *Doctrine of the Incarnation*, p. 7, new edition (London, 1875).

Reflections like these on the ideal of representation current in the world, give certain faint indications of what we might naturally look for in the person of an universal Redeemer. We should look for one of common nature, joined to us by all the sympathies of human kinship and human suffering, and therefore not an angel or spirit, but a man like ourselves. Yet, inasmuch as He is a Redeemer from sin, He must differ from us in this one point,—He must in His sinlessness represent, not the actual depravity of mankind, but the ideal purity which we feel is the design and original state of man. He comes to restore the community and freedom of intercourse betwixt God and man, which has been broken by sin, and to do this He must, as it were, make a fresh departure. He must be man, we feel, but a new man.

It follows also, from what has been already said, that He will be, in some true sense of the term, a Father, a King, a Priest, blessed and blessing others, summing up in Himself all the most gracious relations of humanity. Yet His unique relation to sin cannot but cast a gloom over His life, and all experience shews that He will not be happy, as men usually count happiness.

Such, in fact, is the forecast of Messianic prophecy, of which our text is an example, which alone has built up the fabric of a true portraiture of the Saviour of the world. But fragments of it appear here and there in different ages and countries. Myths of the return of a golden age are not unfrequent, though difficult in many cases to disentangle from the hopes diffused by Jewish prophecy or Christian fulfilment. Thus the Pârsîs have a considerably detailed prophecy of the restoration of true religion under a priest called Pêshyôtanû, and others [28]. The Mexicans expected the return of their gentle king, who had forbidden human sacrifices [29]. The old Germans believed that after the destruction of the gods, Vidar, son of Odin, would arise to avenge his father; while Balder would return from the dead, and all things bright would revive [30]. Again, all here will think instinctively of Virgil's *Pollio*, and of the child who was to be born as a blessing to the world, with whom Justice and Peace were to come back, and in whom a new creation, as it were, was to take its rise:—

> "A mighty line of ages springs anew;
> The Maid returns and Saturn's golden prime;
> From heaven on high a new-born race descends [31]."

We know, indeed, that the oracles of the Cumæan sibyl, from which Virgil professes to draw his

---

[28] *Bahman Yast*, chap. iii. 24 foll. *Sacred Books*, vol. v. (Pahlavi Texts), pp. 224—235.

[29] Quetzalcoatl: see H. Bancroft, *Native Races of the Pacific States*, vol. iii. 260, 444. Cortés was at first taken for him, and a human sacrifice was offered to him, notwithstanding the traditional character of the God, *ibid.*, p. 276.

[30] *Vafthrúdnismál*, 51, 53; *Grimnismál*, 17; *Völuspá*, 57 foll. I do not quote the myth of the Hindu avatâr Kalki, which is probably to some extent traceable to a Christian source. See Hardwick, p. 231.

[31] "Magnus ab integro sæclorum nascitur ordo:
Jam redit et Virgo, redeunt Saturnia regna;
Jam nova progenies cælo demittitur alto."—*Ecl.* iv.
The "Virgo" is Astræa, or Justice: see above, Lect. v. p. 148.

inspiration, were very possibly indebted for their best thoughts to a Jewish hand, yet we can hardly doubt that he here represents a genuine expectation of heathenism, however arrived at.

This is one side of the picture, that of the blessed King and Conqueror; on the other, we have much fainter and rarer indications of Him who was " despised and rejected of men." In the Græco-Roman world Plato stands, perhaps, alone with his vision of the perfectly just man, who is and does not seem to be so; who is the best, and is esteemed the worst; and at the end is put to death with all kinds of tortures [32]. This wonderful gleam of truth is matched only, as far as I know, by that of the Chinese Lao-tse, the elder contemporary and critic of Confucius; expressed, however, in the obscure and artificial language of his school:—

"He who knows the light, and at the same time keeps the shade, will be the whole world's model. Being the whole world's model, eternal virtue will not miss him, and he will return home to the Absolute. He who knows the glory, and at the same time keeps to shame, will be the whole world's valley. Being the whole world's valley, eternal virtue will fill him, and he will return home to *Taou* [33]."

But such beautiful thoughts, whether of poets or philosophers, whether sung by the people or debated

[32] Plato, *Republic*, book ii. p. 361. Cp. Luthardt, *Fundamental Truths of Christianity*, E. T., ed. 3, p. 243 and note.

[33] *Taou-tih-King*, chap. 28; quoted by R. K. Douglas, *Confucianism and Taouism*, p. 195. Cp. Dr. Legge's *Religions of China*, pp. 220 foll., on his teaching about humility; and Hardwick, p. 316.

in the schools, have not power by themselves to satisfy the race of mankind, or to give it any true sense of unity before God. Those who hold them for a few moments seem to lose them again almost at once, and vainly snatch at them like a mocking web of gossamer thrown across their path some dewy morning. The same Virgil who sang so wondrously of the blessed Child, joined in the idolatrous adulation paid to the selfish and politic Augustus. A few years later the master of the Roman world, the crazy Emperor Gaius or Caligula, decreed universal worship to himself; and some generations afterwards, Hadrian ordered his subjects to worship his dead favourite, Antinous. Into such miserable profanity did heathen worship plunge in its most enlightened ages; while, if we turn to other countries, we find, if possible, even lower developments of the belief in incarnations, from which so much might have been hoped.

"One of the worst things in modern India (writes Bishop Caldwell) is the sensual worship of Krishna, as practised by some of the more enthusiastic sects; and this seems to run in parallel lines with one of the highest developments of Christian piety—the personal love of the devout soul to the Divine Saviour of men. That which appeared to be most truly divine in its original shape has become earthly, sensual, if not altogether devilish, by contact with impure minds. Corruptions of the best things are the worst[34]."

But even if we take human ideals at their best, not at their worst, we may be thankful that we are

---

[34] Bp. Caldwell, *Christianity and Hinduism: a Lecture addressed to educated Hindus* (S.P.C.K.), pp. 7, 8—a very valuable paper.

not left to ourselves to frame the pattern of the Godman. Observing what virtues are chiefly valued by mankind, apart from the exceptional and transient thoughts of one or two philosophers, we can easily picture the Christ who would have been created by human imagination. In the first place, He would have been many, and not one. To the Oriental mind generally, He would have been the embodiment of gigantic force; to the Persian, perhaps, of truthfulness and labour; to the Chinese, of regularity and dutifulness; to the Greek, of beauty and intelligence; to the Roman, of imperial majesty; to the Teuton, of calmness and thoughtfulness. Other races would have had other noble thoughts of like sort. Each nation would have endowed Him with the best qualities of its own character, omitting the rest. But the supreme virtues of holiness and humility would have been, to all appearances, omitted by all.

It needed the actual appearance of Christ in the flesh to give unity and reality to these ideals, and to give them those qualities which they all lacked. It needed the manger of Bethlehem, and the village seclusion of Nazareth, and the little success of His ministry in Judæa and Galilee, and the rejection by His own people, and the mocking of Pilate's judgment-hall, and the marring of His visage upon the cross, and the whole life, in its outer seeming, capable of despite and disregard. All this was needed to fulfil God's design in turning men forcibly back from belief in power, and glory, and might, and even duty, and labour, and truthfulness, to belief in simple goodness as the ideal of man's offering to God. Holiness and humility are the foundation of the Christian character, and of all that is best in modern life. Holiness and humility shine out from every page of the New Testament; but the world would have never known and loved them, had they not been visibly set forth in Christ. It is something that the world, to some extent, does love them, and has acknowledged itself conquered by the cross.

There are many, alas! who do not recognize Christ as their representative; and yet how striking are the testimonies to Him which have been uttered by men who could not accept the Church's creed! We have already mentioned the witness of Mahomet. The witness of Spinoza is no less remarkable:—

"I believe (he writes) that no other attained to such perfection (as Moses did) above the rest of mankind, except Christ, to whom the decrees of God, which lead men to salvation, were revealed not by words and visions, but immediately; so that God manifested Himself to the Apostles by the mind of Christ, as He did of old to Moses by the mediation of an aërial voice. And so the voice of Christ, like that which Moses used to hear, may be called the voice of God. And in this sense we may even say, that the wisdom of God, that is, the wisdom which is above human wisdom, assumed human nature in Christ, and that Christ was the way of salvation [35]."

[35] Spinoza, *Tractatus Theologico-Politicus*, cap. i. § 23:—"Quare non credo ullum alium ad tantam perfectionem supra alios pervenisse præter Christum, cui Dei placita, quæ homines ad salutem ducunt, sine verbis aut visionibus sed immediate revelata sunt; adeo ut Deus per mentem Christi sese Apostolis manifestaverit, ut olim Mosi mediante voce aërea. Et ideo vox Christi, sicuti illa, quam Moses audiebat, vox Dei vocari potest. Et hoc sensu etiam dicere possumus, sapientiam Dei, hoc est sapientiam quæ supra humanam est, naturam humanam in Christo assumpsisse et Christum viam salutis fuisse."

Rousseau's sayings concerning Christ and Socrates have often been quoted:—

"What prejudices, what blindness must not a man have to dare to compare the son of Sophroniscus with the son of Mary? What a distance is there between them!" ... "If the life and the death of Socrates are those of a sage, the life and the death of Jesus are those of a God [36]."

It is not, perhaps, so well-known that the founder of the so-called Positivist religion of humanity used daily to read a chapter of Thomas à Kempis, "On the Imitation of Christ," and strongly recommended the practice to his followers, who still pursue it, though in a different spirit to that of Christian devotion [37].

Lately, too, we have been startled by a voice from India, declaring in the name of the Theists of the

[36] J. J. Rousseau, *Émile*, book iv. (*Œuvres complétes*, vol. 4, pp. 240, 241, Paris, 1824): "Quels prejugés quel aveuglement ne faut il point avoir pour oser comparer le fils de Sophronisque au fils de Marie? Quelle distance de l'un à l'autre!" ... "Oui, si la vie et la mort de Socrate sont d'un sage, la vie et la mort de Jésus sont d'un dieu." These words are attributed to the "Vicaire Savoyard."

[37] A. Comte, *System of Positive Polity*, tr. by Congreve, vol. iv. p. 352 (London, 1877):—"The conclusive test of experience induces me to recommend above all the daily reading of the sublime, if incomplete, effort of à Kempis and the incomparable epic of Dante. More than seven years have passed [1854] since I have read each morning a chapter of the one, each evening a canto of the other, never ceasing to find beauties previously unseen, never ceasing to reap new fruits intellectual or moral."

For the method and sense in which Positivists read the *Imitation*, see R. Congreve, *The Religion of Humanity*, Annual Address, p. 5 (C. Kegan Paul, Lond., 1879).

The absence of the name of Christ from the *Positivist Calendar* may, perhaps, be taken as an unconscious tribute of reverence.

Brāhma-Samāj, that England, which has done much for India, has given nothing so valuable as the knowledge of the Lord Jesus:—

"It is Christ who rules British India, and not the British government. England has sent out a tremendous moral force in the life and character of that mighty prophet, to conquer and hold this vast empire. None but Jesus, none but Jesus, none but Jesus, ever deserved this bright, this precious diadem, India, and Jesus shall have it [38]."

Such are a few of the external testimonies to our Saviour as the ideal man. They reinforce our own heartfelt conviction that His willing self-sacrifice makes Him our true representative, the founder of a new humanity. Mahomet, Spinoza, Rousseau, Comte, even Chandar Sen, are all in their way founders, men who have set large movements in progress, men who have had great ideals, different from the ideal of the Church. But all of them have recognized a higher ideal in the person of Christ. The good, the beautiful Shepherd [39], who gives His life for the sheep, has attracted to Himself others besides professing Christians, and we thank them for their honesty in speaking as they have spoken of Him, even though there is a something wanting, a false note, even in their loudest praise.

But to us He is more than an object of admiration.

---

[38] From Keshab Chandar Sen's Lecture, *India asks, Who is Christ?* delivered in the Town Hall, Calcutta, April 9, 1879. This and other passages are quoted by Prof. M. Williams, *Indian Theistic Reformers*, (Royal Asiatic Soc., Jan. 1881).

[39] ὁ ποίμην ὁ καλός, S. John x. 11. See Dr. Westcott's note on this passage (in the *Speaker's Commentary*), bringing out the force of ideal beauty and attractiveness implied by καλός.

His act is ours by faith. His death upon the cross is our death to sin: His resurrection our new birth to repentance. In Him we are brought near to God in a way which is indeed mysterious, but which is consonant with the deepest and most serious reflection that we can make upon the problems of human life. "I am crucified together with Christ," cries St. Paul (Gal. ii. 20). "But it is no longer I that live, but Christ liveth in me. And the life that I now live in the flesh, I live in the faith of the Son of God, who loved me, and gave Himself for me."

3. *Christ the Example for every Man.*

Lastly, I would direct your attention to the great mercy of God in giving each of us, singly and separately, a pattern of holiness in the person of our Redeemer. As we began this Lecture with the thought of God in Christ, walking along the way of holiness, to guide the infirm and simple, so let us end it. He is to us not only the great sin-offering in whose sacrifice we realize the true proportions and the misery of that sin which separates us from God, and the second Adam, the sinless representative, in whom our race is presented anew to its Creator, but He is also the perfect example for each individual.

There is certainly a fitness in this union of offices in Christ which we cannot but acknowledge with adoring gratitude. It is meet that He who represents us all, should be the pattern for each to imitate. But it is a wonderful thing that it is so. A representative such as men could have imagined for themselves, even if he had been supremely worthy of imitation (which is more than doubtful), must, in all probability, have been quite beyond the ordinary reach. The marvellous love of God is shewn by His gift of a Redeemer, whose perfection starts from the level of the most ordinary members of our race; while yet, by stooping so low, He undergoes no real degradation. The pattern of life offered from the manger of Bethlehem to the Cross has points of contact for men, women, and children of all classes. It attracts, by its perfect humility, frankness, and gentleness; so that the meanest of mankind feels in the Gospels a sympathy far removed from the coldness of awful condescension. Yet the same life elevates the highest by its perfect holiness and unselfishness, rebuking pride and luxury with a silent protest, that cannot be unfelt by the most exalted and successful of kings or conquerors.

In the very words, "the Imitation of Christ," there is a freshness and a fragrance that belongs to no other words. We all know something of it. If it is our privilege to be bruised in any degree like Him, as I trust we all may be (let us not shrink from it!), we shall feel this fragrance with tenfold delight and gratitude.

LECTURE VII.

JEREMIAH viii. 11.

They have healed the hurt of the daughter of My people slightly, saying, Peace, peace; when there is no peace.

THE NATURAL DESIRE FOR PEACE, AND THE INADEQUACY OF HUMAN EFFORTS TO ATTAIN IT.

I. Social tendency of mankind.—The family the basis of society.—Obligations to (1) the ideal of paternal government.—High conception of kingship.—Chinese book of history.—The "Great Plan."—(2) The assertion of individual liberty.—Socrates, &c.—(3) The sense of social duty.—Plato's *Republic*.—Education of children.—Higher position of women.

Nevertheless, the State cannot make men really happy.—Impossibility even of preventing war.—Limit to the power of rewarding virtue.—The wants of the soul untouched.

II. Natural alliance between Religion and Politics.—Three theories of their relation, (1) Popular Religion treated as a preservative of Order apart from Truth.—Ancient philosophers.—Polybius on Roman Religion.—Euhemerism.—Varro.—Italian tendency to subordinate Truth to Expediency.—(2) Religious Reformation imposed upon all citizens.—Plato's *Laws*, book x.: his Religious Discipline.—Mahomet.—Formal character of Islam.—Defective theology and morality.—Want of Love.—Character of Mahomet.—His lapse.—Why not a "true prophet."—How far sincere.—Islam, 1. has stereotyped a low form of social life; 2. has opposed religious and intellectual liberty; 3. is a barrier to the Gospel.—(3) Religion a voluntary society, not necessarily co-extensive with the State.—Polynesian Areoi.—Pythagorean clubs.—The Mysteries.—Private guilds.—Buddhism.—Reasons for its success.—Assertion of free-will and the moral Law.—Not really a religion.—Selfishness and apathy.—Failure.

I.

THAT man is formed for social life, not for solitude, is a truth which will hardly be questioned [1]. The hermit life, when it is not a mere singularity or freak of temper, is valuable mainly for its influence on society. It may at times be an important protest against popular corruption. It may be a necessary part of the education of a great teacher. But in both cases men only go into the wilderness with advantage when they come back to regenerate their fellows, like John the Baptist and St. Paul [2], not when they are merely thinking of themselves. Further, it is generally allowed that all society worthy of the name is based on the family. Only in the circle of

---

[1] The social instinct is a commonplace with Aristotle, ἄνθρωπος φύσει πολιτικὸν ζῷον, *Politics*, i. 2, 9; *Ethic. Nic.*, i. 7, 6; ix. 9, 3 (the statement in *Eth. N.*, viii. 12, 7, ἄνθρωπος τῇ φύσει συνδυαστικὸν μᾶλλον ἢ πολιτικόν, is not really inconsistent). Cicero *de Officiis*, i. 4, has a pleasant chapter on the subject. Hobbes is probably the only writer of name who has maintained the paradox that the state of nature is a state of war. Cp. Mr. Eaton's note on the passage of the *Politics*.

[2] It is not necessary here to discuss the value of monasticism, which is, in its origin, a re-assertion of the social instinct in those who have had a common impulse to retire from the world. But I suppose that most English Churchmen would agree in condemning that monasticism which had as its object the salvation only of the brethren of the order, and in admiring that which (under proper restrictions) had the salvation of the souls of others as its principal aim. This is the principle laid down, for instance, by a writer in the *Chr. Remembrancer*, vol. 55, p. 35, Jan., 1868, reviewing Montalembert's *Monks of the West*, who traces the failure of the great monastic system to "the abandonment of the Evangelization of Society, in order to the pursuit of individual perfection."

the home, founded by a single pair, do we find that warmth of mutual love and cherishing protection which are necessary to develope human character at its best: and, as a matter of fact, all civilized communities have been formed by a sort of imitation and enlargement of the family, through the ties of kinship and dependence[3]. The elements of all politics are present in every household. The father is the natural type of the chieftain of a clan or tribe, and the ruler of a nation. The members of a family, the wife, the children, the dependents, with their several offices and positions, are analogous to the citizens of a state, falling naturally into orders and classes. The common life of the household, pursued for common ends, and occupied with common property, is an image of that of larger social communities with their united rights and duties.

The morality of civil life is also little more than an extension of that which gives dignity and gladness to the home. Obedience to authority, right

[3] Plato traces the development of the state from the family with some picturesqueness (*Laws*, book iii. pp. 680 foll.), taking as his text the description of the Cyclopes in the *Odyssey* (ix. 114), amongst whom "everyone is the judge of his wife and children." Aristotle quotes the same passage, and goes over much the same ground, of course with natural difference of manner, in his *Politics*, book i. 2, 7, &c. The modern reader will consult Sir H. Maine's *Early History of Institutions* (Lond., 1875), and other similar books. It is unnecessary to discuss the question whether mankind, or any large part of it, has ever lived promiscuously in a state inferior to that of many beasts and birds. Even if such a form of life could be proved to have existed, it has never directly produced, and never could produce, true civilized humanity. The family is a necessary pre-supposition of any society worthy of the name. The Oneida Creek experiment is, I believe, found too artificial and painful to continue.

conduct of self, and the performance of social duty, are the three special virtues of the citizen, as they are of the member of a family. Whatever happiness and peace man can find in common life, are found where these are practised. Let us consider in a very summary manner the blessings which we owe to each of them.

(1.) Obedience to authority, though never out of date, is more essential in the early stages of society than in any others, because it is the foundation on which all corporate union rests. A sovereign authority is no result of compact, but is the natural acknowledgment of a superior, and is as necessarily pre-supposed in the state as the headship of a father in the family. The lessons, too, which are learnt in both cases are similar. The father is the natural instrument by whose means children acquire an exalted idea of the godlike qualities of strength, wisdom, will and power, of justice and tenderness combined. Through the father they are taught to repose on a superior guidance in the affairs of life, a watchful providence working for their benefit, even though the means may be painful or unintelligible. The transference of this idea to a wider area, and the observation of these qualities in the head of a large patriarchal clan, the chief of a tribe, or the ruler of a nation, has constantly been the first means of lifting masses of men above themselves and their petty or grinding cares. Men naturally gather round him and beg him to help them, as their Father and their Shepherd. In certain conditions of life repose upon a strong arm is the one thing felt to be needful. Men perceive themselves too weak to stand alone; they want some personal object to which they may cling, and on which they may rely. He who gives such support is often madly and foolishly idolized: but devotion to a sovereign, even when not too worthy, has fostered trustfulness and trustworthiness, fidelity, loyalty and chivalry, humility and patience, in a way that no other motive in our experience could have done. We have already seen in former lectures [4] how this high idea of kingship has been in past times associated with a revelation of divinity, often, it must be allowed, to the great detriment of true worship. Yet even the divinised monarchs of those huge and overbearing empires, which Scripture likens so forcibly to wild beasts and birds of prey [5], may be thought of as instruments in God's hand to prepare the way for the kingdom of Him who comes "as a Son of Man [6]," the true father and ruler of the human race. "Nebuchadrezzar my servant," "Cyrus my shepherd," are titles of holy writ for sovereigns of two of these fierce imperial powers, while to St. Paul the Roman emperor is "the minister of God for good [7]." Nor can we be wrong in believing that the marvellous continuance of the Chinese Empire, to which we have already called attention [8], is a fulfilment of the promise of length of days and permanence of dwelling given to those who obey the Fifth Com-

---

[4] Lect. III., pp. 84 foll.; cp. Lect. VI., p. 210.
[5] *Daniel* vii. 3 foll.; *Ezekiel* xvii. 3, 7; *Isaiah* xlvi. 11.
[6] *Daniel* vii. 13, 'k'bar enosh' "as a Son of man" (not "*the* Son"), in contrast with the "great beasts" previously described.
[7] *Jeremiah* xxv. 9; xxvii. 6; xliii. 10: cp. *Ezekiel* xxix. 18—20 (Nebuchadrezzar's service against Tyrus): *Isaiah* xliv. 28: *Romans* xiii. 4.   [8] Lect. III., p. 86.

mandment. In that country filial duty is the highest law of morality, both in the family and the state; and those classics, which to some extent fill the place of sacred books in China, shew that this feeling of the paternal and divine character of government has taken deep root amongst the rulers as amongst the ruled [9]. "From heaven," says their ancient book of history,—the Shû King, in one of its earliest chapters,— "From heaven are the (social) relationships, with their several duties [10]." These are the five relations between husband and wife, father and son, ruler and subject, elder brother and younger, friend and friend,—a list in which we notice that the political relation takes (no doubt intentionally) the central position amongst those of private and domestic life. "When (sovereign and ministers shew) a common reverence and united respect for these, lo! the moral nature (of the people) is made harmonious." . . . "The business of government!—ought we not to be earnest in it? ought we not to be earnest in it [11]?"

This earnestness in government is the prevailing tone throughout the whole of this very remarkable book. In it we have the Instructions and Announce-

---

[9] So much is this the case, that the precept, "Therefore shall a man leave his father and his mother, and shall cleave unto his wife" (*Gen.* ii. 24; *Matt.* xix. 5, &c.), seems to be a serious obstacle to some Chinese enquirers after Christianity. The position of women in China is, on the other hand, far from satisfactory. The wife is too often a drudge in her husband's family.

[10] *Sacred Books*, vol. iii. p. 55. The documents in this book relate to the early period, B.C. 2357—627, yet Dr. Legge argues strongly for its general credibility. See his Introduction, pp. 12, 15, &c.   [11] Ibid., p. 56.

ments of one sovereign and statesman after another, the earliest of them more than two thousand years before our era, sometimes harshly reflecting on their predecessors or opponents, but all breathing a like spirit of devotion to the good of the people. The "one man," as the king is frequently called, is seen realizing his commission from Heaven in no light or arrogant manner. His position towards the men of the "myriad regions" under his rule fills him with awe, and even with terror[12]. He not unfrequently describes himself as "the little child;" he calls upon the people to sympathise with his anxieties, and to imagine his solicitude on their behalf; he is struck with the worth of the relationship between himself and his subjects. It is useless unless it produces mutual respect and reverence; and so misrule is treated as a great opportunity for virtue thrown away by the sovereign, as well as an actual offence moving the indignation of heaven.

Expressions like the following occur again and again, and with a force and variety which convinces us that they are not merely conventional:—

"The virtue of the ruler is seen in his good government, and that government in the nourishment of the people," (p. 47).

"I wish to help and support my people." (p. 58).

"It was the lesson of our great ancestor:—'The people should be cherished, and not looked down upon. . . .

"The ruler of men—

"How should he be but reverent of his duties?" (p. 79).

---

[12] See, for example, the striking language of the Emperor Thang, quoted above, p. 165, note 54. Cp. *Shû King*, pp. 108, 110, for the "anxieties" of a king.

"The sovereign without the people has none whom he can employ; and the people without the sovereign have none whom they can serve. Do not think yourself so large as to deem others small. If ordinary men and women do not find the opportunity to give full development to their ability, the people's lord will be without the proper aids to complete his merit," (p. 103).

"Heaven and earth is the parent of all creatures; and of all creatures man is the most highly endowed. The sincerely intelligent (among men) becomes the great sovereign; and the great sovereign is the parent of the people," (p. 125).

The ideal state of China is naturally nothing else than the sovereignty of an ideal king. This state is sketched in the short treatise called *The Great Plan*[13], which makes more claims to the character of a Divine revelation than most of the documents in the "classics." The central point of this strange little book, which contains a sort of philosophy of the Universe, is called "Of Royal Perfection," which is thus described:—

"The Sovereign having established (in himself) the highest degree and pattern of excellence, concentrates in his own person the five (sources of) happiness, and proceeds to diffuse them, and give them to the multitudes of the people. Then

---

[13] It forms Book iv. of the *Shû King*, and is ascribed to Yü, the semi-mythical king. "To him Heaven gave the Great Plan, with its nine divisions; and the unvarying principles of its method were set forth in their due order."—*Sacred Books*, vol. iii. p. 140. As Dr. Legge says, there is only a "shadowy resemblance" between this book and the Pythagorean treatise, *On the Universe*, which bears the name of Ocellus Lucanus (written probably in the first century B.C.), to which it has been compared. The latter contains no speculations on government, which are the main subject of the *Great Plan*.

they, on their part, embodying your perfection, will give it (back) to you, and secure the preservation of it. Among all the multitudes of the people, there will be no unlawful confederacies, and among men (in office) there will be no bad and selfish combinations;—let the sovereign establish in himself the highest degree and pattern of excellence," (p. 142).

The *Great Plan* then goes on to direct how men of different degrees of virtue are to be treated, so as to bring out a reflection of the king's own character:—

"This amplification of the royal perfection," we read, "contains the unchanging (rule), and is the (great) lesson; yea, it is the lesson of God. All the multitudes of the people, instructed in this amplification of the perfect excellence, and carrying it into practice, will thereby approximate to the glory of the Son of Heaven, and say, 'The Son of Heaven is the parent of the people, and so becomes the sovereign of all under the sky,'" (p. 144).

These words would be striking anywhere, but they are specially striking when we meet with them in a practical book of history like this. We admire a brilliant exception like Marcus Aurelius, the philosopher upon the throne, seeking to make himself all that a man should be, and to fulfil his duties as a citizen of Rome and of the world[14]. But I think

[14] In Marcus Aurelius' twelve books of meditations there is a curious absence of any detailed reflection upon his duties as a sovereign to his subjects. The question hardly seems to interest him. In the following passage he comes near it for a moment; but he is generally (if we may say so) too much occupied with the perfection of his private or inner life. In Book vi. chap. 30, he says, "Beware of turning into a Cæsar, of putting on false colours; for such things are (ὅρα μὴ ἀποκαισαρωθῇς, μὴ βαφῇς· γίνεται γάρ).

we ought to admire more these long, anxious, and continued efforts of Chinese sovereigns and statesmen, to bring out the divine and fatherly ideal of royal power. Such efforts must have stored in that people a reserve of force, which will one day tell in directions of which we can now scarcely dream.

(2.) Second to this in logical sequence, as well as in historical succession, comes the assertion of individual liberty, or the right and duty of self-direction.

It needs but few words to recall the debt of gratitude which we owe to those who have vindicated the personal rights of citizens, especially in the old republics of Greece and Rome. The culture of powers entrusted immediately to ourselves, and only in a secondary degree to anyone else, the training of the will and of the sense of separate responsibility, the conception of duty as at times obliging us to place ourselves singly in defiance of our surroundings, are as important in a religious, as they are in a social point of view. The men of old days, who felt it imperative upon them to think and act for themselves, who would not bow to tyranny, or sink under the

---

Keep thyself therefore simple, good, uncorrupt, grave, unaffected, a friend of justice, reverent to the gods, benevolent, affectionate, strenuous to perform thy proper works. Strive to remain such as philosophy designed to make thee. Venerate the gods, save men. Life is short: there is one fruit of existence upon earth, a holy disposition and actions useful to society (διάθεσις ὁσία καὶ πράξεις κοινωνικαί)." Cp. the same book, chap. 44 : " Everything is helped by that which is agreeable to its constitution and nature. Now my nature is rational and social (πολιτική). My city and fatherland, as Antoninus, is Rome, and, as a man, is the world. It is therefore only those things which benefit these cities that I can reckon good."

pressure of caste and custom, stand out before us, and call to us, nay, seem to grasp our hands as brothers from the dim and unimaginable past.

When Socrates, as president of the Athenian assembly, refused to put a vote which his conscience told him was unjust, he elevated the whole conception of personal liberty [15]. No one could hereafter yield on any like occasion without a feeling of shame and wrong-doing. Such conduct has, directly or indirectly, helped many who have faced the anger of a turbulent multitude in a still holier cause. Nay, even the proud plea, "Civis Romanus sum," has been a stimulus to those who, standing before the bar of judgment, have asserted that their citizenship was in heaven, and their highest title that of Christian.

(3.) Thirdly, the conception of a state as being a moral entity, with duties as well as rights, though of slower and more secret growth than either of the foregoing, and hardly yet recognized in its fulness, has been no less real, and no less valuable. It has been obscured by kings and rulers, who, as leaders in war, have almost of necessity grasped the control of foreign politics. It has been obscured in home politics by the conflicts and shifting alliances of class with class, and of one estate with another. But century after century, the thought has grown, that the rights of individuals, whether kings or subjects, the strife

---

[15] The proposal was to condemn to death by a single vote the nine generals who fought at Arginusæ. All the other prytanes yielded to the popular clamour. See Xenophon, *Hist. Græca*, i. 7, 15; *Memorabilia*, i. 1, 18.

of classes, the enlargement of boundaries, were not everything, but that the state as a body had an existence, a conscience, a moral life. We have gradually learnt that the State has a duty to all its citizens, not to attempt the chimerical project of making them all equal, but to give them a fair chance of development in the sphere to which their nature adapts them; to abolish private war and slavery, to protect men impartially from one another, and to protect them no less from themselves. We have learnt, too, from this idea, that the foreign policy of a nation is a matter of conscience, not simply of the instinct of self-preservation, or of aggrandizement; and of conscience which concerns the whole body, not merely the sovereign, the executive government, or the fighting class.

It is the presence of this idea, in a sort of prophetic form, which gives the charm to such a book as Plato's *Republic*. It is not only a noble work of imagination, but it has the practical value of pointing out two great social needs, the elevation of woman to be the companion and helpmeet of man[16], and the education of all children[17], a duty which has never been thoroughly recognized till the present century. That Plato treated the former of these subjects in

---

[16] The equality of women with men, except in bodily strength, is treated in *Rep.*, v. pp. 454—457.

[17] The subject of education occupies really the largest space in the treatise. In *Rep.*, vii. 736, we are told that knowledge is not to be required under compulsion, but the whole tendency of the book is to make it universal. According to the *Laws*, vii. 804, education *is* to be made compulsory, and the same for girls as boys. In *Laws*, vi. 765, 766, a minister of education is to be appointed, and to be accounted the most important officer of state.

a hard and grotesque manner, is not to be denied [18]; and similar extravagance seems too often the fate of those who approach it without the sobering refinement of Christian morality [19]. But no one who looks at social prospects at home and abroad, who sees, for instance, the heroic work of salvation and reformation undertaken by women, sometimes almost single-handed, amongst ourselves, or who sees the Sisterhoods of France almost the only thoroughly effective and popular religious agencies in that country, can doubt that there is a public work for women in the present and in the future, which has only just begun to dawn.

The remarks we have hitherto been making may serve, in some sort, to remind you of the methods and directions in which improvements in politics may conduce to human happiness. The question which immediately arises, and which more directly concerns us, is this: — Can political life, can the State, make men really happy?

[18] Plato pushes the equality of the sexes too far, and enacts a community of wives and children amongst the "guardians:" *Rep.*, v. 457, 462 foll. This is tacitly given up in the *Laws*, in which a higher feeling on this and kindred subjects is observable. Aristotle criticizes the supposed equality, *Politics*, i. 13, § 9, and the community, ii. 2—4.

[19] This appears particularly in A. Comte's theory of an ideal state, though he takes a different line from that of Plato. See his *System of Positive Polity* (tr. by Congreve), vol. iv. p. 96, on the adoration of women, and pp. 59—61, 279, etc., on the so-called Utopia. It is easy to trace here the influence of the exaggerated cultus of the Blessed Virgin, to which he frequently refers as a sort of unconscious prophecy of his own system. The ascription to Mahomet of a high ideal of women is a paradox, not absolutely without foundation, but not borne out by the general tendency of his life and his utterances on the subject. See below, p. 255.

The answer clearly is:—They cannot.

They can, indeed, to a great extent, assure the conditions necessary to outward peace; they can remove some of the graver obstacles to happiness; they can strengthen the feeling of personal independence, and even set before men great ideals; but they can do little, and probably increasingly little, for the life of the soul.

Even the primary condition of outward peace can only be assured to a very limited degree. The politician has to do with states and nations, and rightly enough makes a virtue of patriotism. But the ideal of peace for man, as the Stoics and others have seen, must include the whole race as one family. This antithesis between the practical and the ideal seems not merely accidental or transitory; for there is no apparent tendency of nations to coalesce or form one state. Rather, one of the most striking phenomena of the present century, is the development and revival of nationalities, the accentuating of racial differences, and the tendency to redistribute large conglomerate states according to kinship and other similar affinities. Again, the configuration of the globe and other physical causes make it, in the highest degree, improbable that the present earth will ever be occupied by a single political body. Neither the North American confederacy, nor the growth of the unwieldy empire of Russia, are sufficient instances of a contrary tendency. It is easy, in fact, to see elements of disintegration, and even of collapse, in both.

This being the case, we must always face the

VII.] *Impossibility of preventing War.* 231

danger of the collision of the material interests of separate states, and the occurrence of war, whether for political principle, or in simple defence of such interests, the importance which men feel that foreigners cannot or will not understand. It is possible, indeed, to imagine a federation of nations: but no federation can be a stronger bond than the individual will of each; and as long as there is evil in the world, so long is it possible that selfish passion may take hold of a large body, as well as a small one. Even within the limits of a state it is not so easy to abolish brigandage and private war. The outbreak of serious quarrels between man and man is, to a great extent, only repressed by fear; but it is impossible to bring home the feeling of fear with sufficient force upon a nation under a different government. To put the matter in a simple light. Either the states of the future will be pretty nearly equal in power, in which case nobody will be deterred from war by the absolute hopelessness of success; or they will be unequal, and then the selfishness of the larger state will be under a strong temptation to forcible aggression.

Much, indeed, may be expected from the spread of humane feeling, the closeness of commercial relations between industrial communities, and the healthy experience of a few cases of satisfactory arbitration. It is to be expected that war will become more and more distasteful to the bulk of the people in civilized European states, and that they will be increasingly successful in making their voices heard. But as long as human nature is what it is, as long as a great number of men can only be controlled by the influence of fear, war will always be a possibility, and to engage in it will sometimes be a duty. Politics, at any rate, as distinct from religious influences, have no sufficient motives to enforce its cessation [20].

Again, in the interior working of the State we have to be content with very inadequate results, with the removal of the more serious hindrances to happiness, rather than with the positive production of it [21]. The State is, in fact, more and more forced to occupy a negative position. It can make certain kinds of vice unpleasant or unprofitable; it can absolutely forbid certain crimes, and punish them with a terrible vengeance; it can enforce a certain amount of moral training and discipline upon children, and upon the servants in its own employment; but it can do little to make virtue directly pleasant or profitable to the mass of its citizens.

There is a place, indeed, for public rewards of heroism, sometimes it may be for large spontaneous

---

[20] The reader will find this question discussed in Dr. Mozley's remarkable sermon on *War* in his *University Sermons*, the argument of which I have used in the foregoing paragraphs. Abstractedly speaking, war cannot be prevented, but it would nevertheless be a great misfortune if statesmen should acquiesce in this conclusion, as they are too much inclined to do. It ought (I venture to think) to be as much the general aim of their foreign policy to make war impossible, as it is the object of domestic policy to prevent riot and quarrel among their own citizens, and to change the forcible repression of crime into a healthy control of public opinion.

[21] Delitzsch has a good section on this topic headed, *Beweis aus der Unzureichenheit des Staates*, in his *Christliche Apologetik*, pp. 192—200.

tributes of a nation's generosity, especially in recognition of acts done in the public service, and in the more external and practical branches of it. But even these have to be jealously guarded, lest they have a degrading effect upon the recipients; and the good sense of most nations has shrunk from making such rewards in ordinary cases, more intrinsically valuable than the laurel or parsley crown, the title, the ribbon, and the medal.

The prizes which are sometimes given for acts or states of virtue in private life are generally ridiculous, not because they are given to bad people, but because the best always escape them. The army and the public service form a sort of school, admitting of special discipline, and special rewards. But it is impossible seriously to imagine the world as an academy in which good conduct should be regularly marked, and the results added up at the end of the year, and places changed in consequence.

The reason of course is, not so much the absolute impossibility of imagining such a state, as its inadequacy to meet men's deepest wants. The best would not care for it; and those who seemed satisfied would be degraded by their satisfaction. What our hearts really long for is inward peace, spiritual peace, peace with God; we want to know how to meet the pressure of personal trials and temptations, and to help others to meet them; we want a comfort that no external rewards can give, and a hope of social blessedness that transcends all the dreams of material prosperity. We have to face the hard facts of sickness, accident, trouble, death, which would make just as severe demands upon our nature in a Utopia, as in the present condition of things; and over and above all these we experience the sense of sin and fear of judgment, which immersion in worldly comfort may deaden, but cannot destroy.

II.

A feeling of the insufficiency of social life by itself has led both theorists and practical politicians to look to religion to come to the assistance of politics. It is easy to see how, even to a heathen, the virtues of civil life may take a religious colour, and so become much more powerful and helpful in their action. Thus obedience to authority obviously allies itself with a trust in divine providence; vindication of liberty is closely akin to the sense of moral responsibility to our creator and judge; and the acknowledgment of social duty may lead us to perceive a spiritual power working in the hearts of all our fellow-men. Such an alliance between civil and religious life is, indeed, so natural, that men in early ages have generally assumed it without conscious reasoning. The patriarchal principle that the head of the family should act as its priest is, for instance, instinctively extended to the State. The king, or chief magistrate, sacrifices for his people; the city and nation are purified at stated intervals by ceremonial lustrations; the popular assembly is sprinkled with the blood of a victim before its business commences; the anger of the gods, shewn in great plagues or calamities, is propitiated by special ritual, and great public successes are the occasion of sacred triumphs and thanksgivings. All these circumstances of popular religion answer a deep want in our nature, and that nation is miserable which does not retain them in some shape or other at every stage of its progress. But as time goes on men begin to change and to doubt. The meaning of some ceremonies is lost, and that of others has become gross, or is infected with selfishness. The patriarchal feeling decays, and men recognize more and more clearly that they are responsible for their own souls, and have their own individual peace to make with God. Yet, at the same time, they cannot but feel that religion belongs to society, and ought to leaven it, and that human nature is not at its best without the union and co-operation of soul with soul.

The great problem then is, how to adapt religion to social needs. This has been answered in three very distinct ways.

The first answer which presents itself is to permit the divergence which has grown up between the belief of the enlightened and the religion of the multitude to continue unchecked. This is the method of those who see clearly the difficulty and danger of changes of belief, and who value the power of custom and popular usage as a guarantee of order. Such men will be found ready (like Hobbes and Shaftesbury amongst ourselves) to support a religion in which they have but scant belief, and even to enforce its outward profession on others, if their private speculations are unchecked[22]. This was practically the answer of the greater number of ancient

---

[22] On this principle, adopted both by the pessimist Hobbes and the optimist Shaftesbury, see Leland's *View of the Deistical Writers*, vol. i. pp. 42 foll., 81 foll. (Lond., 1754).

philosophers, and has been tacitly assumed by not a few modern statesmen, who despair of attaining Truth on any large scale, and who think Order a synonym for Peace.

The second answer is that of more earnest and thorough-going persons, who cannot acquiesce in the indolence, cowardice and insincerity of the policy which has just been described. These men do not shrink from the trouble and danger of overturning a popular cult. Their method is one of religious reform, but of reform carried out by political machinery. They would make a religion as near as possible representing abstract truth, and then impose it upon all citizens. This was the method advocated by Plato in his last great scheme of an ideal polity (the *Laws*), and was, of course, actually put in practice on a grand scale by Mahomet. These men know more of Peace, and recognize that it involves Truth, but wrongly think the alliance of the two can be produced by Force.

Thirdly, and lastly, we have the truer view, that though order may seem to gain something by leaving religion unreformed, and though truth may seem to be propagated by a compulsory profession of faith, yet in both cases the loss is greater than the gain. In the interests of human happiness and true morality religious association must be voluntary, and need not necessarily be co-extensive with the State. To this principle we owe a number of minor religious experiments, and the greatest movement of all outside Christianity, namely, Buddhism. This answer is true in itself, but those who give it are apt to be one-sided and unpractical in their idea of Truth, and to sacrifice social order to their private fancies.

Christianity itself, as a social power, will be the subject of the next Lecture. As far as it can be compared with other religions, it belongs of course to the third division, though its supporters have, from time to time, treated it as if it could be assigned to one or other of the former.

Let us now give a few illustrations of the principles and consequences of these different methods of treating religion in its relation to society.

(1.) The first answer will commend itself to few persons at the present day, or, at least, few amongst ourselves will have the courage to own it: yet it is strange how much support it has met with. In aristocratic communities, nurtured under strong conservative instincts and prejudices, it is natural that men should shrink from the danger of attempting a change of popular belief. The civilization of Greece and Rome was of this kind, based upon slavery, which was assumed as a natural institution[23]; and that of

[23] Both Plato and Aristotle treat slavery as natural. Plato takes it for granted, *Laws*, iii. 690; cp. ib., vi. 777, on the treatment of slaves,—the general principle of which is fine, but the details harsh. In ix. 868, it is laid down that a master who kills his slave in anger shall undergo a purification (only): cp. ib. 865. In case the slave has done no wrong, it is, however, considered as murder: ib., 872. Plato sees the danger of the institution, *Rep.*, ix. 578 foll. Aristotle argues at some length that certain men are born for slavery (φύσει δοῦλοι—*Politics*, i. 5 and 6), but his argument is decidedly weak. He defends the institution in general, while he acknowledges that in many cases it produces injustice. Rousseau well replies:—" S'il y a des esclaves par nature, c'est parce qu'il y a eu des esclaves contre nature" (*Contrat Social*, i. 2.) On the other hand, Aristotle differs from Plato in recommending

India is, in some respects, very similar. In all three we have philosophers airily speculating about truth, and the people left in superstition, to which the enlightened are apt, in moments of weakness or compromise, to return. As long as contempt of the masses, and a rigid system of caste prevails, so long men will be ready to tolerate a life vitiated by this hopeless divorce between belief and worship, the destructive and immoral character of which needs hardly to be insisted upon. The antithesis between what is true and what is expedient, hovers about the lips of these philosophers, and penetrates from the lips into the heart, where it justifies all kinds of subterfuge, inconsistency, and cruelty. Educated men begin to think that they have invented religion and invented God, and when they speak of truth, mean only opinion apart from practice. All genuine sympathy is lost, and selfish comfort becomes the chief aim of existence.

This view of religion is strikingly put by the rationalistic Greek historian, Polybius, in whose time it was probably almost a common-place among educated men. He was living in the second century before Christ, and witnessed the social and moral decay of his own people, and of other nations, and the rise of the great power of Rome. He naturally asked what was the reason of this success, and gave the following curious answer [24]:—

"Besides the other advantages possessed by the Roman constitution, the greatest of all appears to me to be their

admonition of slaves rather than punishment (*Pol.*, i. 13, § 14, criticizing *Laws*, vi. 777).
[24] Polybius, Book vi. 56, §§ 6—15.

VII.]   *Order set above Truth. Polybius.*   239

conception about the gods. It is my opinion that superstition[25], which is considered a reproach amongst the rest of mankind, keeps the Roman state together. For this has been invested with such pomp, and has been carried to such a pitch of ceremony, both in their private lives, and in the conduct of public business, that it is impossible for it to be exceeded. Many persons might, indeed, think this a strange proceeding; but I suppose they have done it for the sake of the multitude. For if it were possible to form a state by gathering together wise men, such a method would, perhaps, be unnecessary. But, inasmuch as every multitude is fickle, and full of lawless desires, irrational anger, and violent temper, it is proper to keep such' people in order with unseen fears, and such-like tragic display. Wherefore men of old seem to have introduced and popularized conceptions about the gods, and ideas of what goes on in Hades, not irrationally and accidentally; but rather, men of the present day are rash and irrational in getting rid of them. Hence, not to speak of others, those who manage public money amongst the Greeks, if they are entrusted with a single talent, being checked by ten clerks, and as many seals, and twice the number of witnesses, are incapable of being honest; but amongst the Romans, men who act as magistrates or ambassadors, and are entrusted with a great sum of money, are kept to their duty merely by the sanctity of their oath. And in other nations it is rare to find a man who abstains from peculation, and is pure in such matters; but amongst the Romans it is rare for any one to be discovered in such malversation."

This theory of Polybius and other Greeks, though doubtless untrue as an account of the origin of Roman religion, unfortunately found favour with many in

[25] δεισιδαιμονία. The earliest extant use of this word in a reproachful sense is probably in Theophrastus' 16th character *of the Superstitious Man*, if that is genuine, as I see no sufficient reason to doubt. It is there defined as δειλία πρὸς τὸ δαιμόνιον, "cowardice towards the spiritual world." Cp. pp. 144, 177.

a people much more devoted to practical life and government, than to a love of truth [26]. Even in the first Punic war (B.C. 249), a consul made an open jest of his duty in consulting the auspices before a battle. Men read with eagerness the rationalistic analysis of religion which was given by Euhemerus, and statesmen began to ask how one priest could meet another without laughing [27].

So prevalent was this low view of popular religion, that the most learned and honest of Roman writers, Marcus Varro, made an analysis of theology as the basis of his encyclopædia of religious antiquities, in which he formally recognized this principle. He specifies three kinds of theology: first, the mythical or poetic; secondly, the physical, or philosophic; thirdly, the civil, or popular. The first was full of dangerous or unworthy fables; the second contained the truth; the third, or civil theology, though not true, was expedient for common people, and ought to be kept up by the State [28]. We cannot wonder, then, that Roman religion issued in a mere political worship of dead emperors, and of the genius of the existing monarch, and of the fortune of Rome,—the deification

---

[26] On the decay of Roman national religion, see Mommsen's *History of Rome*, book iii. ch. 13 (vol. ii. pp. 400 foll., E. T.). His apparent condemnation of theology in the abstract is much to be regretted, especially for the author's own sake, to whom all scholars owe so much.

[27] Cicero, *de Divinatione*, ii. 24, 51: "Vetus autem illud Catonis admodum scitum est, qui mirari se aiebat, quod non rideret, haruspex, haruspicem cum vidisset."

[28] Varro was here following Scævola: see St. Augustine *de Civitate Dei*, iv. 27; vi. 5, &c.; and cp. my *Early Latin*, p. 646.

VII.] *Religion of expediency at Rome.* 241

of force and power and outward peace, with scarce a spark of love or moral enthusiasm.

How far this spirit has been propagated to the present day, in the men of Latin races, it is not now the place to enquire at any length. But probably a good deal of the feeling which first prompted, and afterwards justified, the new dogma of Papal Infallibility can be traced, in great measure, to the same sources as that which assisted the deification of the ancient Imperial power. It seemed, perhaps, a necessary centralisation of authority, destined to crown the slowly-built edifice of the Curia; but it was none the less a survival of the wretched old Italian system of subordinating truth to expediency [29].

(2.) The second answer is (as we have seen) propounded by more zealous persons, and is, at first sight, more attractive. They say in effect:—"Find out the truth as carefully and exactly as you can,

---

[29] Out of 921 bishops who had received summons to attend the Council, 767 were present, and of these 276 were from Italian dioceses, representing only some 27 millions. The German and Hungarian bishops were only 67 in number, representing 46 millions of Catholics. See the interesting account of the Council in *The New Reformation*, by Theodorus [J. Bass Mullinger], p. 64, &c. Lond., 1875. "In church matters (said Friedrich) twenty Germans count for less than one Italian." Mr. J. C. Clay, who was in Rome during the Council, puts the number of Italian bishops at 600; but this can hardly be correct, though many Italians might be bishops outside Italy (*Foreign Church Chronicle*, vol. v. p. 137, Sep., 1881). In the 88 who voted non-placet on the famous fourth clause were "beyond all question three-fourths of the most eminent members of the Council,—Schwarzenberg, Mathieu, Darboy, Rauscher, Simor, Ginoulhiac, Mac Hale, Dupanloup, Ketteler, Strossmayer, Clifford, Kenrick, Maret, and Hefele." (*New Ref.*, p. 88.)

and then impose it upon everyone. If it is true, it will be good for them, whether they like it or not, just as the laws which make men peaceable do them good, however reluctantly they may be obeyed." In this way they seek really to propagate truth, and to ensure peace with God, but by means which are in the end subversive of what they desire to establish.

Amongst the ancients, Plato, stands, perhaps, alone in advocating this procedure, a proof amongst many of his originality. In his *Republic*, he had trusted to philosophy to cure the ills of humankind, but he had little hope of ever seeing his ideal brought into being. He is obliged to be content with supposing a pattern of it somewhere laid up in heaven [30].

But in his later portraiture of a model city in the *Laws*, he is more hopeful, because more religious. He felt in his old age that a community founded on

---

[30] *Republic*, book ix. thus concludes (Prof. Jowett's translation):—" Then if that is his motive, he [i.e. the just man] will not be a politician.

"By the dog of Egypt he will! in the city which is his own, though in the land of his birth perhaps not, unless by some providential accident.

"I understand: you mean in that city of which we are founders, and which exists in idea only; for I do not believe that there is such an one anywhere on earth.

"In heaven, I replied, there is laid up a pattern of it methinks, which he who desires may behold, and beholding, may set his own house in order. But whether such an one exists, or ever will exist in fact, is no matter; for he will live after the manner of that city, having nothing to do with any other.

"True, he said."

According to *Rep.*, v. p. 473, the realization of the ideal state is not to be expected "until philosophers are kings, or the kings and princes of the world have the spirit and power of philosophy."

a basis of united faith in the unseen world was the true type of society. He, therefore, formed a creed by abstraction from those simple elements of belief, which seemed to him to be most capable of proof, and most conducive to morality. His credenda are three: 1. That the gods exist; 2. That they take care of men; 3. That no prayers or sacrifices will prevail on them to sanction injustice. These he supports by arguments, which are no slight contribution to the armoury of what, for convenience, may be called "natural religion." He speaks, in really eloquent and persuasive terms, of the sad condition of atheists, and of the immorality of superstition; and, having proved his creed to his own satisfaction, goes on to enact that its articles shall be enforced on all citizens of his ideal polity [31]. Impiety is to be punished by imprisonment; in milder cases, with a hope of reformation; in more extreme ones, as a lifelong confinement. Private sacrifices, divinations, and the like, which are a fruitful source of irreligion, are to be strictly forbidden, and all such

---

[31] The whole of the tenth book of the *Laws* is occupied with this subject. See pp. 885—907 for the proofs of these credenda, and pp. 907—909 for the laws against impiety and on religion. On the third article of Plato's creed, see above, p. 178. J. J. Rousseau, at the end of his *Contrat Social* (book iv. ch. 6), similarly propounds a "civil religion," without which he thinks it impossible for a man to be either a good citizen or a loyal subject. The sovereign should banish from the State whoever does not believe the existence of God and Providence, future rewards and punishments, and the sanctity of the social contract and the laws. He further forbids intolerance (except on these points). Whoever says "There is no salvation outside the Church," should be driven from the State. All this is very like Tindal's principle, in his *Rights of the Christian Church*. Cp. Leslie Stephen, *English Thought in the Eighteenth Century*, vol. ii. p. 151 (Lond., 1876).

acts are to be public, and performed by a public priesthood [32].

It is a strange leap from Plato to Mahomet, though there can be no doubt that at bottom their principle is the same, with the great difference that there is between the speculative and practical intellect. Both were jealous for the honour of God, though Plato speaks vaguely as a polytheist; both were stern enemies of superstition, and desirous of stamping it out by force. Both of them reduced their religious creed to a minimum, eliminating from it the elements of mystery, in the hope of gaining acceptance from the multitude. It is fortunate probably for the reputation of Plato, that he never had the power to put his dream in practice, pure comparatively, and quite unselfish as his creed may have been. The success of Mahomet, while it has made him an idol to his followers, cannot be viewed as an enviable success by those who look on Islam from the outside.

We have already said something of this religion, but it is worth while to recall in this place some of the more prominent defects under which it labours. In the first place, its conception of the Deity is very faulty, being chiefly an enlargement of an imperfect human character. God is represented as perfect power, but not as perfect goodness; as arbitrary will, to whose action we must be resigned (Muslîm), but not as holy love [33]. Consequently, the

---

[32] No very important duties are assigned to this priesthood, either here or in Book VI. p. 759, where there is another mention of them.

[33] E.g. cunning is ascribed to God, *Sura* viii. 30, "They (the unbelievers) plotted, but God plotted, and of plotters, God is the

VII.] *Theology of Islam.* 245

worship of God is almost entirely of an external character, consisting of ceremonies, formal repetitions and recitations, washings, pilgrimages, fastings, almsgivings, and the like [34]. These have a tendency, even more than in other religions, to become mere mechanical acts. The sense of sin in Islam is very slight; the Law is not difficult to keep; God is lenient, because man is weak [35]; He knows what we are, and does not expect much from us; and so the doctrine of a Mediator and Redeemer is banished, as far as may be, from the heart of man [36]. The fall of Adam is to Mahomet little more than the record of a sin, as it was to the more extreme Pelagians, part of Old Testament history, and having no particular influence on his descendants [37].

best." Cp. above, pp. 62 foll., 68, 135 foll. There are some good remarks in Neander's *Church History*, vol. v. p. 117, E. T., ed. Bohn, on the theology of Islam; and a striking passage in Dr. Mozley's *Lectures on Miracles*, pp. 140—143, ed. 3, 1872, already referred to, p. 63. Cp. Abp. Trench, *Mediæval Church History*, Lect. iv. (Lond., 1877).

[34] The five foundations of practical religion are, 1. The recital of the Creed; 2. Observance of the five stated periods of prayer, said without variation every day; 3. The thirty days' fast of Ramazân; 4. The legal alms; 5. The pilgrimage to Mecca. See T. P. Hughes, *Notes*, p. 101, and the details which follow; and Prof. E. H. Palmer, the *Qur'ân*, pp. lxxi. foll.

[35] "God desireth to make your burden light to you; for man hath been created weak." *Sura* iv. (on women), verse 32, &c.

[36] The atonement is specifically rejected, *Sura* ii. 44, 45. The popular worship at the tombs of saints and Marabouts is a sort of protest against this doctrine of the Koran, and some Moslem theologians have attempted to make Mahomet into a mediator. See J. W. H. Stobart, *Islam*, p. 233, note, and *A Mohammedan brought to Christ*, the *Autobiography* of the Rev. Imad-ud-deen, ed. 2, p. 12 (C. M. S. House, London, 1870). Cp. the tradition given on p. 125.

[37] It is related in the Koran, *Sura* vii. 18 foll.; cp. ii. 34 foll.

Further, in its ethical character Islam is a gloomy religion. It has no true heartfelt love of God [38], whom the Moslem is taught to believe and to fear, but not to approach. The feeling of this want has driven many Moslems into a pantheistic mysticism (Sufiism) [39], which is, however, entirely alien from the formal and practical spirit of the Koran. Nor has it any real love for man as man. The general, and what we may call the orthodox, belief is that salvation is secured by good works, and that a work specially pleasing to God, is the extermination of idolaters by the sword, and the subjugation of infidels [40] (including, of course, Jews and Christians),

[38] This is allowed by Mr. R. B. Smith, *Mohammed and Mohammedanism*, p. 199, ed. 2, 1876 : "Mohammed believed in God, feared, reverenced, and obeyed Him according to his light, as few Jews or Christians ever did; but he could hardly be said in the Christian or even the Jewish sense of the word to love God."

[39] On Sufiism see above, p. 62, note. Imad-ud-deen gives an interesting account of his passage through it, and of the ascetic practices by which he sought to obtain peace, l. c., pp. 10—14.

[40] See on this subject in general, which is of considerable importance in its political aspect, the section on Jihád, or religious war, in T. P. Hughes, *Notes*, pp. 206 foll., W. W. Hunter's *Indian Musalmans*, J. W. H. Stobart, *Islam*, S. P. C. K., pp. 191 foll. The quotations from the Koran, with some modern illustrations, are given in the Bishop of Lincoln's sermon, *The Mohammedan Woe, and its passing away*, in his *Miscellanies*, vol. iii. pp. 92 foll. The most important chapter in the Koran relating to it, is the harsh and even ferocious *Sura* ix., delivered shortly before Mahomet's death, which, by what may be called a fortunate accident, wants the opening Bismillah, which is elsewhere regularly prefixed, i.e. "In the Name of God the compassionate, the merciful." (On the circumstances of the delivery of this Sura, see Sir W. Muir's *Life*, iv. pp. 208 foll., 1861.) It orders all idolaters to be killed, unless they embrace the faith of Islam; and proclaims war against "those who have received the Scriptures," i.e. Jews and Christians, till they

VII.]   *Ethics of Islam.*   247

ideas which no doubt have, from time to time, been current among Christians, but are contrary to the letter, as well as the spirit, of the Gospel. This destructive and oppressive character is of the essence of the Koran, certain chapters of which may truly be said to be written in blood.

As a system of ethics, besides these inherent defects, Islam has weighted itself with the necessity of upholding the character of its founder as a perfect model. Mahomet was, indeed, honest enough to confess his own sinfulness on various occasions, and died with a petition for pardon upon his lips[41]. But

pay tribute, and are humbled (verse 29, the clause, "Those to whom the Scriptures have been given," seems wrongly placed by Rodwell; see the quotation in Muir, p. 211, and E. H. Palmer's translation).

In his earlier teaching at Medina (A.D. 623), Mahomet declared that Jews, Christians, and Sabeites (i.e. Mendeans, or "Christians of St. John"), whoever believed in God and the last day, and do what is right, would be saved (*Sura*, ii. 59); but this seems to be abrogated by *Sura*, iii. 79, a few years later: "Whosoever desireth any other religion than Islam, it shall not be accepted of him, and in the next world he shall be among the lost." In his last illness—perhaps in delirium—Mahomet cried out, "The Lord destroy the Jews and Christians" (Muir's *Life*, iv. p. 270. Some authorities omit "and Christians;" but cp. *Sura*, ix. 30, where just the same sentiment occurs). It is easy to make a catena on toleration from the Koran, as Mons. J. B. St. Hilaire has done, *Mahomet*, pp. 329—333; but it is ludicrously unfair to represent such passages as the substance of Mahomet's teaching on the subject. In this and other respects his character got worse as he grew older. Rodwell's translation, which gives the (probable) chronological order of the chapters, is of great value in exhibiting this change. I have generally quoted from it.

[41] Cp. the tradition given above, p. 125, note 21. In *Sura*, xlviii. 2, one of the latest period, we read: "Verily, we have won for thee an undoubted victory, in token that God forgiveth

he evidently thought very highly of himself; and many of his followers, while admitting that his nature was not impeccable, assert (in the teeth of his own words) that he was preserved from actual sin, and treat his example as binding upon themselves, just in the same degree and manner as Christians apply that of Christ [42].

Now the character of Mahomet is simply a human one, of the earth earthy, disfigured by great faults and crimes in the midst of great virtues, as even his admirers confess [43], by inconsistencies and surprises,

---

thy earlier and later faults." In *Sura*, liii. 19, he first made a compromise with idolatry, admitting the three female divinities of the Arabs to the position of intercessors with God; but in a few days he disowned the words as a suggestion of Satan, and described the idols as mere empty names of human invention. In *Sura*, lxxx. ("He frowned"), he refers to his own harshness to a blind enquirer. His last fragmentary words are thus given by Muir (*Life*, iv. p. 279): "Lord, grant me pardon, and join me to the companionship on high" (I suppose that of the angel Gabriel)..... "Eternity in Paradise.".... "Pardon! yes, the blessed companionship on high." See also the conversation with Ayesha, quoted in Mr. R. B. Smith's *Mohammed*, p. 153, ed. 2.

[42] Pfleiderer, *Religions Philosophie*, pp. 641, 642, quoting Kremer, *Geschichte der herrschenden Ideen des Islam*, p. 156; T. P. Hughes, *Notes*, p. 13, ed. 2. Individual Moslems no doubt would be glad to free themselves from this burden: see the letter of Mir Aulad Ali, quoted by R. Bosworth Smith, *Mohammed*, p. 144, note.

[43] The most prominent admirer of Mahomet in this country (since Carlyle) has been Mr. R. Bosworth Smith, whose interesting lectures are in everyone's hands. He has discussed the faults of his character, and the nature of his pretensions (as it seems to me) in much too lenient a spirit in his *Mohammed and Mohammedanism*, pp. 142 foll., &c., ed. 2, 1876. (Cp. the review of the first edition by Dr. G. P. Badger, *Cont. Review*, for June, 1875, vol. 26, pp. 87–102.) Dr. Th. Nöldeke may be considered an apologist of Mahomet, but is less sympathetic than Mr. Smith; see his article s.v.

VII.]   *Character of Mahomet.*   249

by sudden collapses and passionate outbreaks. After living with comparative strictness up to the age of fifty-four, for the last seven years of his life he gave free indulgence to his passions [44]. Throughout his life he was guilty of occasional acts of terrible cruelty and treachery [45]: and, over and above this, his character is darkened by a still more awful suspicion of imposture, when we find him justifying his sins by the pretence of a revelation from God [46].

Muhammed in Herzog's *Encyclopædia*, vol. xviii. pp. 797 foll. (at end of letter Z)., and cp. his *Geschichte des Qorans*. Mons. J. B. St. Hilaire may also, to a great extent, be classed among his admirers. Dr. Sprenger is in some points a very severe judge (cp. Tiele's judgment, *Outlines of the Hist. of Ancient Religions*, §§ 59 foll.). Sir Wm. Muir holds the balance, but censures strongly the latter part of his life. See iv. pp. 318 foll. for a summary of his moral declension at Medina, which has been denied, but without sufficient ground. Part of it is quoted in note 46.

[44] Mahomet (b. *circa* 570 A.D., d. May, 632) was fifty when he lost Khadîja, with whom he had lived happily and faithfully for twenty-five years. After a month he married another wife (Sawda); and three or four years later, at the age of fifty-four, he added a second, Ayesha, a child of ten years of age. In less than five years following this marriage with Ayesha, he brought together a harem, consisting of nine wives and two concubines. Ayesha used to say, "The prophet loved three things,—women, scents, and food; he had his heart's desire of the two first, but not of the last." Muir, *Life*, iv. p. 328. Cp. the saying of Ibn Abbas, "Verily, the chiefest among the Moslems was the foremost of them in his passion for women," *Ib.*, p. 310, where the facts are summarized, and St. Hilaire, pp. 170—176, &c.

[45] These were specially directed against the Jews. See e.g. the assassinations in A.D. 624, after the battle of Badr (Muir, ch. xiii. vol. iii. pp. 130 foll.), and the massacre of the Beni Coreitza in 627 (*ibid.*, iii. pp. 275 foll.). Other acts of cruelty, perfidy, and malice are mentioned by Muir, iv. pp. 307 foll.; cp. Stobart, *Islam*, pp. 158, 165, &c.

[46] Muir says, vol. iv. p. 318, speaking of his moral declension at

Now in the face of these facts it is impossible to admit, as some Christians even are inclined to do, that Mahomet was a "true prophet[47]." This is a high title to which no one outside the range of the sacred writers of our revelation has as yet made good his claim. We deny it to Mahomet on very simple grounds. Not because he was a sinner, for that is common to men; but because being a sinner, he used his position, as a messenger of God, to cloak and even commend his sin, and so made God the author of immorality. The reasonableness of this criticism is obvious. When a man puts forward so grand a pretension as that of being the mouthpiece of the Deity, it is our manifest duty to apply a moral test to his claims. In the case, indeed, of a predictive prophecy, the natural criterion is the fulfilment or not of what is foretold: but even here we are bound to require agreement with the first principles of religion and morality[48]. But in the case of didactic prophecy, which was that which Mahomet claimed

---

Medina: "Messages from heaven were freely brought forward to justify his political conduct equally with his religious precepts. Battles were fought, wholesale executions inflicted, and territories annexed, under pretext of the Almighty's sanction. Nay, even baser actions were not only excused, but encouraged, by the pretended divine approval or command; a special licence was produced allowing Mahomet a double number of wives (*Sura* xxxiii. 49); the discreditable affair with Mary, the Coptic slave, was justified in a separate Sura (lxvi.); and the passion for the wife of his own adopted son and bosom friend was the subject of an inspired message, in which the Prophet's scruples were rebuked by God, a divorce permitted, and marriage with the object of his unhallowed desires enjoined (Zeinab, wife of Zaid, see *Sura* xxxiii. 36)."

[47] See R. B. Smith, *Mohammed*, ed. 2, pp. 344, 345, and index.
[48] Cp. *Deuteronomy* xiii. 1—3.

to utter, there can be no other test than this last; and nowhere is it so necessary as in the delicate and crucial point of unselfishness in respect to the position of the prophet himself. A single lapse in this matter is enough to discredit the whole message, so far as it goes beyond the elements of truth already current in the world. These, of course, will remain true in any case, but a mere enunciation of old truths, in however emphatic language, does not constitute a prophet.

A lapse of this kind, below the supposed prophet's own moral standard and the standard of his day, is quite a different thing from the incompleteness of a confessedly preparatory system, like that of Judaism. It is reasonable, for instance, to defend the permission of acts of imperfect morality (such as the Mosaic Law of divorce), or the utterance of commands which are suitable to, and possible in, one age, but could not be enjoined in another (such as the extermination of the Canaanites, Elijah's calling down fire on the captains, and the like)[49]. What we are bound to insist upon from every one who claims to be a prophet is this— that, while he definitely advances religion and morality in general, he should never fall behind the standard of his own age in particular. Some parts of his message or legislation may become obsolete; some actions of his may not bear repetition in a later

---

[49] See on this topic in general, Dr. Mozley's *Old Testament Lectures*. The principle of St. Augustine, which he adopts, requires careful handling, but seems essentially contained in our Lord's judgment on Moses and Elijah, *Matt.* v. 31, xix. 8 foll.; *Luke* ix. 54 foll. (where the thought appears to be the same whatever reading is accepted.)

stage of progress, but his teaching will never be absolutely immoral or retrogressive, as some Suras of the Koran confessedly are [50].

The appearance of such elements in a man's teaching are like the symptoms of a secret plague or fever. The rest of the body may be fair to outward view, but when we see these few signs of a decidedly morbid character, we know that there is a want of healthiness in the whole. Mahomet's selfish misuse of God's name proves that he was not a true prophet: and having these marks to guide us, we can go on to trace the falseness which runs through the whole of his system.

How far he was himself deceived is a much more difficult question, though it need not detain us long in this place. He had certainly a strong belief in his own mission, and spoke proudly of his truthfulness; but Arab morality was lax on this point,

---

[50] Any attempt that might be made to defend the action of Mahomet, by a parallel with the vindication of Moses for his marriage with the Ethiopian woman (in *Numbers* xii.), breaks down at once, since there is no proof that Moses did anything at all worthy of censure, though he offended his brother's and sister's jealousy or prejudice. The vindication, it may be also observed, did not at first proceed from the mouth of Moses. Mr. Bosworth Smith suggests that it was a justification which Mahomet may have made to himself, but does not quote it as a positive apology for him (p. 134). His half-parallel with our Saviour's breaking the Pharisaic law of the Sabbath (p. 144), seems to me to have a more dangerous tendency. To alter a ceremonial law, or to elevate and strengthen a law of conduct, is a recognized function of a Prophet, not to make the law bend to his own pleasure or advantage. If our Lord had done the latter, no pious Jew could have accepted Him. The Pharisees might perhaps have done so more willingly.

and included a serious admiration for cunning, especially in a good cause, and Mahomet was above all things a genuine Arab. In his later days he was the victim, probably, of his own reputation, and of that power over the minds of his followers which is so hard a strain upon the morality of even the most pious enthusiasts. Even in his best days he had probably been working for himself quite as much as for God. As long as he was moving upward he could practise self-restraint: but success demoralized him, as it has demoralized his followers ever since. He thought (as we have seen) that God is lenient and forgiving, like a large-minded and sagacious man who knows the world, and so he forgave himself in the name of God for faults which all the time he knew to be faults. The whole matter is of a piece with his defective theology, his unworthy conception of the Deity, and his defective idea of sin. Hence it came about that he who, in his earlier years, had cancelled a revelation which his conscience told him was a sinful compromise with idolatry [51], could in his later age give himself selfish privileges, and justify immoral acts with unmoved and serene composure.

That Mahomet, in great measure [52] extirpated idolatry, and introduced certain reforms into the wild and lawless social life of Arabia, is doubtless true. That he and his followers have been a scourge permitted by God upon a corrupted Christianity, is also

---

[51] *Sura* liii. 19. See above, note 41.

[52] Some of the ceremonies of the pilgrimage to Mecca, kissing the Kaaba, &c., are a clear survival and incorporation of a partial idolatry, notwithstanding all his protestations.

probable. But here our gratitude to him, such as it is, must cease. Wherever Islam has prevailed for any length of time, it has had the following threefold ill effects: 1. It has stereotyped a low and unprogressive form of social life; 2. it has paralyzed the intellectual, and especially the religious, development of mankind; 3. it has been a barrier against the Gospel [53].

1. Had Mahomet been contented with the position of a legislator, or tribal chief, he would have left the way open for further improvement; he would have made a beginning which others might have carried on; and so mankind would have been the gainers, though his own success might have been less rapid. Had he been sufficiently humble to use the sources open to him in the Bible, even in the Old Testament, and much more in the New, his reforms might have been of permanent value. But he would follow neither of these courses. He chose to be a prophet, and above all things the last of the prophets, possessed of a final revelation. Though acknowledging himself a sinner, he set himself practically above the sinless Jesus. He shut his eyes to the real contents of the Bible, and (it is said) would not permit his followers to read it [54]; and consequently he condemned a great part of mankind to live in a permanently unprogressive, or rather retrogressive, social state. It was worthy of a legislator to prevent the barbarous

---

[53] This is Sir W. Muir's judgment, *Life*, vol. iv. pp. 321 foll. Cp. Mr. T. P. Hughes, *Notes*, preface, ed. 2, pp. xi., xii.

[54] This is stated by the Rev. Imad-ud-deen, pp. 10, 11, of his *Autobiography*, already quoted.

VII.]   *Retrogressive social Legislation.*   255

murder of female infants, to forbid certain gross crimes[55], to set limits to polygamy[56], to make divorce less frequent by requiring the restitution of the dowry[57], and to ameliorate in other ways the legal condition of women and slaves. All this Mahomet did, or tried to do; though after all it is probable that women "possessed more freedom, and exercised a healthier and more legitimate influence under the pre-existing institutions of Arabia[58]." But to incorporate and establish polygamy, concubinage, and slavery, and a general low treatment and estimate of women in a revelation professing to be final, the last, best, and most merciful utterance of God to man, is to inflict a terrible curse upon society. If Mahomet did not listen to the revelations of Genesis or the Gospel, he could hardly be unaware of what was known to the heathen, and what his own earlier life might have taught him, that a divided household cannot be the home of moral worth and of mutual respect and support, in the same way that the union of a single pair should and may be. Sallust, for instance, writes as justly as a Christian on the evils

[55] Such as the inheritance by the son of his father's wives; see *Sura* iv. 26. He allowed it, however, in cases already existing.

[56] *Sura* iv. 3. No restriction, however, is put on the number of slave concubines (*Sura* lxx. 30, iv. 28); and divorce or exchange is so easy, that the legal value of the restriction is very slight.

[57] But a man is, as it were, invited to put pressure on his wife to remit her rights in this respect; *Sura* iv. 3 and 28. Cp. Dr. Mozley's remarks on this ignoble feature of the legislation, *Miracles*, Lect. vii. note 1. p. 283.

[58] Sir Wm. Muir, *Life*, vol. iii. p. 305, where are some important remarks on the Moslem idea of marriage, which he thinks less sound, in a very marked degree, than the Hindu.

of Moorish polygamy:—"Animus multitudine distrahitur: nullam pro socia obtinet; pariter omnes viles sunt[59]." In such unions all the harem become equally contemptible, or if one is specially favoured, obvious injury is done to the rest; and it is doubtful whether man or woman loses the most terribly by the degradation which follows. Social life is poisoned at its roots.

2. The paralysing influence of Islam upon the religious and intellectual development of mankind is sufficiently obvious in the present state of countries under Mahometan government. It has not, indeed, always been so. In the stir of conquest, or first conversion, and the years which immediately succeed it, there has been also a movement of mind and heart. But whenever the sword has been long laid down, when the novelty of the change to monotheism has passed away, then comes the dreary record of decay, of shutting up the intellect, of hardening the heart. When Mahomet closed the Bible, he closed the source of intellectual, as well as of moral light. He put a crude, dull, rambling, inconsistent, often coarse and selfish rhapsody, with no ideas at all upon some of the deepest questions that interest and agitate the conscience, with no depth of insight into the working of the soul, into the place of the divine Book; and he put his own sinful and narrow character into the place of the inexhaustible riches of Christ's example. Let anyone try to read the Koran through, making

---

[59] Sallust, *de bello Jugurthino* [chap. 80], quoted by J. W. H. Stobart, *Islam*, p. 229, where are some other good remarks on this subject.

VII.] *Islam opposed to Liberty and the Gospel.* 257

allowances for the greater beauty of the original, and let him think of the effect upon himself of taking it as an unsurpassable model, the great treasure-house of wisdom. Let him then read the life of Mahomet, and the laws and customs which have grown up, partly from the Koran, partly from tradition, and he will understand the deadening effects of Islam upon the soul, and its utter antagonism to liberty of any kind [60].

3. The opposition of Islam to the Gospel follows directly from the precepts and practice of Mahomet, and by implication from its retrogressive morality and unspiritual narrowness. It is much indeed that we have certain fundamental points in common with Moslems, their monotheism, ignorant and unloving as it is, their deep belief in the reality of revelation, though it has armed their hands against mankind, and their reverence for the Lord Jesus [61], superficial and unpractical as it has always been. But as long as they believe the Koran, they are bound to hold that Christ is not the Son of God (*Sura* xix. 31—36), that He was never crucified, but was represented by one in His likeness (*Sura* iv. 156), and that He is no other than a servant whom God favoured with the gift of prophecy (*Sura* xliii. 59),

[60] Carlyle's condemnation of the "insupportable stupidity" of the Koran is remarkable in one who chose Mahomet as his type of the "hero as Prophet:" see his *Heroes*, &c., pp. 76, 77, in vol. xii. of his collected works. For the traditions, we may refer to Major R. D. Osborn, *Muhammedan Law, its Growth and Character*, in *Contemp. Review*, vols. 29 and 30, May and June, 1877.

[61] "Devout Musalmans never mention the name of Seyyedna Eesa, or our Lord Jesus, without adding the words, 'on whom be peace.'"—R. B. Smith, l. c., p. 267.

S

and is not to be associated in that worship which is due to God only (*Sura* ix. 31) [62].

It seems hopeless, then, to expect (as Neander and others incline to do) that Islam will be to many "a theistic medium of transition from idolatry, at its very lowest stages, to the only genuine theism of Christianity [63]." On the contrary, one of the greatest dangers to the spread of the Gospel is the rapid conversion of some of the lower races to Islam, which attracts them by its one broad view of monotheism, by its external discipline, and the alliance which it offers with something like a world-wide power; while it makes few demands upon the heart, legalises and justifies a low social morality, and actually destroys the sense of sin which before existed [64]. It offers a simple theory of the universe which enables a man to make the easiest possible compromise between religion and selfishness, and to suppose that there is nothing higher to be found.

Pride of self, satisfaction in having attained the truth, and being able to look down on others, is a strong feeling, I suppose, with most Moslems; and next to this is a worship of success, "a belief that all the enjoyments of sense are the rightful heritage of the faithful, who dare to seize them [65]," and therewith a strong hold on the things of this world, and

---

[62] The passages of the Koran relating to our Saviour, are collected in Stobart's *Islam*, pp. 142—146.

[63] Neander, *Church History*, vol. v. pp. 120 foll., ed. Bohn, 1851.

[64] This is, I have reason to think, the opinion of Bp. Steere, and the result of his experience of negro conversion to Islam.

[65] See Sir Bartle Frere's Lecture, *Christianity suited to all Forms of Civilization*, in *Chr. Evidence Lectures*, series 2, p. 336.

VII.]   *Hopelessness of Islam.*   259

bitter hostility to all who oppose their rule, or weaken it by desertion. Wherever Moslems are the dominant race, their conversion seems all but hopeless; only when pride has been broken, when success is turned into failure, and the need of toleration is experienced in their own case, then there may be some hope that the kingdom which is not of this world may appear to them in a fairer and more attractive form. The failure of Islam to benefit mankind is, as we have seen, specially traceable to its assumption of finality and to its imposition of a harsh, one-sided legislation, under colour of a new Gospel. As an attempt to give happiness to society against its will by means of religion, it is simply pernicious. Mahomet is essentially one of those false prophets denounced in Scripture, who heal the trouble of the human heart "slightly," and who cry "Peace, peace," when there is no peace.

(3.) We now turn to a third answer to the grave question, "How can religion best influence society?" The true principle is no doubt, "Let speculative truth and religious order unite in one community; let entrance into it be voluntary, and let its influence upon politics be that of persuasion, not of force." The success of those who give this answer must, of course, depend on the truth or falsehood of their doctrine; but outside Christianity, they have a dangerous tendency to become anti-social. We have not opportunity to do more than touch very lightly on the minor experiments which have been made in this direction, especially as many of them are really insignificant, while others are shrouded in an intentional obscurity. Secrecy has been the besetting and ruinous fault of the great number of these voluntary religious bodies. Nothing is more certain than the value of the Christian maxim, adopted as fundamental by the Positivists, that it is right to "live openly [66]." Secret societies, for the most part, have been viewed by outsiders either with exaggerated prejudice or with exaggerated respect; while their members have been too apt to consider themselves above or outside the laws of open life. Secrecy produces a sort of delicious intoxication, a greedy delight in the sweetness of "stolen waters," which is one of the most dangerous of human passions; and these associations are apt to be distorted from their legitimate ends into centres of conspiracy or refuges of immorality. Thus the Areoi of Polynesia, the depositaries of sacred lore and literary culture, the members of which are invested with a sort of divinity in this life, and with a claim to happiness after death, have become absolutely immoral [67]. The Pythagorean confraterni-

---

[66] *Matt.* v. 14 foll.: "Ye are the light of the world," &c. *John* xviii. 20: "I spake openly to the world," &c. 1 *Thess.* v. 22: "Abstain from all appearance of evil." (Rev. vers., "every form" with "appearance" in margin.) 2 *Cor.* viii. 21: "Providing for honest things, not only in the sight of the Lord but also in the sight of men." 1 *John* i. 7: "If we walk in the light, as He is in the light, we have fellowship one with another." Cp. *Rom.* xii. 17; xiii. 13; 1 *Pet.* ii. 12, &c. Comte especially applies it to political life, *Positive Polity*, E. T., vol. iv. p. 400.

[67] The Areoi of Tahiti and other islands were clubs of men and women, living licentiously together, and bound by the rule of killing all their children. They went about giving dramatic representations of dance and song, and in this way have preserved

VII.]   *Character of Secret Societies.*   261

ties of Magna Græcia, on the other hand, though we hear nothing but what is favourable of their moral aims, were suspected, perhaps with some reason, of political agitation, and were crushed by violence [68]. Their most enduring effects may probably be found in the influence which they exercised upon the mind of Plato, whose ideal of a state is made up in great measure of elements drawn from the two chief attempts to mould human life on Dorian principles, the constitution of Lycurgus and the life of these Pythagorean brotherhoods [69]. Of the Orphic and other societies connected with the mysteries, we know comparatively little. The idea that they were centres of high dogmatic instruction has long been given up by scholars, but what they actually were is less easy to estimate [70]. At their best they repre-

much of the old mythology. For a collection of what is known about them from Cook, Ellis, Wilson, Moerenhout, &c., see Waitz, *Anthropologie der Naturvölker*, vol. vi. pp. 363—369, ed. Gerland (Leipzig, 1872). He finds the origin of the association in devotion to Oro, the ruler of souls after death, and in the hope of future happiness, p. 368. Cp. Gerland, *Aussterbung der N. V.*, p. 47 (Leipz., 1868).

[68] What is known about the Pythagorean societies has been put together by Zeller, *Pre-Socratic Philosophy*, vol. i. pp. 342 foll., tr. by S. F. Alleyne (Lond., 1881). The fullest collection of Pythagorean fragments is given by Mullach, *Fragmenta Philosophorum Græcorum*, vol. i. (Paris).

[69] See on this point Prof. Jowett's *Plato*, vol. iii. pp. 153 foll., ed. 2, 1875. The actual legislation of Lycurgus is described by Grote, *Hist. of Greece*, vol. ii. pp. 145—156, ed. of 1862. For its influence, both on Plato and Aristotle, see p. 154.

[70] Lobeck's *Aglaophamus* (in three books, 1. *Eleusinia*; 2. *Orphica*; 3. *Samothracia*) has done great service in criticizing and exposing the pretensions which many modern writers had made in behalf of the mysteries, but it hardly enables us to understand

sent the vague theology of music, that spirit which reaches forward into the darkness, and draws a wondering crowd along with it, solaced now with rapturous gleams of light, and now oppressed with melancholy and unintelligible sadness. The myth of Orpheus tells us of one who has actually been into the land of Hades, and has nearly, but not quite, succeeded in bringing back his darling. It lifts the veil only to drop it again. The mysteries were in like manner occupied principally with dramatic pictures, representing two tales of the lower world: one of Demeter looking for her daughter Proserpine, who has been snatched from her by Pluto; the other, that of Dionysus-Zagreus, the infant son of Zeus, who has been torn to pieces and buried, and whose limbs are again brought together on the breast of Demeter,—a myth closely akin to that of Osiris [71]. That these mysteries were moral in any real degree is very improbable, their ascetic prescriptions were external, and often unmeaning or fantastic [72], but

the real character of these celebrated rites. A more constructive account of the Eleusinia will be found in Preller's *Griechische Mythologie*, i. pp. 645—655, cp. ii. 487 foll. on the Orphica (Berlin, 1872). The same subjects are treated at length by Döllinger, *Heidenthum*, book iii., *die Mysterien und die Orphische Religionslehre.* See also Grote's *Greece*, vol. i. pp. 15—37. In these books the reader will find all necessary references.

[71] Crete was probably the medium through which Egyptian theology first passed into Greece: see Döllinger, p. 129. Epimenides, the Cretan Orphic priest, was invited to Athens as early as B.C. 612 (others say 596), to cleanse the city from the stain of Kylon's murder. See *ib.*, p. 132. The identification of Dionysus-Zagreus with a bull also naturally reminds us of Osiris-Apis.

[72] For the prescriptions of the "Orphic life," we may compare the chorus of Euripides' *Minos*, quoted by Porphyrius *de Abstinen-*

VII.]   *The Mysteries.*   263

they served to keep up an aspiration after a future life, and sometimes comforted mourners. Yet even this comfort was degraded by the contempt expressed for the uninitiated, who, without any fault of their own, were doomed to a lower place in another world [73].

Besides these better-known societies, there were a number of smaller guilds, founded usually on some foreign cult, or fanciful and almost accidental enthusiasm, which had great vogue among the lower classes in Greece [74], and would have developed at least as

tia, iv. 19. The bull representing Zagreus was torn in pieces, and his flesh eaten raw, a sort of act of communion with the deity, by which rebirth was assured. But after this, abstinence from animal food was enjoined,—an idea probably connected with a doctrine of transmigration. The Pythagorean prohibition of eating beans was also Egyptian in character (Herod., ii. 37).

[73] Like the Areoi, those devoted to the gods of Hades in this life were supposed to be their special favourites after death. See the passages in Lobeck, pp. 69 foll., and Döllinger, pp. 175 foll. The following is one of the most important, *Hom. Hymn. in Cererem*, 480 foll. :—

ὄλβιος ὃς τάδ' ὄπωπεν ἐπιχθονίων ἀνθρώπων·
ὃς δ' ἀτελὴς ἱερῶν ὅς τ' ἄμμορος, οὔποθ' ὁμοίως
αἶσαν ἔχει φθίμενός περ ὑπὸ ζόφῳ εὐρώεντι.

Plutarch *De audiendis Poetis*, 4 (tom. ii. p. 21 = vol. i. p. 81, Wytt.), quotes a story of Diogenes ridiculing the distinction of initiated and uninitiated; but he refers to the hope given by the mysteries in his letter of *Consolation to his wife* on the death of their daughter Timoxena, ch. 10 (tom. ii. p. 611 = vol. 3, p. 464, Wytt.).

[74] The best authority on this subject is P. Foucart (now President of the French Archæological School at Athens), *Des Associations Religieuses chez les Grecs* (Paris, 1873). The most important existing document on these societies is the inscription of Andania in Messenia, B.C. 93, which may be found in P. Cauer's *Delectus Inscr. Græcarum*, pp. 19—27 (Leipzig, 1877), and elsewhere.

largely in Italy but for the jealousy of Roman lawyers and statesmen, who perhaps tried to reduce them to the position of mere burial-clubs [75]. All had the great merit of being free associations for a religious end, and as such they admitted women, slaves, and foreigners to participate in their benefits; and most of them had a special tendency to give a more distinct hope of a future life, a hope which was closely connected with their provisions for decent and careful funeral rites. They had besides, something of a sacramental system, joining rich and poor in common worship and in a common festal meal; while some of them assisted their members by loans of money without interest, and in this way took, in some slight degree, the place of our modern benevolent institutions.

On the other hand, their importance and charitable influence have been often exaggerated [76], sometimes with a polemical intention of depreciating the Christian Church. It is also clear that too many of them, if not immoral in principle, put no real check on immorality, but rather gave scope for it in their nightly meetings and promiscuous assemblages, and that they were fruitful sources of superstition, satis-

---

[75] On the Roman guilds see Th. Mommsen *de Collegiis et Sodaliciis* (Kiliæ, 1843). The attempt to check their growth is clear, but it is conjectured, rather than demonstrated, that *only* burial-clubs were permitted: see Mommsen, l. c., pp. 88 foll. Renan assumes this too absolutely as proved, *les Apôtres*, pp. 355, 356, ed. 1, 1866.

[76] As by Renan, *les Apôtres*, pp. 351 foll., following Wescher. These exaggerations are well criticized by Foucart, l. c., ch. xv. pp. 139 foll.

VII.] *Private Guilds and Burial-clubs.* 265

fying their members by formal purifications and incantations, without any evidence of change of heart. Every little accident of domestic life sent the superstitious man or woman to the Orphic or Oriental mystery-monger, who was frequently the centre of such a confraternity. For two obols they could get a prediction on any future event, large or small, serious or ridiculous. A philtre or a conjuration of evil came with equal readiness. The wills of gods and men were supposed to be subject to the meanest class of magicians, and we know (sometimes by actual experience in our own country) the miserable degradation that follows.

All these societies, however interesting to the student of antiquity, are but insignificant and ephemeral when compared with the great movement of Eastern Asia, which still numbers as its adherents perhaps 500 millions of mankind[77]. Buddhism is the only voluntary association, or church of believers, which can be at all compared with Christianity as to the purity and loftiness of its moral teaching, at least in details, or as to its power of expansion. It no longer exists indeed in India, the country of its birth, where it was extinguished after many centuries, partly by internal decay, partly (it is thought) by persecution[78]. But as early as the third

[77] See above, p. 92.

[78] This extinction took place gradually, between the 7th and 12th centuries A.D., when the last blow was given by Moslem conquest. What little is known of these events is told in Rhys Davids' *Buddhism*, pp. 242 foll. The later history of Buddhism in India is extracted almost entirely from the travels of three Chinese pilgrims, Fan Hian, A.D. 400; Sung Yun, A.D. 518; and

century B.C. it had spread to Ceylon, whence it was propagated to Burma and Siam, the three countries which retain it in its most original form, and where it is still the national belief. Its introduction into China was not much later, and in the fourth century of our era it became the State religion, and is now professed in some form or other by a very large proportion of the people. From China it made its way to Corea and Japan, and other islands, losing no doubt many of its original features, but still retaining much that is characteristic.

Northern Buddhism in Tibet is of later growth, and has suffered much greater alteration, taking the form of the worship of a living Buddha,—the Dalai Lāma, and being mixed up with much eclectic superstition, while in Nepāl it has formed a sort of fusion with the worship of Śiva.

In view of this immense outward success, we naturally ask the reasons of such a wide expansion? We shall find them perhaps equally in the truth and the falsehood of Buddhist principles. On the one side there are the two great verities, that religious association should be voluntary and open to all men, and that moral conduct conduces to happiness or misery more absolutely than anything else. The dignity of human nature is, in fact, the basis of all that is good in Buddhism. Caste is abolished, women are ad-

---

Hiouen Thsang, A.D. 629—648, translated by Rémusat, Beal, Stanislas Julien, and others. Mons. A. Barth, in his remarkable article on Indian religions (in Lichtenberger's *Encyclop. des Sciences Religieuses*, vol. vi. pp. 571 foll., Paris, 1879), traces the decay of Buddhism to its own 'senility' rather than to persecution. Proofs of the latter certainly appear slight.

mitted to the society, a mass of superstition is lifted from the mind, and the moral law (especially that which answers to the second half of the Ten Commandments) is re-asserted with a force and persuasiveness that no other system, except the Christian, can shew. Man's free-will to do right or to do wrong, not any external fate, not any performance or non-performance of ceremonial acts, is that which decides his destiny, for happiness or misery. We can easily imagine the healthy and refreshing effects of such a proclamation in Eastern society, which tends so readily to fixity of life, which is wont passively to let unreal barriers grow up between class and class, to grow torpid under the delusions of pantheistic fatalism, and to acquiesce in a lazy formality of religious action as a substitute for energetic moral sympathy with goodness. No wonder that Gotama seems a godlike teacher, stooping down with infinite gentleness and compassion to make men once more brethren, and to bring them back to simple rules of life, to help them again to respect themselves and all living creatures, and to take their proper place in this bewildering and ever-changing world.

This is the good side of Buddhism[79]. Its great defect is that it is a philosophy, not a religion, while it claims to supply the place of religion. The Buddha means "the enlightened one", he who knows; and escape from ignorance, not from sin against God

[79] Mons. J. B. Saint-Hilaire has an interesting chapter on the merits and defects of Buddhism, pp. 141—182 of his *Le Bouddha et sa Religion*, ed. 3 (Paris, 1866).

or injury to man, is the great object set before his followers. The practical denial of God the creator, and the narrowing down of human interest to the field of conduct within one's own control, has flattered the so-called common-sense of mankind, and made them content with a very feeble and futile ideal of peace and happiness. Buddhism is a kind of Positivism, without the motto, "Live for others," which the latter has borrowed from Christianity. The Buddha, indeed, had great sympathy for mankind, and many Buddhists, like him, have been ardent self-denying missionaries [80], and have doubtless reaped the reward of their devotion. But his doctrine sets up the purely individual object of perfection of self as the end of life, without any reference to God, or to the good of other souls. The Positivist equally omits the glory of God as a moral motive, but lays great stress on our absolute duty to humanity, a belief which is indeed illogical and in-

---

[80] The following words are attributed to Gotama just before his famous sermon at Isipatana, near Benares:—

"I now desire to turn the wheel of the excellent Law.
For this purpose I am going to that city of Benares
To give light to those enshrouded in darkness,
And to open the gate of immortality to men."

See Rhys Davids' *Buddhism*, p. 43 ; and cp. *Sacred Books, Buddhist Suttas*, vol. xi. pp. 146 foll. The same energetic missionary spirit appeared in the purer school of Buddhism, the Hînâyana, the system of the "small conveyance." The Mahâyana, or school of the "great conveyance," produced a very different type, that of metaphysical subtlety. See E. J. Eitel's *Buddhism: Three Lectures*, pp. 37 foll., 2nd ed. (Honkong, 1873). King Asoka established a board for foreign missions, which he supported with his political influence, and his own son, Mahendra, went as a missionary to Ceylon: *ibid.*, p. 19.

VII.] *Selfishness of Buddhist Doctrine of Merit.* 269

effective without belief in God, but certainly renders the Positivist scheme of morals superior to that of the Buddhist. It is true that the latter is bound to respect and help other men, but (theoretically) this is only a means to increase his own merit; and therefore gratitude for generous acts is not necessary, since the merit of the act—which is in his eyes the only thing worth considering—rests entirely with him who does the kindness.

Hence Sin is viewed as a misfortune, which happens to you and delays your perfection, rather than as an offence against God or man, and it is even possible to keep a daily profit and loss account of merit and demerit, as is done by some Chinese Buddhists [81].

In consequence of this theory of sin and merit, based on the absence of a Creator, there are no primary motives to good conduct except fear or self-love. It rests with a man's self whether he will save himself now, or in some future rebirth; whether he will barter a limited period of punishment in hell for so much present indulgence. The moral Law, indeed, exists outside him, and the unseen world and its terrors is very real to him; but the execution of the Law depends entirely on his own determination. No one suffers except himself by his non-fulfilment of it, or, at least, the suffering of others makes no difference to him, except as it interferes with his acquisition of merit. There is no real solidarity of in-

[81] R. Spence Hardy, *Manual of Buddhism,* p. 507 (Lond., 1853); Eitel, *Lectures,* p. 63. On merit-making in Siam see the interesting observations of a modern Buddhist in H. Alabaster's *Wheel of the Law,* pp. 53 foll. (Lond., 1871).

terests between man and man here or hereafter. How attractive such a theory may be to human selfishness is obvious to any one who will think of what he himself is like in his meaner moments.

Another reason for the spread of Buddhism in the Eastern world is to be found in the tedium of life and the enjoyment of simple inactivity, which a Western can hardly understand as a motive prevailing over great masses of men. This can only have been felt where the idea of endless transmigration has taken a firm hold of the imagination, and been long believed without an effort. In countries where this is the case,—as in India after the Vedic period,—the merely negative rest of Nirvāna, and the absence of all activity and sense of want, comes as a great relief. According to the most probable theory of original Buddhism, entrance into Nirvāna was to be found in this life in the cessation of all ignorance and desire [82], to be followed after death by extinction of name and form, differing little, if at all, from absolute annihilation [83]. Human nature has naturally

---

[82] See Appendix I.

[83] Professor Max Müller calls attention to the more positive meaning of Nirvāna as a state of life in this world, and supposes that Buddha himself held a view somewhat more like the one now popular in Buddhist countries of the state after death, which was subsequently given up by his more metaphysical followers. "It represented the entrance of the soul into rest, a subduing of all wishes and desires, indifference to joy and pain, to good and evil, an absorption of the soul in itself, and a freedom from the circle of existences from birth to death, and from death to a new birth."—See *Buddhist Nihilism*, in *Selected Essays*, vol. ii. p. 305, and other Essays in that volume. Buddha's own view must at present remain uncertain. According to the *Sutta-Nipáta*, however, when

VII.] *Doctrine of Nirvāna.* 271

revolted from this prospect, and perhaps the majority of Buddhists have either ceased to desire Nirvāna as a practical object (as in Siam)[84], or they have turned it into a positive state of happiness, something like the Moslem paradise, as in Tibet and China[85].

But whether Nirvāna be considered as absolutely negative or not, the whole tendency of the Buddhist system is to set the highest moral value on an anti-social state of indolence and inactivity—to stamp despair of the world with the whole force of its approval. Gotama's original idea was apparently that of a houseless hermit-life of absolute apathy[86], which soon passed

asked "if consciousness would exist," he replied that "as a flame, blown about by the violence of the wind, goes out, and cannot be reckoned as existing, even so a Muni, delivered from name and body, disappears, and cannot be reckoned (as existing)." ... "For him who has disappeared there is no form; that by which they say he is, exists for him no longer." (*Sacred Books*, vol. x. pt. 2, pp. 198, 199.)

[84] Alabaster, *l. c.* p. xxxviii., says: "The ordinary Siamese never troubles himself about Nirwana, he does not even mention it. He believes virtue will be rewarded by going to heaven (Sawan), and he talks of heaven, and not of Nirwana. Buddha, he will tell you, has entered Nirwana, but, for his part, he does not look beyond Sawan."

[85] The Paradise of the Western Heaven, believed in by the worshippers of Amitâbha Buddha, is well described in Eitel's *Lectures*, pp. 97 foll. He thinks it may have had its origin "in Gnostic or Persian ideas, influencing the Buddhism of Cashmere and Nepaul," *ib.*, p. 102. Cp. Edkins, *Religion in China*, p. 99; *Chinese Buddhism*, pp. 233 foll., &c.

[86] According to the *Sutta-Nipâta* (see Fausböll's *Introduction*, p. xv.), the highest life is that of the Muni, "one who forsakes the world and lives in a houseless state, because from house-life arises defilement. .... He is not pleased nor displeased with anything. He is indifferent to learning. He does not cling to good or evil. He has cut off all passion and all desire. He is

into a Sangha, or brotherhood of mendicants (bhikshus). Of course laymen had also to be tolerated, but only as an afterthought, and in a secondary degree of virtue. Women also were admitted after a time to take the vows, but (it is said) that they cannot attain Nirvāna without being first reborn as men [87].

Buddhism thus differs from all other religious systems, which have become popular, in being founded on monasticism and developed out of it. In other religions it is an accretion, not a necessary part of the life. They can do just as well without it as with it. But should men decline any longer to take the yellow robe, or should the world cease to provide the monks with the daily bread, on which they live without working for themselves, the whole system must collapse [88]. Buddhism is thus, even more than other voluntary societies which we have mentioned, profoundly anti-social. The human race exists that there may be monks; and the object of the monastic life is to annihilate the race. This is indeed to make a solitude and call it peace.

Of course the system is not fully carried out. The monastic life may be laid down at pleasure, and is not a lifelong yoke on those who find they have no vocation for it. In some countries the robe is assumed for a short period of life by the greater part of the population. The Buddhist re-assertion of

free from marks and possessionless." He is without consciousness or sensation, and without breathing, i.e. lives in a state of absolute apathy.

[87] Eitel's *Lectures*, p. 63: cp. p. 111 of the same book.
[88] See the remarks of a "modern Buddhist" in Alabaster's *Wheel of the Law*, p. 54.

VII.]   *Character of Buddhism.*   273

human freedom has also, in the earlier centuries of its propagation, led to great and often beneficent activity. To it is due the building of stone temples of striking architecture, the erection of monuments of very remarkable sculpture, the building of valuable tanks, the foundation of hospitals, the writing of chronicles and inscriptions,—not to speak of the more religious movements of councils and missions. Buddhist literature, though full of tedious repetitions, and wanting in higher poetical elements, is comparatively natural and popular; its teaching is suited to the ears of common men, and consists largely of fables or parables and illustrations from life [89].

This activity has now, to a great extent, ceased. The Law is little understood by those who read it, much less by those who listen, and missionary energy is all but extinct. The teaching in Buddhist schools is very elementary and trifling, and little is written of any value [90]. Superstition has settled down again

---

[89] It is now matter of general knowledge that much of the collection of Planudes (in the fourteenth century), known to us as Æsop's Fables, is Buddhist in origin, being founded on the *Gātakas*, in which the Buddha in some previous birth is the hero of every tale. See Rhys Davids' *Buddhist Birth Stories,* pp. xxix. foll.; and cp. Max Müller *on the Migration of Fables,* in *Selected Essays,* vol. i. pp. 500—547. The *Gātaka* stories themselves may be earlier or later than Gotama. Dr. Frankfurter has seen a MS. in which the moral verses exist apart from the fables. See Appendix I.

[90] Mr. Alabaster replies very inaptly to M. St. Hilaire's criticism of the literary incapacity of Buddhist nations (*Le Buddha et sa Religion,* p. 180, Paris, 1866, referred to in *Wheel of the Law,* pp. liii., liv.), by instancing the literature of China and Japan, countries which are only Buddhist in a very partial manner. He refutes his own statement as far as Siam is concerned, on p. 4 of

T

upon the common people wherever Buddhism prevails, often (as in Ceylon) in the gross form of the worship of evil spirits; and the degradation and ignorance of Northern Buddhism is almost proverbial [91]. The impressions we receive of Buddhist countries differ, no doubt, somewhat according to the character and position of the reporters, but on the whole we cannot be wrong in charging Buddhism with terrible mental apathy, and practical unfruitfulness. It has been said that this is due to climate. But Buddhism, as we have seen, could once be active; and native criti-

---

his own book, both from his own observation, and that of the Siamese statesman whose work he is translating. The latter says: "The course of teaching at present followed in the temples is unprofitable." "Our Siamese literature is not only scanty, but nonsensical," &c.

Mr. Alabaster does not deny the second charge, that Buddhism is incapable of organising equitable and intelligent societies, but only retorts with some remarks upon French politics, and the want of happiness in European states.

[91] Sir James Emerson Tennant wrote in 1850, in his *Christianity in Ceylon:* "Both socially and in its effect upon individuals, the result of the system in Ceylon has been apathy, almost approaching to infidelity. Even as regards the tenets of their creed, the mass of the population exhibit the profoundest ignorance, and manifest the most irreverent indifference. In their daily intercourse and acts, morality and virtue, so far from being apparent in practice, are barely discernible as the exception, &c. (p. 228)." "The Buddhist priests connive at demon worship, because their efforts are ineffectual to suppress it; and the most orthodox Singhalese, whilst they confess its impropriety, are still driven to resort to it in all their fears and afflictions (pp. 231, 232)." The expression of the priests or monks in Ceylon and elsewhere, is described by several writers as one of mental inertness, approaching idiotcy. (R. Spence Hardy, *Eastern Monachism*, pp. 311, 312. Lond., 1860.)

Northern Buddhism is picturesquely described in Eitel's *Three Lectures*, pp. 84 foll.

cism of its effects in China shews how much it may alter character irrespective of external conditions. To the Confucianist, as well as to the Christian, it appears as foolishly destructive of what is natural and useful, through fear of the misuse, and as fatal to a performance of social and domestic duty [92].

Buddhism has been extirpated in the country of its birth, and we are inclined to think that this fate has not been undeserved. Better even the degraded theism of the Brāhmans than the elevation of man above God,—of this religion without a basis and without a hope. Hopeless as it is for the individual, so also it foresees its own extinction. Gotama (it is said) prophesied that in five thousand years his relics would be burnt up, and all knowledge of his doctrines would disappear from off the earth. It is also a belief that as long as the system flourishes in the sacred land of Ceylon, it will flourish everywhere; but when it falls there it will fall throughout the world [93]. God has given us this sacred land, the key, as it were, to the religion of five hundred millions. If we have faith in God and in the worth of our own lives, as His instruments and subjects; if we will use the means of Buddha, the pure persuasion of holy words, and the example of a self-denying and compassionate life, we may win back to belief

[92] On this Confucianist criticism, see Edkin's *Chinese Buddhism*, pp. 200, 201. Dr. Legge has kindly pointed out to me an interesting Chinese comment on this subject, which he has quoted in the notes to *The Announcement about Drunkenness* in the *Shú King* (*Chinese Classics*, vol. iii. pt. 2, p. 402, Honkong, 1865).

[93] For these traditions, see R. Spence Hardy, *Eastern Monachism*, pp. 430, 431.

in their Creator, not the men of this land only, but an almost innumerable multitude of immortal souls.

Such, then, is the failure of these great human efforts to attain peace by bringing religion to bear upon society. Men have tried to secure order without regard to Truth, and have ended in simple idolatry of outward Tranquillity. They have attempted to impose a minimum of Truth by force, and have bound society in chains. They have withdrawn from the world, and cultivated what they held for Truth in anti-social secrecy or selfish retirement. They have tried all these methods, with grand opportunities and on a broad scale. The religion of Rome, Islam, and Buddhism represent enormous forces and vast external successes; but the Peace which they have preached is no Peace proceeding from God, no Peace for man.

LECTURE VIII.

ST. JOHN xiv. 27.

Peace I leave with you, My peace I give unto you: not as the world giveth, give I unto you. Let not your heart be troubled, neither let it be afraid.

THE PEACE OF THE CHURCH AS WORTHY OF GOD WHO GIVES IT AND AS SATISFYING THE NEEDS OF MAN.

Recapitulation.—I. Notes of the Church as representing the Divine Nature: (1) *Unity*, (2) *Holiness*, (3) *Catholicity*.

(1.) *Unity*, its double sense, singleness and concord.—Other systems based on human concord.—The Church rests on the Unity of the Blessed Trinity.—Difficulty of present disunion.—Reference to the invisible Church not a sufficient reply.—Answer, 1. the early Church was visibly one.—Tübingen theory not borne out by facts.—2. Unity, on points of faith still very profound.—The schismatic temper, a sort of check on heresy.—3. Prospects of future unity, much advanced by the loss of secular power.—A new period of history began in 1870.—Position of the Church of Rome.—Of our own Church.—The Royal Supremacy.—Future conflict on fundamental truths. — Possible mediation by Church of England.

(2.) *Holiness*, not self-culture or outward law, but the assimilation of divine life.—Coincidence of obedience and freedom in Christ.—Approach to it in Christians, especially near death.—Gradual sanctification of nations.—Christianity and national character. — Christian legislation. — Constantine. — Self-corrective power.—Repentance for negro slavery.—Other social reforms.

(3.) *Catholicity*, an image of God's omnipotence and omnipresence.—Definition of St. Cyril of Jerusalem. — 1. Influence of the Church on *action* in social and civil life.—The Crusades.—2. Influence on *thought* in doctrine of the Logos.—Necessary overthrow of Scholasticism.—Successive tendencies to Deism,

Pantheism, and Positivism.—Demand for a Christian philosophy.
—3. Education of *feeling*.—Art and Literature.—Call to repentance: work of religious orders.—Place of the charismata.
II. The Church as satisfying Human wants.—Symbolism of the Ark and its contents.—Contrast with Dionysiac enthusiasm.
(1.) *Doctrine.*—Faith and scepticism.—Theology recognizes all classes of fact.—Peace given to the Intellect.
(2.) *Sacraments.*—Analogies in heathenism.—Christian Sacraments "an extension of the Incarnation."—Practical value.—St. Cyprian on Baptism.—The Eucharist.—Other sacramental rites.
(3.) *Discipline.*—The Church called *Apostolic.*—The Gospels "the Institution of a Christian Ministry."—Realization of Christ's presence.—Practical influence.—Conclusion.

IN our last Lecture we sketched some of the most striking and characteristic attempts which have been made to secure the Peace and Happiness of mankind, first by means of social and political instruments, and then by the aid and influence of religion outside Christianity. Both, we saw, had failed; the first necessarily, because they confined their scheme of blessedness to this earth, "ad fructum pacis terrenæ in terrena civitate;" and even in this sphere they were found confessedly incompetent, either to prevent war, or to make life really happy.

The failure of those who attempted to secure Peace by means of religion was traced to different causes. Some, like many in ancient Greece and Rome, were found subordinating Faith and Truth to Expediency, and treating Religion as an instrument of police. Others, like Mahomet, limited themselves by a one-sided and retrogressive formula, and did violence to the conscience by persecution. Lastly, those who recognized the truth, that Religion, to have

VIII.]   *Worthy of the Nature of God.*   279

any moral worth, must be accepted by a voluntary act of Faith, were observed in practice to have an anti-social character. This is the case both with the smaller secret societies, and with the great monastic system of philosophy, which has been so strangely destined to occupy the larger part of Eastern Asia. The cynical worshipper of Imperial Rome, the bitter Moslem, who narrows down his belief in God to the proud and selfish utterances of a false prophet, and the hopeless, vacuous recluse of Buddhism, are striking and manifest types of the failure of human endeavours to build up a system of peace without the Spirit of God. We now turn to the brighter picture of the Peace which is given by the Church on earth, leading upward to the Church in heaven.

In treating this subject, we shall continue to follow the method previously adopted, and endeavour to display the gift of Peace, first, as worthy of Him who offers it as His own, saying, "Peace I leave with you, My peace I give unto you;" and, secondly, as the true satisfaction of the wants of man who receives it.

I.

The Gift of Peace as worthy of the Nature of God.

What are the attributes of the Divine Nature which are most clearly represented in the Church? They can, I think, best be described in the words of one of the oldest creeds[1], I believe "in One Holy

---

[1] The Creed of Jerusalem: see St. Cyril of Jerusalem, *Catechesis* xviii. at the beginning. The Creed of Constantinople runs:—

Catholic Church." Let us take the three attributes in the order in which they stand.

(1.) *Unity*, as a divine attribute, and as applied to the Church, is obviously capable of two senses. On the one hand, there is what we may call the primary sense of singleness in comparison with multiplicity, the one true God as opposed to the many false ones, the unique Church as contrasted with the variety of defective religious systems. On the other hand, it may mean oneness, in the secondary sense of harmony as opposed to discord, the internal concord of the divine nature as opposed to the vacillation of created wills, the Peace of the Church as contrasted with the strife of human societies. The first implies an external contrast, the second describes an internal state.

In both senses, unity is a mark or note of the Church, and the two naturally run into one another; as, for instance, in the great passage where St. Paul urges the Ephesians to "keep the unity (that is, concord) of the Spirit in the bond of peace:" and then adds the reason, "There is one (and only one) body and one spirit, even as ye are called in one hope of your calling; one Lord, one faith, one baptism, one God and Father of all, who is above all, and through all, and in you all" (Eph. iv. 3—6). It is important to remember this double sense of

---

"And in One Holy Catholic and Apostolic Church." The omission of "Holy" in the English "Nicene Creed" has been supposed accidental, but see *Church Quarterly Review*, viii. 378 foll., where it is ascribed to a critical use of the books on Councils open to the Reformers.

unity in thinking of the Church, because in the necessary connection of the two lies one of the radical differences between the Christian and other ideals of Peace. They approach the subject chiefly from the secondary sense of unity, namely, concord, and view it chiefly as the result of a co-operation of human wills. This is an obvious criticism on the merely state ideals, whose object is the fruit of earthly peace. It is true also of the polytheist or heathen, who regards religion as a national peculiarity, securing a certain earthly blessing to its followers. The Moslem scheme sounds grander from its proclamation of "one God," and yet it is bound fast to earth by its requirement of adhesion to Mahomet as the exponent of divine truth, and by its use of force to produce belief; while Buddhism is, as we have seen, more absolutely Pelagian and individual in its aims, more reckless of God and of a future life than any other religious system. The Church alone rests not upon man's ordinance or compact, but upon the divine unity. In every act and thought it takes us up to God. Its root is in the unity of the Blessed Trinity, into whose name every Christian is baptized, one in singleness of nature far above all creation, and one in the divine concord of love, which knows no will and no good outside the will and the blessedness of the common nature. It is unique, because there is but one God who has said to His people, "Look unto Me, and be ye saved, all the ends of the earth: for I am God, and there is none else" (Isaiah xlv. 22); and again, "I will dwell in them, and walk in them; and I will be their God, and they shall be My people" (2 Cor. vi. 16, &c.). It is united in love, because "God is love, and he that dwelleth in love dwelleth in God, and God in him" (1 John iv. 16).[2]

It will be said, indeed, by an objector, that "this attribute of unity is beautiful and God-like, and just such as we should expect in the body of Christ, but it is not possessed as a fact by the Church. Look at the divisions of Christendom; look at the secularity of some Churches, and the intrusion of the State into others, where Peace is only maintained by the Civil Power."

To this obvious difficulty the reply has been often made that visible unity is not to be expected in this world; that the Church never professes to be complete at any given moment of time, but lives as an heir of eternity; and that unity is an attribute rather of the invisible, than of the visible, body. Our atten-

---

[2] There is no doubt some very definite reason why the cube was chosen as the type of the dwelling of God, both in the Old Testament and the New. This was the form of the Holy of Holies, both in the Tabernacle and the Temple, and probably in the temple of Ezekiel (see the commentators on *Exod.* xxvi. compared with Josephus, *Ant.*, iii. 6, § 3, 4; 1 *Kings* vi. 20; *Ezek.* xli. 2 and 4, and Fergusson's interesting article, *Temple*, in *Smith's Bible Dictionary*). This, too, was the appearance of the heavenly city, the new Jerusalem, as described in *Rev.* xxi. 16. We may suppose that it was chosen (1) as a type of external strength, evenness, solidity, and compactness, somewhat as "four-square without a flaw" (τετράγωνος ἄνευ ψόγου) was to the Greeks the description of a perfect man (see the poem of Simonides in Plato's *Protagoras*, p. 339, alluded to by Aristotle, *Eth. Nic.*, i. 10, 11; *Rhet.*, iii. 11, 2). It is also (2) the simplest solid of three dimensions, length, breadth, and height; a type, therefore, of internal unity and co-equality. Cp. *Eph.* iii. 18.

tion is called off from earth to the unseen Communion of the Saints of all lands and all ages, whom God is gathering into his treasure-house of Paradise, and will one day exhibit in its perfect sum, when Christ returns to gather His own around Him, and to judge the world. But, easy as this explanation is, and comforting as the doctrine of the Communion of Saints, and of Christ's second coming must especially be in times of disunion, it is hardly satisfactory and complete. It is true, but not the whole truth. Rather we should reply to an objector, 1. that the visible Church for many centuries shewed a power of union which was a new thing in the world, and that this union lies at the basis of all Church-life; 2. that even in the present there is a deeper union of belief among Christians of all persuasions, than the appearance of discord produced by the different government of sects and churches would lead outsiders to believe; 3. that in the future the prospects of union are real and rational, however obscured at the present moment. Our Lord, indeed, prophesied that tares would be sown amid the wheat of His sacred field, and that both would grow together till the harvest. We cannot therefore expect a perfectly united Church, but we may expect and labour for a much greater measure of concord than we see at present.

1. The union of the early Christian Church is a fact which is specially remarkable when we consider the discordant social and religious elements out of which it was compacted. The chasms between Jew and Gentile, between freeman and slave, were greater than any with which most of us are fami-

liar. Yet in the first half of the second century of our era, within about a hundred years of the Ascension, the Catholic Church was established all round the Mediterranean sea, under the same form of episcopal government, and with a doctrine substantially the same as that now held among ourselves. The theory of the Tübingen school, of the long continuance of the strife between a so-called Petrine or Ebionite, and a Pauline or Gentile Christianity, will not bear serious examination, though it has served a useful purpose in drawing minute attention to the early records of Church History[3]. This detailed investigation has brought out most clearly the substantial unity of the early Church, and the readiness with which Catholic doctrine was accepted. He who is "our peace," made both Jew and Gentile one, broke down the middle wall of partition, and slew the enmity which divided them, even in the lifetime of the first Apostles (Eph. ii. 14 foll.). This is a topic upon which we cannot now enlarge; but what has once been under such difficult circumstances can be again. All sects and churches look to the early period of Church History as common ground. The more closely they study it, the greater will be their agreement: the more clearly they will see that visible unity, without absolute uniformity, is a natural and possible attribute of the Church.

2. Even at this moment the union of belief

---

[3] The English reader, who may possibly be unfamiliar with this theory, will find it explained and satisfactorily refuted in [Bp.] J. B. Lightfoot's *St. Paul and the Three*, an Essay attached to his Commentary on St. Paul's *Epistle to the Galatians*.

among Christians is very deep, far deeper than that of the superficial creeds which bind other men together. No sect has clearly established its right to the name of Christian which does not accept the most profound doctrines of the Trinity, the Incarnation, the Atonement, the Resurrection, Ascension, and Second Coming of Christ, the Inspiration and Authority of Holy Scripture, and the indwelling in some form or other of the Holy Spirit in the Church. As a sign of this faith the Sacraments of Baptism and Holy Communion are acknowledged as a bond of union by all except the Society of Friends, who are daily becoming a less important exception, while they still maintain a hold on central truths, and have done not a little for the cause of Christian peace and holiness. The Socinians and Unitarians, who cling to the skirts of Christianity, shew evident traces of their inability to hold their ground between supernatural religion and Deism, shifting readily from one into the other.

It is true that there is much individual doubt and even heresy, probably, in all Christian communions, but there is no powerful Church which is heretical on the fundamental doctrines of the faith. The great schisms are largely due to differences on points of doctrine such as the *Filioque*, which touch regions of theology of extreme difficulty, and do not bear very obviously on practical conduct; or they have turned in a great measure upon questions of Church government and discipline. And where more practical differences of doctrine have been the main cause, reunion has been seriously hindered by the intrusion of the secular spirit on the one side,

and the resentment against it on the other. But
even these deplorable and humiliating divisions bear
witness to the intense reality of belief in the Christian body; its desire for the primary, if not the secondary kind of unity; its wish to hold fast even in
minor points to the Faith once for all delivered to
the Saints. Nor can it be denied that the schismatic
temper, ungrateful and captious though it is, has
often acted as a critical check upon heresy. No
Church feels itself absolutely free to follow its own
developments. It has to meet opposition and censure,
and to defend itself in the open court of Christian
controversy. It has to fall back upon the common
ground of Scripture, and even in the midst of its
aberrations it must confess that there is a general
unity above that of its own portion of the field. It
is hardly possible for professing Christians to fall behind and below the level of those great doctrines
which we have mentioned. The Church can never
wake up, as it did after the Council of Rimini (A.D.
359), and find itself groaning under the shame of an
Arian creed. There is, indeed, a real danger of novel
falsities in another direction. But even if one portion of the Church invents new dogmas, it cannot
claim the consent of the Christian world without
a glaring and obvious untruthfulness, which in the
end must tell upon its own members. We may
hope that a sense of this unreality may, in some day
of grace, be a reason for the withdrawal and reconsideration of the doctrines in question.

The operation of this check is visible already to
some extent. It will, no doubt, be felt more de-

cidedly in the future, when superstition passes away before a wider diffusion of intelligence and civil liberty, and when what are now comparatively small bodies (like some of those which make up the Anglican communion) have attained their full growth and power.

3. This thought leads us on to a forecast of the future. Here, as we have said, we have real and rational, though not brilliant, prospects of closer unity. The main causes of schism are two, and those intimately connected:—1. The intrusion of the secular spirit into the Church; and 2. its correlative opposite, the Pelagian or individual tendency, which dislikes the whole principle of human mediation. The Church of Rome has been the great offender under the first head, by turning her own spiritual power into a secular one: while the Eastern and Anglican Churches, with the Lutherans of the Continent, have been more in danger of treating secular and royal power as if it were spiritual. The Protestant sects, on the other hand, have resented this intrusion of secularity, in whatever form, by their tendency to the contrary error of denying the spirituality of the body, and localizing it in the individual. But the cloud of misconception which has made such different errors so common seems slowly lifting with altered circumstances.

In the first place secular rule, which has been so closely associated with the Church since the time of Constantine, has all but entirely departed from it. The temporal power of the papacy, which was the most distinct embodiment of this union, passed away about eleven years ago as quietly and quickly as a dream[4]; but the abolition of the scattered remnants of spiritual jurisdiction in temporal affairs had been long in process throughout the world. With the Vatican Council, the last effort of Papal aggrandisement, and the entrance of the Italian troops into Rome, which followed it so closely, an entirely new period of Church History has begun[5]. In that Council the Court of Rome decreed her own destruction, by shewing the natural outcome of her tendency to spiritual pride in an act of flagrant self-assertion. Rome has done a grand work in the past as a centre of social power, keeping mankind together, and giving them a lift above the divisions of nationality[6]. For this work, we may presume, God has spared her for three centuries after the Council of Trent, when danger was so thick about her. He may spare her yet again. But as surely as Nebuchadnezzar pronounced his own degradation when he said, "Is

---

[4] The dogma of Infallibility was proclaimed at Rome, July 18, 1870, the same day that the declaration of war on the part of France was made known at Berlin. This opened Rome to the Italians by the withdrawal of French support; the troops entered the Porta Pia in September, and in October the city was annexed to the Italian kingdom. If the war was the result of Jesuitical or other Roman influence on French politics (as Bismarck asserted in 1874), the connection of the two events is even more striking. See his speech in the Prussian chamber, quoted in the *New Reformation*, p. 91.

[5] "Future historians," says Quirinus, "will begin a new period of Church history with July 18, 1870, as with October 31, 1517:" l. c., p. 90.

[6] Cp. the striking passage of Guizot, *Lecture* xii. p. 230, quoted by Dean Church, *Influences of Christianity on National Character*, p. 105; and Abp. Trench, *Mediæval Church History*, p. 154.

VIII.] *The Churches of Rome and England.* 289

not this great Babylon which I have built?" as surely as Herod Agrippa incurred the doom of those who suffer idolatrous adulation of themselves, so surely did the Pope's proclamation of his own Infallibility condemn him to the fate of those who ignore their own human frailty when exalted to the highest position as ministers of God. It may be long ere the full effect of this capital error is visible; but of this we are certain, that the sword of persecution, whoever henceforth may wield it, has for ever passed away from the grasp of the Roman Pontiff.

This revolution which has taken place with regard to the Church of Rome extends more or less to all other Churches having a connection with secular power. We cannot tell exactly how far the change will go, but it is morally certain that toleration for all opinions not absolutely anti-social must be granted, sooner or later, in every civilized country. How far a national profession of religion will be given up as a result of this toleration, is a problem likely to be decided differently by different nations, according to their greater or less common-sense. Where it still happily continues, it will probably be rather in the form of a distinctly realized compact between two separate powers, than the confusion of offices which at present to some extent exists. The Royal Supremacy, for instance, would be less dangerous to the peace of mind both of Churchmen and Dissenters, if it could be realized as the fatherly authority of the highest lay dignitary of the Church, a nursing fatherhood like that of Hezekiah or Josiah, not the prerogative of the Sovereign as a representative of merely secular power, who, like Nero, "bears the sword" to enforce civil obedience upon all his subjects. Such a power as the last must indeed exist and control the Church, as far as it possesses temporalities; not, however, as a result of the Royal Supremacy, but as a necessary part of all sovereignty, belonging to the office of a ruler, whatever his religion. But the Royal Supremacy belongs only to the Sovereign as a Christian, as the member of a spiritual, not a secular body; and if exercised as such,—for example, by providing that spiritual causes should only be tried by Christian judges, fully and freely approved by the Church and familiar with her laws,—the strongest objections which are made to it would vanish.

However this may be, it is clear that in any case one great barrier to union will be removed by the loss of any power of persecution on the part of the Church. The transference of power to her enemies, and to the enemies also of all dogmatic belief, which has in some cases taken place, ought also to strengthen internal union. It is clear that the great conflict of the immediate future will be one on the most fundamental doctrines of religion and morals, on the existence of God, on the truth of a future life of rewards and punishments, and on the supremacy of an external law of conduct. A feeling of agreement on these points, joined to a clearer consciousness of the reason of this agreement, ought to drive all Christians closer together in the face of a common enemy. The value of unity, and of the blessings

VIII.] *Duty of English Churchmen.* 291

which we receive through the Church, must needs grow plainer in the midst of this conflict. Men will learn that without revelation they could not even be certain of these primary truths, and that without the grace which comes through the body of Christ, the highest discipline of society cannot be long maintained[7]. They will cease to cling to their mere individualism, and will no longer think it strange that God should have ordained a continuous ministry from above, when they perceive its value as a guarantee of purity of doctrine and independence of moral teaching. When the great obstacle of individualism is removed, it is probable that an independent body like the Anglican Church will grow enormously in strength, and will be able to influence the future of Christendom as a mediating power in a way as yet scarcely conceived.

Such an expectation does not want striking analogies in its favour. When we think how widely the English Constitution has served as a political model for other countries; when we remember how the material inventions of our engineers have assisted the friendly intercourse of all nations, and the commerce of wealth and knowledge by land and

[7] Renan, for instance, admits the danger—though too much in the spirit of Polybius and Varro—in the following striking words:—
"Jouissons de la liberté des fils de Dieu; mais prenons garde d'être complices de la diminution de vertu qui menaçerait nos sociétés, si le christianisme venait à s'affaiblir. Que serions nous sans lui? Qui remplacera ces grandes écoles de sérieux et de respect telles que Saint-Sulpice, ce ministère de dévouement des Filles de la Charité? Comment n'être pas effrayé de la sécheresse de cœur et de la petitesse qui envahissent le monde?"—*Les Apôtres*, p. lxiii. ed. 1, 1866.

sea,—why should we fear to imagine that our Church may have a like influence on Christian unity? It is, and must remain in some details, the Church of a single nation, but it may nevertheless be a source of light and hope to other nations; a shining proof that order and liberty, faith and reason, can be united in a bond of Christian love.

In the meantime it is ours to cultivate a spirit of unity, to recognize God's work wherever it appears, to look upon those that are separated from us with eyes of affection, to admit that they sometimes have gifts and energies that we have not, and that they realize fragments of truth of which we have lost sight. The time has not yet come for a fusion, except in some small degree. We have a precious deposit of primitive truth which we have no right to surrender, a heritage of catholicity and order which we must not part with for an artificially-compacted unity. But in God's good time will come the drawing together of all who really labour for peace.

(2.) The attribute of *Holiness*, like that of Unity, does not take its rise from human nature, but from divine grace. The moral beauty of Christian life is not a development of our ordinary powers, such as the Utopian and the Socialist dream of, whereby all goodness shall be brought out by culture and civilization, as graceful varieties and delicate blossoms are raised by careful gardening from a coarse and common flower. Mere human goodness of this kind is little to be relied upon. It makes a fair outside, but it is liable to sudden collapse, and to be destroyed by a violent burst of wildness and intemperance from within. At its best, this orderly, social sort of goodness is closely akin to selfishness, to a love of comfort, to a wrong view of pain and suffering, and is ignorant or intolerant of the fact of sin. Hence those who make morality spring from below, not from above, generally avoid the term holiness altogether, or travesty and misapply it as the Positivists do in speaking of the "holy city of Paris."

Nor is the holiness of the Church, on the other hand, a result of law and discipline, imposed from the outside by a legislator. Discipline is indeed a necessary part of Church-life, but the object of the kingdom of God is not outward but inward fulfilment of the Law, by assimilation of a Divine life. Holiness to the Christian means union with Christ, justification by faith in Him, forgiveness of sins, followed by the sanctifying work of the Holy Spirit. The Church does not look upon Christ so much as a Lawgiver or Founder of a religion, but rather as being the religion in His own person. The Church is not only His kingdom, but His body, in which His heart beats and His divine life circulates. To be holy is to partake of this life, in which there is an absolute coincidence of free-will and obedience, an acceptance of sacrifice as the natural work of a human being.

For just as in the Unity of the divine nature there is no before and after, no priority of will to goodness, or of goodness to will, but a perfect eternal coincidence of the two, so it is also in the life of Christ. In it there is no strife of motives; but He obeys, and yet at the same moment acts with perfect freedom.

Thus He tells us, "My meat is to do the will of Him that sent Me, and to finish His work" (John iv. 34), that is to say, it is a perfect satisfaction of His own desires; and of His atoning sacrifice, of laying down His life, He says: "No man taketh it from Me, but I lay it down of Myself. I have power to lay it down, and I have power to take it again. This commandment have I received of My Father" (John x. 18).

The Church, then, is a society of the redeemed, of those who look to Christ for forgiveness of sin, and who strive to become like unto Christ, and to be one with Him. "Being justified by faith we have peace with God." This is the ideal of holiness, which is very far from being attained by the majority of Christians. But the reality is reached by some, the glory of it rests in their better moments on a much larger number, and the germ is present, we believe, in all. The hidden life, in the stir and bustle of the world, cannot, perhaps, be displayed very frequently; but it is attractive even when it is covert, and often when we mourn in the chamber of a dying friend do we first learn that the secret of his winning, magnetic power was a constant remembrance of the presence of God, a robe of holiness worn beneath the outer garb. Often, too, as death draws near, do Christian men and women really seem to touch upon that perfection for which their lives have been but a preparation, losing all their former reluctance to mould their wills entirely by God's will. How many have expired with "Thy will be done" on their lips and in their hearts! How many martyrs have received their sentence of death, like St. Cyprian, with a simple "Deo gratias," more eloquent than the most fervent exhortation which they may have longed to utter[8]! How many, like Monica, the mother of St. Augustine, have died in a foreign land, giving up the cherished thought of burial among their dearest kindred, and saying, "Nothing is far from God[9]!" How many have left their fondest plans unfinished, resigning them contentedly into the hands of Him who gave the power to begin them—"Qui cœpit opus iste perficiet[10]!" How many strong and ambitious men have gently met the hard fate that came suddenly to cut short a grand career! We may perhaps recollect Lord Strafford's speech upon the scaffold: "I come here to submit to the judgment that is passed against me: I do it with a very quiet and contented mind: I do freely forgive all the world; a forgiveness, not from the teeth outward, but from my heart. I speak it in the presence of Almighty God, before whom I stand, that there is not a dis-

---

[8] *Cæcilii Cypriani Acta Proconsularia*, cap. 4. The proconsul read the sentence, "Thascium Cyprianum gladio animadverti placet." Cyprianus episcopus dixit: "Deo gratias." He had hoped, it seems, to be inspired to prophecy, writing in his last letter (*Ep.* 81), "quodcumque enim sub ipso confessionis momento confessor episcopus loquitur, aspirante Deo, ore omnium loquitur;" but no such gift of prophecy was vouchsafed to him. Cp. Bp. E. W. Benson's article, *Cyprianus*, in Smith and Wace's *Dict. of Chr. Biograyhy*, vol. i. p. 754.

[9] St. Augustine, *Confessions*, ix. 11.

[10] "Confidens hoc ipsum, quia qui cœpit in vobis opus bonum, perficiet usque in diem Christi Jesu." *Philip.* i. 6, Vulg. The words in the text were used by S. Francis de Sales on his death-bed. See his *Life*, by Mrs. Lear, p. 264.

pleasing thought that ariseth in me against any man[11]." This was surely a triumph of Christian holiness; and hardly less striking are the words of Joseph Scaliger, whom perhaps we think of merely as a scholar of enormous learning and overbearing temper: "I begin to feel and perceive the joys of eternal life. I shall soon behold Him who was sacrificed for men; I long for the blessed sight. All else to me is dross: there is nothing that could make me wish to live one hour longer[12]."

These are visible proofs of the peace of God ruling in single hearts. Nor are they wanting in larger bodies of men. The precepts to "honour all men" (1 Pet. ii. 17), to see in every human being, however weak, a "brother for whom Christ died" (1 Cor. viii. 11), an immortal soul capable of serving God in heavenly glory, have slowly made themselves felt in general politics as well as in private life. There is something like a gradual sanctification of nations, however incomplete it appears when measured by an ideal standard. Christianity gave to the Greek races, for instance,—as the many centuries of Byzantine history go to prove,—a seriousness and earnestness of character, a sense of equality and brotherhood, a permanence of resolute hope, which philosophy had quite failed to impart to them. It has stirred the powerful, sluggish souls of the Latin races, and given

[11] Quoted more at length by Dr. Mozley, *Lord Strafford* in *British Critic*, vol. xxxiii. p. 534, 1843 = *Essays*, vol. ii. p. 101, 1878.

[12] See Dr. W. Kay, *Promises of Christianity*, in the Calcutta *Missionary*, vol. iv. p. 261; since reprinted (Parkers, 1855), and containing much material bearing on the subject of this lecture.

them a new capacity of the affections, of feeling, loving and imagining. It has developed in the Teutons of the north that respect for truthfulness, manliness, and hard work, that reverence for law and liberty, that delight in the pure and tender charities of home, of which the germs were discerned by Tacitus[13]. Such—as has been well remarked—are its prominent moral effects upon the three greatest of western peoples, and a similar influence may be observed in all others. It is true that much remains still undone, that there are survivals of brutal and ferocious instincts in all Christian nations, and that some of the greatest crimes, and the most fatal blunders, have followed a misuse of what were taken to be Christian principles. Yet we can most surely trace in history not only a direct carrying out of Gospel precepts in legislation, but also an ever germinant sense of right, lying dormant perhaps for centuries, but ready to spring up, to suggest improvement, and to correct mistake and crime, so that no Christian nation is without hope from within.

If we look to direct effects, it is certain that the legislation of the Roman empire after Constantine bears witness to a sense of the honour of humanity and of the holiness of human life, very different from that which was before perceptible. We observe at once the prohibition of infanticide, a better treatment of prisoners, an abolition of certain atrocities

---

[13] I have here summed up the thesis of Dean Church's three Lectures, *On some Influences of Christianity upon National Character*, (Lond., 1873,) to which the reader is referred for many beautiful illustrations.

of punishment, an attempt to stop the gladiatorial spectacles, the suppression or alleviation of the most degrading kinds of slavery and the facilitation of enfranchisement, the weakening of the despotic power of the father of a family, the elevation of the law of marriage, the check put upon divorce and the like [14].

Slavery was not, indeed, prohibited directly by any precept of the Gospel. It was a greater triumph, a wiser and nobler policy, to effect this momentous revolution in peace, to draw out the good side of the relation, and make the master gentle and the slave hopeful and courageous, than to proclaim a servile war. But the abolition of slavery has been the necessary, though gradual, result of any real assimilation of Christian principles [15].

It is true that a new kind of servitude is an invention of Christian Europe, of English and Spanish adventurers; and that negro slavery in the West Indies was even promoted, by Las Casas and others, on distinct grounds of a mistaken Christian philanthropy. But the conscience of Christendom, though it seemed to sleep, at last awoke, and the general

[14] I have put together some details of this legislation in my article on *Constantine*, in Smith and Wace's *Dict. of Chr. Biography*, vol. i. pp. 635—637.

[15] On the relation of Christianity to slavery the reader should specially consult H. Wallon, *Histoire de l'esclavage dans l'Antiquité*, tom. iii. chaps. i. and viii.—x., New. Ed. (Paris, 1879.) Cp. also Prof. Goldwin Smith's powerful pamphlet, *Does the Bible Sanction American Slavery?* (Oxford, 1863.) The Ellerton Essay for 1869, *Slavery as affected by Christianity*, by E. S. Talbot (now Warden of Keble College), contains a judicious summary of the whole subject of ancient and modern slavery. It is, unfortunately, only privately printed.

VIII.] *Self-corrective power of Christianity.* 299

abolition of slavery and the repression of the slave-trade is the work mainly of this century. The germinant self-corrective power of our religion asserted itself, and the terrible reproach has been rolled away. The great crime and the great blunder has been repented of, and the sacrifice, we trust, accepted.

It would be easy to point to other cases of Christian principle gradually asserting itself to sanctify society. We see it, for instance, in the different treatment of the lower races, where Christian perceptions are strong, and where they are weak. Extermination, depression and contempt on the one side, preservation, sympathy and elevation on the other, mark the two opposite modes of treatment. Professing Christians have, alas! often been guilty of the one, but scarcely any but Christians have attained to the other [16].

Much yet remains to be done to roll away other reproaches, as, for instance, with regard to national

---

[16] On this subject see Sir Bartle Frere's Lecture, referred to above, pp. 311—316.

The fair treatment of the Ainos by the Japanese government, is described by Miss Bird, *Unbeaten Tracks in Japan*, vol. ii.; but they are left, nevertheless, in a state of hopeless ignorance.

The evil influence of Europeans on the native races, is well described by Gerland, *Das Aussterben der Naturvölker*, which should be read by all missionaries. He lays e.g. great stress on the depressing, melancholy effect of an overbearing civilization suddenly transplanted into the midst of an uncultured race. It is now fairly understood that a very gradual alteration in the mode of social life is necessary, if religion is to take a firm hold of a people. We hear from all quarters—India, Japan, New Zealand, Melanesia, Zanzibar, &c.,—of the difficulty of this problem. The history of the conversion of Saxon England is one of the most hopeful examples of what may be done to meet it.

intemperance, the opium traffic [17], and the protection of women [18]. Great blunders are made still, and great crimes committed and palliated for a time. But the conscience is not absolutely dormant. Self-interest and selfishness will be driven to take refuge in corner after corner, and in the end holiness and justice will prevail. Or at least, if they do not, history teaches in the largest letters, that punishment and destruction must fall on the guilty nation. Christ came to bring peace, but He also came to bring a sword. Holiness He will have; and the sacrifice, if not salted with salt, will be salted at least with fire.

(3.) *Catholicity* is the third of those great attributes of the Church, which reflect the image, and testify to the indwelling, of the Divine Nature. As the Church

---

[17] For an eloquent and well-grounded statement of the national guilt of this traffic, the reader may be referred to an article on *The Opium Trade with China* in the *Church Quarterly Review* for Oct., 1876, vol. iii. pp. 1—33 [an expansion of a paper read before the Oxford Missionary Association of Graduates by Mr. H. S. Holland], and, for suggestions as to what may be done to clear ourselves from it, to Sir Bartle Frere's paper read at the Newcastle Church Congress, Oct. 5, 1881, and a letter of Dr. Kay's in the London *Guardian*, Oct. 26, 1881. Sir B. Frere advises, as a first step, giving up the Calcutta monopoly, and assimilating the practice in Eastern India to that in Bombay and elsewhere. Dr. Kay, Dr. Legge, and Cardinal Manning advocate the retention of the monopoly, and a gradual reduction of opium cultivation on our side, under treaty with China permitting her to prohibit the import entirely within a given number of years.

[18] For a summary of what has been done by legislation for the protection of women, and for suggestions of further measures, see the " (confidential) statements prepared for the Committee of the Lower House of the Convocation of Canterbury" by Admiral A. P. Ryder, forming Appendices A. and B. to the *Chronicle of Convocation*, session May 17, &c., 1881, published by Rivingtons.

is one, because the Blessed Trinity is one, in singleness and concord, and as it is Holy by the assimilation of the Divine Life, so it is Catholic because God is omnipotent, omnipresent, and eternal, and because Christ has been exalted in His human nature to the right hand of God, and has thence sent forth the Holy Spirit into all our hearts. Catholicity is the working of that mighty uplifting power, that transcendant energy which raised our Lord from the dead, after that He had descended into the lower parts of the earth, and exalted Him far above all heavens, that He might fill all things from highest to lowest. It is the power of the Resurrection, that power of God, which "hath put all things under His feet, and gave Him to be head over all things to the Church, which is His body, the fulness of Him that filleth all in all" (Eph. i. 22, 23; iv. 9, 10, &c.).

"The Church is called Catholic," says St. Cyril of Jerusalem (in his *Catechetical Lectures*, xviii. 23), "because it extends through all the world, from one end of the earth unto the other; and because it teaches catholically, and without defect, all doctrines which ought to come to the knowledge of all men, both about things visible and invisible, in heaven and on earth; and because it subjects every race of men to true religion, both rulers and ruled, learned and unlearned; and because it universally treats and heals every species of sins that are committed by soul and body; and because it has in possession every kind of virtue that is named in deeds and words, and every sort of spiritual gifts."

To the notion of extent with which St. Cyril begins this summary, we should, I suppose, add universality of time, and so enlarge the idea of place as to include the invisible world; and then his fivefold description will be no imperfect picture of the ideal comprehensiveness of the Church. It embraces the whole world, visible and invisible, past, present, and future, the dead, as well as the living; it teaches and harmonises all truth; it disciplines all mankind, without distinction of race or class; it heals all sin; it consecrates every virtue and faculty of the soul. Merely to aim at this ideal is a Divine work; so broad in its scope and measure, that the name Catholic has often been chosen as the most distinctive epithet of the Church, as the one emphatic term which most fills the imagination, and stimulates the moral life.

Actual fulfilment falls no doubt very short of the ideal. Life, as we see it, is fragmentary, inchoate, and confused. God (as we are learning from all sides) does no work suddenly, but patiently, and, as we are apt to say, naturally. The simplest civilization is a work of long time, how long we can perhaps only guess. Much more does the work of the Church, a higher, holier, harder, less intelligible work, require many generations for its full issue. What the Church has done is only a foretaste, a prophecy of what it is to do. But think of what it has done, what it is clearly called to do in the great provinces of *action*, *thought*, and *feeling*, which embrace, in some sense, the whole of human life.

1. In the first place, the Church is the chief, though not the only, organ by which the human race has felt its common nature, and has been roused to *common action*. The Church has proclaimed the Fatherhood of God, of which men knew somewhat by nature,

with a fresh emphasis, and in a new sense. It has taught men of different castes and orders that they were all members of one family. It has penetrated into all the relations of life, and vivified them by a sense that they depend upon kinship through the eternal Father. It has specially given new strength to family ties, abolishing polygamy, and making each home a centre of purity. It has enforced the dignity and the absolute duty of labour, according to St. Paul's maxim, that "if any would not work, neither should he eat" (2 Thess. iii. 10; cp. 1 Thess. iv. 11). It has set its seal, not only on the more conspicuous and brilliant virtues, but on the social qualities of courtesy, cheerfulness, and contentment. It has led men to take an interest in society, and in the business of government, since we are "all members one of another." By its Councils, it demonstrated to the world the value of the system of representation; by its internal discipline, it has led the way to a more rational legislation; by its hospitals, its leper-houses, its penitentiaries, by its societies for the redemption of captives [19], by its homes and refuges for the distressed, the Church has proclaimed the worth of weak or degraded human lives, and that in centuries when it was not a little corrupt and darkened; by its schools and colleges it saved the culture of the old world from the destructive flood of barbarism; it has, for the most part, stood in the forefront of learning, and has never been content to fall entirely into the background; by its

---

[19] On such Societies during the Middle Ages, cp. Abp. Trench, *Mediæval Church History*, pp. 411—413.

missions, destined to make disciples of every people, it has broken down the barriers of nationality, binding all its members by subjection to one Lord, and by rules of conduct far higher than the laws or customs of earthly kingdoms.

That the organization thus created has been in many respects weak, and in many quarters maimed and broken, that the action has not always been an unmixed good, we know only too well. Sometimes the working of the deepest and most sacred emotion upon large bodies of men has been disfigured, as in the Crusades, by much that is selfish, and has ended in apparent failure. But the Crusades (which we may take as an example of these mixed effects of Christianity) were, nevertheless, a great common religious enterprise, full of happy consequence. To them is due a consciousness of unity among the nations of the West, like that which the tribes of Greece are said to have gained by combining in the Trojan war, a consciousness which all subsequent wars and jealousies have not destroyed [20]. It was surely a great, we may even say, an incalculable, gain, that Moslem arms, then threatening Western civilization, were driven back for two centuries from the walls of Constantinople. It would also be mere affectation and insensibility to what is noble to despise the religious consecration then given to the profession of arms, and the virtues of chivalry, which have done so much to make modern warfare better than it was of old. In spite of all mistakes, there

---

[20] Thucydides, i. 3. Cp. Abp. Trench, *Mediæval Church History*, pp. 142—144.

VIII.] *The Church and Philosophy.* 305

has been a healthy motion and a stir in all quarters of the Christian world, restlessly seeking for peace, the only temper that can give hope for the future.

2. In the world of *thought*, again, the Church has had an equally important mission, giving a wholly new coherence to knowledge and history by its doctrine of the Word made Flesh, the Divine Logos, who is manifested in the whole order of the Universe, and by whom we are invested with a glorious freedom, so that all things are ours in Him. We have not, indeed, by any means experienced the full light that issues from this doctrine. We can point, no doubt, with gratitude to the works of the early fathers, especially to the broad and generous grasp of this doctrine by the Church of Alexandria, and to the immense systematic labours of the mediæval schoolmen, as evidences of what has been done to found a universal Christian philosophy. But it is also true that, since the rise of the modern spirit in philosophy and the prominence given to the inductive method of investigation, the doctrine of the Logos has been too much thrown into the background, and the cold shadow of Deism has spread over great part of the intellect of Europe [21].

This seems at first sight most disheartening—a

[21] Bacon himself was not a Deist, but rather a man to whom the Biblical revelation was very real, and Mr. Wace goes so far as to state his opinion, "that the doctrine of the Logos is at the very root of Baconian thought." Nevertheless he was clearly and perhaps necessarily anxious to separate the provinces of religion and science, and it is worthy of remark, that his friend and secretary, Thomas Hobbes, was the father of Deism in England. The tendency of English natural philosophers to Arianism, when not distinctly to Deism, is also very marked.

withdrawal of Christ from the world of thought. Yet, even in this obscuration, faith must recognize the Divine agency of the Logos, preparing the way for a fuller and riper system. The scholastic philosophy, confusing the heterogeneous mass of mediæval doctrines with entire Catholic truth, and hampered with an excessive reverence for antiquity, had become a tyranny, a burden upon thought. Men were taught, *a priori*, how things ought to be, and must be; primary Christian truths, and secondary and one-sided developments were thrust upon students, with an equal assurance of certainty; notwithstanding some brilliant exceptions, the study of nature was neglected; and it was necessary to overthrow, or at least to veil, the dominant system, that men might see with their own eyes how things really were.

If sunlight for a time seemed withdrawn from the field of science, if men have since confined themselves too much to special studies, yet their merit is to have really worked, really to have interrogated nature, and to have laboured calmly and without fear or distraction [22]. The history of their work is also full of instruction and encouragement. Since the fall of the scholastic philosophy, to which Bacon so much contributed, the generalisations, commonly called the Laws of Nature, have been slowly and gradually built up. At first they struggled hard for tolera-

---

[22] On the absolute duty of work upon what is close about us, as set forth by Bacon, with reference to the commands to Adam in the early chapters of Genesis, see the excellent remarks of Mr. Wace, Note 7a, pp. 268—275, of his Bampton Lectures.

tion; then they won a difficult but complete victory; and again, when accepted, seemed likely to exercise as harsh and as stiff a tyranny as the *a priori* systems which they supplanted. But a corrective has gradually been supplied in the historical and comparative methods,—the observation of succession and analogy,—which have, in recent times, so largely supplemented the purely inductive method.

The idea of Law, conceived as a formula capable of enunciation once for all in set terms, and having an eternal, changeless validity, has gradually given way before that of Process in almost all departments of scientific observation. The most solid facts are found to undergo a change; the realm of life, or of growth analogous to life, is seen expanding marvellously before our eyes, till every thing appears to be involved in it. Many minds have in consequence swung back from Deism to Pantheism, and Evolution has, to some men, taken the place of God. But Deism and Pantheism are both so irrational, so utterly inadequate to explain the simplest facts of our moral and spiritual life, that neither of them can long hold mankind together. Positivism, which has made a systematic and memorable attempt to fill the gap, itself bears witness to the craving of human nature for some stronger bond than such systems can supply; while its appreciation of the necessity of religion, gives it an importance not possessed by mere Agnosticism.

Yet it is impossible to look at an encyclopædic attempt to grasp all knowledge and all history, such as that made by the founder of Positivism, without a deep, oppressive sadness. That all this effort, so powerful and so penetrating in many of its parts, however grotesque and open to criticism in some of its details, should end in so puerile a result as the deification of humanity, seems to strike one with despair, as to the benefits to be expected from thought and knowledge apart from faith.

Can men heap fact upon fact, and connect science with science in a splendid hierarchy, and find no better end than this? Is such a review to come to this, that we must worship either actual humanity, with all its meanness and wickedness, or ideal humanity, which does not yet exist, and if this world is all in all may never come into being? Are we to worship either vice and wickedness, side by side with goodness, or a mere hope of something which on the Positivist hypothesis must always remain weak and ignorant?

For ideal humanity, however moral and enlightened, if unaided by God, as the Positivist holds, is still earth-bound and sense-bound. It clearly can never understand the simplest of the laws or processes of nature on this earth; much less can it understand the nature of the Universe, which is nightly displayed to our contemplation, when earth is shadowed in darkness, as if to draw our eyes by force from fixing ourselves on what we have too close about us. Science, while it opens many things to us, discloses also, *pari passu*, the narrow limits of our powers of knowledge. We are told that it is common sense to recognize that much is beyond us.

Perfectly true. But it is not common sense to worship an ignorant and weak humanity, which certainly made nothing, and has in itself no assurance of continuance in the future, nay, rather, a very clear probability of destruction, if simply left to itself.

What Positivism surely needs to give it hope and consistency is the doctrine of the Logos, of the eternal Word and Reason, the Creator, Orderer, and Sustainer of all things, who has taken a stainless human nature that He might make men capable of all knowledge. This divine humanity of the Logos, drawing mankind into Himself, is, indeed, worthy of all worship. In loving Him, we learn really what it is to "live for others." In looking to Him, we cease from selfishness and pride. Such a worship of humanity is not a mere baseless hope, but a reality appearing in the very midst of history, a reality apprehended by Faith indeed, but by a Faith always proving itself to those, and by those, who hold it fast in Love [23].

There is room then, ample room, and a loud demand for the re-establishment of a Christian philosophy, based upon the Incarnation. It must clearly accept all known facts, but must be very careful to remember that the hypotheses of science are always in process of correction. It must not confound truth with transitional inferences from facts of Nature, any more than with secondary and one-sided developments of Theology. But even with this cau-

---

[23] On the relations of Positivism to Christianity, the reader should consult Dr. Westcott's Essays in the *Contemporary Review*, vols. vi. and viii. in the numbers for Dec. 1867, and July, 1868.

tion such a philosophy will by no means be a substitute for the Bible and the Creeds. The form it takes, like that of scholasticism, may pass away. It may reign for a time, and do good work, and then be found wanting. But it is clearly demanded of the Catholic Church that it should now provide such a step towards the stronger and riper knowledge, which, in the fulness of time, the Son of God will reveal to those that love Him; that, when that time comes, we may have minds exercised and prepared to receive the glorious message. The form of knowledge will vanish away; but the capacity for it, and the temper suitable to its reception, must be fully educated, if the Church on earth is to be the seed-plot of the Church in Heaven.

3. We have spoken of the Catholic Church as an organizer of active life, and as a teacher of philosophic truth. But little need be said of its obvious functions as an educator of *feeling*. Whether we consider feeling as an objective sense of beauty, or as an inward personal emotion, the Church has confessedly had command of both regions of the heart. Beauty has been recognized and loved with a new and unselfish love, as a divine gift, and the power of art has been venerated as an operation of the Holy Ghost, who gives a new spirit to the wise-hearted and cunning craftsman. Some arts have, indeed, been shunned or practised with less success in Christendom, partly through fear of their misuse, partly because they were less capable of giving expression to any deep movement or varied tone of feeling. Thus the Eastern Church has been left

in a low stage of artistic culture, chiefly, we may suppose, through a fear of the heathen associations which clung to many forms of art; while the stage has never wholly cleared itself in any country from the atmosphere of degradation into which ancient Rome had plunged it. Sculpture, again, has suffered both from puritanical prejudice and from its apparent incapacity to express many of the more subtle and intimate emotions which Christianity has been particularly destined to propagate.

Hence music, painting, and architecture have become specially Christian arts, and have flourished nowhere so thoroughly as when they have been handmaids of religion. Side by side with these arts, poetry and imaginative literature have imbibed a wholly new spirit and a new sense of pathos, distinguished specially by a reverence for weakness as well as strength, a perception of joy springing out of sorrow, a hope of resurrection, an acceptance of the life of Christ as the acme of beauty as well as the law of conduct. This spirit is visible not only in the hymns of the Church, which ring in the ears of the sick and dying, when all other sounds are stilled; not only in such distinctly Christian poets as Dante and Milton,—one the greatest, the other among the greatest minds, of their respective nations,—but also in the tone of refinement and of true human brightness spread over the greater part of modern literature. It is this which is the secret of the undying power of writers like Shakespeare and Scott, who do not make a special show of religion, and of the comparative failure of others of scarcely less genius, who are disfigured by hopelessness, coarseness, or an affected paganism. The importance of the hold which the Church has upon society through such means as these can scarcely be over-estimated; but we cannot be satisfied with what has been already done. It is a truly noble ambition to sanctify all arts, to bring all that is beautiful into the service of Christ, to infuse into all that attracts the eye or charms the ear or delights the mind the joy and peace of the Holy Ghost.

The cultivation of interior feeling or sentiment is equally the work of the Church. All the keys of the human heart, from the tumultuous passion of repentance to the refinement and grace of a placid and unruffled life, are given by our Lord to His Body. But specially the call upon the sinner to save his soul and join himself to Christ, and to receive the Holy Ghost into his heart, as into a temple, with all the intense emotion and searching of spirit that follows this appeal, is ever sounding throughout the Church. It is a call to resurrection, necessary not only at the first conversion of a nation, but as a constant regenerating power. If the regular ministry of the Church fails in its duty to make this appeal, then an irregular agency springs up to do it,—sometimes, as in the Middle Ages, in an order of monks or preachers, sometimes in a more sectarian body. Such agencies are indeed very uncertain in their work, and are exposed to great temptations. The Benedictines, after several centuries of wonderful success, lost their missionary ardour, and confined themselves to their wide domains and cloistered studies. The Mendicant orders who arose to do their work, after a period of extraordinary brilliancy, fell into comparative disrepute. The Dominicans, with misguided zeal, threw themselves into the terrible fallacy of the Inquisition, the "compelle intrare," towards which even St. Augustine had led the way [24]; while the Franciscans, having brought religion back to the homes of the people [25], became all too soon a proverb for greediness and superstition. The Waldenses, on the other hand, were forced against their will into schism, and into a sort of partnership with heresy. It was a sense of this failure that very largely contributed to the Reformation, a sense that no Church can be doing its work unless it has its hold continually upon the hearts of the people.

Since the Reformation the Jesuits, and other preaching and teaching orders in the Church of Rome,—the Moravians in Germany, the sects, and especially the Wesleyan Methodists in England, —have attempted to take up the work that fell from the hands of the monks and friars of earlier days. It is easy enough to point out the grave faults, and the one-sidedness of temper of these very different attempts. But they are manifestations of

[24] St. Augustine at first had opposed the compulsion of the Donatists by the civil power, but he afterwards changed his opinion, as he tells us in his *Retractations*, ii. 5. He gives his reasons in two of his *Epistles*, 93, *ad Vincentium*, and 185, *ad Bonifatium*,— a very disastrous misuse of his great power of argument, the substance of which has been repeated again and again in succeeding centuries. We must not, however, forget the protests of St. Bernard against the persecution both of Jews and Waldenses.

[25] See especially the late Mr. J. S. Brewer's preface to the *Monumenta Franciscana*, in the Master of the Rolls' Series.

spiritual life which deserve deep attention. Some instruments of the kind the Church must have if it is to be truly Catholic; something answering to those manifold gifts of the Holy Ghost, the charismata, the possessors of which in the early days worked side by side with the regular ministry of the Church. The warning, "Quench not the Spirit: despise not prophesyings" (1 Thess. v. 19, 20), is constantly needed. Thank God, we in the Church of England are becoming daily more alive to the danger of this neglect.

II.

The Gift of Peace as satisfying the Wants of Man.

We have been speaking hitherto of the more general and comprehensive attributes of the Church which reflect the fulness of the Divine nature. We now turn naturally to the second part of our subject,—its specific adaptation to human wants. What are the great instruments by which the Peace of the Church is secured, the outward forms by which it fulfils its mission to the world? They are acknowledged all but universally to be three, namely (in the words of our Ordinal) the Doctrine and Sacraments and Discipline of Christ.

It is easy to see the obvious necessity of such a triple adaptation to our nature. Man wants peace for his intellect and reason, and finds it in a creed delivered with authority as revealed Truth. He wants peace for his heart and affections, and finds it in union with the divine life implanted by Baptism and renewed by Holy Communion. He wants

VIII.] *Symbolism of the Ark and its Contents.* 315

peace for his will, and finds it in submission to the rule and discipline of the Good Shepherd, exercised by the Apostolic ministry in His name. He wants these things, not only in idea and invisibly, but through a visible medium, the counterpart of Christ's life on earth. He wants them historically and permanently enshrined in facts, and such as he wants them God in His condescending mercy has given them.

An evident type and symbol of this threefold gift was set before the ancient people of God in the contents of the ark, or rather, was hidden from their eyes behind the veil, waiting till Christ should open the way to their meaning. Like all the symbolism of the ancient Church of Israel, the ark, with its contents, has a striking relation both to the forms of Heathenism about it, and to the Christianity which was to succeed it. To the first it has a superficial outward likeness and an inward contrast, while to the second it stands in a relation of transition and prophecy. The two tables of the covenant therein preserved, with the pot of manna and Aaron's rod that budded, were at once direct historical memorials of things past, and pregnant and forcible emblems of what was to come. There was the monument of the fiery lawgiving of Sinai in the tables of stone; there was the pot of manna, the bread from heaven that sustained their weary desert pilgrimage; there was the marvellous rod that blossomed amongst the dry staves of the other tribes, with its reminiscences of the gainsaying of Korah, and the establishment of the authority of one priestly household. What a world of history and prophecy was enclosed in that little space! How solemn, too, and forcible, were these plain memorials, compared with the gross and dubious symbols of the sacred chests of the Egyptian or Greek deities, to which an outsider might have compared them [26]. Let us, for the sake of impressing the contrast, try to throw ourselves into the position of a heathen who wished to make the best of his religion, a Plutarch or a Porphyry. Setting aside the coarser symbols, which play such a horrible part in the earth-bound fancies of polytheism, what was the best that we could have learnt from the higher emblems,—the thyrsus, the pomegranate, the ears of corn, the balls of wool, and the rest? What was the essence of this religion as a gift of God to man? We see Dionysus, the joyous reveller, waving his wand and taking possession of his votaries, and intoxicating them with a sense of the beauty and the charm of nature. As we look at the trains of graceful figures, with their light and easy motion, upon some precious vase or richly-carved sarcophagus; as we read the wild choruses of Euripides, and the sweet and stirring poems of Catullus or Keats; as we gaze upon the moving canvases of Titian and Tintoret, we feel what an attraction there is, not merely for the artistic temperament, in this Dionysiac enthusiasm. We perceive that it touches that inborn passion for wildness and freedom, for triumphing with nature, for being at one with the spirit of

---

[26] On the contents of the mystic chests, see Clement of Alexandria, *Protrepticus*, 2, §§ 21, 22; and cp. Döllinger, *Heidenthum*, p. 168, § 107.

the world, both physical and animal, which is akin to something noble, something really beautiful in man. Yet look at it a little closer, a little more coldly,—what was it really in its effects? We see crowds of fanatics leaving their homes, women deserting their husbands and children, tearing some poor animal limb from limb to make a cruel sacrament, and dancing by the glare of torchlight upon the mountains till faintness and exhaustion overpowered their sinking bodies. The thyrsus is thus a sort of enchanter's wand, a Circean magic, turning human beings into an artificial state of savagery, scarcely even picturesque in its reality, and anything but a rod of divine discipline. In the pomegranate, again, with its many seeds, we seem to see little more than an emblem of physical fruitfulness, with perhaps a faint outlook towards the hope of a future life. We catch some more distinct intimations of the dignity and usefulness of labour in the ears of corn and the balls of wool that Demeter taught mankind to produce in the field and by the fireside, and this is certainly the best side of the mysteries. But all is obscure and hazy, where it is not strange and dangerous. In these rites the idea of prophecy and inspiration, of discipline and instruction, is travestied by bacchantic frenzy; sacraments are misrepresented by sensual or savage ordinances; and a law of moral duty is only dimly inferred as a labouring for the meat that perisheth, instead of being clearly written on the stones of Sinai.

But what the heathen in vain felt for, what the

Jew had only in part, or in type and prophecy, that Christ has given us, opening the way within the veil, and disclosing the fulness of His treasures.

(1.) It needs but few words to point out the great value of the Christian ordinances as instruments of Peace. As regards the first of the three, namely, *Doctrine*, we have already spoken in former Lectures of the marvellous power of the Bible over the human heart [27], of the repose and strength that follows an acceptance of Christ's authority [28], and of the sustaining, satisfying power of the Creed [29], and it is unnecessary to repeat it here. We have also remarked upon the striking agreement as to the great mysteries of the Creed, which unites the divided portions of Christendom. The power of Christian doctrine is an eloquent fact which no one can gainsay, though only those who have tasted the peace and joy of believing can really understand its fulness.

It has, however, been sometimes said or implied that the restful, believing temper of the Church is less sympathetic, less practically useful than the sceptical and restless spirit. All advance in philosophy, we are reminded, begins in doubt, and science is constantly revising its hypotheses, and ever on the watch for indications of omitted phenomena, which may help it to define more accurately what it only knows in part. But even those who are caught by the attractive side of scepticism, are obliged to make a stand somewhere; as, for instance, those in the very lowest stage of belief are forced to assume that

---

[27] Lect. iv. p. 121.   [28] Lect. iv. pp. 130 foll.
[29] Lect. vi. p. 187 foll.

knowledge is possible, and that there will be some continuity between the future and the past. They are obliged, that is to say, to admit that the theological virtues of hope and faith are practically necessary to knowledge; and most of them will not wish to exclude love, though they may differ from us as to its object. Many of them also will be ready to agree with Bacon "that there is hardly any other approach to the kingdom of man, which is founded on the sciences, than that which leads to the kingdom of Heaven, into which entrance is not granted except under the likeness of a little child" (*Nov. Org.*, aph. 68). Science, in her serious moods, agrees with faith in thinking that to be "ever learning and never coming to the knowledge of the truth" is misery and failure. We, on our part, are also perfectly ready to admit that an enquiring temper, which you may, if you choose, describe as sceptical, is useful up to a certain point. If it is necessary to science, it is necessary also to theology, to remind us of the fragmentariness of our knowledge, and to correct the tendency to carry single principles to extremes. It requires, for instance, a sort of healthy scepticism to perceive the danger of such developments as Papal Infallibility or Bibliolatry, as Calvinism or modern Universalism. The only difference, then, between us and those who are not Christians, if we view the matter entirely from the intellectual side, is as to range and occupations of faith and doubt respectively. We say that their faith is not broad enough to give peace, and is exposed to the great temptation of indolence. If a man believes that knowledge is possible at all, he cannot, without stunting and maiming his intelligence, leave out of his view the obvious facts that the world cannot be self-created, that evolution is a process, which is described, not a cause of anything, and that human free-will has a potential energy outside all the limits of experience and observation. When these primary truths have been taken into account, let him consider further the witness of the conscience with regard to sin, the unique position of Israel in history, the character of Jesus Christ, the witness to the Resurrection, the existence of the Church, and all the other facts which lie so close together in this connection. We may then ask, which really gives truer peace to the intellect, a doctrine that harmonises all these very important facts, or a scepticism to which they are so many knots and insoluble problems—nay, it may be, even a list of subjects, the discussion of which must be tabooed and evaded? We ask, for instance, again and again, "What think ye of Christ?" and sceptics again and again shirk a full enquiry. They have no theory that will the least bear criticism in detail [30]; and they take refuge in vague generalities about possible processes of self-deception and illusion, loose probabilities of weakness or even wickedness and imposture, in the Evangelists and other writers of the New Testament. What would be said of such conduct as this in any other region of thought? Is not wilful neglect of Biblical and theological study rightly described as immoral, when we think of the

[30] See additional note, page 336.

great issues which underlie acceptance or rejection of the Creed?

It is true that the Church is content to leave much unexplained, and so far (as we have said) has a seeming point of contact with scepticism. But then it has a rationale of this contentment to offer. It is a scepticism of faith, not of doubt; or rather, it is an acceptance of a position which is itself part of the Creed, namely, that God is our teacher, and we always learners from Him. We believe that "when that which is perfect is come, then that which is in part shall be done away" (1 Cor. xiii. 10). This position should certainly make us sympathetic with all those doubters who have so far advanced as heartily to accept this principle that they are learners from God. They are not, indeed, good Christians, but they are inchoate Christians. They begin to feel with us "the peace of God that passeth all understanding," a weight taken off the spirit, a hopefulness as to the triumph of good over evil, which will lead them onwards and upwards. But it is only a full possession of the Creed enabling believers to feel that they are workers together with God, which gives them an absolutely untiring energy in work, and a readiness to take up any labour, however humble, because they know that He will mould everything into His plan, and that the task of the least is essential to the glory of the greatest.

There is indeed, we admit, such a thing as a selfish, lazy faith, and the comfort of which it boasts is no real example of the peace given by Christian doctrine. It is true also that there are some religious-minded men, who look with earnestness for peace, and yet never seem to reach it in this world. Such exceptions of both kinds are a trial and an enigma, which, we doubt not, will be solved and set straight in another state of being. But, for the present, we must look, here as elsewhere, at the general result. Acceptance of Christian doctrine does give a reasonable and harmonious peace to the mind; it enables us to comprehend, as far as our imperfect thought can, all classes of facts, it sets us free from a perpetual irritation about first principles, which often impedes decisive action at critical moments, and it leaves quite a sufficient sense of incompleteness in our knowledge to give a healthy activity and humility to the intellect.

(2.) The peace given by the *Sacraments* of Christ is equally adapted to the wants of the heart and affections. Almost all nations testify to the instincts which underlie the two universal Sacraments of Baptism and the Holy Eucharist, and there are not a few widespread analogies to the other Sacramental rites of the Church [31]. Forms of initiation, purification, and dedication, often by water [32], festivals of communion

---

[31] The inauguration of Numa, in which the augur laid his right hand upon the king's head and prayed to Jupiter for a sign, is described at length by Livy, i. 18, and Plutarch, *Numa*, 7, p. 64 B. Mommsen doubts whether this ceremony was really used at the accession of a king, but as it appears to me without sufficient reason, in his *Römisches Staatsrecht*, vol. ii. p. 8. Inauguration was in use without doubt for the rex sacrificulus and the flamines: see Labeo in Gellius, *Noctes Atticæ*, xv. 27, 1, and Livy, xxvii. 8; xl. 42.

[32] E. B. Tylor, *Primitive Culture*, ii. pp. 430 foll., cites numerous cases of the lustration of children, often in connection with the

VIII.]   *Heathen Sacramental Rites.*   323

with the deity, by partaking of a sacrifice just offered [33], are known wherever religion has attained or retained any hold over mankind. They have given a constant sense of brotherhood and companionship, of dependence on the Divine love, often strong enough to raise men above the divisions of national life. Thus all distinctions of caste are abolished amongst those who meet in the temple of Jagannāth in Orissa, and the sacred food of his offerings passes without reserve from hand to hand, even among men of hostile nationalities and differing faiths [34].

To many of the heathen every meal is in some sort a sacrament, since a small portion or libation is offered to the deity generally before men set their hands to it [35]. Amongst the Romans, a silence was observed between the two courses of their principal meal, whilst this little sacrifice was being performed,

ceremony of naming, generally at some fixed time after birth. Cp. also above, p. 161, and note 44.

On the "dies lustricus" of the Romans see J. Marquardt, *Privatleben der Römer*, pp. 81 foll. (Leipzig, 1879).

[33] Cp. Tylor, l. c. pp. 394—396; Döllinger, *Heidenthum*, pp. 209 foll., 373, 535 foll., &c. St. Paul, 1 *Cor.* x. 16—21, grounds his prohibition of eating things offered to idols on the sense of communion with the supposed deity. It is striking that sin-offerings (*hostiæ piaculares*) among the Romans, were only eaten by the priests, just as amongst the Jews. See J. Marquardt, *Röm. Staatsverwaltung*, iii. pp. 179 foll., and *Leviticus* vi. 26, 29, x. 17.

[34] The sacred food is called Mahāprasād (*lit.* great favour). See W. W. Hunter's *Orissa*, vol. i. pp. 85 foll. At present, some low castes are excluded, contrary to the original institution. *Ibid.* pp. 135 foll. The worship of Jagannāth is part of the Vaishnava reforms already referred to, p. 97, note 54. Mr. Hunter's two chapters on this subject should be read by every one. The misery endured by the crowds of pilgrims is described with great force.

[35] Tylor, l. c., &c.

to do honour to the presence of the Gods[36]; and surely Christians cannot suffer themselves to be behind the heathen in thus consecrating the gift by remembrance of the giver[37].

There is a real beauty, nay, sometimes a potent charm, about some of these rites, though too often they have the hideous spectres of lust or cruelty lurking in their shadow; and even when they are purest, they wholly lack the force of the Christian sacraments. Heathen sacraments are at best arbitrary and fanciful; they are the result of a vague groping after God in myth and symbol. But the two great Christian Sacraments rest on the express commands of Christ, and are intimately connected with the historical facts of His manifestation to men, and a backward reference to much in the religious life of Israel. They have often and rightly been called an "extension of the Incarnation[38]," that is to say, they are natural means by which the power of Christ is present to us, just as His visible body was the instrument of divine grace to the first disciples. As

---

[36] See the quotations in J. Marquardt, *Röm. Staatsverwaltung*, iii. p. 124, esp. Servius *ad Æneid*. i. 730:—"Apud Romanos etiam cena edita sublatisque mensis primis silentium fieri solebat, quoad ea quæ de cena libata fuerant, ad focum ferrentur et igni darentur, ac puer deos propitios nunciasset, ut diis honor haberetur tacendo. Quæ res cum intercessit inter cenandum Græci quoque θεῶν παρουσίαν dicunt."

[37] The Christians of Papinenipalli in Southern India have the beautiful custom of putting a small portion of maize into the offertory pot, suspended from the roof, every time that any is ground for cooking. The contents are presented every Sunday.

[38] Bp. Jeremy Taylor's *Worthy Communicant*, i. 2, an idea clearly in the mind of Hooker, *Eccl. Polity*, v. ch. 51 foll. Cp. R. I. Wilberforce, *On the Incarnation*, ch. xiii.

VIII.] *Practical Value of the Sacraments.* 325

He has united the Finite to the Infinite by His birth in human flesh, so in these simple physical elements He has taken up and consecrated nature and daily life, and has given us a foretaste of the divinised realm of nature, the new heavens and the new earth wherein dwelleth righteousness, which are in God's good time to rise from the ashes of the old. Those who accept Christ as the Mediator, will also thankfully accept the rites which He has instituted as channels of His mediatorial grace.

This is not the place for a full discussion of the practical blessings of the Sacraments. Their value as a bond of union between man and man is obvious, so obvious, that others besides Christians are drawn to adopt something of the kind. We have lately seen in France a miserable parody of Baptism in an assembly of democratic atheists; and the Theists of the Brāhma-Samāj have now instituted a communion service, the elements of which are rice and water.

That the Christian Sacraments have, over and above this, an educational value peculiar to them, is also acknowledged by many who are slow to accept the creeds[39]. The careful preparation which they exact, or ought to exact; the solemnity of their celebration; the awe and hush that falls upon the worshippers; the tenderness of the emotion which they excite, even among those who take the low views of a mere charitable expectation in Baptism, or a historical commemoration of the death of Christ in the Eucharist,—all this gives comfort to the soul of many wearied with intellectual strife, or incapable

[39] Cp. Hooker, *Eccl. Polity,* v. 57. 2.

of understanding controversy. But deeper far is the peace of those who can accept the language of the Prayer-Book, thanking God from their hearts that the newly-baptized "is regenerate and grafted into the body of Christ's Church;" and that in Holy Communion He doth "assure us" of His "favour and goodness towards us, and that we are very members incorporate in the mystical body" of His Son. We feel that necessary as faith and the preparation of the heart certainly is, delightful as is the communion of prayer and the response of the Spirit's inward motion, yet in the Sacraments there is an outward gift, an act, a motion of the divine love towards us, which it is impossible for us to have invented or controlled, which is ready to lay hold of us and transform us, if we will only let it do its holy work. We understand the feeling with which St. Cyprian wrote, directly after his baptism, describing his former and his present state. He tells us first, you may remember, how he thought the doctrine of new birth "a hard saying," how impossible it seemed to him to get rid of the obstinate defilement of nature and the ingrained habits of vice; and then he continues as follows:—

"Such were my frequent musings: for whereas I was encumbered with the many sins of my past life, which it seemed impossible to be rid of, so I had used myself to give way to my clinging infirmities, and, from despair of better things, to humour the evils of my heart, as slaves born in my house, and my proper offspring. But after that life-giving water succoured me, washing away the stain of former years, and pouring into my cleansed and hallowed breast the light which comes from Heaven, after that I drank in the Heavenly Spirit, and was created into a new man by a second birth,—then marvellously what before was doubtful became plain to me,—what was hidden was revealed,—what was dark began to shine,—what was before difficult, now had a way and means,—what had seemed impossible now could be achieved,—what was in me of the guilty flesh, now confessed that it was earthy,—what was quickened in me by the Holy Ghost, now had a growth according to God [40]."

Not less is the peace of mind which follows a devout reception of the Holy Eucharist. Through it we join the society of the holy angels, and enter into the repose of the blessed dead. All good influences of the communion of saints surround us. The offertory united to the oblation of the elements is a symbol of the dedication of our natural life and substance to God, and to the purposes of His kingdom of Peace and charity towards all men. The consecration, shewing forth the Lord's death, and pleading it as a sacrifice for sin, implies a parallel oblation of the worshipper as a member of the crucified body of Christ, ready in all things to submit his will to his Father's will. The act of communion crowns these acts by an assurance given to us that the strength and solidity of the Redeemer's glorified life, the purifying and vivifying power of His love, is ready to pass into ours if we will but receive it. Christ is present to us, with us, and in us, as really as when He walked the earth in human flesh. In touching Him we find health, and rest, and joy. Men may not understand these feelings, or be able to enter into

[40] St. Cyprian *ad Donatum*, 3 (*Library of the Fathers*, vol. iii. p. 3).

this experience, but they cannot doubt their reality or their energy.

There is a like power also in the other sacramental ordinances through which the Church acts as a channel of divine grace. The gift of individual strength in Confirmation, and of authority in Ordination, are manifest aids to those who receive them [41]. How much of our social purity and happiness is due to the grace to keep the marriage vow given by God to those who ask the Church's blessing, is evident by the laxity which follows its rejection. Nor can the misuse of the grace of absolution, and the degradation of the ancient system of penance, excuse us in shutting our eyes to the crying want of the human heart, especially in its weakness and disease, which is met by an external assurance of God's pardon for sin confessed [42].

(3.) The acceptance of the *discipline* of Christ by the will of man completes the work of Peace, which is begun in his nature by the tranquillizing effect of the Creed upon the intelligence, and carried on by the influence of sacramental grace upon the heart. It is the exercise of discipline which specially gives the Church the name and title *Apostolic*, inasmuch as our Lord committed the government of His Church

---

[41] Cp. Dr. Liddon's Sermon at Oxford, Dec. 22, 1867, *The Moral Value of a Mission from Christ* (Rivingtons, 1868).

[42] There is an interesting sermon on *Absolution* in F. W. Robertson's *Sermons, Third Series*, pp. 61—76, ed. 1878, which may help some persons to understand this truth who are inclined to shrink from it. Cp. F. D. Maurice, *Kingdom of Christ* (ed. 2, vol. 2, pp. 191 foll., Lond., 1842), section headed, "Objections to an Absolving power in Ministers."

to the Apostles. Without, therefore, going into details of law and custom, it is necessary to say a few words on that ministry, which is confessedly the chief instrument and organ of Discipline. So clear is it that our Lord desired to establish a body of officers in His Church, that (as has been well said), "if we called the Four Gospels 'the Institution of a Christian Ministry,' we might not go very far wrong, or lose sight of many of their essential qualities[43]." The careful and even elaborate education given step by step to the Apostles—as a body in the Galilean ministry recorded by the first three Evangelists, as individuals in that which is the special subject of St. John—is inexplicable, unless our Lord was training them for an office, that is, for a permanent function in His Church. For Christ speaks of His Church over and over again as a kingdom, working in the world though not of the world, and a kingdom implies an abiding constitution. Order is everywhere His delight, as we see, not only in His words in support of the Jewish functionaries, the priests and scribes[44], but also in the pleasure which He shewed when the principle was recognized by others, as by the Centurion of Capernaum[45]. To have spoken, therefore, and acted as He did would have been indeed misleading, unless, as all Christendom

---

[43] F. D. Maurice, *The Kingdom of Christ*, vol. ii. p. 148, ed. 2. The whole section is striking and effective.

[44] "Go shew yourselves unto the priests," *Luke* xvii. 14; "The Scribes and the Pharisees sit in Moses' seat," &c., *Matt.* xxiii. 2, and elsewhere.

[45] *Matt.* viii. 10; *Luke* vii. 9.

for many centuries agreed, He was making provision for a government that was to last for all time.

It was clearly our Blessed Lord's "plan" (if we may use the term with reverence) to employ the Apostles rather than Himself as visible instruments of salvation. He might have made a multitude of converts all on the same level of equal relations to Himself, but He did not do so. His method was to lay down general principles of doctrine and morality, and to commit the application of them to the Apostolate, not to impose a minutely-defined and all-sufficient rule of life like Mahomet, or to create a crowd of individual saints like Gotama. He refuses to be made a king by the crowd, that is to say, He discards all ambition to make His name widely known by His visible presence, and resigns the work of proclaiming it to a limited number of persons—the Twelve and the Seventy—trained by lengthened contact with Himself, from which other men are in great measure debarred. To the Apostles especially He gave the assurance, "As My Father hath sent Me, even so send I you," and the promise as to remission and retention of sins that follows (John xx. 21 foll.)[46]; and He speaks of their ministry as lasting till His second coming: "Who then is that faithful and wise steward, whom his Lord shall make ruler over his household, to give them their portion of meat in due season? Blessed is that servant whom his lord when he cometh shall find so doing"

---

[46] This assurance is implied in many places, e.g. *Matt.* x. 40; *Luke* x. 16; *John* xiii. 20; xvii. 18.

(Luke xii. 42, 43). I need not remind you how these words are re-echoed by St. Paul, who describes the ministry as a special gift of Pentecost to educate the body of Christ, "till we all come in the unity of the faith and of the knowledge of the Son of God, unto a perfect man, unto the measure of the stature of the fulness of Christ [47]."

There were dangers no doubt in this unique method, and those clearly foreseen by our Divine Master; dangers lest His ministers should strive to become lords over God's heritage, or that the truths they preached might be set at naught with the obscurity of their persons. But the method has surely been justified by the event. Christ's perpetual presence with His Church has been brought home to age after age by the Apostolic ministry with a force that no diffused impression committed to a multitude could ever have attained. Our Lord desires us to think of Him as an ever-present ruler, absent temporarily from sight, but with us invisibly, and at any moment about to return again in visible majesty. Is not the sense of this kept up most powerfully by the ministry, which is taught and teaches that it holds office directly from His hands? Had the ministry been left to grow up as a human afterthought, developed merely by social necessities, and receiving its commission from below, it is probable that Christ's perpetual presence in His Church would soon have been disparaged or denied. The Sacraments might have remained as outward signs, but they would have

[47] *Ephes.* iv. 11 foll.

surely been reduced, as the sects too much tend to reduce them, to *tesseræ* of mutual fellowship between man and man.

Christianity might have become a powerful religious society of either of the three types mentioned in our last lecture, but it would hardly have been the kingdom of the living Christ. At best it would have been dependent for its sense of His presence upon the uncertain activity of the inward motions of the Spirit, like those on which the Society of Friends has relied, or upon sudden outbursts of the charismata. We have already observed how untrustworthy these outbursts are, and to what dangers they are exposed (p. 311), though controlled, as they have been, directly and indirectly, by the regular ministry. Even in the last generation we have seen a bold attempt to revive a separate and temporary Apostolate, in a society closely similar to that of the Montanists of earlier days, and we have also seen the institution pass away, and leave the world very nearly where it was before.

Let those, then, who are inclined to think lightly of Apostolical succession, and who misconceive the ministry as interfering with the priesthood of Christ, consider rather how little they would have known of that priesthood as a present reality, without the representation of it which is constantly before their eyes in those ministers who have a true sense of their mission.

There is a false sacerdotalism, but there is also a true one [48]. The false gives those who imbibe it

---

[48] Cp. F. D. Maurice, *l.c.*, pp. 135—138.

an overbearing sense of their own importance, an idea that, like the Brāhmans of India, they are to lord it over their brethren in spiritual and often in secular things. The true sacerdotalism claims the right to be in all things like unto Christ, who came not to be ministered unto but to minister, and to give His life a ransom for many. The false theory again strives to keep the conscience of others in bondage, to make them slaves or weaklings, daring not to stir a finger except under direction of the priest: the true realizes that almost its first duty is to absolve, that is, to free the conscience, to put forward the ministry of reconciliation, to give a sense of joy and liberty to the soul, a joy as in the presence of the Redeemer of all men.

The office of the ministry, as our Lord designed it, may then be summed up in one word as bringing home to man the presence of Christ. It would take too long to exhibit this in detail; but consider for a moment the action of the Episcopate in binding men together with a sense of unity, as all subjects of Christ our king. If it were only an instrument linking province to province and country to country, it would be simply indispensable as an organ of Christian feeling.

To use the words of a writer already quoted:—

"The overseers or Bishops of the Christian Church have felt themselves to be emphatically the bonds of communication between different parts of the earth. The jurisdiction of each has been confined within a certain district; but by the very nature of their office they have held fellowship, and been obliged to hold fellowship, with those who lived in other districts, who spoke different languages, who were bound together by different notions or customs [49]."

Think of it again as a careful steward and dispenser of doctrine, and an independent witness to morality; as a mouthpiece of the Church in working upon public opinion; as a guarantee for the constant and reverent performance of the services of public prayer and praise and the due administration of the Sacraments. Without the Apostolic ministry, doctrine is apt to become a matter of private interpretation, to bend to the heretical bias of the moment, and to cease to be proclaimed in its fulness; and morality tends all too surely to be reduced to the level of social custom [50]. Ministers who receive their commission only from the people are notoriously under a temptation not to teach or to condemn, except in agreement with the popular voice. They are tempted to shrink from boldly representing Christ either to their flocks or to the civil rulers: and as to the gathering together to meet the Lord in public worship, it is certain that where the commission from Him is disregarded, there anything like

---

[49] F. D. Maurice, *l.c.*, p. 138.

[50] The extraordinary prevalence of divorce in the puritan states of New England is a terrible proof of this danger. See the *Church Quarterly Review* for April, 1881, on *Christian Marriage*, vol. 12, pp. 20 foll. Deducting Roman Catholics,—who, to their honour, do not contribute to these statistics,—the ratio of divorces to marriages is said by Dr. Allen to stand thus:—"In Massachusetts, 1 to 15; in Rhode Island, 1 to 9; in Connecticut, 1 to 8; in Vermont, 1 to 13." (*North American Review*, June, 1880, p. 557.)

frequency of public prayer and Holy Communion is also generally dropped [51].

Such, then, are the outward means by which our Lord has deigned to apply His kingdom of Peace to our crying human wants. With a statement of these means, we have arrived at the conclusion of our long argument. I have striven to shew to those who seek to find rest in religion that there is one and one only, as far as we know, that fulfils the conditions naturally demanded by the reason, and that that religion is the Christian. I have attempted to demonstrate that it alone presents a doctrine of the Divine Nature, which is capable of standing against the assaults of Pantheism on the one side, and of Deism on the other. I have shewn also that in its contents it fulfils the general expectation of mankind. All religions have for their aim and object Truth, Holiness, and Peace. The Christian Revelation alone exhibits them in a manner which is worthy of God who gives it, and satisfactory to the nature of man who receives it. The Bible and the Creeds, the Person and Work of Christ, and His Kingdom of Peace, are manifestations of the Divine glory and mercy of the Creator and Father of all men, who wills to draw His erring children to Himself with cords of love. These precious gifts are ours in Christ: we may hold fast

---

[51] The reader will find the question of the results of Episcopacy *versus* Presbyterianism as it appears in Scotland, forcibly stated by Bishop Charles Wordsworth of St. Andrews, *Outlines of the Christian Ministry*, Lect. III., *Argument ex consequenti* (Longmans, 1872). The divine origin of the ministry is defended in the former Lectures, and in his *Remarks on Dr. Lightfoot's Essay on the Christian Ministry* (Parkers, 1879).

to them and hand them on to others, or we may loosen our hold of them and make the faith of others weak. May God grant that none who hear these Lectures may have the misery of parting from their Saviour, or of detaching other souls from Him. May He give His blessing and His presence to those truths which have been learned from His Word and the teaching of His Church, however imperfectly and weakly expressed, and bring all who hear or read these words to "follow peace with all men, and holiness, without which no man shall see the Lord" (Heb. xii. 14).

Additional note to p. 320.

For the most recent sceptical criticism of the Gospels, see an article entitled *Études d'Histoire religieuse: critique des récits sur la vie de Jésus*, par M. Ernest Havet, de l'Institut de France (*Revue des deux Mondes*, Avril, 1881, tome 152, pp. 582—622). M. Havet attacks the credibility of the most received facts of the life of our Lord, and reduces His intellectual character to the lowest possible level, leaving the Church without any intelligible origin. For a specimen of the reply to which this criticism is open, directed to a single point, see Mr. R. H. Hutton's able article, *Christ's Prophecies of His own Death*, in the *Expositor* for July, 1881, second series, vol. i. pp. 457—472.

APPENDIX I.

BUDDHISM, *by Oscar Frankfurter.*

To understand the success which the teaching of Gotama the Buddha had among the people of India, we must go back to the earliest history of this country. We cannot, indeed, give any account of India in these old times but such as we can extract from the literary monuments, and as they are only of a religious character, and touch very slightly on history, much must, of course, remain hypothetical. The sources of our information as to the earliest ages lie in the sacred hymns which the ancient Hindus used to chant at their festivals. It is scarcely necessary to add, that the hymns of the *Rig* Veda do not all belong to one period. Whilst we must date the main substance of some of them as early as the sixteenth century B.C., the composition of others approaches very nearly to the age of Gotama himself, who was destined to overthrow a system which bore in its later stages the germs of its own decay and destruction[1].

The first glimpses afforded us by the hymns of the *Rig* Veda shew us the Indian people, after the separation from their other Āryan brethren, settled in the northern part of India, and not divided into castes. Their language was what is now called Vedic Sanskrit, which was then a spoken dialect. They were an agricultural people, enjoying life, and sacrificing to the gods, who were expected, in return for these sacrifices, to grant the prayers which the faithful addressed to them. The father of the family was also the priest, who prayed to the gods for a long life and a numerous progeny. This primitive state, however, did not last long. In their migration farther south, they met with aboriginal peoples, perhaps possessed of comparatively greater civilization. These, so far as we can infer from the hymns, they subjugated after hard struggles. The next result of the intercourse with these aboriginal races, for such we must consider the Dasyus, was that the language in which

[1] Brahmanism, which followed Buddhism, after the latter was expelled from India, cannot and must not be regarded as the continuation of the Vedic religion. It was simply Buddhism, adapted to Brahmanical prejudices, with all the superstition which had crept up when Buddhism ceased to be in India the grand spiritual movement.

the earliest hymns were addressed to the gods became unintelligible to the people. In a few families, the old mode of reciting the hymns was maintained; on the other hand, through the constant wars, a warrior caste (the Kshattriyas) sprung up, whilst the bulk of the people still kept to agricultural pursuits (Vaisyas).

To these hymns, which were handed down intact from father to son, a certain sacredness was attached, and it was believed that the gods would not understand them, if only a single word was altered. New hymns were, however, added to the stock, which reveal, from more than one aspect, their comparative lateness. To one of these belongs the famous Purusha-sūkta (R.V. x. 90), which gives the earliest account of the origin of castes (see Appendix III., p. 356). It was composed when the Indians were settled in the heart of India. The only seasons mentioned in it are spring, summer, and autumn, and no mention is made of the winter, which is counted as one of the seasons by writers of the earliest age. Its lateness is moreover shewn by the fact that the Dasyus, under the name of *S*udras, must have been fully recognised by the Hindus, as they also are considered to have originated from Purusha. A century later, the hymns were not even understood wholly by the Brahmans (the priests), and it is to that time that we must ascribe the final redaction of the Vedic hymns, with their commentaries (about 600 B.C.).

A characteristic of the Indian mind, in the age of which we are speaking, is its deep religiosity. It was, certainly, not always so; but, doubtless, as soon as the conquest of India was accomplished, as soon as the condition of the people was settled again, the Indian mind concentrated all its powers on the development of religion. Together with this religious feeling we notice a deep reverence for antiquity. The hymns of the *Ri*g Veda, after having been once recognised as the one source from which all information had to come, were made the starting-point of all kinds of speculation. It was still in the main the same Veda in the seventh century, as it was in the fifteenth or sixteenth century B.C., but the interpretation of it had become a different one.

The science of the Vedas (if this tautology be allowed) was for the people at large a book with seven seals. Within the Brahmanic caste, however, on the other hand, every philosophy was based on the Veda; and every one of these philosophies, based on the Veda and its earliest commentaries, the so-called Brāhma*n*as, and more especially the Upanishads, which form the philosophical part of the Āra*ny*akas, was considered orthodox. The latter may best be described as a sort of super-commentary to the Veda. A wide range was left for individual speculation; and from the highest spiritualism down to the grossest materialism, systems were founded on the authority of the Veda as a revealed book.

The religious wants of the people remained, however, unsatisfied. The Brahmans usurped an intolerable tyranny over the masses of the people, which they defended by the theory of the migration of souls—a doctrine of which no traces can be found in the Vedic hymns, while allusions to it are frequently met with in the Upanishads [2].

We can, therefore, scarcely wonder that out of the caste which for a long time struggled with the Brahmans for supremacy, the Kshattriyas, reformers should arise, who, setting aside caste, ascribed to the Vedas, as means of religious knowledge, only a limited authority.

This brief sketch has brought us down to the middle of the fifth century, when, through the appearance of Gotama, the old Brahmanism received its death-blow.

We purpose in the following pages to give a short account of the history and doctrines of this eminent reformer.

The reformers of the Kshattriya caste were called *S*rāma*n*as. To address the people, they used the vernacular languages of India, commonly, or without adequate reason, called by the native grammarians, Prak*r*ita, as derived from Sanskrit. None of these systems but that of Gotama (if we except that of Niga*nth*a Nā*t*aputta, the founder of the Jain religion, the sacred books of which have scarcely begun to be published) can have had any very brilliant success. We scarcely know more of these systems than the occasional allusions made in the Buddhist scriptures to some of their doctrines. But we gather that they must have been very numerous; and that their followers were generally mendicants, who were convinced of the vanity and futility of life, and tried to make the best of things by withdrawal from the world.

Renewed researches might possibly lead to the discovery of manuscripts, from which we could learn more about these early sects. We must, however, remember that literary property was not much respected in India. When a sect succeeded in stamping out the doctrines of another, it also tried to destroy the books in which these doctrines were propounded: while, on the other hand, if a certain reputation was once attached to a name, additions were

---

[2] [Was not this doctrine of transmigration perhaps borrowed from the lower creed of the aboriginal tribes?—J. W.]

made to conform the doctrine to the standard of the day. These additions were always made in a dead language, by men who belong to a nation who are grammarians κατ' ἐξοχήν, and so it is most difficult to fix the date of any Indian book, sometimes within several centuries; and much must be left to internal evidence and subjective reasoning. The best example of this composite work is, perhaps, the grammatical literature which goes under the name of Pāṇini; or, to speak of Buddhist literature, the Commentaries which are known under the name of Buddhaghosa.

We are in a better position as regards Buddhism itself, and though we cannot attempt to give the exact date of the time when its sacred writings were compiled, we can within a few years fix the period in which Gotama lived. This is certainly due to the fact that Buddhism was a popular religion, which, as we shall see later on, did not give much, if any, scope to the gods to form men's destiny, and considered the conduct of life of higher value than any other Indian religion did. Through the famous edicts of Asoka, about the middle of the third century B.C., taken together with the information contained in the sacred books themselves, we are able to fix the death of Gotama within six years, viz. between 483—477 B.C., and his attaining to the highest wisdom in 543 B.C., the beginning of the Sinhalese era. If the account given in different books is right, and we have no reason to doubt it, Gotama attained to this wisdom when he was twenty-nine years of age, and this would therefore fix his birth to the year 572. We further learn from the Buddhavaṁsa, one of the sacred books of the Khuddaka Nikāya,—the statements of which, though evidently of a later date, and already intermixed with some myths, are confirmed by the other sacred writings,—that Gotama was the son of Suddhodana, the King of Kapilavatthu, and his wife Māyadevī, that he was married to Saddakaḵḵānā, from whom he had a son Rāhula. His two chief disciples were Kolita and Upatissa; his personal attendant, Ānanda; whilst Khemā and Uppalavaṇṇā are given as the names of his female disciples [3]. We learn further, that he was brought up in the house of his father with great splendour, but that, tired of a life of idleness, he forsook the world. His determination is poetically illustrated by four sights he had, shewing

---

[3] The admission of female disciples, though belonging to Buddha's own time, is considerably later than the institution of the order of mendicants. The Kullavagga relates that Gotama could not be persuaded to institute an order of female mendicants till after the repeated requests of Mahāpajāpatī Gotamī, his aunt and foster-mother.

the misery of man's life,—a decrepit old man, a leper, a dead body, and a recluse; most likely, however, political combinations were the principal cause for his resolution to become a mendicant. Wassiliew, *Buddhism*, p. 12, refers to a legend, according to which, whilst Gotama was preaching the law, the whole tribe of the Sākya was extirpated by the Virūdhakas. He asks whether this event did not, perhaps, take place before Gotama left his home.

After he attained Buddhahood [4], he preached his first sermon (he inaugurated the dominion of the law, or in Buddhist phraseology, he turned the wheel of the law) at a place near Benares, called Isipatana. This sermon is still to be found in the sacred writings. It has lately been translated by Mr. Rhys Davids in the series of Sacred Books of the East, vol. xi. p. 146, and is called the Dhamma-*K*akkappavattana-sutta.

Before we attempt to give the outlines of Gotama's doctrines, it will, I think, not be out of place to state briefly the opinion Gotama held of himself as a religious teacher. For these we are dependent solely on the sacred writings, or Pi*t*akas. A few words upon the date and character of these writings are also necessary in this connection.

It is a well-known fact that the Sacred Books of the Buddhists, as they are now extant, embrace three great collections, which are respectively called the Vinaya-pi*t*aka, treating on the outward discipline of the order of mendicants, and the Sutta and Abhidhamma pi*t*akas, treating of the doctrine. Tradition would have us believe that two of these great collections were already in the shape in which we now have them, a few months after the master's death, when a rehearsal took place. The concluding chapter of the *K*ulla Vagga tells us that this was performed at an assembly convened in consequence of the heretical tendencies of Subhadda. Now the *K*ulla Vagga is the only book which gives such an account, whilst the Mahā-parinibbāna-sutta, which relates the death and obsequies, and the distribution of the relics of the Buddha, keeps silence on this fact. It has been very well pointed out by Professor Max Müller, in opposition to Dr. Oldenberg, that the not mentioning of this Council does not necessarily imply that it did not take place, as an account of the Council would be somewhat out of place in such a connection. Most likely, therefore, it did take place, but scarcely to rehearse the whole

---

[4] The period which elapsed from the time of his determination to forsake the world until his attainment of the highest wisdom, is given differently in various books, varying from a few hours to six years.

of the Scriptures, but to fix some rules for the guidance of the
mendicant order, and to lay the foundation of the Dhamma. This
was highly necessary, as the Buddhist Church soon became a pro-
selytizing body. There was no time in Buddha's lifetime to fix
the text of the Scriptures, as he was wandering about until the
very last moment, preaching his law, and trying to gain converts
to the new doctrine. We find evidence of this in the Scriptures
themselves. The Sutta and Vinaya-pi*t*aka both introduce his
teaching frequently, the former always with the words: "Thus
it was heard by me." "Once upon a time the Blessed One lived,"
or "Once upon a time when the Blessed was wandering about
with his alms-bowl."

It therefore remains to be seen if we can discover among the
extant Scriptures such as would be likely to form the foundation
on which the others were based. In the case of the Vinaya, we
are (thanks to the acumen of Dr. Oldenberg) in a position to point
to such a book. It is the Pātimokkha, the Office of the Confession
of male and female mendicants, which forms the basis of the
Vibhaṅga. A book which forms the foundation of the other two
books, the Mahā Vagga and the *K*ulla Vagga, was certainly once
extant. At present, we can only suppose that it was a treatise
similar in contents to the Kammavā*k*a, which contains ecclesiasti-
cal rites and formulas, such as are treated in greater length in
the Mahā Vagga.

Our knowledge of Buddhism is not yet far enough advanced to
say with equal certainty which books form the foundation of the
Dhamma. We must keep in mind, leaving it for future investigation, that at the first so-called Council mention is made only of
the Dhamma and the Vinaya. Now the title of Abhidhamma for
the last of the three collections is of a later date; and if it is quite
true that in the Abhidhamma several very late works were included, (such as the Kathāvatthu, of which it is expressly stated
that it was added to the collection by Moggalīputta at the third
Council, about 247 B.C.), we find in it, nevertheless, some very
simple books which contain a *resumé* of Gotama's doctrine, propounded in a most unattractive and matter-of-fact form, which
might be earlier than the Sutta Pi*t*aka, and form its foundation.

To get a clear idea of what the original doctrines of Buddhism
consisted, we are therefore, as far as the Dhamma is concerned,
dependent on internal evidence. This internal evidence can even
now be brought to a very high degree of probability, for the simple
reason that those doctrines which may be considered as really and

thoroughly Gotama's own teaching, will occur over and over again in different parts of the sacred books; whilst those which were added later appear only once in the books.

Between the first Council at Rājagaha, if Council it can be called, to the second Council, which took place at Vesālī about 383 B.C., and for which we have historical evidence, the great bulk of the Buddhist Scriptures were composed. This Council was convened for the purpose of settling ten questions, on which a dispute had arisen among the priesthood. Only one of these questions is mentioned in the Vinaya as it is now before us. We must, therefore, infer that the Vinaya, as we have it now, is older than the Council at Vesālī. We shall, therefore, be right if, in accordance with Dr. Oldenberg, we place the main substance of the Sutta and Vinaya literature about 400 B.C. When the text was finally completed, as we now have it, is much more difficult to determine. We have already alluded to the fact that the Indian philosophers liked to make additions to the writings of their great men, in order to impart a certain sacredness to their own opinions.

Of course, allusions to Gotama's opinion of himself will but rarely occur. Happily, however, we find some few instances from which we can not only gather what others thought of him, but what he thought of himself. The discourses (suttas) almost always represent an unbeliever who belongs to the Brahmanical caste as coming to Gotama, whom he addresses simply and disrespectfully as Bho Gotama, in order to get up a dispute with him, which he commences by putting a knotty question; as a matter of course also, the unbeliever is converted. The Brahmans, it may also be inferred, felt a painful awe of this new teacher, who did not belong to their own caste, and who tried successfully to destroy the privilege of caste by addressing himself to the people. They did all in their power to blemish his character, and their false accusations of incontinence and other vices are frequently the subject of Buddhist books. It is needless to say that all these are triumphantly refuted.

It is on such occasions that he speaks of his own character; and he does so likewise, if, as in the case of the King of Magadha, A*g*atasattu Vedehiputta, he is asked for advice, or for the outlines of his doctrine. Furthermore, when Māra, the evil spirit, appears to tempt him, he is ready to speak of his own abilities. We have, of course, in this last instance, only the outcome of the popular belief in his powers entertained by the members of his own sect. All the three instances, however, go far to shew that he did not attribute his doctrine to any supernatural revelation. It was a firmly established fact with him, as with his followers, that the doctrine which he propounded was the outcome of faculties acquired in different characters in previous births. For the wisdom he had attained he had only to thank himself. What he speaks most of is his kindness and charity towards all living creatures; and confronting his doctrines with those of other sectarians, he maintains that theirs are based on tradition, and thus liable to be perverted, whilst the effects of his own are immediate, unlimited by time, conducive to salvation, attractive to all comers, a fitting object of contemplation. He has freed himself from all sensual desires, and is thus able to free all living creatures from them, in shewing them the path which leads to their highest bliss.

We have, however, now to ask what made the doctrine of Gotama spread so rapidly. We have already spoken shortly of the state of Indian affairs in Gotama's time, and of the religious wants of the people. High-minded philosophers were eager to minister to these wants, and the names of several such reformers are given in the Buddhist scriptures. We shall best be able to judge of the success of Gotama's doctrine when we compare the answer he gave to the question, What were the fruits of a religious life? to that given by others.

Some of these reformers maintained that a holy or unholy life has no reward or punishment, and that as the greatest crime may be committed without any result, so also a religious life and works of charity are of no avail. Or they preached a law of fatality, to which every being is subject: he has to run through the course of migration, and the wise and the fool will arrive at the same goal after they have completed these migrations. Or again, as man is made of the four elements, earth, water, fire, air, so after his death the constituent parts of the body will become those four elements again, but for good or bad deeds he will not have any rewards or punishments. The answer Niga*th*a Nā*t*aputta gave, also avoiding the question, was, that the Niganthas are well defended in four directions. They restrain sinful propensities by general abstinence from evil; they weaken the evil by controlling it; they spare the evil; they are under self-control.

No one of all these philosophers grappled with the difficulties of a reward for good deeds in the present life. Gotama, when asked the question about the fruits of a religious life, shewed the advantage of that conduct, which makes even the man in a humble condition respected. He shews, furthermore, that a religious life leads to the keeping of the laws, which bear in themselves the germ of self-satisfaction, as they lead to the destruction of passions. Not only the mendicant who keeps the precepts, but also the layman, is happy and rewarded. In what, then, consists the happiness of a religious life? We find the answer most poetically given in the following quotation from the Gātakatthavannanā:—

"By what can every heart attain to lasting happiness and peace? To him whose heart was estranged from sin the answer came: When the fire of lust is gone out, then peace is gained; when the fire of hatred and delusion are gone out, then peace is gained; when the troubles of mind arising from pride, credulity, and all other sins have ceased, then peace is gained."

The peculiarity of this answer is self-evident; it is, however, quite in accordance with the other tenets of Buddhism. A Buddhist, not knowing of any supreme external power by which salvation could be attained, had necessarily to look for salvation to an internal power. This power is found in the subjugation of passions, which is considered by Buddhists as amounting to the highest state of blessedness (beatitude).

In order to understand fully this doctrine, we have to turn our attention first to one of the earliest tenets of Buddhism, the so-called Chain of Causation. This doctrine is said to have been taught by succeeding Buddhas[5].

Before commenting on this Chain of Causation, it will perhaps be better to give a literal translation of the passage in which it is described. It is always difficult to translate philosophical terms. The expressions used may suggest associations with others already known from another philosophy, and impart thus an entirely wrong idea. It is more difficult still in the Buddhist philosophy. A native Hindu has naturally different ideas on this subject from one whose early training and surroundings have been entirely different.

"From ignorance spring the conditions of existence; from the conditions of existence spring consciousness; from consciousness the individual, consisting of mind and body; from the individual,

---

[5] It is well known that the orthodox Buddhist belief is that Gotama was not the only Buddha, but that other Buddhas preceded him; and that when the world is relapsing into wickedness, other Buddhas will follow to save it. We have thus in the Buddhava*m*sa, one of the sacred books, the history of twenty-four Buddhas, besides that of Gotama himself. Also a twenty-sixth Buddha is said to reside in the so-called Tusita heaven. Allusions are likewise made in various other parts of the Pi*t*akas.

the six organs of sense; from the six organs of sense, contact; from contact, sensation; from sensation, craving; from craving, attachment; from attachment, continued existence; from existence, birth; from birth, decay and death, sorrow, lamentation, pain, grief, and despair."

Ignorance, which, as the main cause of existence, is put at the head of the list, is explained to mean the ignorance of the four great truths on which the whole Buddhist philosophy is based,—the nature of suffering, the cause of suffering, the cessation of suffering, the path leading to the cessation of suffering. Without knowing these four truths, no beatitude can be brought about.

In ignorance, then, the conditions of existence have their origin. The term which I have translated "conditions of existence" has been rendered in different ways. Its meaning, however, appears clear: it is meant to signify that which causes a living being to be born in one of the Buddhist worlds, in a position determined by his previous thoughts, words, and actions.

The next link in the chain is consciousness, consisting of the consciousness of the eye, ear, nose, tongue, touch, and mind. This consciousness unites with the embryo in the mother's womb, and produces the individual, consisting of mind and body. These two links are thus united to each other; the existence of either of them is dependent on the other. Without consciousness, the individual cannot be produced; without the individual, no consciousness.

In the individual, the six organs of sense have their origin, which consist of the abstracts,—form, sound, odour, taste, contact, and ideas. These abstracts give rise to contact, which consists equally of six divisions corresponding to the above, viz. eye, ear, nose, tongue, body, and mind. It will be seen that for the five senses of our philosophy Buddhism has six, adding *mind* to them.

From contact springs sensation. We learn that this sensation is threefold,—pleasant, unpleasant, neither pleasant nor unpleasant. It gives rise to craving. Though later works enumerate a great number of cravings, all may be fairly divided into three groups,—craving for sensual pleasure, for continued existence, and for non-existence.

Craving is the cause of attachment, which is fourfold. Its divisions are sensual pleasure, wrong doctrines, ritualism, and self-consciousness. This attachment is the immediate cause of continued existence in one of the Sattalokas, the abode of living beings, of which there are thirty-one. A new birth arises from

Buddhism. 347

this continued existence, out of which follow decay, death, sorrow, lamentation, pain, grief, and despair.

It has been well said that this way of accounting for the continuance of existence is a somewhat arbitrary one. It is quite true that one thing does not necessarily follow out of the other, that the chain extends practically over three births, the first beginning with ignorance, the second with consciousness, and the last with attachment, as the cause of continued existence. But we should certainly considerably underrate the great reasoning-power of Buddhists, were we to suppose that they believed the links of the chain to follow strictly one out of the other. They are simply twelve reasons for continued existence which is *set on fire through the passions of lust, hatred, and delusion.*

An opportunity to free himself from this chain (which, for the world as a whole, is practically eternal, for birth follows birth) is given to the individual.

Questioned in what Beatitude (Nirvāna) consists, Gotama returns the answer, "In the extinction of the three fires of lust, hatred, and delusion;" and further questioned how the individual could attain to this beatitude, he returns the answer, "*Through the noble eightfold path,*" of which he thus enumerates the single divisions: right views, right aims, right speech, right conduct, right livelihood, right exertion, right-mindedness, and right meditation.

These terms are wide and general, and they would, without any explanation, embrace the substance of a holy life. However we find, though evidently in later parts of the Pitakas, an explanation of the path, which mostly substitutes technical expressions for the wide and general terms.

We learn thus that Buddhists considered right views as the knowledge of the four great truths, the ignorance of which, as we have shewn above, is the immediate cause of existence. Right aims are explained to be such as are free from malice and cruelty, and such as tend to a renouncing of the world.

The following three divisions, right speech, right conduct, and right livelihood, refer more to the practical part of the Buddhist life. Right speech and right conduct contain in themselves the essence of those of the Ten Commandments which treat of the duties towards our neighbours. Right speech is explained as to abstain from lying and slander, and from the use of harsh and frivolous language; right conduct, as to abstain from destroying life, from theft, and from unchastity. The third, right livelihood, takes a still more practical turn, as it enforces the gaining of a livelihood, which will not in any way harm a fellow-creature, or one's own mind or body. To gain a livelihood as a butcher would certainly be against this law. Other modes of gaining a living are open to objection, and the commentator enumerates, in the first instance, the livelihood which a dancing-girl gains by her occupation.

The explanation of the last three divisions occurs in the same way in the Abhidhamma-pi*t*aka; we may consider those three, therefore, as the earliest attempt to explain the terms which in the course of time had become unintelligible. As to the other explanations of the Abhidhamma-pi*t*aka, we must at present refrain from giving an opinion of them, as very little is known of the books in which they are contained.

The explanation of the last three divisions breathes again more of the philosophy of later Buddhism. We are told that right exertion means an occupation that shall so interest the mind, as to prevent any possibility of an evil condition of mind from arising, and also will dispel any sinful state or thought already in existence, thus producing a healthy condition both of mind and body.

Right-mindedness is explained to mean the continual recollection of the natural weakness and impurity of the body, the evils of sensation, the evanescence of thought, and the conditions of existence.

Right meditation, finally, is said to mean those profound meditations by which the believer's mind is purged from all earthly emotions, but no thought of any higher being is ever suggested.

We have purposely refrained from every polemic. Our statements have been taken from the earliest sacred writings of the Buddhists themselves, and we hope that they will tend to clear the way to a more correct understanding of Nirvā*n*a than is perhaps general [6].

The question has often been asked, whether Buddhist philosophy acknowledges the existence of a God who, as a supreme ruler,

---

[6] The common notion that Nirvā*n*a is annihilation, is certainly due to the fact that it is difficult for a European mind to imagine a state of blissful existence in life. Nothing in the Buddhist scriptures, as far as they are at present known, tends to confirm the idea that annihilation is the desired end of life. Another notion of Nirvā*n*a, where it is said to mean a blissful existence after death, is mostly propounded by writers on modern Burmese Buddhism. This we have reason to ascribe to the fact that one of the existences in heaven, as reward for a pious life, was mistaken for the final goal to which every Buddhist aspired as the *summum bonum*.

governs mankind and all sentient beings, and who is the framer of man's destiny? We have already drawn attention to the influence which the Vedic mythology exercised on the popular belief of the Indian people; how, in return for the sacrifices, the Hindu expected the granting of those wishes for which he asked. The *popular* Indian belief never raised itself to such a height of speculation as to acknowledge the simple notion of a single Creator. The notion always remained behind that only in return for sacrifices one could expect the fulfilment of wishes. In his pity for all living beings, Gotama disallowed sacrifices, and the next consequence was that man was not made dependent for the fulfilment of his wishes on the free-will of the gods. However, the belief in these gods was deeply rooted in the Indian mind, and was transferred to Buddhism, just as the belief in Thor, Wodan, Balder, and the rest prevailed among the Teutonic nations even after their conversion to Christianity. In our own fairy tales and epic poems we have a case exactly analogous. It is well known that Beowulf, Sigfrid, Kriemhild and Brunhild of the Nibelungenlied, are representatives of the gods of the old Norse mythology. They have become good Christians in the course of time, just as the Vedic gods became good Buddhists. Many a characteristic of their old power nevertheless still remained, and many a true and beautiful word and deed are related of them, not unworthy of their previous dignity. On the other hand, just as the Teutonic nations pitied the water-sprites because they could not be saved, the Buddhist would feel pity for some of the old Vedic gods because they could or would not listen to the teachings of the Buddha. The gods, however, seldom act from their own initiative, but nevertheless such a case is related in the later legend, when, after the attainment of Buddhahood, Gotama hesitates for a while to communicate to mankind the truths he has discovered, Mahā Brahmā quitted the Brahma world and appeared before him, and loosing his robe from one shoulder in token of respect, and falling upon one knee, implored the sage not to keep back from man the knowledge of the way of beatitude. A god has only a temporal existence, and he ranks of course below the Buddhas. The existence as a god is a reward for a pious life, but according to his kamma he will be born in a lower or higher station; he may, once upon a time, become a Buddha, and be thus able to release mankind and gods from all bonds of suffering. Thus the legends relate that Gotama himself was born four times as the god Indra (Sakka Inda devānam).

One can, in my opinion, neither blame Buddhism for its atheism or agnosticism, nor, on the other hand, pretend that Buddhism was a monotheistic religion. The reproach of atheism would only be justified if it could be proved that Buddhism received from another religion the notion and strict proof of the existence of a supreme being, which it wilfully ignored. Such is, however, not the case; no more is the notion of monotheism in accordance with the tenets of Buddhism. The Brahman, which the later Hindus raised to the dignity of an abstract supreme being, to whom they wished to be united, was in Buddhism still only one deity amongst many. As such, he had a temporary existence, as every other god of the Vedic Pantheon, and was subject to birth and decay. Moreover, the Buddhist did not recognise a soul in man, without which the idea of monotheism is not conceivable. It substitutes for soul the kamma of man (the outcome of his words, deeds, and thoughts), much in accordance with the Latin proverb, "Fortunæ suæ quisque faber est," and the well-known maxim of modern philosophy, that every being is only the outcome of the accumulated deeds of his ancestors[7].

The existence of living beings was not restricted to the earth, as the Buddhist world-system embraces innumerable abodes for living beings, in which they are born according to their kamma. The older theory of the migration of the soul maintained that the soul remained the same, and migrated as such to different corporeal forms. Buddhism, denying the soul, but admitting the *kamma*, the *individual* outcome of words, deeds, and thoughts, had the strange theory, in conformity with the older one of soul, that the kamma was accumulated in a new being.

It has often been asked how this theory of kamma, and the denial of the existence of a soul, can be brought into agreement with the fact that Gotama knew in what particular characters he had previously appeared among living beings, and how he could preserve consciousness, such as is related of him in the Gātakatthava*n*na*n*ā. This book contains, as is well known, fables and fairy tales, which are put in the mouth of the teacher with the purpose of enforcing a doctrine in a humorous way. Their ori-

---

[7] Cp. also Goethe's *Iphigenie auf Tauris*, Act I. Scene 3:—

"... Es erzeugt nicht gleich
Ein Haus den Halbgott noch das Ungeheuer;
Erst eine Reihe Böser oder Guter
Bringt endlich das Entsetzen, bringt die Freude
Der Welt hervor."

gin is doubtless due, "for the most part, to the religious faith of the Indian Buddhist of the third or fourth century B.C., who not only repeated a number of fables, parables, and stories, ascribed to the Buddha, but gave them a peculiar sacredness and a special religious significance, by identifying the best character in each with the Buddha himself in some previous birth" (Davids' *Buddhist Birth Stories*, vol. i. p. lxxxii.).

It has until lately been assumed that the *G*ātaka without the commentary is no longer extant; but I have seen a MS. of the *G*ātaka simply containing the verses, which gave the commentator an opportunity to relate the stories which he puts in the mouth of Gotama, and in which he makes him play a prominent part. It is, therefore, the commentator who is responsible for the perversion of the original doctrine. All vague assertions about the non-agreement of the denial of the soul with the fact of Gotama's knowledge of his previous existences are worthless. It is to be inferred, therefore, that through taking the *G*ātaka with the commentary as the original, the opinion arose that what the Buddha knew of his previous existences was due to the knowledge he had of the future, present, and past, which was one of the attributes of Buddhahood.

We have in the preceding paragraphs collected together such facts as can be considered firmly established about the life of the Buddha, and the law he preached. It remains now for us to describe the character of the community (Sangha) to which Gotama, in the first instance, directed his teachings. It has already been briefly noticed that orders of mendicants (bhikkhus) were not unknown at the time when Gotama commenced his teaching, and to such mendicants he addressed himself. The source of our knowledge of the discipline of the Buddhist community, lies in the Vinaya Pi*t*aka, which contains a collection of rules regulating the outward conduct of the Sangha and bhikkhus. It has been shewn on page 342, that the Pātimokkha, and a collection of rites form the main substance of the Vinaya, on which, in the course of time, in the form of a Commentary, the Vibhanga and Mahā-Vagga, have been enlarged. To obtain, therefore, a notion of earlier Buddhism, apart from historical researches, it will only be necessary to consult these two books.

We may take it for granted that Gotama, in the first instance, was the founder of a sect of mendicants, to whom he propounded his doctrine. He wandered about with them from place to place begging for alms, and caring little for the wants of the morrow. In the beginning of his teaching no fixed rules for the admission to the order of mendicants were laid down: but the ever-growing influx of his followers made it necessary to supply this want. Admission to the order was only granted to those who were free from all bodily ailments, and free from debt; who had received the permission of their parents, and were of the full age of twenty. These different laws shew that an abuse must have prevailed for some time, and in the Vinaya some stories are related which make it apparent that the laying down of these rules was highly necessary.

Food was collected *daily for the day* in an alms-bowl, one of the necessary requisites of a Buddhist monk, and no other food was allowed to be eaten. But of course, as time advanced, exceptions were granted, which made the rules valueless. It was then allowed to partake of meals which were offered to the whole order, or to a certain portion of it. Further, if a mendicant received a spécial invitation, he was allowed to go, and he received also permission to partake of the meals offered on certain days, as on the full-moon days, and the days following full-moon. His robes were to be taken from rags found on a dust-heap, or in a cemetery; but also here we find many exceptions to the rule. Robes made of linen, of cotton, of silk, of wool, of hemp, and of flax, were allowed to be worn, especially when offered as a gift of honour to a mendicant. He had to lodge at the foot of a tree. This rule, in its simplicity, shews us clearly that at the beginning the community was a wandering one, whilst the exceptions make it evident that Buddhism soon became a missionary body, anxious to make converts, and to obtain a permanent footing in the country. It was allowed to mendicants to dwell in monasteries, large houses, houses of more than one storey, houses surrounded by walls and rock-caves.

For his ailments he was only allowed to use cow's urine; doubtless a relic of Brahmanical superstition, where, as it is well known, the cow was considered a sacred animal. But in this case also later exceptions made the rule irrelevant; and if a modern physician might perhaps smile at the remedies, they could, at any rate, do little harm. They were clarified butter, butter, rape-oil, honey, and sugar-juice. Nay, legends even seem to prove that the art of medicine must have been greatly advanced. Thus a story is told of *G*īvaka, in the *G*ātakas, who, after he had been instructed by his teacher, was sent out by him to collect, in a circuit of several yo*g*anas around the town, such herbs as were *utterly useless* in medicine. The pupil returned saying that there was not a single herb which was useless.

No sexual intercourse was allowed to the monk, and the slightest breach of this commandment was followed by exclusion from the community. "Just as a man whose head has been cut off is unable to live, so does a monk who has indulged in sexual intercourse cease to be one, or to be a son of Sākya." Theft was rigorously forbidden: not a blade of grass was the monk to take; and a later addition enforces that if he should take a piece of silver of the worth of two shillings, he ceases to be a monk, or a son of Sākya.

The destruction of life was likewise forbidden; not even an ant must be killed. Abortion was considered, in a later addition of the law as amounting to the murder of a human being, and on this latter crime expulsion from the order followed.

To put a check to bragging about perfection, it was enforced that no mendicant should lay claim to more than human perfection; not even by saying that he delighted in solitude. Hereto were added, in the course of time, other regulations, which enforced that a monk, who for sake of gain untruly and falsely lays claim to these perfections, should be expelled from the community.

An institution belonging to the earliest Buddhism, is the assembly of the disciples twice a month, at full and new moon, to confess the sins which they had committed. According to their gravity, exclusion from the order, or temporary separation, followed the confession, or the offender had to give up the object with which he sinned. Thus, to give an instance, it would be an offence to wear a spare robe longer than ten days after a set of robes is finished; or, on the other hand, it is considered an offence if a monk accepts a robe from a nun, who is not related to him. Other offences, again, require confession and absolution, or confession alone.

In speaking of offences, it is, perhaps, worth noticing that those laws which a monk is required to observe when he first enters the order, are given under different headings. Unchastity is enumerated both as a deadly sin and as a fault, including temporary exclusion from the order; and in the same way theft is considered as a deadly sin, except in petty cases where it may be only a fault requiring confession and absolution. Only the destroying of life in a human body is considered a deadly sin, whilst taking of life falls under different general headings.

APPENDIX II.

The Notion of Conscience amongst the Zulus,
By Bishop Callaway.

The early missionaries found no word in the Zulu language for "conscience." Clearly the working of conscience was found amongst them; but we had no word to express what we mean by conscience. We could not tell a man, for example, to obey "the dictates of his *conscience:*" nor that he was misled by a debased conscience. If we used Inhlizingo (heart), we should be at once struck with the impropriety of telling him to do what, perhaps, we were continually warning him not to do, to listen to the dictates of his own heart; which he was always perfectly disposed to do, and claim the dictate of his heart as a sufficient reason and justification for any kind of evil. "My own heart told me to do it," was with the native a sufficient valid reason for doing anything. We were obliged to use cumbersome circumlocutions. I observed that they would use a saying, in speaking of a thoroughly bad, wilful evil-doer, as a reason for his abiding evil-doing, *Udhliwe Ugovana*, "He has been devoured (eaten up) by Ugovana," that is, all the good in him has been as utterly eaten up, as the cattle, &c., of one smelt out by the witch-doctor, have been eaten up by a party of Zulus, sent against him by Ketchwayo, for the purpose.

"Ugovana?" I enquired, "who is he?"

"Oh!" it was answered, "Ugovana is the *bad man* in us, and Unembeza is the *good man* in us."

This not very lucid answer might have led one in a hurry to conclude that the Zulu was speaking of a good and evil spirit, of whose working within him he was conscious. But on further enquiry, I found that Ugovana was the personification of an evil heart, and Unembeza of a good heart; "for," said my informant, "every man has two hearts in him, one urging him to do evil, and to leave off good, that is Ugovana; the other, not to do evil, but to do good, that is Unembeza. Ugovana comes to us with a big, blustering, but lying voice. He almost frightens us into doing evil; and calls us fools for not doing what we wish to do, and our hearts tell us to do; and asks us why we have wishes and feelings given us, if not to gratify them? But just as we are about to do the evil, Unembeza comes with a little tiny voice, so little, that we scarcely hear him amid the noise Ugovana is making, and says, 'No, no! do not that wicked thing. You know it is wicked! Do it not.' But we usually listen to the more noisy importunity of Ugovana."

Having mastered the two words, in order to test my proficiency, and see if I could speak a little more impressively on the subject of conscience than hitherto, I determined to use the words in a sermon. On a Sunday morning, at our usual congregation, when I introduced the words, every eye was at once turned to me, and, as I proceeded, I had the command of every one present; every face was raised to mine, aud every mouth slightly opened in rapt attention and interest. I knew they all understood me.

On leaving church, I said nothing to the Christian natives. I thought I would rather speak on the subject to a heathen-man who had been present, and proceeded to walk up the village; when I met the man, an old soldier of Dingan, I asked, "Jabisana, did you understand my sermon to-day?"

He replied, his face all beaming with a smile, "Yes, indeed I did, and here is a proof of it," turning aside his blanket, and exposing a four-pronged fork.

"But," said I, perplexed, "what has that fork to do with my sermon?"

"Oh," he said, "a great deal, as I will shew you; I was walking along by these houses, and saw this fork lying on the ground, and picked it up. Ugovana said, 'You are lucky to-day, Jabisana, you have found a fork. No one saw you pick it up. Hide it under your blanket, and take it home!' But Unembeza said, 'No, Jabisana, that would not be right. It is not your fork; it has an owner. Find him, and give him back the fork!'" And he added laughing, "I intend to obey Unembeza."

APPENDIX III.

The Purusha-Sūkta (*Rig-Veda Sanhitā*, Book x., Hymn 90; from Muir's *Sanskrit Texts*, vol. i. p. 9 foll.)

[This hymn is generally allowed to be comparatively modern, i.e. later than the main part of the Rig-Veda, both on account of its diction and grammatical structure, the philosophical terms employed, the mention of the three seasons in the order, spring, summer, autumn (*R.-V.*, x. 161. 4, has autumn, winter, spring), the description of the origin of the four castes, which are not mentioned elsewhere in the Rig-Veda, and similar reasons. It is, however, an interesting monument of early Hindu philosophy and cosmogony, before the rise of Buddhism.]

1. Purusha had a thousand heads, a thousand eyes, a thousand feet: on every side enveloping the earth, he overpassed (it) by a space of ten fingers.

2. Purusha himself is this whole (universe), whatever has been, and whatever shall be. He is also the lord of immortality, since (or when) by food he expands.

3. Such is his greatness, and Purusha is superior to this. All existences are a quarter of him; and three-fourths of him are that which is immortal in the sky.

4. With three-quarters Purusha mounted upwards. A quarter of him was again produced here: he was then diffused here everywhere, over things which eat and things which do not eat.

5. From him was born Virāg, and from Virāg, Purusha. When born, he extended beyond the earth, both behind and before.

6. When the gods performed a sacrifice with Purusha as the oblation, the spring was its butter, the summer its fuel, and autumn its (accompanying) offering.

7. This victim, Purusha, born in the beginning, they immolated on the sacrificial grass. With him the gods, the Sādhyas and the *Ri*shis, sacrificed.

8. From that universal sacrifice were provided curds and butter. It formed those aërial (creatures), and animals both wild and tame.

9. From that universal sacrifice sprang the *Rik* and Sāman verses, the metres and the ya*g*ush.

10. From it sprang horses and all animals with two rows of teeth; kine sprang from it; from it goats and sheep.

11. When (the gods) divided Purusha, into how many parts did they cut him up? what was his mouth? what arms (had he)? what (two objects) are said to have been his thighs and feet?

12. The Brāhman was his mouth; the Rāganya was made his arms; the being (called) the Vaisya, he was his thighs; the Sūdra sprang from his feet.

13. The moon sprang from his soul (*manas*), the sun from his eye, Indra and Agni from his mouth, and Vāyu from his breath.

14. From his navel arose the air, from his head the sky, from his feet the earth, from his ear the (four) quarters; in this manner (the gods) formed the worlds.

15. When the gods, performing sacrifice, bound Purusha as a victim, there were seven sticks (stuck up) for it (around the fire), and thrice seven pieces of fuel were made.

16. With sacrifice the gods performed the sacrifice. These were the earliest rites; these great powers have sought the sky, where are the former Sādhyas, gods.

By the same Author.

FRAGMENTS AND SPECIMENS OF EARLY LATIN, with Introductions and Notes; Oxford, at the University Press, 1874. 1 vol., 8vo., price 18s.

LECTURES INTRODUCTORY TO THE HISTORY OF THE LATIN LANGUAGE AND LITERATURE; Oxford, 1870. Price 2s. 6d.

UNIVERSITY SERMONS ON GOSPEL SUBJECTS; Oxford, 1878. Price 2s. 6d.

KEBLE COLLEGE AND THE PRESENT UNIVERSITY CRISIS.—A pamphlet; Oxford, 1869. Price 6d.

THE CHURCH AND THE UNIVERSITIES: a Letter to C. S. ROUNDELL, Esq., M.P., *with Postscript;* Oxford, 1880. Price 1s.

ERASMUS; SIVE THUCYDIDIS CUM TACITO COMPARATIO.—A Prize Essay; Oxford, 1866. Price 1s.

INDEX.

A few Corrigenda will be found on p. xiv.

Aaron's rod, 315 foll.
Abbott, Dr., *Through Nature to Christ*, 140 foll.
Abraham, faith of, 34 *n.*; promise to, "thou shalt go to thy fathers in peace," 147 *n.*
Absolution, value of, 328.
Academics, only admit probability, 100.
Ackermann, C., *The Christian Element in Plato*, 97 *n.*
Adam, ordered to work, 306 *n.*
Aditi, personification of Infinity, 78.
Agni, Hindu fire-god, 76.
Agnosticism inferior to Positivism, 307.
Ainos, position of the, 299.
Aisvarikas of Nepâl, 91.
Alabaster, H., *Wheel of the Law*, on merit-making in Siam, 269 *n.*; on Buddhist literature, 273 foll. *n.*; Buddhist social incapacity, 274 *n.*
Alcestis and Admetus, 165.
Alcestis, idea of Death in the, 155.
Alexandria, doctrine of the Church of, 305.
Altar to the "Unknown God," 144 foll.
Amenophis II., remarkable language of, 85.
Amitâbha Buddha, 271 *n.*
Andania, inscription of, 263 *n.*
Anglican Church, future of the, 287 foll., 291 foll.; possible mediation by, 291.
Anselm, St., *Cur Deus Homo*, 185 *n.*, 194, 195, 196.
Apollo, 78; purification by, 157.
Apostles, training of the, 329 foll.; assurances given to, 330.
"Apostolic," a title of the Church, 328.
Apostolic ministry, 315, 328 foll., 332.
Apostolic Succession, 333.
Areoi of Polynesia, 260 and *n.*
Aristotle, deistic tendency of his moral philosophy, 60; on desire of knowledge, 70; on human misery, 149; his idea of God, 191; on the social instinct, 218 *n.*; on the growth of Society, 219 *n.*; criticism of Plato's *Republic*, 229 *n.*; on slavery, 237 foll. *n.*

Ark, contents of the, 315 foll.
Arnold, Edwin, *The Light of Asia*, 123 foll.
Art-culture in the Church, 310 foll.
Asoka, king, council of, 92 *n.*; missions of, 268 *n.*; inscriptions of at Babra, 92 *n.*; elsewhere, 179 *n.*
Assyrian lamentation of a sinner, 157 foll.
Asva-medha, 164 *n.*
Athanasius, St., on Sabellianism, 53 *n.*
"Âtmadâ," meaning of, 172 *n.*
Atonement, heathen efforts after, 156—177.
Atonement, The, of Jesus Christ, attractiveness of, 185; its grandeur and breadth, 186 foll.; and God's Love, 191 foll.; and God's Justice, 197 foll.; its willingness, 198, 294; a revelation of the guilt and danger of sin, 200 foll.; a representation of all men, 204 foll.; union with, 215, 327.
Augustine, St., on Porphyry, 103; attacks both Pelagians and Manichæans, 114; on Varro and Scævola, 240 *n.*; on Old Testament morality, 251 *n.*; on death of Monica, 295; justifies persecution, 313 and *n.*
Aurelius, Marcus, his idea of duty, 225 and *n.*
Authority, nature of, 122; instinct for, 127 foll.; gives strength, 131.
Authority, tendency to disregard, 26.
Avatârs of Vishnu, 86.
Avesta, character of the, 94; Spiegel's, 159 *n.* See Pârsîs, Vendîdâd.
Avidyâ, principle of, 46 *n.*

Bacon, Francis, and the Logos doctrine, 305 *n.*; on the duty of work, 306 *n.*; on the need of humility, 319.
Balder, revival of, 208.
Bancroft, H., *Native Races of the Pacific States*, refs. in notes, 83, 147, 159, 161, 167, 169, 174, 175, 208.
Banerjea, Rev. K. M., *The Arian Witness*, 171 foll.; cp. 163 *n.*
Baptism, 322; heathen rites of, 161 *n.*,

322 n.; parody of, 325; emotion excited by, 325; S. Cyprian on, 326.
Barker, Joseph, on character of atheists, 13 n.
Barth, A., on extinction of Buddhism, 266 n.
Beauty, sense of, 310.
Benson, E. W., Bp. of Truro, on St. Cyprian, 295 n.
Berkeley, Bishop, on the supposed defect of evidence for revelation, 5.
Bernard, St., on love, 19 n.; against persecution, 313 n.
Bible, admits the thought of injustice, 5; superiority of its idea of God, 37, &c.; comprehensiveness of, 113, 114 n.; and other religious books, 119 foll.; union of fact and symbol in, 137.
Bird, Miss, *Unbeaten Tracks in Japan*, conversion at Otsu, 142; treatment of the Ainos, 299 n.
Bishops instruments of Christian fellowship, 333. See Episcopal.
Blasche quoted by H. L. Mansel, 104 n.
Blood, offering of, 162 foll.; washing in, 163.
Brahmâ, myth of, 84.
Brâhma-Samâj, the, 97 n., 214, 325.
Brewer, J. S., *Monumenta Franciscana*, 313 n.
Browning, R., *The Confessional*, 10 n.; *A Death in the Desert*, 20.
Buddha, Amitâbha, 271 n.
Buddha, Gotama, life of, 87; date of his death, &c., 88 n.; sympathy with humanity, 88, 267, 268; doctrines of, 88 foll., 266—272; audacity of, 89; pessimism of, 90, 271; Pelagianism, 90, 114, 281; his doctrine of Nirvâna, 270 n.; worship of, and romantic legend, 91 and n.; his triumph-song, 123; pretensions to apathy, 124; on evil in the human heart, 150; godlike condescension of, 267; meaning of Buddha, *ib.*; his missionary spirit, 268; words at Isipatana, 268 n.; supposed prophecy of the extinction of his religion, 275; his means recommended to Christian missionaries, 275 foll.; contrasted with our Lord, 124, 330.
Buddhahood, how attainable, 124; Buddha's words on attaining, *ib. n.*
Buddhism, and the non-existence of the soul, 90 n.; three refuges of, 188; selfishness of, 204; the greatest voluntary association outside Christendom, 265; extinguished in India, 265; its wonderful expansion, 266; northern, 266, 271, 274; its two great verities, *ib.*; its moral power, 265, 267; its great defect, 267 foll.; compared with Positivism, 268 foll.; two schools of, *ib. n.*; missionary spirit of, *ib.*; doctrine of sin and merit, 269 foll.; indulges tedium of life, 270; highly anti-social, 271 foll.; developed out of monasticism, 272; early activity of, 273; literature of, *ib.*; modern apathy of, 273 foll.; Chinese, criticised by Confucianists, 274 foll.; in Ceylon, 274; tradition and prophecy about, 275.
Buddhism, *Sacred Books of*, see Dhammapada, Gâtakas, Lalita-Vistara, Mahâ-parinibbâna-Sutta, Suttanipâta; writers on, see Alabaster, Davids, Edkins, Eitel, Frankfurter, Hardy, Legge, Müller, Saint-Hilaire.
Buddhist Sacred Books, their date, 92 n., 341 f.j; theory of the origin of sacrifice, 179 n.; pilgrims, 265 foll. n.; Nirvâna, 90, 270 foll., 347.
Buddhists, number of, 92, and n., 265.
Burial-clubs at Rome, 264.
Burnet [Bp.], *Life of Rochester*, 141 foll. n.
Bushmen, 28 n.
Butler, Bp., *Analogy*, on reason, 18; on a state of probation, 24; on natural cures of evil, 184; on repentance, 185; on rash judgment, 189; on innocent suffering for the guilty, 197.
Byzantine Greek character, 296.

Cain, the sign given to, 157.
Caldwell, Bp., on worship of Krishna, 210.
Callaway, Bp., on religious ideas of the Kaffirs, 35 n.; on Kaffir idea of conscience, 151 n., and App. II.
Calvinism, sometimes an occasion of unbelief, 9.
Carlyle, T., on Positivism, 128 n.; on the Koran, 257 n.; cp. 248 n.
Carter, Rev. T. T., *On the Divine Revelation*, 196 n.
Caste, influence of, 238; cp. 338; abolished by Buddhism, 266; superseded in temple of Jagannâth, 323.
Catholicity, attribute of, 300 foll.; connected with the resurrection, 301; St. Cyril on, *ib.*; in action, 302 foll.; in thought and philosophy, 305 foll.; in art, 310; in literature, 311; in sentiment, 312 foll.
Cato's saying about the haruspices, 240 and n.
Centurion, the, of Capernaum, 329.

Cerinthus, unites Ebionism and Docetism, 65 n.
Ceylon, 266, 268 n., 274 foll.
Chaldean astrology, 75.
Chandar Sen, Keshab, his testimony to Christ, 214.
Charismata, the, 314; cp. 332.
Cheyne, T. K., on Cyrus and Darius, 50; on Isa. xxxv. 8, 182 n.
Children, sacrifice of, its reason, 168.
China, state religion of, 57 foll.; its great defect, 58; wanting in ideal elements, 135. See Confucius, Edkins, Legge.
Chinese Buddhism, 266, 269, 271, 274 foll.
Chinese empire, unique position of, 86, 221; deification of emperors, 85; ideal of government, 222—226; Emperor Thang offers himself, 165.
Chinese primitives, date of, 30.
Chiron and Prometheus, see corrigenda, xiv., 165, 199.
Christ, our Lord, His claims, 125 foll.; contrast with Buddha and Mahomet, 124 foll., 330; the Atonement of, 185 foll.; willing sacrifice of, 198, 294; the revealer of judgment, 202 foll.; our representative, 203 foll.; our example,215 foll.; coincidence of freedom and obedience in, 293; His presence in the Eucharist, 117, 327; His "plan" as to the ministry, 330 foll. See Atonement, Incarnation, Logos.
Christ, Jesus, the character of in literature, 311; evidence given by, 320; sceptics shirk enquiry into, 320; cp. 336 n.
Christ, Mahomet's testimony to, 125; Moslem reverence for, 257 and n.; but cp. 256, 257 foll.; Spinoza's testimony to, 212; Rousseau's, 213; Chandar Sen's, 214; the, of imagination and the real, 211; the *Imitation of Christ*, how read by Positivists, 213 and n.
Christlieb, Th., *Modern Doubt and Christian Belief*, 43 n.
Christology, Eutychian, 54; Ebionite, 63, 124; Nestorian, 65; cp. 211.
Christology, ideal, without the creed, 129, 141.
Church, notes of the, in the Creed, 279 foll. See Lecture VIII. *passim;* and cp. Peace.
Church, Dean, on *Sacred Poetry*, 120 n., 161 n.; *Influences of Christianity on National Character*, 288 n., esp. 297 n.
Church Quarterly Review, *Theodore of Mopsuestia*, 65; *Nicene Creed*,

280 n.; *Opium Trade*, 300 n.; *Christian Marriage*, 334 n.
Cicero, *de Natura Deorum* quoted, 100; *Tusculans*, on wilful immorality, 151; *de Officiis*, on the social instinct, 218 n.; *de Divinatione*, Cato on the haruspex, 240.
Civilization, its work under God, and its connection with mental and moral changes, 3; ancient, based on slavery, 237; does not produce Holiness, 292; its depressing effect on native races, 299 n.
"Civis Romanus sum," 227.
Clarke, Dr. Samuel, on necessity of Miracles, 127 n.; Revelation agreeable to Reason, 132 n.
Clay, J. C., on the Vatican Council, 241 n.
Cleanthes, sin an impiety, 153.
Clement of Alexandria on Buddha, 91 n.; on the mystic chests, 316 n.
Clementines, author of the, 130.
Clergy, reproaches against, 11; connexion with the Universities, *ib.*
Clifford, Prof., *Ethics of Belief*, 24 n.
Codrus, dying for his people, 165.
Coleridge, quoted by J. S. Mill, 19 n.
Communion of Saints, 283.
Communion, Holy, 322 foll., 325, and esp. 327 foll.; heathen and other parallels, 322 foll.; cp. 264.
Comprehensiveness of Christian Doctrine, 110, 112 foll.
Comte, Auguste, quoted by H. L. Mansel, 105 n.; sympathy with Romanism, 128; recommends the *Imitation of Christ*, 213; and Dante, *ib.* n.; on adoration of women, &c., 229 n.; on living openly, 260 n. See Positivism.
Confession, 157—161, 328.
Confirmation, 328.
Confucius, coldness of his character, 58; date of, 88 n.
Congreve, R., on reading *the Imitation*, 213 n.
Constantine, legislation of, 297 foll.
Contemporary Review, *Greek Mind and Death*, 148 n.; *Muhammedan Law*, 257 n.; *Positivism and Christianity*, 309 n.
Copleston, R. S. [Bp. of Colombo], preface, ix.
Corn-ears, in the mysteries, 316 foll.
Cotton, Bp. of Calcutta, his prayer, iv.
Councils, Church, influence of, 303; Buddhist, 273.
Crates, some evil in every man, 150.
Creed, sustaining power of the, 187 foll.; cp. 318 foll.; of the Church of Jerusalem, 280 and n.; of Constantinople, *ib.*; 'Nicene,' *ib.*

Crete, medium between Egypt and Greece, 262 n.
Cross in Mexican sacrifice, 175.
Crusades, the, their results, 304.
Cube, symbolism of the, 282 n.
Cyprian, St., his martyrdom, 295; on baptism, 326.
Cyril, St., of Jerusalem, on the Creed, 280 n.; on Catholicity, 301.
Cyrus and Darius, 50; called "my shepherd," 221.

Dale, R. W., *On the Atonement*, 199 n.
Darmesteter, James, 50 foll., 155.
Darwin, Mr., and the Fuegians, 28 n.
Davids, T. W. Rhys, on Buddhism, quoted in the notes, 87—92 *passim*; on its extinction in India, 265 n.; on Buddha's sermon, 268 n.; on *Buddhist Birth Stories*, 273 n.
Death, a friend in the golden age, 147; an avenger, 154; impurity of, 154 foll.
Deism, Anthropomorphic, puts God outside the world, 55; its connection with Judaic, or Ebionite elements, 44, 61 foll.; in modern philosophy, 305 and n.
Delhi, religious function at, 204.
Delitzsch, F., *Christliche Apologetik*, on the idea of death, 154 n.; on sacrifice, 162 n.; on Rabbinical Jewish sacrifice, 164 n.; on Chinese sin-offerings, 166 n.; on self-sacrifice, 169 n.; on the incompetence of the State, 232 n.
Delphi, oracle of, 78, 79.
Demeter, myths of, 262; her emblems, 317.
Developments, one-sided, 319.
Dhammapada quoted, on 'self,' 90 n.; has no reference to marvels, 91 n.; preface to, on Buddha's date, 88 n.; on power of men over themselves, 114 n.; on evil in the heart, 150; on uselessness of sacrifice, 179 n.; on the three refuges, 188 n.
Diodotus, speech in Thucydides, 150.
Dionysus-Zagreus, 262 foll.
Dionysiac Enthusiasm, 316 foll.
Disunion of Christendom, 282 foll.
Divorce, Moslem, 255 and n.; in America, 334 n.
Doctrine, Christian, union with respect to, 285; an instrument of peace, 318 foll.; cp. 121, 130, 187.
Dodona, oracle of, 74.
Döllinger, Dr., *Heidenthum*, referred to in notes, on the Delphic oracle, 79; danger of myths, 98; slight hope of immortality, 101; impurity of death, 155; Egyptian confession, 161; sacrifice, 163, 164, 167; on the mysteries, 262; on mystic chests, 316; heathen sacraments, 323.
Dominicans, 313.
Dorian principles, 261.
Dorner, J. A., *System of Chr. Doct.* on Hegel, 47 n.; Schleiermacher, 53 n.; Scotus, 63 n.; modern heresy, 65 n.; *Person of Christ*, on Sabellius, 53 n.; Scotus, 63 n.
Douglas, R. K., 46 n., 209 n.
Dualism, characterized, 49 foll.
Dubois, Cardinal, 10.

Eaton, J. R. T., *Politics*, 218 n.
Ebionite Christology, 63, 124; cp. 284.
Edda, Saemund's, 84 n., 208; Snorri's, 94 and n.; cp. Grimm, Odin.
Edkins, Dr., on Imperial worship in China, 57 n.; worship of Amitâbha Buddha, 271 n.; Confucianist criticism of Buddhists, 275 n.
Egypt, knowledge of, goes back to B.C. 3000, acc. to Mr. Renouf, 30 n., 84; esoteric doctrine pantheistic, 48 and n.; negative confession of sin, in the *Book of the Dead*, 161.
Egyptian Kings deified, 84 foll.
Eitel, Dr., refs. in notes to his *Buddhism*, on the Hînâyana, 268; paradise of western heaven, 271; position of women, 272; Northern Buddhism, 274.
Eleusinia, accounts of the, 262.
Ellicott, Bp., *the Being of God*, 49 n.
Emperor, Roman, worship of, 85, 128, 210, 240 foll. See China, King.
England, influence of its constitution and inventions, 291. See Anglican Church, New England.
Epimenides, altar erected by, at Athens, 145 n.; introduces Orphic mysteries from Crete, 262 n.
Episcopal government, early spread of, 284; necessary to the Church, 333; results of, contrasted with Presbyterianism, 334 n.
Eskimo, 28 n.
Eucharist, see Communion, Holy, 322, 327.
Euhemerism, 240.
Euripides, *Ion*, 78 n.; *Cresphontes*, 149; *Alcestis* and *Hippolytus* on impurity of Death, 154 foll.; *Minos* on Orphic life, 262 n.; cp. 316.
Eutychian heresies tend to pantheism, 52, 54 foll.
Evolution, influence of the theory of, 307; a process not a cause, 320.

INDEX. 363

Faith suitable to a moral being, 24; connected with awe by Hindus, 74; Christian, see Lect. IV. *passim;* its contact with scepticism, 321; sometimes selfish, *ib.* See Creed, Doctrine, Truth.
Fall, the, its effects, 194.
Fan-Hian, 265 *n.*
Fatherhood, influence of the idea on society, 220 foll.
Fergusson on the Temple, 282 *n.*
Feuerbach quoted by H. L. Mansel, 104 *n.*
Filioque controversy, 285.
Fire-gods, 76.
Forgiveness, Divine, not a mere release, 195.
Foucart, P., *Des Associations Religieuses*, 263.
Francis, St., de Sales, words of, 295.
Franciscans, 313.
Frankfurter, Dr. O., on the date of Buddha, 88 *n.*; on the Gātakas, 273 *n.* See pref. ix., and App. I.
Free-will and grace conciliated, 113.
Frere, Sir Bartle, *Christianity suited to all forms of Civilization*, 141 *n.*; on Moslem character, 258; on treatment of lower races, 299 *n.*; Paper at Newcastle on Opium Trade, 300 *n.*
Friends, Society of, and Christian Unity, 285; and spiritual life, 332.
Fuegians, conversion of the, 28 *n.*

Gardner, Percy, *the Greek mind in the presence of death*, 148 *n.*
Gâtakas, or Buddhist Birth-stories, 273 *n.*
Gâyatrî, Hindu prayer, 76 *n.*, 161 *n.*
Genesis, early chapters of, 137 foll.; on marriage, 255; on the duty of work, 306 *n.*
Gerland, G., *das Aussterben der Naturvölker*, on human sacrifice, 166; on the Areoi, 250 *n.*; on melancholy of native races, 299 *n.*
"Great Plan" of the Shû King, 225.
Gnosticism, 51 and *n.*; early and modern, 139—141.
God, idea of, as arrived at by the reason, 36; wonderful relation of men towards, 71; His action often excluded from history of religion, 72; always our teacher, 25 *n.*, 321; our power as fellow-workers with, 321; condescension of, in creation a key to other mysteries, 176; His love, 191 foll.; His mercy, 195; His justice, 197; Fatherhood of, and Christian action, 302 foll.; cp. 321. See Monotheism, Theism, "I am that I am."

God, name of in Chinese, 57 *n.*; mean idea of in the Koran, 63, 244 foll., 253; Plato's idea of, 98, 191; Aristotle's, 191; "unknown" to the heathen, 145 foll.; sense of separation from, Lect. V. *passim.*; the Creator overlooked by Buddhism, 89, 268, 348 foll.
Gods, living and travelling amongst men, 83; passing away of the, 96 *n.*
Golden age, myths of, 146 foll.
Gospels, criticism of the, 320, 336 *n.*; "the Institution of a Christian Ministry," 329.
Gotama, the Buddha, 87 foll.; his godlike condescension, 267; facts of his life, 340. See Buddha.
Grace and Free-will equally asserted in the Bible, 113.
Granth of the Sikhs, 119 *n.*
Greek myths of golden age, 146 foll.
Greek religion, superficial sense of sin in, 148; melancholy idea of life, 148 foll.
Grimm, *Teutonic Mythology*, 74 *n.*, 84 *n.*; horse sacrifice, 164 *n.*; human sacrifice, 167 *n.*, 168 *n.*
Guilds, private religious, in Greece, 263; in Italy, 264.
Guizot on the mediæval Church, 288 *n.*

Hades, legends of, 203, 262; Gods of, protect their favourites, 263 *n.*
Hardwick, Archd., *Christ and other Masters*, pref., vii., 84, 86, 91, 209.
Hardy, R. Spence, *Manual of Buddhism*, 124 *n.*; on merit-making, 269 *n.*; *Eastern Monachism* on mental inertness of Buddhists, 274 *n.*; prophecy of the extinction of Buddhism, 275 *n.*
Havet, Ernest, on the Gospels, 336 *n.*
Hegel, his definition of Religion, 47 *n.*; on the Fall, 194 *n.*
Hegelianism, its pantheistic tendency, 46 foll.; cp. 65 *n.*
Heimdall, 84.
Heliogabalus reintroduces human sacrifice, 167.
Heraclitus, on oracles, 80.
Herbert, George, *The Pulley* quoted, 105.
Herbert, Lord, of Cherbury, 64; his book, *de Veritate*, and *Autobiography*, 129.
Heresy, various types of, see Lecture II., and the Table, 68; on fundamental doctrines, how far limited, 285.
Hermit life, 218.
Hesiod, on ignorance of prophets, 103; on the golden age, 147 foll.

Hindu philosophy, pantheistic character, 48, 267; cp. 238; religion characterized, 134 foll., 238; confession of sin, 161 n.; identification of victim and sacrificer, 163; sacrifice and austerity ascribed to the gods, 170 foll.; human sacrifice, 166 n., 169 n. See Banerjea, Jagannâth, Muir, Müller, Vedas, Vishnu, Wilson, Williams.
Hiouen Thsang, 266 n.
Hippolytus, St., on Ebionites, 124.
Historical character of the Christian Creed, 136 foll.
History, Biblical, compared with popular mythology, 137.
Hobbes, Thomas, and the Canon of Scripture, 65; on the origin of society, 218 n.; supports State religion, 235; the father of Deism, 305 n.
Holiness, desire for, see Lect. V., VI.
Holiness, of the Church, rests on divine grace, 292 foll.; in individuals, 294 foll.; in nations, 296 foll.; required by Christ, 300.
"Holiness" misapplied by Positivists, 293.
[Holland, H. S.], on Opium Trade with China, 300 n.
" Holy," a title of the Church, 280 n.; 292 foll.
Holy Spirit, the, His work in art, 310 foll.; in the call to repentance, 312; the charismata of, 314.
Homer, on human misery, 148.
Homeric poems and the Bible, 121 n.; hymn to Demeter quoted, 263 n.
Hooker, R., on the Sacraments, 324 n., 325 n.
Hope remaining after the other Gods, 148 n., 184.
Horace, on wilfulness, 154 n.; on sacrifice, 180.
Horse sacrifice, 164.
Hughes, Rev. T. P., Notes on Muhammadanism, on Divine decrees and Sufiism, 62 n.; on the Koran, 119 n.; on Mahomet's acceptance of miracles, 125 n.; on his sinfulness, ib.; on practical religion of Islam, 245 n.; on Jihâd, 246 n.; on character of Mahomet as binding Moslems, 248 n.; ill-effects of Islam, 254 n.
Humility, appreciated by Plato and Plutarch, 153 n.; Celsus on Christian, ib.; by Lao-tse, 153 n., 209; Christ's, 211 foll.
Hunter, Dr. W. W., Orissa, on Jagannâth, 169, 323 n.; Indian Musalmans, 246 n.

Hutton, R. H., Christ's prophecies of His own death, 336 n.
Hwang-Ti, imperial title in China, 85.

I am that I am, the words commented on, 38, 49 n.
Idolatry extirpated by Mahomet, 253; partial survival in Islam, ib. n. See Emperor, Positivism.
Idol-meats, why forbidden, 323 n.
Ignatius St., to the Smyrneans, on the fact of our Lord's death and resurrection, 139.
Ignorance, especially of religious truth, sinful, 7; of philosophers and poets, their confessions of, 99—104; escape from, the object of Buddhism, 267.
Imad-ud-deen, Rev., Autobiography of, 245 n., 246 n.
Imitation of Christ read by Positivists, 213; cp. 216.
Imposition of hands in sacrifice, 163; in the inauguration of Kings and Priests at Rome, 322 n.
Incarnation, The, of Christ, 176, and Lect. VI. passim; philosophy founded on the, 309; connection with the Sacraments, 324.
Indian religion, flexible and unhistorical, 134 foll.; contrasted with Islam, 135. See Hindu.
Indra, faith in, 74.
Inexhaustibility of Holy Scripture, 118 foll.
Infallibility, Papal, artificial character of, 118 n.; how justified, 241; its proclamation condemns the Papacy, 288 foll.; remarkable coincidence in dates, 288 n.
Infinity and Personality of God combined, 38 foll.; how this truth may be received, 40 foll.
Inspiration, natural belief in, 92 foll.
Intellectual avarice, 23.
Intellectual coldness, 17.
Intellectual indolence, 14 foll.
Intellectual pride, 22.
Intellectual recklessness, 21.
Intelligibility, characteristic of truth, 131.
Invisible Church, 282 foll.
Irenæus, St., on the continuance of faith and hope, 25 n.
Isaiah xxxv. verses 7, 8, "the way of holiness," 181 foll.
Islam, acknowledges the Scriptures, 34 n.; its doctrine of divine decrees (Taqdi'r), 62 n.; its deistic temper, 62 foll.; creed of, does not come home to natural reason, 132; contrast with Indian Pan-

INDEX. 365

theism, 135 foll.; unprogressive, 136; absence of miracles in, 125 n., and 142 n.; defective theology of, 244 foll.; formal character, 245; banishes doctrine of Redemption, 245; gloomy ethics, 246; good works, ib.; harshness, 246 foll.; weighted with character of Mahomet, 247 foll.; ill effects of, on society, 254 foll.; paralyses intellectual and religious development, 256; opposes the Gospel, 257. See Hughes, Koran, Mahomet, Sir W. Muir, R. B. Smith, &c.
Israel, history of, 138 foll.; what they found in Canaan, 140 n.; unique position of, 320. See Jews.
Italian spirit in religion, 241.

Jagannâth, car of, 169; worship of, in Orissa, 323.
Japan, 142, 266, 299 n.
Jeremiah, on God's power and man's free-will, 113.
Jesuits, their supposed influence on Franco-German war, 288 n.; their work, 313.
Jews, Rabbinical, sacrifice of, 164; St. Bernard and, 313 n. See Ark, Israel, Moses.
Jihâd, religious war, 246 n.
Job, book of, admits a sense of injustice into the Bible, 5.
Joinville, on the sceptical master of theology, 5.
Jowett, Prof., his translation of Plato quoted, 153, 242; on Dorian influences on Plato, 261 n.
Judgment, revealed by the Saviour, 203.
Justin Martyr, conversion of, 130.

Kaffir death-song, 35; a, on idea of God, ib.; idea of conscience, 151, and Appendix II., 354.
Kakravarti, title of, 92.
Kalki, avatâr of Vishnu, 208 n.
Karma, Buddhist doctrine of, 90, 184, 350.
Kay, Dr. W., *The Missionary*, on Pantheism, 45 n.; *Promises of Christianity*, 296 n.; policy as to opium trade, 300 n.
Kings, deification of, 84—86. See Emperor.
Kingship, idea of, 220 foll.
Knowledge, a duty as well as a natural desire, 6, 7; cp. 310; limits of, 308.
Koran, respect for the, 119; put forward by Mahomet as a miracle, 125 n.; cunning ascribed to God in, 244 n.; character of God in, 245; atonement rejected in, ib. n.; the Fall, ib.; ferocious Sura ix. and other passages on religious war, 246 n., 247; how far tolerant, 247 n.; a witness to Mahomet's sinfulness, 247 foll. n.; cp. 253; Suras giving licence to Mahomet, 250 n.; against certain crimes, 255; on polygamy, &c., ib.; its character, esp. as taking the place of the Bible, 256 foll.; denies our Lord, 257 foll.
Krishna, 87; sensual worship of, 210.

Labour, duty of, 303; cp. 306.
Lactantius, on Seneca as a witness against heathenism, 152.
Lalita-Vistara, legend of Buddha, 96 foll. n.
Lamech's wives, not a solar myth, 137 foll. n.
Lao-tse, on humility, 209; cp. 153 n.
Las Casas and slavery, 298.
Lasaulx, *die Sühnopfer*, 167 n.
Latin character influenced by Christianity, 296. See Roman.
Laws of nature, 306 foll.
Legge, Prof. James, on date of Chinese primitives, 30 n.; on name of God in Chinese, 57 n.; quotation from Chinese prayers, 57 foll.; on Confucius, 58; on idea of inspiration in China, 59 n.; on title Hwang-Tî, 85 n.; on Emperor Thang, 165 n.; on Lao-tse, 209 n.; Chinese criticism of Buddhism, 275 n.; on opium-trade, 300 n.
Leland *on the Deists*, 235 n.
Lenormant, François, *Origines de l'Histoire d'après la Bible*, 137 n.; on Cain's confession, 157 n.
Liberty, vindication of, 226 foll.
Liddon, H. P., preface, x; on the Bible, 114 n.; on our Lord's claims, 123 n.; on the sense of sin, 149 n.; on mission from Christ, 328.
Lightfoot, J. B. [Bp. of Durham], St. Paul and Seneca, 60 n.; on the Tübingen theory, 284 n.
"Live openly," a Christian motto, 260.
Lobeck, *Aglaophamus*, its value and defects, 261 n.
Locke, John, on human ignorance of God, 37; on miracles, 127.
Logos, The, working in History, 108; doctrine of the, 305 foll., 309; and Lord Bacon, 305 n.
Loki, 84.
Love, necessary to understand the language of Love, 19; its power in extending and intensifying personality, 41; true character of, 192 foll.
Lucan, Cato's speech in, quoted, 45.

Lucian, Pseudo-, *Philopatris*, on the "unknown God," 145.
Lustration of a city, 234.
Lustrations, imply taint of sin, 161. See Baptism.
"Lustricus, dies," 323 *n.*
Luthardt, *Fundamental Truths*, 10 *n.*, 209 *n.*; *Saving Truths*, 149 *n.*, 165 *n.*; *Moral Truths*, 149 *n.*
Lycurgus, legislation of, 261.

Mahâ-parinibbâna-Sutta quoted, on the Buddha's age, 87 *n.*; on the noble truths, 88 foll.; on the three refuges, 89; date of, 92 *n.*; salvation attained by each for himself, 114 *n.*
Mahomet, did not claim miracles, 125 *n.*, and 142 *n.*; contrasted with our Lord, 125, 330; admitted the sinlessness of Christ, 125 *n.*; cp. 247; his principle of enforcing religion, 236, 244 foll.; low idea of the Fall, 245; a mediator to some of his followers, 245 *n.*; did not love God, 246 *n.*; his attitude to idolaters, Jews and Christians, 246 foll. *n.*; confesses his own sinfulness, 247 and *n.*; his mixed character, 248; his moral lapse, 249—251; his harem, 249 *n.*; acts of cruelty, *ib.*; why not a true prophet, 250 foll.; relations to Mary and Zeinab, 250 *n.*; how far sincere, 252 foll.; his reforms, 253, 255; not content with his proper position, 254; establishes a low social state, 255; closed the Bible, 256; puts his own character in the place of Christ's, 256; false teaching about Christ, 257; false prophecy of Peace, 259, 276, 278.
Mahomet, writers on, referred to in the notes:—T. Carlyle, 248, 257; T. P. Hughes (q.v.), 125, 248; J. B. Mozley (q.v.), 63, 245; Sir W. Muir (q.v.), 249, 250; Th. Nöldeke, 248; J. B. Saint-Hilaire (q.v.), 247, 249; R. B. Smith (q.v.), 246, 248, 250, 252; Sprenger, 249; Stobart, 245, 246, 249, 258; Tiele, 249.
Mahometans acknowledge the Scriptures, 34. See Islam, Moslems.
Maine, Sir H., *Early History of Institutions*, 219 *n.*
Manco Ccapac sacrifices his child, 168.
Manna, the, as a type, 315.
Manning, Cardinal, on opium, 300 *n.*
Mansel, H. L. [Dean], on Anthropomorphism, 43 *n.*; on Gnostics, 51 *n.*; on ignorance of Modern Philosophers, 104 *n.*
Mâra, the Buddhist Tempter, 124 *n.*
Marquardt, J., *Privatleben der Römer*, 323 *n.*; *Staatsverwaltung*, 323 *n.*, 324 *n.*
Marriage, Moslem idea of, inferior to Hindu, 255 *n.*; Christian, 303, 328, 334; cp. 219. See Polygamy, Divorce.
Martensen, *Christian Dogmatics*, 191 *n.*
Maurice, F. D., *Religions of the World*, preface, vii.; *Kingdom of Christ*, on absolution, 328 *n.*; on the Ministry, 329; sacerdotalism, 332 *n.*; Episcopacy, 333.
Megasthenes on Buddha, 91 *n.*
Merit, Buddhist doctrine of, 269 foll.
Merivale, Dean, on the Perusinæ aræ, 167 *n.*; on the cessation of sacrifice, 178 *n.*
Messianic prophecy, 207 foll.
Mexican mythology, 83; confessions of sin, 159 foll.; baptism of infants, 161 *n.*; human sacrifice, 166 foll.; cp. 160, 169 *n.*; reaction against, 169 *n.*; sacrifice of gods Huitzilopochtli and Xiuhtecutli, 174. 175 *n.* See also Quetzalcoatl.
Mill, John Stuart, his dejection and collapse, 19.
Milman, Bp. of Calcutta, *Love of the Atonement*, 203 *n.*
Ministry, Christian, its value, 291, 315, 331 foll.; institution of in the Gospels, 329 foll.; brings home Christ's presence, 331—333; influence on doctrine and morals, 334. See Ordination.
Minucius Felix, on natural monotheism, 34 *n.*
Miracles, asked for by Pharisees and Sadducees, 61 foll.; necessary for a Revelation, 127 *n.*, 142 *n.*; Christ's admitted by Mahomet, 125; absence of, in Islam, 125 *n.*, and 142 *n.*
Missionary alphabet, xiii.
Missions, Church, 304; cp. preface, viii. foll. See Oxford.
Mitra, God of day, 77.
Moab, King of, sacrifices his son, 168.
Moloch, sacrifice to, 167, 168 *n.*
Mommsen, Th., on decay of Roman religion, 240; *de Collegiis*, 264 *n.*; *R. Staatsrecht* on inauguration, 322 *n.*
Monasticism, value of, 218 *n.*, 313 foll.
Monica, death of, 295.
Monotheism, natural, 33 foll.; only

INDEX. 367

publicly held by those who possess the Scriptures, 33 foll., 37.
Moravians, 313.
Moses and the Ethiopian woman, 252 n.
Moslems, character of, 258 ; their regard for Mahomet, 248 n.; Muslîm, meaning of, 244. See Islam, Mahomet, Koran.
Mozley, J. B., preface, vii.—ix.; his classes for graduates, 65 n.
Mozley, J. B., on the duty of hope and noble wishes, 21 n.; on selfish love of Truth, 23 n.; on Mahomet's idea of God, 63, 245 n.; *Essay on Oracles*, 79 n.; on the necessity of Miracles, 127 ; on the Sacrifice of Isaac, 168 n.; on the Atonement, 197 ; on War, 232 n.; on the morality of the Old Testament, 251 n.; Lord Strafford, 295 n.
Muir, Dr. John, *Sanskrit Texts*, refs. in notes, 74, 75, 76, 77, 84; theories of inspiration, 95; cp. 146; Purusha-Sûkta, Appendix III., 356.
Muir, Sir W., his judgment of Mahomet, 249 foll. n.; quotations from his *Life*, 246 foll.; on ill effects of Islam, 254 n.; puts Hindu above Moslem marriage, 255 n.
Müller, Prof. F. Max, his missionary alphabet, xiii. foll.; refs. in notes, his series of *Sacred Books*, 30 ; his judgment on them, 120 (text); on faith of Abraham, 34; on Parsi monotheism, 51; name of God in Chinese, 57; *Hibbert Lectures* quoted, 75, 78 ; on date of Buddha's death, 88; Buddhist doctrine of the soul, 90; worship of Buddha, 91; number of Buddhists, 92; passing away of the gods, 96 ; on supposed primeval revelation, 146 (text); Vedic confessions of sin, 161; on *Buddhist Nihilism*, &c., 270 ; *Migration of Fables*, 273.
[Mullinger, J. B.,] *the New Reformation* quoted, 241 n., 287 n., 288 n.
Muni, life of a, 271 n.
Murder, guilt of, 156.
Music, theology of, 262 ; in the Church, 311.
Myers, F. W. H., *Essay on Oracles*, 75 n., 79 n.
Mylne, L. G. [Bp. of Bombay], *On Theodore of Mopsuestia*, 65 n.; preface, ix. n.
Mystery to be expected in our view of the Divine Nature, 41 foll. ; of scientific truths, 115 ; of human nature, 116 ; of Christian truth, 117; false of the Immaculate Conception and Papal Infallibility, 118 n.
Myths, confession of the danger of, 98 and n.

Nature, Voices of, 74; Laws of, 306 foll.
Neander, *Church History*, on Gnosticism, 51 n.; on theology of Islam, 245 n.; hopes for Islam, 258 n.
"Nebuchadrezzar my servant," 221 ; pronounced his own degradation, 288.
Nestorianism and Pelagianism, 65.
Neubauer, Dr., on Isa. xxxv. 8, 182 n.
New England, divorce in, 334 n.
Newman, J. H., *Grammar of Assent*, on false candour of sceptics, 17 n.; strange connection of the cultus of the B.V.M. with Arianism, 63 foll.
"Nicene Creed," 280 n.
Nineteenth century, *Religion of Zoroaster*, 50 n. ; *Modern Parsis*, 51 n.; *Odinic songs in Shetland*, [not Scotland], 173 n.
Nirvâna, Buddhist, 90, 270 foll.; probable theory of, 270, and 347 foll. ; Max Müller upon, 270 n.; *Sutta-Nipâta* on, *ib.*; neglected by many modern Buddhists, 271; women, incapable of, directly, 272.
"Nuk pu nuk" in Egyptian, what it really means, 49 n.

Obedience, virtue of, 220.
Ocellus Lucanus, 224 n.
Odin, *the High one's Lesson*, 173 foll.
Offertory, the, 327.
One-sidedness in religion, 110.
Opium trade with China, 300 and n.
Order, our Lord's delight in, 329.
Ordination, 328. See Ministry.
Origen on "mere faith," 18 n. ; on the office of faith in human life, 25 n.; on moral danger of unbelief, 128 n.
Ormazd and Ahriman, 50 n.
Orpheus, myth of, 262.
Orphic societies, 261 ; life, 262 n.; mystery-mongers, 265.
Osborn, Major R. D., *Muhammedan Law*, 257 n.
Osiris, myth of, 174; and Dionysus-Zagreus, 262.
Ovid, on the propensity to evil, 151 ; on identity of victim and sacrificer, 164.
Oxford Missionary Association of Graduates, pref. viii., 28 n., 300 n.

Pantheism in the Church connected with heathen elements, 44; its destructive character, 47 foll.

Pantheism and Deism contrasted, 43 to end of Lecture ; cp. 307 ; mutually exclusive, 111 ; modern tendency to, 307.
Pantheistic interpretation of myths of suffering gods, 175 foll.
Papacy, self-condemned, 288 foll. See Infallibility, Romanism.
Papinenipalli, Christians of, 324 n.
Pârsîs, modern monotheistic, 34 n., 50 foll. and n. ; on impurity of death, 155 ; confession of sin, 158 foll. ; confession of faith, 188 ; expect a deliverer, 208.
Pascal, "qu'il faut aimer les choses divines pour les connaître," 19 n. ; on the negligence and "bassesse de cœur" of infidels, 21 n ; Christianity a combination of the internal and external, 109 n.; on the Incarnation, 202.
Patets, Pârsî confessions, 159.
Patriarchal principle, 234; cp. 220 foll.
Paul, St., his speech at Athens, 69, 107, 143 foll.; co-ordinates grace and free-will, 113 ; rests on historical fact of the Resurrection, 139 ; blames Athenian superstition, 144 ; thought highly of the natural evidences of religion, ib. ; enforces labour, 303 ; on the ministry, 330.
Peace, natural desire for, see Lect. VII. passim ; cannot be assured by civil society, 230 ; failure of threefold attempt to secure, 236 foll., 276, 278 foll.
Peace of the Church, see Lect. VIII. passim, 277 foll.; unity, 280 foll. ; Holiness, 292 foll.; Catholicity, 300 foll., — in action, 302 foll. ; thought, 305 foll. ; art, 310 ; feeling, 312 ; Doctrine, 318 foll. ; Sacraments, 322 foll.; Discipline, 328.
Pelagianism, its connection with Nestorianism, 65 ; Pelagian character of Buddhism, 90, 114, 281 ; Pelagian tendency of modern schism, 287 foll.
Penitentiaries, etc., 303 ; cp. 300.
Permanence, an attribute of Truth, 133 foll.
Persecution, loss of the power of, 289, 290; fallacy of, 313.
Persian Dualism, 50.
"Perusinæ aræ," 167 n.
Pêshyotânû, expectation of, 208.
Pfleiderer *Religions philosophie* on Schleiermacher, 54 n.; on the Fall, 194 n.; on Mahomet, 248 n.
Pharisaism deistic, 61 ; cp. 252 n.
Philosophers confess ignorance, 104.

Philosophy, Christian, 305 foll. ; demand for, 309 foll.
Pindar, on the counsels of the Gods, 103.
Plato, on the art of divination, 82 ; forbids admission of the Poets, 97 ; on the Idea of Truth, 98 ; his hope of a Divine Word, 99 ; idea of a golden age, 146 foll. ; on the strife of good and evil in the soul, 150 ; on divine justice and likeness to God, 153 ; respect for humility in, 153 n.; against superstition and immoral theology of sacrifice, 178, 243 ; his idea of God, 191 ; the ideal just man, 209 ; on the growth of society, 219 n. ; his *Republic* on education, 228 ; on position of women, 229 ; on slavery, 237 n.; on the pattern of the Ideal State, 242 ; his creed in the *Laws*, 243 ; to be made compulsory, 243 foll. ; inadequate idea of a priesthood, 244.
Plutarch, on the Stoic polity, 27 n. ; on oracles, 79 n. ; on birth and death, 149 n. ; on superstition and atheism, 177 ; on the mysteries, 263 n. ; cp. 316.
Poetry, Christian, 311.
Polybius, his rationalistic view of Roman religion, 238 foll.
Polygamy, Mahomet's, 249 ; Moslem, 255 ; evils of, 255 foll.; Sallust on Moorish, 256 ; abolished by Christianity, 303. See Marriage.
Pomegranate, 316 foll.
Pope, Alex., pantheistic lines of, 46.
Positivism, its worship of Humanity, 128, 308 ; its mottoes, 260, 268 ; its morality compared with Buddhism, 268 foll. ; superior to Agnosticism, 307 ; its failure, 308 ; what it wants, 309 ; Dr. Westcott on, 309 n. See Comte.
Porphyry, his collection of oracles, 102, 128 ; his confession of uncertainty, 103 ; *de abstinentia*, 147 n., 168 n., 262 n.
Prajâ-pati called âtmadâ, 172.
Prayer, neglect of, 15 foll.
Preller. *Griech. Myth.*, 147, 165, 167, 262 ; *Röm.*, 163, 164, 167.
Prichard, J. C., on unity of human race, 29 n.
Probation, life a state of, 24.
Prometheus, see corrigenda, xiv., 76 and n., 165.
Psalter, use of the, 120.
Punishment, future, 202 foll.
Purânas, date of the, 87 n.
Purusha-Sûkta, 95 and n. See Appendix III., 356.

INDEX. 369

Pythagoras, date of, 88 n.
Pythagorean societies, character of, 260 foll.; influence on Plato, 261.
Pythia, the, at Delphi, 79.

Quatrefages, A. de, on unity of human species, 29 foll. n.
Quetzalcoatl, the gentle god of Mexico, 84 n.; happy life under, 147 n.; forbade human sacrifices, 169 n.; his return expected, 208; Cortès mistaken for, ib. n.
Quirinus, on Vatican Council, 288 n.

Râvana, power of, 170.
Rägnarök, xiv. and 96.
Reason, true place of, 17 foll.
Redeemer, character expected in a, 207. See Christ.
Religion, unity of, 27; a matter of moral choice, 66; history of, mistake often made in tracing, 72; as an influence on society in non-Christian States, 234 foll.; three methods of applying, 235 foll.
Religions, three fundamental ideas of all, 31, 335.
Renan, E., his demand for a miracle at Paris, 61 n.; his peculiar position, 64 foll. n.; exaggerates importance of Roman collegia, 264 n.; on the necessity of religion to society, 291 n.
Renouf, P. le P., on our knowledge of Egypt, 30 n.; on "nuk pu nuk," 49 n.; on divinity of Egyptian kings, 84 foll.
Repentance, limited power of, 184 foll.
Representation, principle of, 204 foll.; of two kinds, 205; natural, 206.
Resurrection, the, its connection with Catholicity, 301 foll.; influence on literature, 311; call to in the Church, 312.
Revelation, natural expectation of, 72 foll.; both ideal and practical, 109 foll.; needed to enforce primary truths, 33, 37, 291; Moslem regard for, 257.
Rewards for virtue, how limited, 232 foll.
Richter, F., quoted by H. L. Mansel, 104 n.
Rimini, Council of, 286.
"Rishi," Vedic seer, 172 n.
Rita, ideal Duty, 78.
Robertson, F. W., the Illusiveness of Life, 140 n.; Absolution, 328 n.
Rochester, Earl of, his conversion, 141.
Rodwell's Koran, 247 n.
Roman Emperor, deification of, 85, 128, 210, 240 foll.

Roman history, later, a record of crime, 151 foll.
Roman religion, common sense of, 169 n.; described by Polybius, 238 foll.; decay of, 240; Varro on, 240; inauguration of a king, 322 n.; sin-offerings in, 323 n.; consecration of daily food, 324 n.
Romanism, its deistic side, 63 foll.; artificial mysteries of, 118; and Positivism, 128; subordinates truth to expediency, 241; secularity of, 287 foll.; work of mediæval, 288. See Infallibility.
Rousseau, J. J., Émile, on Christ and Socrates, 213; Contrat Social, on "Natural Slavery," 237 n.; on " Civil Religion," 243 n.
Ryder, Admiral A. P., on the protection of women, 300 n.

Sabellian and Eutychian heresies, 51 foll.
Sabellianism, its pantheistic tendency, 52 foll.
Sacerdotalism, false and true, 332 f.
Sacraments of the Church, 322 foll.; an extension of the Incarnation, 324; the ministry necessary to, 331 heathen, 322 f., 324; cp. 264, 317. See Baptism, Communion.
Sacred Books of the East, 30 n.; criticism of, 120.
Sacrifice, element of self-denial in all, 162; for sin, ideas underlying it, ib.; offering of blood, 163; imposition of hands, ib.; identified with the sacrificer, 163 foll.; of white bull, ram, horse, 164 and n.; willingness to die required in, 164; human, 165—169; as voluntary self-surrender, 165 foll.; as ritual institution, 166 foll.; feelings that lead to, 168; reaction against, 169 foll.; forbidden at Rome, 167 n., 169 n.; to Jupiter Latiaris, &c., 167 n.; of children, 168; of a king and of a guest, ib.; ascribed to the gods in India, 170; of self of the " Lord of Creatures," 171; of Purusha, 172; of Odin, 173; of Mexican gods, 174 foll.; of Osiris and others, 174; principle involved in these myths, 176; tendency to give up as useless, 178 foll.; Buddhist opinion of, 179 n.; Horace, Odes, iii. 23, on, 180; at Roman meal, 323; Christ's, pleaded in the Eucharist, 327 (see Atonement); union with, 215, 327.
Saint - Hilaire, J. Barthelémy, admires Mahomet, 249 n.; on his

B b

toleration, 247 n.; on Buddhism, 267 n.
Sâkyamuni, 87. See Buddha, Gotama.
Sallust, on Moorish polygamy, 255 foll.
Sarasvatî, river goddess, 75.
Savi*tri*, prayer to, 76.
Sayce, A. H., *Accadian Psalm*, 158 n.
Scaliger, Joseph, his dying words, 296.
Scepticism, its attraction, 318 foll.; connection with faith, 319 foll.
Schism, some chief causes of, 285 foll.; schismatic temper a check on heresy, 286.
Schleiermacher, his pantheistic and Sabellian leanings, 53 and n.
Scholasticism, its great efforts, 305; why it failed, 306.
Schopenhauer, quoted by H. L. Mansel, 104 n.
Scotland, religion in, 334 n.
Scott, Sir W., his power, 311.
Scotus, Duns, his theory of the Incarnation, 54 n.; Deistic tendencies of, 63 and n.
Sculpture, neglect of, 311.
Sea-Gods, oracular, 75.
Secrecy, natural passion for, 260; cp. 70 foll.
Secret societies, their danger, 260.
Secularism, a result of Deism, 56.
Secularity in the Church, 287 foll.
Seneca, on Immortality, 101; on the wickedness of his times, 152.
Servius, on silence at Roman meals, 324 n.
Seventy, the, 330.
Shaftesbury, Lord, (the philosopher) supports state religion, 235.
Shakespeare, his power, 311.
Shang-Tî, in Chinese, 57.
Shelley's idea of illusion, 46.
Shepherd, the good, 214; cp. 147, 220.
Shû-King, The, character of, 222 foll.
Siam, Buddhism in, 269, 271 n., 273 n.
Sibyl, the, 208 foll.
Simonides, on the perfect man, 282 n.
Simplicity, not a necessary mark of truth, 111.
Sin and unbelief connected by our Lord, 6; of voluntary ignorance, 6, 7.
Sin, secret inclination to, 12 foll.; heathen sense of, 149—154; connected with death, 154 foll.; confession of, 156—161, 328; its work in the world, 193 foll.; revelation of its guilt and danger, 200 foll.; slight sense of in Islam, 245, 253;
Buddhists view it as a misfortune, 269.
Sinlessness of the Redeemer, 207; falsely ascribed to Mahomet, 248.
Sin-offerings, 162 foll.; Roman and Jewish, 323 n.
Sins of the intellect, 14—23.
Slavery, abolition of, 198, 298; Greek and Roman civilization based upon, 237; Plato's and Aristotle's views of, 237 foll. n.; Rousseau on, *ib.*; Mahomet legalizes, 255; influence of the Gospel on, 297 and n.; negro, institution of, 298; repentance for, *ib.*
Smith, Goldwin, Mansel's *Letter to*, 43 n.; *Does the Bible sanction American Slavery?* 298 n.
Smith, John, *Select Discourses*, 82 n.
Smith, R. Bosworth, *Mohammed and Mohammedanism*, Mahomet did not love God, 246 n.; admires M., 248 n.; thinks him a "true prophet," 250; letter from Mir Aulad Ali, 248 n.; tendency to justify M., 252 n.; on Moslem reverence for our Lord, 257 n.
Society, natural to man, 218; an extension of the family, 219; influence of religion on, 234 foll.
Socinians, 285.
Socrates, his relation to the oracles, 80 foll.; his inward monitor, 82; trial and death of, 98; compared with Christ, 213; his independence as a citizen, 227.
Solon, on concealment of the mind of the gods, 103.
Soma, Hindu god, 76 n.
"Son of Man" in Daniel, 221.
Sophocles, *Antigone* on wondrousness of man, 184; *Œd. Colon.* on birth and death, 149 n.; on intercession, 165 n.; *Antigone* on man's power of conquering evil, 184.
Spinoza, his one substance, 45; Hegel on, 47 n.; Schleiermacher on, 53 n.; his testimony to Christ, 212.
State, origin of, 219; conception of, 227 foll.; cannot give happiness, 230 foll.; its negative position, 232.
Steere, Bp., *Attributes of God*, 185 n.; on conversion to Islam, 258 n.
Stephen, Leslie, *English Thought in 18th century*, 243 n.
Stoics, their deistic side and connection with Judaism, 60 and n.; on oracles, 81 n.; polity and ideal of Peace, 27 n., 230.
Strafford, Lord, his speech on the scaffold, 295.

INDEX. 371

Strauss, D. F., his connection with the Eutychian school, 54; quoted by H. L. Mansel, 104 n.
Sufiism, 62 n., 246.
Sun-gods, Vedic, 76 and n.
Superstition, blamed by St. Paul, 144; compared to Atheism by Plutarch, 177; praised by Polybius as a political instrument, 238 foll.; use of the term in Greek, 239 n.
Supremacy, Royal, suggestion about, 289 foll.
Sutta-Nipâta, quoted, on "Karma," 90 n.; levitation in, 91 n.; on origin of sacrifice, 179 n.; on the three refuges, 188 n.; on hermit-life, 204 n., 271 n.; on Nirvâna, 270 foll. n.

Table, comparing different religious systems, 68.
Tables of the Law, 315 foll.
Talbot, E. S. [Warden of Keble Coll.], preface, xi.; on Slavery, 298.
Tao, its pantheistic character, 46; cp. Lao-Tse.
Taoism in China, 59.
"Tapas," austerities, power ascribed to, 170.
Taurobolia and Criobolia, 163.
Taylor, Jeremy, on the Sacraments, 324 n.
Temple, form of the Jewish, 282 n.
Tennant, Sir J. E., on Buddhism in Ceylon, 274 n.
Terence, "Homo sum," etc., xiv., 27.
Tertullian, the place of Reason, 17 n.; the soul naturally Christian, 33.
Testament, Old, points to Christ, 126; morality of, 251 and n.; Mahomet's neglect of, 254. See Bible, Genesis.
Testament, New, criticism of the, 66, 320. See Gospels. Revised version quoted, 144 n., 260 n.
Teutonic mythology, see Grimm, Edda, Odin; national character and Christianity, 297.
Tezcatlipoca, in Mexico, seats left for, 83.
Thang, Chinese Emperor, ready to die for his subjects, 165; cp. 223 n.
Theism, Biblical. See Lect. II.
Theodore of Mopsuestia and Modern Thought, 65 n.
Theognis, on Hope, 148 n., 184 n.; on birth and death, 149 n.
Tholuck's *Guido and Julius*, 104 n., 149 n., 202 n.
Thompson, J. C., 48 n.
Thor, 74, 84.
Thoro the Dane sacrifices his child, 168.

Thucydides on the Trojan war, 304.
Thunder, gods of, 74; oracles from, 75.
Thyrsus, the, of Dionysus, 316 foll.
Tî, or Shang-Tî, 57.
Tiele, *Outlines of Rel.*, 119 n., 249 n.
Tindal, *Rights of the Christian Church*, on civil religion, 243 n.
Transliteration of Oriental words, xiii. foll.
Transmigration, 270; cp. 339.
Transubstantiation, artificial, 117.
Trench, R. C. [Abp.], *Hulsean Lectures*, 114 n.; *Mediæval Ch. Hist.*, on influence of Rome, 288 n.; on works of mercy, 303 n.; on the Crusades, 304 n.
Trinity, doctrine of, a bulwark of the divine Personality, 52 foll.; mystery of, 112; intelligibility of, 132 foll.; unity of the, its relation to the Church. 281.
Trinity of the Buddhists, 188 n.
Trumpp, Dr. E., on the *Adi Granth*, 119 n.
Truth, Christian pursuit of, 23; natural passion for, 70; an element in all widespread belief, 111; Christian, comprehensive, 110 foll.; mysterious, 115 foll.; inexhaustible, 118 foll.; authoritative, 122 foll.; intelligible, 131 foll.; permanent, 133 foll.; a source of freedom, 131; subordinated to expediency, 236—241; imposed by force, 236, 241 foll.; sought in voluntary societies, 236, 259 foll.; failure of these three attempts, 276, 278 foll.
Truths, the four Noble, of Buddhism, 88.
Tübingen School of criticism, 64, 65; on the early Church, 284.
Tylor, E. B., *Primitive Culture*, on human sacrifice, 166 n.; lustration of children, 322 n.; heathen sacraments, 323 n.

Ueberweg, *Hist. of Philosophy*, on Schleiermacher, 53 n.; Scotus, 63 n.; Plotinus, 102 n.
Unbelief and Sin, 6.
Unbelief, its moral causes, 8—23.
Unitarians, 285.
Unity of the Church, its double sense, 280 foll.; rests on the Unity of the Blessed Trinity, 281; of the early Church, 283; present, on points of doctrine, 284 foll.; prospects of, 287; office of the Church of England towards, 291 foll.
Unity of the Godhead the basis of Christian Unity, 280 foll.; coinci-

INDEX.

dence of will and goodness in, 293.
Unity of the human race, 28—30.
Unity of religion, 27; heathen view of, 27 n.
"Unknown God" at Athens, &c., 145.
Upanishads, Pantheism of the, 45. and n.
Utopias, inadequacy of, 233 foll.

Vaishnava reforms, 97 n., 323 n.
Varro, Marcus, on religion and theology, 240.
Varuna, 77.
Vasishtha, 77.
Vâta, hymn to, 75.
Vatican Council, composition of the, 241 n.; striking synchronism respecting, 287 n.; new period begins with, 288.
Vaughan, *The Trident*, &c., 173 and n.
Vedantism, the converse of Hegelianism, 46.
Vedas, The, 94 foll.; theories of their inspiration, 95; importance of knowing, 96.
Vedic gods, 74—78.
Vedic hymns, depth of mysterious ideas in the, 77 foll.; formulæ of confession in, 161.
Vendîdâd, on purification, 155 foll. n.; on confession, 158.
Vigfússon, Dr. G., on Odin's song, 173 n.; on Rägnarök, xiv.
Vidar, son of Odin, 208.
Virgil, 79 n., 155 n.; *Pollio*, 208.
Virgin, the Blessed, cultus of, 63; connection with Arianism, 64 n.; influence on Positivism, 229 n.
Vishnu, avatârs of, 86; sacrifice of, 173. See Vaishnava.
Voltaire on the Christian religion, 10; his deism, 64.

Wace, H., preface, x.; on cavils against Christianity, 10 n.; on Prof. Clifford's *Ethics of Belief*, 24 n.; on Bacon, 305 n., 306 n.
Waitz, Theodor, on unity of human species, 29 n.; cp. 166.
Waldenses, 313; cp. note.
Wallon, H., *Histoire de l'Esclavage*, 298 n.
War, impossibility of preventing, 230—232.
Water-gods, oracular, 75.
Wesleyans, 313.
Westcott, B. F., on the Pharisees and Sadducees, 62 n.; on the "good shepherd," 214 n.; on Positivism, 309 n.
White, Blanco, *Autobiography*, 23 n.
Wilberforce, R. I., *on the Incarnation*, quoted, 206; on the sacraments, 324 n.
Wilmanns, *Inscr. Lat.*, 145 n.
Williams, Prof. Monier, on the Hindu Philosophy, 48; on Zoroaster, 50; the Pârsîs, 51; Hindu Theistic Reformers, 97, 214; Hindu confession, 161; asva-medha, 164; human sacrifice, 169; Râvana, 170.
Wilson, Prof. H. H., quoted, 87 n.; on human sacrifice, 166 n.
Wind, "The Breath of the Gods," 75.
Women, low position of, in China, 222 n.; ideas about in Plato's *Republic*, 228 foll.; Comte's theories about, 229 n.; work of, in modern society, 229; Mahomet's passion for, 249 n.; degraded by Islam, 255; Buddhism on, 272; protection of, 300. See Polygamy.
Wool, balls of, in the mysteries, 316 foll.
Wordsworth, Charles, Bp. of St. Andrews, on the Christian ministry, 334 n.
Wordsworth, Chr., [Bp. of Lincoln], *Letters to Gondon*, 18 n.; *the Mohammedan Woe*, 246 n.
Wordsworth, Wm., *Ode to Duty*, 78.
Work, duty of, 303, 306; vaguely recognized by heathens, 317; power of, among Christians, 321.
Worship, public, neglect of, 15; the ministry guarantees, 334; heathen, 234.
Wurtz, Prof. Ad., *On the Atomic Theory*, 115 n.

Xenophanes, Pantheism of, 45.
Xenophon, on Socrates and the oracles, 81 foll.; on the "two souls" in men, 150 foll.; on the noble independence of Socrates, 227.
Xiuhtecutli, Mexican god of fire, 175.

Yggdrasil, symbol of the world, 174.
Yogis, asceticism of, 170.

Zeller, on Xenophanes, 45 n.; on date of Pythagoras, 88 n.; on Plato, 98 n.; on Pythagorean societies, 261 n.
Zoroastrian confession of faith, 188. See Avesta, Pârsî, Persian, Vendîdâd.
Zulus. See Kaffirs.